STECK-VAUGHN
GED

READING LITERATURE AND THE ARTS

Popular Literature
Classical Literature
Commentary

Susan D. McClanahan, Educational Consultant
Donna D. Amstutz, Special Advisor

STECK-VAUGHN ADULT EDUCATION ADVISORY COUNCIL

Donna D. Amstutz
Asst. Project Director
Northern Area Adult Education
   Service Center
Northern Illinois University
DeKalb, Illinois

Roberta Pittman
Director, Project C3 Adult Basic
   Education
Detroit Public Schools
Detroit, Michigan

Elaine Shelton
Consultant, Competency-Based
   Adult Education
Austin, Texas

Lonnie D. Farrell
Supervisor, Adult Special Programs
Los Angeles Unified School District
Los Angeles, California

Don F. Seaman
Professor, Adult Education
College of Education
Texas A&M University
College Station, Texas

Bobbie L. Walden
Coordinator, Community Education
Alabama Department of Education
Montgomery, Alabama

Meredyth A. Leahy
Director of Continuing
   Education
Cabrini College
Radnor, Pennsylvania

Jane B. Sellen
Supervisor, Adult Education
Western Iowa Tech
   Community College
Sioux City, Iowa

Steck-Vaughn Company
A Subsidiary of National Education Corporation

Product Design and Development: McClanahan & Company
with PC&F, Inc.

Project Director: Bonnie Diamond, Ed. D.

Assistant Project Director: Patricia Carlin

Design/Production Director: Judi Baller

Editorial Development: Ann Craig, Frank McClanahan,
Catherine Podojil, Marion Meade,
Winifred Davis, Patricia Parmalee

Photograph Credits: Cover Photograph by Rick Patrick
Photoresearch by Photosearch, Inc.
pg. 16 Omikron, Photo Researchers
pg. 25 Berenice Abbott, Museum of the City of New York
pg. 154 Anestis Diakopoulos, Photo Researchers
pg. 232 Nancy J. Pierce, Photo Researchers

Illustration Credits: PC&F, Inc.

ISBN 0-8114-1898-7   4 5 6 7 8 9 0 PO 91 90 89 88

Contents

To the Student

The GED test offers you an opportunity to

1. Keep or get a better job in government, industry or business
2. Increase your earning powers
3. Expand educational opportunities in trade, technical, vocational, or apprenticeship programs
4. Fulfill your personal goals

It awards a certificate that is the equivalent of a high school diploma. It measures your mastery of skills and general knowledge in Writing Skills, Social Studies, Science, Reading Literature and the Arts, and Mathematics.

The Steck-Vaughn program prepares you for success on the GED exam by:

- Teaching appropriate concepts and skills that will provide a solid foundation for your general knowledge
- Providing practice in the GED format
- Emphasizing the reading skills that will be tested on the GED exam—those that require you to apply, to analyze and to evaluate as well as to comprehend what you read
- Offering test-taking tips to build your confidence
- Applying concepts and skills in practical and realistic settings
- Building vocabulary by highlighting and defining new terms
- Teaching reading, writing and problem-solving skills to make you better readers
- Frequently using charts, tables, graphs, diagrams, maps and figures, which are part of the GED test, and instructing you how to gain meaning from them.

It does this through an easy-to-follow, predictable Four Step Plan that includes

- Introducing and teaching a concept
- Applying a particular reading or problem-solving strategy to the concept
- Practicing the concept in the GED test format
- Testing and checking your answers

(Answers and Explanations to both the Practice and GED Mini-Test items provide further instruction through explanations of why choices are incorrect as well as why a given choice is correct.)

The following table summarizes the contents of the GED tests.

The Tests of General Educational Development

Test	Content Areas	Number of Items	Time Limit (minutes)
Writing Skills	PART ONE Sentence Structure Usage Mechanics	55	75
Writing Sample	PART TWO Essay	1	45
Social Studies	United States History Geography Economics Political Science Behavioral Science	64	85
Science	Life Science Earth Science Physics Chemistry	66	95
Reading Literature and the Arts	Popular Literature Classical Literature Commentary	45	65
Mathematics	Arithmetic Measurement Number Relationships Data Analysis Algebra Geometry	56	90

How To Use This Book

The Book:

A sequentially organized program

The Pretest

- Tells you what content and skills you have already mastered and
- What content and skills you need to work on—a real aid to planning your time and increasing your studying efficiency
  (See the Pretest/Posttest Diagnostic Chart in the back of this book)

The Overview

- Explains each major section of the book
- Provides definitions of vocabulary terms and concepts that relate to material in each major section

The Study Plan

HINT ▷ a practical reminder when applying a concept

TIP a practical reminder related to test-taking

A predictable seven-page lesson that includes:

- An **Introductory** teaching page
- A **Strategy** page that teaches and applies a related reading skill to increase understanding and aid mastery
- **Practice** pages that review and reinforce the particular content and the reading skill in GED format
- **Mixed Practice** exercises in the Mathematics and Writing texts that review previously learned material
- A multiple choice, GED format test (**GED Mini-Test**) that measures higher-level thinking skills
- **Answers and Explanations** for both the Practice and the GED Mini-Tests that give *immediate* feedback and pinpoint possible errors or weaknesses

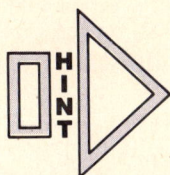

The Review

- Summarizes the instructional content of a section
- Provides more practice items in GED format

The Posttest

- Simulates the actual GED test
- Alerts you to the need for possible further study
  (See the Pretest/Posttest Diagnostic Chart in the back of this book)

Test-Taking and Study Skills

Test-Taking Skills

The _AIM_ of the Steck-Vaughn GED program is to prepare you to take and to pass the GED examination with ease and confidence. You bring to the program your own personal style and your life experience.

With these as a base, use the preparation material and the suggestions that follow to build and strengthen your academic skills, test-taking ability and study skills.

The Steck-Vaughn program is designed to provide numerous test taking situations in the multiple-choice GED format. GED items appear in:

- Pre- and posttests for each book
- Practice and test pages for each lesson
- Reviews for each major book section

The more opportunities you have to practice the GED test format, the more you will increase your confidence in test taking. _You learn about the test by preparing for the test._

Some key test-taking skills are:

- Set goals
- Plan your test-taking time
- Read for understanding
- Analyze the test questions carefully before answering them
- Pace yourself

Reviewing the helpful Steck-Vaughn GED Mini-Test Tips that are part of each lesson will help you gain more confidence in test taking.

Study Skills

The Steck-Vaughn program aids in developing and improving your study skills. They are an important element in successful test taking.

Some important study skills to remember are

- Improve your vocabulary
- Use your text as well as other resources, including maps, charts, graphs and diagrams to help you learn
- Plan your study time
- Take notes and use your notes to study from; your notes can be a map or an outline or any form that is most helpful for you
- Make a check-list of the areas that give you trouble and refer to this list so you practice what is difficult for you
- Problem solve:
  - discover what the problem (question) is
  - list two or three possible solutions
  - choose the one best answer
  - try it out
  - re-think and research if it does not work.

Try to find out why a solution is wrong and keep that in mind to apply to future material you read.

The on-going repetition and review of both the test-taking and study skill strategies and the constant practice will give you confidence and self-assurance as you prepare for and take the GED exam.

PRETEST
Literature

DIRECTIONS: Choose the one best answer for each item below.

Items 1–4 refer to the following passage by Mark Twain.

WHAT DOES IT TAKE TO BECOME POPULAR?

They had borrowed a melodeum—a sick one; and when everything
was ready a young woman sat down and worked it, and it was pretty
shreeky and colicky, and everybody joined in and sung, and Peter was
the only one that had a good thing, according to my notion. Then the
(5) Reverend Hobson opened up, slow and solemn, and begun to talk; and
straight off the most outrageous row busted out in the cellar a body
ever heard; it was one dog, but he made a most powerful racket and he
kept it up right along; the parson he had to stand there, over the coffin,
didn't seem to know what to do. But pretty soon they see that long-
(10) legged undertaker make a sign to the preacher as much as to say, "Don't
you worry—depend on me." Then he stooped down and begun to glide
along the wall, just his shoulders showing over the people's heads. So he
glided along, and the powwow and racket getting more and more outrageous all the time; and at last, when he had gone around two sides of
(15) the room, he disappears down cellar. Then in about two seconds we
heard a whack, and the dog he finished up with a most amazing howl or
two, and then everything was dead still, and the parson begun his
solemn talk where he left off. In a minute or two here comes this undertaker's back and shoulders gliding along the wall again; and so he glided
(20) and glided around three sides of the room, and then rose up, and shaded
his mouth with his hands, and stretched his neck out towards the
preacher, over the people's heads, and says, in a kind of a coarse
whisper, *"He had a rat!"* Then he drooped down and glided along the
wall again to his place. You could see it was a great satisfaction to the
(25) people, because naturally, they wanted to know. A little thing like that
don't cost nothing, and it's just the little things that makes a man to be
looked up to and liked. There warn't no more popular man in town than
what that undertaker was.

1. The writing style in this passage would be
best described as

   (1) friendly and colloquial
   (2) angry and serious
   (3) formal and pompous
   (4) reserved and uncomfortable
   (5) snobbish and amused

2. The undertaker becomes popular because

   (1) he is the town politician
   (2) he performs a simple task
   (3) everyone watches him
   (4) he shows great courage
   (5) he is friends with the preacher

GO ON TO THE NEXT PAGE.

3. In which of the following places is this scene *most* likely set?

    (1) an African desert
    (2) New York City in the 1960s
    (3) Paris during World War II
    (4) a Mississippi village in the early 1900s
    (5) Alaska in the present

4. As used in this excerpt, the word "racket" means

    (1) a fight
    (2) a conference
    (3) the whispers from downstairs
    (4) tennis equipment
    (5) loud noises

Items 5–8 refer to the following passage by Annie Dillard.

WHAT HAPPENS WHEN YOU ENCOUNTER A WILD ANIMAL?

Weasel! I'd never seen one wild before. He was ten inches long, thin as a curve, a muscled ribbon, brown as fruitwood, soft-furred, alert. His face was fierce, small and pointed as a lizard's; he would have made a good arrowhead. There was just a dot of chin, maybe two brown hairs'
(5)   worth, and then the pure white fur began that spread down his underside. He had two black eyes I didn't see, any more than you see a window.

The weasel was stunned into stillness as he was emerging from beneath an enormous shaggy wild rose bush four feet away. I was
(10)   stunned into stillness twisted backward on the tree trunk. Our eyes locked, and someone threw away the key.

Our look was as if two lovers, or deadly enemies, met unexpectedly on an overgrown path when each had been thinking of something else: a clearing blow to the gut. It was also a bright blow to the brain, or a sud-
(15)   den beating of brains, with all the charge and intimate grate of rubbed balloons. It emptied our lungs. It felled the forest, moved the fields, and drained the pond; the world dismantled and tumbled into that black hole of eyes. If you and I looked at each other that way, our skulls would split and drop to our shoulders. But we don't. We keep our skulls.
(20)   So.

He disappeared. This was only last week, and already I don't remember what shattered the enchantment. I think I blinked, I think I retrieved my brain from the weasel's brain, and tried to memorize what I was seeing, and the weasel felt the yank of separation, the careening
(25)   splashdown into real life and the urgent current of instinct. He vanished under the wild rose. I waited motionless, my mind suddenly full of data and my spirit with pleadings, but he didn't return.

5. Why does the author assert that her encounter with the weasel "felled the forest, moved the fields, and drained the pond" (lines 16–17)?

    (1) to show the natural setting
    (2) because that is what happened
    (3) to heighten the importance of the scene
    (4) to prove the weasel's wildness
    (5) no one would believe her otherwise

6. The author uses this encounter to illustrate

    (1) how wild animals are friendly but nervous
    (2) how to collect scientific data efficiently
    (3) the stunning stillness of the weasel
    (4) how instinct draws animals towards humans
    (5) the intimate connection between man and animal

GO ON TO THE NEXT PAGE.

7. As used in line 15, what does "grate" mean?

  (1) a metal grid
  (2) a sign of intimacy
  (3) a high, squeaking sound
  (4) friction between two surfaces
  (5) conflict

8. What does the author do to cause the weasel to slip away?

  (1) She moves too suddenly.
  (2) She tries to memorize what she saw.
  (3) She plans aloud her next step.
  (4) She loses interest in the weasel.
  (5) She starts to retrieve something she lost before she saw the weasel.

Items 9–12 refer to the following excerpt by Marsha Norman.

WHAT DECISION DOES ARLENE HAVE TO MAKE?

RUBY: Well, you don't want to trust him, that's for sure.

ARLENE: We spent a lot of time together, me an Carl.

RUBY: He live here?

ARLENE: No, he jus broke outta Bricktown near where I was. I got word
(5) there sayin he'd meet me. I didn't believe it then, but he don't lie, Carl
don't.

RUBY: You thinkin of goin with him?

ARLENE: They'll catch him. I told him but he don't listen.

RUBY: Funny, ain't it, the number a' men come without ears.

(10) ARLENE: How much that diswashin job pay?

RUBY: I don't know. Maybe seventy-five.

ARLENE: That's what he said.

RUBY: He tell you you was gonna wear out your hands and knees grub-
bin for nuthin, git old and be broke and never have a nice dress to

(15) wear? (*Sitting down*)

ARLENE: Yeah.

RUBY: He tell you nobody's gonna wanna be with you cause you done
time?

ARLENE: Yeah.

(20) RUBY: He tell you your kid gonna be ashamed of you an nobody's gonna
believe you if you tell em you changed?

ARLENE: Yeah.

RUBY: Then he was right. (*Pauses*) But when you make your two nickels,
you can keep both of em.

GO ON TO THE NEXT PAGE.

9. You can infer that Ruby and Arlene

    (1) have had children
    (2) have been in prison
    (3) are experienced dishwashers
    (4) are sisters
    (5) have escaped from prison

10. When Ruby refers to the number of men that come without ears, she means

    (1) men do not listen
    (2) men are funny
    (3) many men are born without ears
    (4) men are deaf
    (5) men's ears look funny

11. You can infer from the excerpt that

    (1) Carl is Arlene's brother
    (2) Carl often lies
    (3) Carl has escaped from prison
    (4) Carl is Ruby's brother
    (5) Carl and Arlene hardly know each other

12. Ruby's last speech means that, though Arlene's life on her own may be hard, she can

    (1) be a good mother
    (2) collect coins
    (3) have her independence
    (4) learn dishwashing
    (5) be lovable

Items 13–16 refer to the following review from Newsweek.

WAS VINCENT VAN GOGH A MADMAN OR A SAINT?

There was a tension between the two forces within Vincent, the force of dissolution, and the force of creativity. This tension peaked in these last months when Vincent was in Dr. Peyron's asylum in Saint-Remy and later under the care of Dr. Gachet at Auvers. After all, Holly-
(5) wood and Kirk Douglas didn't create van Gogh's "mad genius" syndrome. "You certainly paint like a madman," was Cezanne's comment when Vincent showed him some of his work. And Pissarro said that "this man will either go mad or outpace us all. That he would do both, I did not foresee."
(10) What in fact was this legendary madness? That malady was diagnosed, during his lifetime and after, in a hodgepodge of medical-psychiatric terms that included schizophrenia, syphilis, epilepsy, catatonia, dromomania (an obsession with traveling), xanthopia (seeing yellow everywhere) and just plain turpentine poisoning. But even Karl Jaspers,
(15) the noted psychiatrist and philosopher who thought Vincent schizophrenic, also characterized him as having a "mentality of the highest moral character, the expression of an absolute veracity . . . an infinite love, a generous humanity." The clue is here: behind the psychiatric jargon Vincent's madness may have been the result of the
(20) extreme pressure put on him by an ethical development far in excess of the normal.
Van Gogh's art, which lasted only ten years of his life, was his last attempt to live an ideal ethical life, a life of altruistic love. Before then he had failed at everything: selling art, love affairs, school-teaching,
(25) preaching. As an evangelist, he tried to help the poor coal miners of the Borinage area in Belgium; he went into the pits with them, taught their children, gave away everything he owned to them, nursed them after a terrible explosion. For such excessive zeal he was dismissed by the evangelical authorities. Decidedly, he was mad, said his sardonic friend Gau-
(30) guin: "Contrary to the teachings of his instructors, the wise men of Holland, Vincent believes in a Jesus who loved the poor." Embarrassing as it may be to admit it, Vincent was a failed saint who finally found a way to give shape and power to his balked love for humanity—his art.

GO ON TO THE NEXT PAGE.

13. Within van Gogh there existed a tension between

    (1) turpentine poisoning and schizophrenia
    (2) the force of madness and his failures
    (3) evangelical zeal and a love of humanity
    (4) disintegration and the power of creativity
    (5) failure at selling art and success at love

14. According to the author, van Gogh's madness may have been caused by

    (1) his inability to paint well
    (2) his excessive ethical development
    (3) his excessive love of art
    (4) his dismissal by evangelical authorities
    (5) his stay at the asylum at Saint-Remy under the care of Dr. Peyron

15. Van Gogh the evangelist and van Gogh the painter had in common

    (1) a love of nature
    (2) their dismissal by authorities
    (3) experience teaching children
    (4) altruistic love of others
    (5) a desire to be happy

16. Which of the following choices *best* describes the author's opinion of van Gogh?

    (1) a failure at everything he did
    (2) a man with many mental illnesses
    (3) a great immoral artist
    (4) a successful evangelist
    (5) a man with a love of humanity

Items 17–22 refer to the following passage by William Kennedy.

WHAT DO YOU THINK OF WHEN YOU HEAR AN OLD SONG?

"On second thought," said Helen, "I want to sing one for Francis for buying me that flower. Does your friend know 'He's Me Pal,' or 'My Man'?"

"You hear that, Joe?"

(5) "I hear," said Joe the piano man, and he played a few bars of the chorus of "He's Me Pal" as Helen smiled and stood and walked to the stage with an aplomb and grace befitting her reentry into the world of music, the world she should never have left, oh why did you leave it, Helen? She climbed the three steps to the platform, drawn upward by (10) familiar chords that now seemed to her to have always evoked joy, chords not from this one song but from an era of songs, thirty, forty years of song that celebrated the splendors of love, and loyalty, and friendship, and family, and country, and the natural world. Frivolous Sal was a wild sort of devil, but wasn't she dead on the level too? Mary (15) was a great pal, heaven-sent on Christmas morning, and love lingers on for her. The new-mown hay, the silvery moon, the home fires burning, these were sanctuaries of Helen's spirit, songs whose like she had sung from her earliest days, songs that endured for her as long as the classics she had committed to memory so indelibly in her youth, for they spoke (20) to her, not abstractly of the aesthetic peaks of the art she had once hoped to master, but directly, simply, about the everyday currency of the heart and soul. The pale moon will shine on the twining of our hearts. My heart is stolen, lover dear, so please don't let us part. Oh love, sweet love, oh burning love—the songs told her—you are mine, I (25) am yours, forever and a day. You spoiled the girl I used to be, my hope has gone away. Send me away with a smile, but remember: you're turning off the sunshine of my life.

Love.

GO ON TO THE NEXT PAGE.

17. What do "frivolous Sal" (line 14) and "heaven-sent Mary" (line 15) and the "silvery moon" (line 16) all have in common?

   (1) They can all be seen in the bar.
   (2) Helen grew up with them.
   (3) They all originate in songs.
   (4) Joe has sung to Helen about them.
   (5) Helen has sung to Francis about them.

18. With which of the following statements would the author *most* likely agree?

   (1) Helen should never have given up music.
   (2) Helen's life is better than the lives in songs.
   (3) It was all for the best that Helen gave up singing.
   (4) Those old songs are all sad.
   (5) Old songs are not worth taking seriously.

19. As used in line 21, what does "currency" mean?

   (1) the money Helen makes singing
   (2) the value of the heart and soul
   (3) the cost of her musical education
   (4) her standard of living
   (5) the money Francis spent on flowers

20. When Helen sings she imagines she is singing

   (1) to Francis about her sorrow
   (2) a song her mother used to sing
   (3) a song she never knew before
   (4) a song about a pale moon
   (5) an era of songs celebrating love

21. Which of the following characteristics *best* describe Helen?

   (1) pathetic but proud
   (2) young and pretty
   (3) jolly and off key
   (4) old and hopeless
   (5) hopeful but naïve

22. The old songs celebrate *all* of the following *except*

   (1) love
   (2) the natural world
   (3) friendship
   (4) nostalgia
   (5) country

Items 23–26 refer to the following poem by Gwendolyn Brooks.

WHY DOES THIS GIRL WANT TO GO DOWN THE ALLEY?

A Song in the Front Yard

I've stayed in the front yard all my life.
I want a peek at the back
Where it's rough and untended and hungry weed grows.
A girl gets sick of a rose.

(5) I want to go to the back yard now
And maybe down the alley,
To where the charity children play.
I want a good time today.

GO ON TO THE NEXT PAGE.

They do some wonderful things.
(10) They have some wonderful fun.
My mother sneers, but I say it's fine
How they don't have to go in at quarter to nine.
My mother, she tells me that Johnnie Mae
Will grow up to be a bad woman.
(15) That George'll be taken to Jail soon or late
(On account of last winter he sold our back gate).

But I say it's fine. Honest, I do.
And I'd like to be a bad woman, too,
And wear the brave stockings of night-black lace
(20) And strut down the streets with paint on my face.

23. What does the "back yard" mean to this poet?

(1) an elegant garden
(2) a jail
(3) a place populated by exciting people
(4) a place where dishonest people live
(5) the streets of the city

24. What does "A girl gets sick of a rose" mean?

(1) Roses smell too sweet.
(2) Her mother makes her pick them.
(3) She wants to stay out till quarter of nine.
(4) She tires of the wholesome life.
(5) A rose represents the bad women.

25. Which of the following characteristics *best* describes the speaker of this poem?

(1) curious and naïve
(2) content and serene
(3) happy and cooperative
(4) satisfied and reclusive
(5) furious and vindictive

26. Which of the following actions would this author choose to do?

(1) tend her mother's garden
(2) live a simple, proper life
(3) go to jail with the other exciting people
(4) never wear makeup
(5) go out on the town and have fun

Items 27–30 refer to the following excerpt by Lanford Wilson.

WHY ARE THESE PEOPLE IN THE SOUTHWEST?

VITA: (*Entering*) Niles? Are you all right?
NILES: (*Offstage*) Just a minute.
VITA: (*Notices the pill bottle, picks it up . . . Calling*) Where have you got to? (*Puts the bottle in her purse*)
(5) NILES: (*Offstage*) I found a water faucet I'm sure hasn't been opened in twenty years. I'll die of typhoid, but I'll die refreshed. (*He re-enters, wiping his face with a damp handkerchief*) I must have half of New Mexico on my face.
VITA: You were beginning to look a little like a cinnamon doughnut, yes.
(10) NILES: Sixty miles on a dirt road with nothing to look at except sagebrush, only to be turned back by the highway patrol and have to look at the same sagebrush all over again from the other side. You told Dr. Singer we'll be a day late?

GO ON TO THE NEXT PAGE.

VITA: He's in a meeting. His secretary has gone to the bank.

(15) NILES: At twelve hundred dollars a day per shrunken head, you'd think Singer's institute would own the bank by now.

VITA: I left the number of the pay phone out there.

NILES: Darling, I'm not going to stand in a church in the middle of the wilderness waiting for some secretary to return our call.

(20) VITA: If we don't hear in ten minutes, I'll try again. (NILES *notices the pill bottle is gone*) I've got it.

NILES: Good. I may need it. (*Looks at his watch*) We'll give her five minutes. (*He spreads a handkerchief on the deep sill of the window, and sits*) Even when we get there, Phoenix is going to be no fun for you. Liv-

(25) ing down the road from the asylum—in some sleazy motel.

VITA: Holiday Inn. No surprises.

NILES: Probably be crowded with husbands and wives of the other patients, all brightly pretending nothing is wrong. Keeping active and interested and fit. Forming a slow-pitch softball team. I see T-shirts

(30) emblazoned with WIVES OF THE LOONIES.

VITA: I'll skip that, I think. I might even get some work done.

27. This scene takes place

(1) at Singer's institute
(2) in a sleazy motel
(3) in a church in the southwest
(4) in a Holiday Inn
(5) along a dirt road

28. You can infer that Vita and Niles

(1) are visiting old churches in the southwest
(2) are vacationing at the Holiday Inn
(3) are traveling pill salespeople
(4) have been delayed on their way to Singer's institute
(5) have taken a wrong turn on a dirt road

29. You can infer that Singer's institute

(1) teaches taxidermy
(2) treats injured softball players
(3) offers psychotherapy
(4) teaches motel management
(5) teaches investment banking

30. From Niles' words you can tell that he is mainly worried about

(1) being late to the institute
(2) being seen by others as crazy
(3) losing Vita's love
(4) the high cost of the institute
(5) Vita's boredom in Phoenix

Answers and Explanations

Literature Pretest *pp. 5–12*

1. **Answer:** (1)   Choice (2) is wrong because this passage is witty, not serious. The incorrect grammar and colloquial words show that the writing is not formal, choice (3). The author is not embarrassed, choice (4), nor does he make fun of the characters, choice (5).

2. **Answer:** (2)   There is no mention of the undertaker being a politician, choice (1), nor that he is a particularly good friend of the preacher, choice (5). Although everyone watches him, choice (3), that is not why he is popular. The task he performs does not require great courage, choice (4).

3. **Answer:** (4)   The setting for this passage seems to be a small community where people know each other. The colloquial language is definitely American, so choices (1) and (3) are ruled out. While such small communities exist in America today, choice (5), the use of antiquated words such as "melodeum" suggests this takes place long ago.

4. **Answer:** (5)   While the fight, choice (1), is the source of the racket, it doesn't define that word. Choice (2) implies a meeting of sympathetic parties, which clearly the meeting of the dog and the rat is not. Choice (3) contradicts the description of the fight downstairs. Choice (4) is a definition for racket that, while correct in other circumstances, does not apply to this use of the word.

5. **Answer:** (3)   Although saying the encounter "felled the forest" does show the natural setting, choice (1), that is not the purpose of the statement. Choices (2) and (5) suggest that the author needs to lie to be believed, which is untrue. Choice (4) is irrelevant.

6. **Answer:** (5)   Choices (1) and (4) contradict the experience of encountering the weasel. There is no mention of a scientific experiment, choice (2). While this encounter does show the stillness of the weasel, choice (3), that is not the author's central point.

7. **Answer:** (4)   A grate can be a metal grid, choice (1), but that is not the meaning in this context. Choices (2) and (5) place a value on what is essentially a neutral action. A high squeaking sound, choice (3), may result from the friction between two surfaces, choice (4), but does not define grate.

8. **Answer:** (2)   There is no mention of her moving too suddenly, choice (1), planning her next step, choice (3), or literally retrieving something she lost, choice (5). Nor does she lose interest, choice (4), as is clear from the last line of this excerpt.

9. **Answer:** (2)   This is correct because of Ruby's reference to doing time. No other choice is supported by the passage.

10. **Answer:** (1)   This is correct because Ruby's description is figurative language for men's inability to listen to women. The other choices are not supported by the passage.

11. **Answer:** (3)   This is correct because Arlene says Carl broke out of Bricktown. Choice (2) is contradicted by the passage, and choices (1), (4) and (5) are not supported by the passage.

12. **Answer:** (3)   Ruby's words are another metaphor, this time for independence. Arlene undoubtedly wants choices (1) and (5), but these are not what Ruby talks about. Choices (2) and (4) are not supported by Ruby's words.

13. Answer: (4) Turpentine poisoning and schizophrenia, choice (1), are both possible causes of van Gogh's illness, but do not answer this question. Madness and lack of success, choice (2), and evangelical zeal and love of humanity, choice (3), existed in van Gogh, but not as opposites, which the use of the word "tension" requires. Van Gogh did not have success at love, so choice (5) is incorrect.

14. Answer: (2) Choice (1) is incorrect because van Gogh was well respected by the two other painters quoted in this excerpt. There is no mention of his loving art too much, choice (3), nor of the effects of his stay at the asylum, choice (5). While his dismissal by the evangelical authorities, choice (4), might have pushed him towards madness, it was not the most important factor.

15. Answer: (4) While choices (1) and (3) may be true, they do not show a grasp of the author's central point. Van Gogh's painting was not dismissed by authorities, choice (2). While he may have always wanted to be happy, choice (5), this sentiment is not mentioned by the author.

16. Answer: (5) Choice (1) is incorrect because van Gogh was tremendously successful as a painter. Although he suffered from mental illness, choice (2), the author's opinion of him is not based solely on this fact. Choices (3) and (4) contradict the excerpt.

17. Answer: (3) These different images cannot literally be seen in the bar, choice (1), nor did Helen actually grow up with them, choice (2), although she has known about them through songs since childhood, choice (3). There is no evidence Joe has sung to Helen before, choice (4), or that Helen has sung to Francis before, choice (5).

18. Answer: (1) The author suggests that the world described in songs is more splendid than everyday life, making choices (2), (4) and (5) incorrect. In line 8, the author writes that Helen should never have quit singing, making choice (3) wrong.

19. Answer: (2) There is no mention of Helen being paid, choices (1) and (3), nor is her singing related to her standard of living, choice (4). She sings to thank Francis for flowers, but this does not involve currency, choice (5). The author uses currency in line 21 to define the qualities or values of the heart.

20. Answer: (5) There is no mention of singing about sorrow, choice (1), nor of Helen singing a song her mother used to sing, choice (2), nor a specific song about the moon, choice (4). The songs are clearly ones she has known before, choice (3).

21. Answer: (1) Helen could not be young, choice (2), because she remembers the old songs. She does not seem jolly, choice (3), and, while singing, she is not hopeless, choice (4). Because she has lived through a great deal and looks back on the old songs, we know she is not naïve, choice (5).

22. Answer: (4) In lines 12–13, the author lists that the songs celebrate love, choice (1), the natural world, choice (2), friendship, choice (3), and country, choice (5). The only choice not mentioned is nostalgia, choice (4), although Helen feels nostalgic about the old songs.

23. Answer: (3) There is no mention of an elegant garden, choice (1), or busy streets, choice (5). The girl's mother suggests that if the girl goes into the back yard she will encounter people headed for jail, choice (2), and dishonest people, choice (4), but the girl disagrees with her mother, so only choice (3) is correct.

24. Answer: (4) Choices (1) and (2) are not mentioned in the poem. The girl wants to stay out past a quarter to nine (line 12) and not just until that time, although in either case the question of time does not define the rose. Choice (5) suggests the opposite of the meaning implied in the poem.

25. Answer: (1) Choices (2), (3) and (4) all suggest the girl has no complaint with her life, although the poem clearly expressses her desire for something she does not have. She does not show vindictiveness, choice (5). Choice (1) best describes her childlike frustration.

27. Answer: (3) Niles refers to New Mexico and to standing in a church in the middle of the wilderness. The locations in the other choices are all mentioned in the passage, but are not the site of the passage.

29. Answer: (3) Niles, because of his nervousness and need for pills, is obviously in need of emotional treatment. His humorous references to shrunken heads and Singer's owning the bank makes choices (1) and (5) tempting, but still incorrect. There is no support for either choices (2) or (4) in the passage.

26. Answer: (5) Choices (1), (2) and (4) are all options the girl's mother would choose for her, not actions the girl wants for herself. From her innocent description of the "bad" people, it is clear she does not consider going to jail, choice (3), a possibility.

28. Answer: (4) Both Niles and Vita refer to trying to call Singer's to tell them about the delay. None of the other choices is supported by the passage.

30. Answer: (2) Niles' use of the terms "shrunken heads," "asylum," and "loonies" suggest that he is worried about being crazy or being thought crazy. Choices (1), (4) and (5) state other concerns of Niles, but not his main one. Choice (3) is not supported by the passage at all.

To figure out your score, count the problems you missed. Then subtract the number of problems you missed from the total number of questions on the test. If half or more are correct, you may consider that you have passed the test. To organize your study time efficiently, turn to the Pretest/Posttest Diagnostic Chart in the back of this book.

A city newspaper stand filled with popular reading material.

fiction
writing of moderate length, such as stories or novels, that is based upon something the author imagined

nonfiction
writing of any length that is based on facts

In the following lessons you will study the various types of writing that make up popular literature. These include prose writing, **fiction** and **nonfiction**, as well as poetry and drama. You will also study the techniques used by writers of popular literature and learn to identify the effects created by these techniques. You should know, however, that what makes popular literature different from any other literature is simply that it is recent, and not that it employs techniques that are different. So as you work through the lessons, remember that the skills you learn will help you answer any questions on the GED exam that deal with reading or with literature of any sort. If you can read and understand popular literature, you can read and understand the classics.

There is no reason for you to be uneasy about any questions about literature that appear on the GED exam. You will learn to handle them.

In the lessons that follow, you will learn strategies for reading fiction, nonfiction, **poetry** and **drama.** You will learn to read and analyze passages that cover the full range of popular literature. The passages you will read are similar to those you will find on the GED exam. The questions you will be asked about those passages are also similar to those that will appear on the GED exam.

As you work through the lessons, keep in mind that the main thing you will be tested on in the GED literature section is your ability to understand what you read. Understanding what you read is your key to success on the GED exam. Authors write because they have something to say. They want you to understand them. So your first and most important goal is to grasp the author's basic meaning. To do this you will have to understand what the words mean and how to guess the meaning of the words you do not know from the clues the author gives you. You will learn to do this by using the clues in the **context.** You will then be able to figure out the author's **main point.**

Once you have figured out the author's main points, you can concentrate on recognizing the techniques the author uses to get his or her points across. Do not worry if you are not able to define literary techniques. The GED exam will not test how good you are at remembering definitions. What is important is that you be able to understand the *effects* created by the literary techniques used.

Another skill that flows from understanding the meaning of a piece of writing is the ability to take the author's ideas and apply them in a *new* context. The lessons that follow provide practice in this skill. Once you understand the author's ideas, you can apply them in a new setting. As you see, it is most important to understand what the author is saying.

The lessons and drills that follow will teach you many things. They will give you confidence by showing you that you have the capacity within yourself to perform well on the GED exam. They will help you learn how to make your native common sense and the experience you have gained by living work for you as you read and analyze popular literature.

poetry
writing that is generally short and emotional and expresses a new or different point of view in an unusual way

drama
writing that is meant to be performed, such as plays or scripts for movies or television; if it is funny, it is called comedy—if it is serious, it is simply called drama

context
the place in a passage where a word appears, or how it is used, which may provide the reader a clue as to its meaning; context may also refer to where or how lines fit into a passage

main point
the same thing as main idea; refers to the central idea of a passage, or some part of a passage; it may be explicit, which means that it is stated directly, or it may be implicit, which means that it is not stated directly

1 Fiction

Fiction differs from other kinds of writing in that the author is trying to create a world through imagination, rather than simply from fact. Even if there is some basis in fact, the real message will be something the author imagined.

Some authors' works take place wholly in an invented world— as in Lewis Carroll's *Alice in Wonderland,* for example. Other authors may deal with imaginary characters in an invented world, but a world invented out of scientific facts—as in science fiction. One author may write about actual figures from history, but will invent episodes and mix imaginary characters with the real ones—as in historical fiction. Another author will write about the life of a real person, but invent conversations, incidents and personal characteristics—as in fictional biography. The selection below is a form of fictional autobiography.

When you read fiction you may find that the author is writing about things you do not know. Often, though, you can figure out the author's meaning from context, from parts of a sentence or paragraph that help you. You will find clues that set the time and place the author is writing about. This process is called **getting meaning from context.**

Read the following passage by Gore Vidal. Try to get meaning from context as you read. Remember that the way words are used in the passage will give clues to what they mean. Use the Purpose Question above the passage to help you.

HOW DO THE REPUBLICANS AND FEDERALISTS DIFFER?

During the last session of the Third Congress I led the battle in the Senate against ratification of Jay's treaty with England. The treaty was clumsily drawn and to our disadvantage. It actually contained a clause forbidding us to export cotton in *American*
(5) ships. In effect, the treaty made us a colony again. It also revealed for the first time the deep and irreconcilable division between the Republican and Federalist parties—and they were now actual political parties, no longer simply factions. One was pro-French; the other pro-British. One wanted a loose confedera-
(10) tion of states, the other a strong central administration; one was made up of independent farmers in alliance with city workers; the other was devoted to trade and manufacturing. One was Jefferson; the other was Hamilton.

Strategies for READING

═══ Get Meaning from Context ═══

This skill involves using the words and phrases surrounding a new word to provide clues to its meaning. These surrounding words and phrases may be within the same sentence, or within a group of sentences.

If you are faced with a word you do not know, look for clues in the **context**—the surrounding text—to help you figure out what the word means. Sometimes the context will *define* a word, as "context" was defined in the preceding sentence. Sometimes the context will *compare* an unusual word to a known word. Or the context provides a *contrast* to a new word in such a way as to give a clue to its meaning.

Perhaps the context may even give the meaning of a word or words by using *examples*. Again, an author may use the context to *repeat the meaning* of a word, using words or phrases that are more familiar. Sometimes you will find that the context will include *details* that give clues to the word's meaning.

Even if you cannot figure out the exact meaning of a word or group of words, clues from the context will improve your ability to make a good guess.

Examples

DIRECTIONS: Use the information on this page and the passage by Gore Vidal on the preceding page to choose the <u>one</u> best answer for each item below.

1. Which phrase below *best* describes the meaning of the phrase "irreconcilable division" (line 6) in the passage?

   (1) difficult to understand
   (2) difficult to separate
   (3) totally opposed
   (4) almost identical
   (5) barely opposed

Answer: (3)   Choices (4) and (5) are wrong because they suggest similarities, and everything in the passage indicates great differences. Choices (1) and (2) are wrong because no clues anywhere in the passage support them.

2. Which phrase in the passage gives a clue to the meaning of "factions" (line 8)?

   (1) "Third Congress"
   (2) "against ratification"
   (3) "actual political parties"
   (4) "one was pro-French; the other pro-British"
   (5) "a strong central administration"

Answer: (4)   Choice (4) describes the opposing viewpoints of two political groups. No other choice correctly defines the word.

Practice

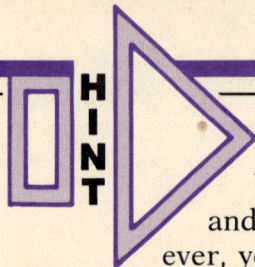

HINT

Look for key words that help to *define*—
because, that is, means, such as, is called—
and key words that help to show *contrast*—however, yet, still, nevertheless, but, instead of, while.
These key words provide clues to the meaning of new
or less familiar words.

DIRECTIONS: Choose the one best answer for each item below.

Items 1–6 refer to the following passage by James Michener.

WHAT CAN YOU FIND IN THE NIGHT SKY?

When he first stepped into the night he did what astronomers
had been doing for some two million years before the invention of
the telescope: he stood in the middle of the open land behind his
house and slowly surveyed the heavens, orienting himself as to
(5) the stars at this latitude, at this longitude and at this hour. He
thus became one with the ancient Assyrians, with the wondering
men who erected Stonehenge, and with the Incas of Peru. He
looked only briefly to the north, for he had long since mastered
the polar stars that never set; there was Polaris, friend of
(10) mariners, the two Bears, and the Dragon that wound its tortuous
way between them. He knew each of the stars in the Big Dipper
by its Greek designation and its characteristics, but his interest
tonight was in the stars of the west, which would soon be setting,
to be lost for half a year as they moved into proximity with the
(15) Sun, whose light would obscure them during the daytime hours.

And as he stood there, face up to the sky, he savored that
mysterious moment when the glow of twilight disappeared into
true darkness, allowing light from distant stars to reveal itself.
Low on the horizon stood Arcturus, glowing red like some mighty
(20) furnace, and he wanted desperately to bring it first into his
glasses, but he realized that the flickering atmosphere would
diminish the star, so he turned his gaze higher, and after a while
the whole panoply opened up, stars innumerable in brilliant con-
figurations and colors.

(25) Curiously, he did not bother with the bright half-Moon, for he
judged correctly that this was a garish nearby phenomenon which
he could always study at will; what he yearned to see were the
stars, those scintillating messengers from immortal distances. So
for some moments he surveyed his heavens, looking now at one
(30) high star, then another, until finally he settled upon the one
which he would first see with his new glasses.

GO ON TO THE NEXT PAGE.

1. The word "astronomers" in line 1 of the passage means

   (1) people who were mariners
   (2) people who studied the stars
   (3) people who invented the telescope
   (4) people who stood in their backyards
   (5) people who lived two million years ago

2. The word "proximity" in line 14 of the passage means

   (1) closeness
   (2) opposition
   (3) separation
   (4) orbit
   (5) calculation

3. Why was the man in the passage interested in the western stars?

   (1) They soon would be lost for half a year.
   (2) The sun was about to rise.
   (3) He knew their Greek designations.
   (4) Astronomers had watched them for two million years.
   (5) He had already seen Polaris.

4. What did the Incas and the Assyrians have in common?

   (1) Together, they built Stonehenge.
   (2) They lived at the same latitude and longitude.
   (3) They were both mariners.
   (4) Both surveyed the stars.
   (5) They looked only briefly at the northern stars.

5. "Arcturus" in line 19 is

   (1) a statue on the horizon
   (2) a mighty glowing furnace
   (3) a bright star
   (4) a brilliant configuration of stars
   (5) a large red planet

6. The word "panoply" in line 23 means

   (1) a brilliant display
   (2) a single bright star
   (3) a large door
   (4) the flickering atmosphere
   (5) twilight

Items 7–8 refer to the following passage by Mary Renault.

WHO ARE THESE CHILDREN?

Their mahouts, who had come with them from India, and knew them as a mother knows her child, had worked on them all yesterday in the high thatched elephant-sheds among the palm-trees; crooning and clucking and slapping, washing them in the canal; painting on their foreheads, in ochre or scarlet or green, sacred symbols enlaced with elaborate scrollwork; draping their wrinkled flanks with tasseled nets brilliantly dyed and threaded with gold bullion; fastening jeweled rosettes through slits in their leather ears; grooming their tails and toes.

7. The word "mahouts" means

   (1) Indian wise men
   (2) painters
   (3) decorators
   (4) elephant trainers
   (5) Indian kings

8. The word "ochre" means

   (1) a monster
   (2) elaborate scrollwork
   (3) a jewelled rosette
   (4) toenails
   (5) a color

Before you take the GED Mini-Test, check your answers on pages 23–24.

1

TIP

As you take the GED Mini-Test, relax. Remember it is designed to help you build your confidence in test taking. Set your goals for this test. Then use the Answers and Explanations to help you analyze how you did.

DIRECTIONS: Choose the one best answer for each item below.

Items 1–6 refer to the following passage by James Michener.

WHEN WAS THE EARTH CREATED?

He based his persuasive reasoning on two books which a Mississippi clergyman of some erudition had brought to his attention. The first was by Philip Gosse, an English writer, who argued simply that there were fossils, yes, and there were dinosaur bones, and there were geological

(5) strata, and everything was exactly as Darwin and the geologists described it. The secret was that in the year 4004 B.C. God had created the world exactly as Genesis said, and had hidden all these bits of evidence in the rocks and in the dinosaur bones as a kind of temptation to man's intellectual presumptions. Gosse explained everything in such sim-

(10) ple and beautiful terms that Strabismus said, 'No further discussion is necessary. The record is exactly what the atheistic professors at Yale say. It has to be, because God placed it there on the day of Creation.'

The second book was extremely useful when arguing with people from the universities who had a smattering of knowledge. It was George

(15) McCready Price's *The New Geology*, which Marcia Strabismus sold for ten dollars a copy, to those who sought the truth. It was a formidable essay, well founded in scientific jargon and difficult to rebut. Its major thesis appealed to all who suffered from the tyranny of science, and when Strabismus translated this into his own terms it made a persua-

(20) sive argument:

'These here scientists try to tell us that fossils found in rocks always grow from primitive forms to complex forms like you and me. And to prove this they show us that the primitive forms always appear in the earliest rocks, and the complex forms in later rocks. But how do they

(25) date the layers of rock? You stop right now and tell me how they date the layers of rock.

'They do it by seein' that primitive forms are in what they call the older layers. And the complex forms in the younger. Don't you see that they's arguin' in a great big circle. It's jest like a boy tellin' his girl,

(30) "You ought to kiss me because it's Valentime's Day, and Valentime's Day became special because that's when girls kissed boys."

'That's crazy reasonin' and the boy knows it, and the scientists know it, and they's pullin' the wool over the eyes of the public. I say it's time to stop.'

GO ON TO THE NEXT PAGE.

1. The word "geologists" in line 5 means

   (1) clergymen
   (2) people who study rocks
   (3) professors at Yale
   (4) English writers
   (5) dinosaurs

2. The word "atheistic" in line 11 means

   (1) beautiful
   (2) believing in God
   (3) not believing in God
   (4) intellectual
   (5) argumentative

3. The word "formidable" in line 16 means

   (1) childish
   (2) powerful
   (3) lacking detail
   (4) expensive
   (5) easy to rebut

4. Those who suffer from the "tyranny of science" are

   (1) George McCready Price and Marcia Strabismus
   (2) people who could not read
   (3) people from the universities
   (4) Darwin and Philip Gosse
   (5) men of God

5. How do scientists date the layers of rock?

   (1) They use carbon 14.
   (2) They look for fossils in the rock.
   (3) They compare them to moon rocks.
   (4) They start from 4004 B.C.
   (5) They draw circles around them.

6. What does Strabismus mean by "They's arguin' in a great big circle" (line 29)?

   (1) The method scientists use to date rocks assumes the truth of evolution.
   (2) Scientists are well-rounded people.
   (3) All scientific reasoning is circular.
   (4) Scientists assume that complex forms always grow from primitive forms.
   (5) Scientists cannot tell old rocks from young rocks.

Check your answers to the GED Mini-Test on page 24.

Answers and Explanations

Practice *pp. 20–21*

1. **Answer:** (2) While it is true that the passage refers to mariners as in choice (1), the inventors of the telescope as in choice (3), people who stood in their backyards as in choice (4) and people who lived long ago as in choice (5), these are all merely descriptive details. The one common thought in this passage is observing the stars.

2. **Answer:** (1) The only way the light of the sun would obscure the stars of the west for half a year is if they were close to the sun, so you know that choices (2) and (3) are wrong. It is plain from the context of the passage that choice (5) cannot be correct. Choice (4) would be a reasonable guess, but the passage does not really support it.

3. **Answer:** (1) There is no support in the passage for choice (2). Choices (3) and (4) may be true statements, but they do not answer the question. While choice (5) is also a true statement, and would be a good guess, it is clear from the context that choice (1) is a better answer.

4. **Answer:** (4) The common thought that links all the people who are mentioned by the author in this passage is that they all watched the stars. Also, you can eliminate every other answer, since no other answer is specifically supported in the passage.

5. Answer: (3)   Choice (2) is a description of how the author thinks Arcturus looks, but it is not a definition. Choice (4) uses language taken from the passage, but this language does not describe Arcturus. There is no support in the passage for choice (1). Choice (5) would be a good guess, but if you read the passage carefully, it is plain that Arcturus is a star.

7. Answer: (4)   Although choices (1) and (5) both use the word "Indian" from the passage, there is no other information to indicate that "mahouts" are either wise men or kings. There is information to indicate that they both paint and decorate the elephants, choices (2) and (3). The passage, however, indicates that mahouts do much more than merely paint and decorate. Thus, choice (4) is the best answer.

6. Answer: (1)   Choice (3) has no support in the passage. The only reason this answer would seem plausible at all is because of the word "opened." Choice (4) is a phrase from the passage, but clearly not the answer to the question. Choice (5) is wrong because the events in the passage occur after twilight has disappeared. Choice (2) is closer to correct, but the phrase "stars innumerable" makes it plain that choice (1) is the right answer.

8. Answer: (5)   There is no support in the passage for choice (1), although the word is close to "ogre." Choice (4) also has no support in the passage. Both choices (2) and (3) refer to items that are mentioned in the passage. But it is plain from the context that these items do not have the same meaning as "ochre." Choice (5) is also supported by the phrase "or scarlet or green," which are both colors.

GED Mini-Test   *pp. 22–23*

1. Answer: (2)   It is plain from the context that this passage is about fossils, dinosaur bones and other things found in rocks. Choice (5) is clearly wrong. Choices (3) and (4) could be correct, but it appears from the context that the term "geologists" is a broader term than described by these answers. Choice (1) is also wrong from the context, which makes it plain that the geologists and the clergymen are at opposite extremes.

3. Answer: (2)   The passage makes it plain that choice (5) is wrong, since it states the opposite. In the same way, choice (3) is clearly wrong from the context. Choice (1) has no support in the passage, and would make no sense. Choice (4) would be a possible guess, but even as a guess it would make much less sense than choice (2). Thus, choice (2) is the only answer that really fits the context of the passage.

5. Answer: (2)   You may know from your independent knowledge that choice (1) and possibly choice (3) are both true statements. However, neither of these answers finds any support in the passage, which is focused on fossils. There is no support at all for choice (5), and not really for choice (4), either, although choice (4) does make reference to a date that appears in the passage.

2. Answer: (3)   There is no support in the passage for choice (1), although "atheistic" looks like "aesthetic." Choices (4) and (5) would be reasonable guesses since both of those choices describe qualities that professors might possess. However, if either of these choices were correct, they would add little to the passage. This reduces the alternatives to choices (2) and (3), and it is clear from the context that choice (3) is the right answer.

4. Answer: (3)   Choices (1) and (5) describe people who clearly do not suffer from the tyranny of science, since these are the people with the same views as Strabismus. Choice (4) is also wrong because it is clear from the context that Darwin and Philip Gosse have nothing in common. Choice (2) has no support in the passage, and would not make sense from the context.

6. Answer: (1)   Choice (3) would be a good answer except for the word "all," since the passage is not about all scientific reasoning. There is no support for choice (2). Choice (5) may be true, but it does not answer the question. Choice (4) is true, but it is not what Strabismus means. What he means is that when scientists use this assumption to prove evolution, they are arguing in a circle.

2 Fiction

As you learned in the last lesson, fiction is a form of writing that tells a story. All authors tell stories through sentences combined into paragraphs. Each sentence expresses at least one idea, and each paragraph expresses at least one main idea.

In fiction, the main idea of a paragraph is the one idea the author is trying to focus on—the purpose of the paragraph, a sort of summary. The main idea may be stated in a single sentence anywhere in the paragraph. Or it may be a combination of several sentences, each of which provides a detail.

Read the following passage by Louis Auchincloss. Look for the main idea as you read. Try to state it in your own words. Use the Purpose Question above the paragraph to help you.

WHAT DOES THE FUTURE HOLD FOR MADGE?

Madge Dyett felt that the year 1937, which had marked for so many of her friends a turning point in the Great Depression, seemed only to confirm its permanent doom for herself and her parents. They continued to live in the shabby, four-storey, red
(5) brick house on East Thirty-fourth Street, but only because they could not sell it, and the top floor was rented to an uncle and aunt. Her father was out of work and prattled all day, with a self-confidence that nothing could justify, of his financial prospects and plans. Madge had had to give up college and take a job teach-
(10) ing at Miss Fairfax's School, of which she and her mother were alumnae. Her only future seemed to be to stay there until she was old enough to retire.

Henry Street looking west from Market Street, Manhattan; November 29, 1935.

Identify the Main Idea

The main idea is the most important point an author is trying to make. It is stated at the beginning, middle or end of a paragraph.

In many paragraphs the **main idea** will be clearly stated in a single sentence. This sentence often is at the beginning or at the end of the paragraph. If it is at the beginning, then the rest of the paragraph will simply add details that support the main idea. If it is at the end, then the details will be given first and then summarized.

When you read a paragraph for the main idea, you should focus on the first and last sentences. If either the first or last sentence seems to "sum up" the paragraph, then it expresses an explicit, or clearly stated, main idea.

There may also be an explicit main idea in a sentence in the middle of the paragraph. You can look for such a sentence if the first and last sentences of a paragraph seem to be details. If there is no single sentence that "sums up" the paragraph, then the paragraph does not have an explicit main idea. All the passages in this lesson have explicit main ideas.

Examples

DIRECTIONS: Use the information on this page and the passage by Louis Auchincloss on the preceding page to choose the <u>one</u> best answer for each item below.

1. Which of the following sentences states the main idea of the paragraph?

   (1) Madge's father was out of work.
   (2) The Depression was over.
   (3) Madge would retire soon from her teaching job.
   (4) Madge and her parents seemed permanently doomed by the Great Depression.
   (5) Things were looking better.

Answer: (4) Choices (1) and (2) are facts, but they are only details, not the main idea. Choice (3) is false. Choice (5) is false as to Madge and her parents, though true for others.

2. Which of the following sentences does *not* support the main idea?

   (1) Madge had to give up college.
   (2) Her parents had to rent out part of their house.
   (3) Madge's father could not cope.
   (4) Things would be better when Madge's parents sold their house.
   (5) Madge had only her retirement to look forward to.

Answer: (4) All the other answers support the main idea. The problem with selling the house is only a detail to support the main idea of doom.

Practice

HINT

Often the main idea of a paragraph will appear at the beginning of the paragraph. It may also appear at the end. Always read the whole paragraph before you try to find the main idea.

DIRECTIONS: Choose the one best answer for each item below.

Items 1–2 refer to the following passage by Garrison Keillor.

HOW DO LAKE WOBEGONIANS CHOOSE THEIR CARS?

In Lake Wobegon, car ownership is a matter of faith. Lutherans drive Fords, bought from Bunsen Motors, the Lutheran car dealer, and Catholics drive Chevies from Main Garage, owned by the Kruegers, except for Hjalmar Ingqvist, who has a Lincoln.
(5)   Years ago, John Tollerud was tempted by Chevyship until (then) Pastor Tommerdahl took John aside after church and told him it was his (Pastor Tommerdahl's) responsibility to point out that Fords get better gas mileage and have a better trade-in value. And he knew for a fact that the Kruegers spent a share of the Chevy
(10)   profits to purchase Asian babies and make them Catholics. So John got a new Ford Falcon. It turned out to be a dud. The transmission went out after ten thousand miles and the car tended to pull to the left. In a town where car ownership is by faith, however, a person doesn't complain about these things, and John
(15)   figured there must be a good reason for his car trouble, which perhaps he would understand more fully someday.

1. Which sentence below *best* describes the main idea of the paragraph?

  (1) Most of the Lutherans in Lake Wobegon drive Fords.
  (2) Most of the Catholics in Lake Wobegon drive Chevies.
  (3) Most people in Lake Wobegon buy cars based on their religion.
  (4) The author of the passage does not think Fords are good cars.
  (5) There is a Lincoln dealership in Lake Wobegon.

2. Why does the author of the selection tell the story about John Tollerud?

  (1) He tells the story to show how people make choices based on religion.
  (2) He wants to point out that Fords get good gas mileage.
  (3) He wants to show how religion taught John not to complain.
  (4) He wants to show that Fords have bad transmissions.
  (5) He wants to show how John was punished for wanting a Chevy.

GO ON TO THE NEXT PAGE.

Items 3–6 refer to the following passage by Larry McMurtry.

WHY DID THE WIFE EAT IN THE LOFT?

She seldom did eat with them. It bothered July a good deal, though he made no complaint. Since their little table was almost under the loft he could look up and see Elmira's bare legs as he ate. It didn't seem normal to him. His mother had died when he

(5)   was six, yet he could remember that she always ate with the family; she would never have sat with her legs dangling practically over her husband's head. He had been at supper in many cabins in his life, but in none of them had the wife sat in the loft while the meal was eaten. It was a thing out of the ordinary, and

(10)   July didn't like for things to be out of the ordinary in his life. It seemed to him it was better to do as other people did—if society at large did things a certain way, it had to be for a good reason, and he looked upon common practices as rules that should be obeyed. After all, his job was to see that common practices were

(15)   honored—that citizens weren't shot, or banks robbed.

Joe didn't share July's discomfort with the fact that his mother seldom came to the table. When she did come it was usually to scold him, and he got scolded enough as it was— besides, he liked eating with July. So far as he was concerned,

(20)   marrying July was the best thing his mother had ever done. She scolded July as freely as she scolded him, which didn't seem right to Joe. But then July accepted it and never scolded back, so perhaps that was the way of the world. . . .

3. Which statement reflects the main idea of the first paragraph?

(1) Common practices should be obeyed.
(2) It is not a good idea to complain.
(3) A wife should eat with her family.
(4) Banks should not be robbed.
(5) Elmira should wear stockings.

5. Which statement *best* describes July's beliefs as stated in the first paragraph?

(1) Everyone should be free.
(2) Wives should do what their husbands tell them to do.
(3) There is a good reason for society's rules.
(4) If something bothers you, you should discuss it.
(5) He does not like Elmira.

4. Which statement is *not* supported in the selection?

(1) July had eaten in many cabins.
(2) July was probably a sheriff.
(3) July's mother had died when he was six.
(4) July liked surprises.
(5) July's cabin had a loft.

6. Which statement *best* describes Joe's beliefs as stated in the second paragraph?

(1) Joe did not like to eat with Elmira.
(2) Joe's mother scolded him a lot.
(3) Joe did not respect July because Elmira scolded him.
(4) Women scolded; men stayed out of the way.
(5) Joe hoped July liked him.

Before you take the GED Mini-Test, check your answers on pages 30–31.

GED Mini-Test

2

TIP
When you are reading for the main idea, remember to look for a key sentence that "sums up" the whole paragraph. It may be anywhere in the paragraph.

DIRECTIONS: Choose the one best answer for each item below.

Items 1–6 refer to the following passage by John Knowles.

WHY DOES THE WAR STILL LIVE FOR THE AUTHOR?

Everyone has a moment in history which belongs particularly to him. It is the moment when his emotions achieve their most powerful sway over him, and afterward when you say to this person "the world today" or "life" or "reality" he will assume that you mean this moment,
(5) even if it is fifty years past. The world, through his unleashed emotions, imprinted itself upon him, and he carries the stamp of that passing moment forever.

For me, this moment—four years is a moment in history—was the war. The war was and is reality for me. I still instinctively live and
(10) think in its atmosphere. These are some of its characteristics: Franklin Delano Roosevelt is the President of the United States, and he always has been. The other two eternal world leaders are Winston Churchill and Josef Stalin. America is not, never has been, and never will be what the songs and poems call it, a land of plenty. Nylon, meat, gasoline, and
(15) steel are rare. There are too many jobs and not enough workers. Money is very easy to earn but rather hard to spend, because there isn't very much to buy. Trains are always late and always crowded with "servicemen." The war will always be fought very far from America, and it will never end. Nothing in America stands still for very long, including the
(20) people who are always either leaving or on leave. People in America cry often. Sixteen is the key and crucial and natural age for a human being to be, and people of all other ages are ranged in an orderly manner ahead of and behind you as a harmonious setting for the sixteen-year-olds of the world. When you are sixteen, adults are slightly impressed
(25) and almost intimidated by you. This is a puzzle finally solved by the realization that they foresee your military future, fighting for them. You do not foresee it. To waste anything in America is immoral. String and tinfoil are treasures. Newspapers are always crowded with strange maps and names of towns, and every few months the earth seems to lurch
(30) from its path when you see something in the newspapers, such as the time Mussolini, who almost seemed one of the eternal leaders, is photographed hanging upside down on a meathook.

GO ON TO THE NEXT PAGE.

1. Which statement *best* describes the main idea of the first paragraph?

    (1) Reality is what you make of it.
    (2) Time is like a river.
    (3) Fifty years is like a heartbeat.
    (4) Emotions are powerful.
    (5) Every person has a special moment.

2. Which statement is *not* supported in the first paragraph?

    (1) Some moments last forever.
    (2) Each person has his own reality.
    (3) Reality is converted to emotion.
    (4) All men are brothers.
    (5) Some emotions are timeless.

3. Why does the author still clearly remember the war?

    (1) Franklin Delano Roosevelt was President.
    (2) It was his personal reality.
    (3) There was not much to buy.
    (4) The war would never end.
    (5) America was not a land of plenty.

4. Which statement *best* describes the author's feelings about the war?

    (1) It was very real for him, yet he was not actively involved.
    (2) It was real for him because he was a soldier at that time.
    (3) It was very unreal to him.
    (4) The war was very disruptive to the people at home.
    (5) The war was very close to home.

5. Why does the author think adults are impressed with sixteen-year-olds?

    (1) Adults would like to be young.
    (2) Sixteen-year-olds do not waste things.
    (3) Sixteen-year-olds read newspapers.
    (4) They will be fighting soon for adults.
    (5) Sixteen is a natural age to be.

6. Why does the author say string and tinfoil are treasures?

    (1) The war has made them scarce.
    (2) They are useful to sixteen-year-olds.
    (3) He liked them when he was sixteen.
    (4) People are very wasteful.
    (5) They help him to solve puzzles.

Check your answers to the GED Mini-Test on page 31.

Answers and Explanations

Practice   *pp. 27–28*

1. **Answer:** (3)   Choice (1) is a true statement from the passage. Choice (2) is also a true statement from the passage. However, choice (3) is a broader statement than either choice (1) or (2). Both choices (1) and (2) are *illustrations* of the principle in choice (3). Choice (4) may be true, but it is not supported by the passage. Choice (5) is not supported by the passage, either, and is not even a reasonable inference from the information given in the passage.

2. **Answer:** (1)   There is support in the passage for choices (2) and (4), but these answers do not support the main idea of the paragraph. They are only details. There is no support in the passage for choices (3) and (5). They are related to the main idea, but only because they use key words from the passage and not because they have a real connection.

3. **Answer:** (1) Choices (3) and (4) are true statements, but they are not the main idea; they are details to support it. There is no support in the passage for choice (5). Choice (2) may be what July thinks, but there is no indication it is what the author thinks.

5. **Answer:** (3) Choices (1) and (4) are both false. Choices (2) and (5) may be true, but the passage does not support them. There is direct support for choice (3).

4. **Answer:** (4) All the other choices are supported directly or indirectly by the passage. Choices (1) and (3) are direct statements from the passage. Choices (2) and (5) are reasonable inferences. Only choice (4) has no support at all.

6. **Answer:** (4) Choice (1) is a possible inference from the passage, but not a direct inference, and *not* the main idea. Choice (2) is a true statement, but it is a detail to explain Joe's beliefs and not really a statement of those beliefs. Choice (3) is contradicted by the passage. Elmira's scolding had more to do with how Joe felt about her than about July. Choice (5) is a true inference. However, choice (4) has direct support and is thus the best answer.

GED Mini-Test *pp. 29–30*

1. **Answer:** (5) Choice (1) may be both profound and true, but there is no support in this passage for it. Choice (2) is symbolic language and may also be true, but there is neither direct nor indirect support for it in the passage. Choice (4) is a reasonable inference from the passage, but not really related to the main idea, which is connected with time. Choice (3) is related to time and so seems to be close to the main idea. But choice (3) is simply a detail about time and not the main idea.

2. **Answer:** (4) Choice (2) is simply a restatement of the main idea of the passage and thus is supported by the passage as a whole. Choices (1) and (3) are each details from the passage that support the main idea. Choice (5) is an inference from the passage that directly supports the main idea and is very close to it. Thus, the only statement that is not supported is choice (4).

3. **Answer:** (2) Although this question does not specifically ask for the main idea, this choice is the main idea of the passage. It is what the author is really trying to say. All the other choices are things that the author remembers from the war. But they differ from this choice in that they are only details that he remembers. The reason that he remembers details of the war at all is because it was his own personal reality, his own moment in time. Thus, choice (2) is the only correct answer.

4. **Answer:** (1) Choice (2) is false only because the author was not a soldier. Choice (3) is false because the passage makes it plain the opposite is true. Choice (5) is also directly contradicted by the passage as a whole and by specific statements in the passage. Choice (4) may be a true statement. The passage, however, does not support the truth of this statement and this statement does not describe the way the author remembers the war.

5. **Answer:** (4) Choice (1) is probably a true statement, but it is not the reason why adults are impressed with sixteen-year-olds. Choice (2) may also be true, but again, it does not answer the question. Choice (3) may be a fact and also an inference from the passage, but it does not answer the question either. Choice (5) is clearly something the author believes. But the passage does not support this choice as the best answer to the question. Thus, by a process of elimination, choice (4) is the best answer.

6. **Answer:** (1) Choice (2) is a possible inference from the passage, but there is no real support for this inference. Choice (3) is a possible inference but has even less support than choice (2). There is no support at all for choices (4) and (5). They are not even reasonable inferences, although choice (4) might be true. Thus, by a process of elimination, it is plain from reading the passage and the question that choice (1) is the only possible answer.

3 Fiction

When a paragraph does not clearly state the author's main idea, it should have an **implicit** main idea.

As you learned in the last lesson, most paragraphs will have a main idea. However, the main idea is not always clearly stated. Sometimes there is no single key sentence in a paragraph that sums up the paragraph. The author wants you to fill in the blanks, as it were, by yourself. You must figure out what the author is trying to say; you are not told directly. Yet there still is a main idea—an *implicit* main idea. You must **infer** it, figure it out from the hints and details in the passage.

Read the following passage by M. M. Kaye. Look for the implicit main idea as you read. Try to state it in your own words. Use the Purpose Question above the passage to help you.

WHAT CHANGED THE WORLD FOR THIS MAN?

Months ago he had told Wally that he could never fall in love again because he was cured of love forever—immunized to the disease like a man who has recovered from smallpox. And only a few hours ago, eight at most, he would have repeated that state-
(5) ment and been confident that it was true. He still could not understand why it should no longer be so, or how it had come about. His feelings for the child Juli, though protective, had certainly never been either fond or sentimental (small boys being sel-dom interested in, let alone deeply attached to little girls much
(10) younger than themselves) and given the choice he would undoubt-edly have preferred a playmate of his own age and sex. Besides, he had known who she was when he carried her through the river and stood holding her for an unconscionably long time in the dusk; yet his only emotion had been impatience . . .
(15) Two nights later, staring at her in the durbar tent and dis-covering with amazement that she was beautiful, his pulses had not quickened or his emotions been stirred; and when she came to his tent he had been suspicious, irritated and vaguely sen-timental by turn, and ended up feeling angry and embarrassed. So
(20) why on earth should a few minutes in which she had sobbed in his arms, and the sight of her wet, distorted face, change the world for him? It did not make sense—yet it had happened, all the same.

═ **Identify an Unstated Main Idea** ═══

This skill identifies the most important point an author is trying to make. An unstated main idea is hinted at. It is implied.

Before you look for an implicit, or implied, main idea, first make sure that the passage does not have an **explicit** main idea—a key sentence that sums up the paragraph. If not, you will need to look for an **implicit main idea**—one that is suggested or hinted at without being actually stated. To do this, you must read all the information. You must infer what the author's main idea is. To **infer** means to make a good guess, based on available information. To infer the main idea of a paragraph:

1. Decide what the paragraph is about (the topic).
2. Decide what point the supporting details make about the topic.
3. Combine the topic with the point the details make about it.

Examples

DIRECTIONS: Use the information on this page and the passage by M. M. Kaye on the preceding page to choose the <u>one</u> best answer for each item below.

1. What is the main idea of the passage?

   (1) He could never fall in love again because he was cured of love forever.
   (2) His feelings for Juli were neither fond nor sentimental.
   (3) He was surprised to find himself in love again.
   (4) He discovered his only emotion was impatience.
   (5) Juli made him feel angry and embarrassed.

Answer: (3)   Choices (1) and (2) refer to the man's feelings from a long time ago. Choices (4) and (5) refer to his more recent feelings. Only choice (3) refers to his feelings as of the time of the passage. The other choices are contrasts to the main idea.

2. How long has the man in the passage known Juli?

   (1) He has known her for several months.
   (2) He has known her since he was a small boy.
   (3) He has known her for two days.
   (4) He has known her for about eight hours.
   (5) He has known her since he had smallpox.

Answer: (2)   There is no support in the passage for choice (5). All the other choices refer to times mentioned in the passage, but none of these reflect how long he has known Juli.

DIRECTIONS: Choose the <u>one</u> best answer for each item below.

Items 1–8 refer to the following passage by Garrison Keillor.

WHAT CAN YOU DO WITH A CUP OF CLOROX?

When I left Lake Wobegon, Donna Bunsen and I promised each other we'd read the same books that summer as a token of our love, which we sealed with a kiss in her basement. She wore white shorts and a blue blouse with white stars. She poured a
(5) cup of Clorox bleach in the washing machine, and then we kissed. In books, men and women "embraced passionately," but I didn't know how much passion to use, so I put my arms around her and held my lips to hers and rubbed her lovely back, under the wings. Our reading list was ten books, five picked by her and five by me,
(10) and we made a reading schedule so that, although apart, we would have the same things on our minds at the same time and would think of each other. We each picked the loftiest books we knew of, such as Plato's *Republic, War and Peace, The Imitation of Christ,* the *Bhagavad-Gita, The Art of Loving,* to have great
(15) thoughts to share all summer as we read, but I didn't get far; my copy of Plato sat in my suitcase, and I fished it out only to feel guilty for letting her down so badly. I wrote her a letter about love, studded with Plato quotes picked out of Bartlett's, but didn't mail it, it was so shameless and false. She sent me two postcards
(20) from the Black Hills, and in the second she asked, "Do you still love me?" I did, but evidently not enough to read those books and become someone worthy of love, so I didn't reply.

Two years later she married a guy who sold steel supermarket shelving, and they moved to San Diego. I think of her lovingly
(25) every time I use Clorox. Half a cup is enough to bring it all back.

1. Which of the following statements reflects the main idea of the paragraph?

(1) True love is always sealed with a kiss.
(2) The man in the passage liked to read a lot.
(3) The man in the passage loved Donna less than he thought.
(4) Young love always ends in sorrow.
(5) The man in the passage did not keep his promises.

2. How does the man in the passage feel about Clorox?

(1) He feels that half a cup is enough.
(2) It makes him feel sad and lonesome.
(3) He thinks it is the best product on the market.
(4) The smell of it brings back loving memories of Donna.
(5) It reminds him of the great books of the world.

GO ON TO THE NEXT PAGE.

3. Which of the following details does *not* support the main idea of the passage?

   (1) Donna married and moved to San Diego.
   (2) Donna and the man in the passage promised to read the same books all summer.
   (3) Donna wore white shorts and a blue blouse.
   (4) The man in the passage did not answer Donna's postcards.
   (5) The man in the passage and Donna wanted to think of each other all summer long.

4. Why did the man in the passage and Donna pick lofty books to read?

   (1) They wanted to impress each other.
   (2) They wanted to have great thoughts to share.
   (3) They wanted to further their educations.
   (4) They wanted to spend all their time reading.
   (5) Lofty books reminded them of each other.

5. What does the context tell us about Bartlett's?

   (1) Plato read Bartlett's.
   (2) Bartlett's is shameless and false.
   (3) Bartlett's is a love story.
   (4) Bartlett's is a lofty book.
   (5) Bartlett's is a source of famous quotations.

6. Which of the following details supports the main idea of the passage?

   (1) Donna went to the Black Hills.
   (2) Donna's husband sold supermarket shelving.
   (3) In books, men and women "embraced passionately."
   (4) The *Bhagavad-Gita* and *The Art of Loving* are lofty books.
   (5) Donna and the man in the passage wanted to have the same things on their minds at the same time.

7. Why did the man in the passage not mail the letter he had written to Donna?

   (1) He was embarrassed because he had not read Plato's *Republic*.
   (2) He spilled a half a cup of Clorox all over the letter.
   (3) He knew that she was on a trip somewhere in the Black Hills, but he did not know her mailing address.
   (4) He thought that she was shameless and false.
   (5) He had decided over the summer that he really did not love Donna after all, but he did not have the heart to tell her of his changed feelings.

8. Why did the man in the passage not reply to Donna's postcard?

   (1) He was too busy to take time for things like writing letters.
   (2) The only book that he took with him was Bartlett's.
   (3) He thought that he was unworthy of love.
   (4) He had moved to San Diego and did not get the postcard in time.
   (5) He did not know her address until two years later, when she was already married to someone else.

Before you take the GED Mini-Test, check your answers on pages 37–38.

DIRECTIONS: Choose the one best answer for each item below.

Items 1–6 refer to the following passage by Louis Auchincloss.

WHAT DO PEOPLE DO ON A CRUISE?

The Foxens, like most of the passengers, lived in the past. But it was not, Betty noted, necessarily the real past. It was rather a past that was being constantly edited, smoothed, brightened, touched up. It was a past studded with the little victories of the person who was in the process of
(5)   creating it. Ned Foxen loved to relate to her how cleverly he had dealt with this or that ornery customer of his Buick agency in Rochester and how he had steered a bill to passage in the Albany assembly by playing both sides against the middle. And Roseanne enjoyed telling her how often she had been right in warning her married children not to do the
(10)   things that they had then done and later regretted. The past had been purged of thorns and bitterness; it was now an unending source of complacency.

And the future? Well, of course, there was not so very much of that to look forward to. It was better to divide one's time between a semific-
(15)   tional past and an artificial present. The world of the cruise was a world that had abolished all the bogies of old people: the difficulty of cooking and cleaning without servants, the problem of how to use leisure time, the ache of loneliness. On board the *Stella Maris,* obsequious Italian stewards administered to their every need; their working
(20)   hours were filled with a gentle round of cocktail parties, card parties, lectures, movies and deck games; and there was no end of ears in which to plant their reminiscences, no end of tongues to offer them those of others. It was a world in which the only imaginable task was that of mixing the drinks oneself if one entertained in one's cabin. Even death,
(25)   if it came on the cruise, was easy. There were several fine coffins, inlaid with satin, ready for emergency, in the hold.

1. Which statement *best* describes the main idea of the first paragraph?

   (1) The Foxens lived in the past.
   (2) The past got better with time.
   (3) Ned Foxen loved to tell stories.
   (4) Ned Foxen was a clever man.
   (5) The Foxens were retired.

2. Why does Roseanne enjoy talking about her children's problems?

   (1) She is a mean person.
   (2) She just likes to talk.
   (3) It is her way of editing the past.
   (4) She does not have anything else to talk about.
   (5) Her children do not have good sense.

GO ON TO THE NEXT PAGE.

3. Which statement *best* describes the main idea of the second paragraph?

   (1) There is not much to do on a cruise.
   (2) Cruises are set up to fill the empty lives of old people.
   (3) Cruises are a lot of fun for young people.
   (4) Old people have many bogies.
   (5) Life on a cruise is easy.

5. Why do the people on the cruise not like to think about the future?

   (1) They are too busy having fun.
   (2) It is hard to cope without servants.
   (3) They are entertaining in their cabins.
   (4) Death will soon overtake them.
   (5) They are worried about the problems of their children.

4. From the context it is clear that the word "bogies" in line 16 does not mean

   (1) medical problems
   (2) empty hours
   (3) cleaning
   (4) loneliness
   (5) cooking

6. Which statement does *not* support the main idea of the passage?

   (1) On the cruise there were stewards who administered to every need.
   (2) Mixing drinks was the only task that anyone on the cruise would ever have to do without help.
   (3) Even death was made easy for the passengers on the ship.
   (4) There was always another passenger to listen to reminiscences.
   (5) The cruise ship was named the *Stella Maris*.

Check your answers to the GED Mini-Test on page 38.

Answers and Explanations

Practice   *pp. 34–35*

1. Answer: (3)   Although the passage uses the phrase "sealed with a kiss," choice (1) is clearly not the main idea. Choice (2) is simply a detail about the man in the passage. Choice (5) is also a detail, and is closer to the main idea than choice (2). But choice (3) is a better answer, because the reason he did not keep his promises is that he loved Donna less than he thought. Choice (4) may be true, but as in choice (1), the word "always" is a clue that this answer is not the right one.

3. Answer: (3)   Choice (5) is very close to the main idea of the passage, and is thus clearly wrong. Choice (4) is a detail that directly supports the main idea and is thus also wrong. Choices (1) and (2) are details that only indirectly support the main idea. Choice (3), however, does not support the main idea at all.

2. Answer: (4)   Choice (1) is a direct statement from the passage, but it is not the main idea. Choice (2) is the opposite of the way he feels about Clorox. Choice (3) may be a true statement, but there is no support for this answer in the passage. Choice (5) may also be true, since the author's memories of Donna are connected to the books they were going to read. However, choice (4) sums up the whole passage in a sentence, and is thus clearly the best choice for an answer.

4. Answer: (2)   Although choice (3) might be true, it is not the reason given in the passage. Choice (4) may also be true, but it is not the reason given in the passage either. Choice (1) might be a reasonable inference from the passage, but choice (2) is clearly a better answer. Choice (5) is not supported at all in the passage.

5. Answer: (5)   Choice (1) is wrong because there is no indication in the passage that Plato read Bartlett's. Choice (2) is wrong because it is the letter, not Bartlett's, that is shameless and false. There is no support in the passage for choices (3) and (4). There is neither any indication that Bartlett's is a love story nor that it is one of the lofty books.

7. Answer: (1)   There is no support in the passage for choice (2). Choice (4) is also wrong because there is no indication that Donna was shameless and false. Choices (3) and (5) would both be reasonable guesses, but choice (1) is supported by the sentence in which the letter is mentioned.

6. Answer: (5)   Choice (1) is a detail from the passage, but it does not support the main idea. The same is true of choices (2) and (3); they are details, but they have nothing to do with the main idea. Choice (4) is an inference from the passage, but like all the other choices it does not support the main idea. Thus, choice (5) is the only correct answer.

8. Answer: (3)   You can tell this is the right answer from the sentence where it states that he did not reply to the postcard. Also, although all the other answers might be reasonable explanations for why he did not reply to the postcard, they are all guesses. None is supported in the passage.

GED Mini-Test   *pp. 36–37*

1. Answer: (2)   Choices (3) and (4) are true statements from the passage, but both are merely details that support the main idea and are not the main idea itself. Choice (5) is a reasonable inference from the information in the passage, but is also merely a detail. Choice (1) is closer to the main idea, but a reading of the passage as a whole reveals that choice (2) is a better answer.

3. Answer: (2)   Choice (1) is clearly false. Choice (3) may be true, but the passage really makes no reference to young people. The whole focus of the passage is on old people and their problems. Choices (4) and (5) are both true. However, these choices are details that support the main idea and are not the main idea itself.

5. Answer: (4)   Choice (1) is false. Choice (5) may be a true statement, but it has nothing to do with the future. Choice (2) is not supported by the passage at all. Its only connection to the passage is the word "servants." Choice (3) is close to the right answer, but it is not supported by the passage.

2. Answer: (3)   There is no support in the passage for choice (1), since there is no indication that she is a mean person. Choices (2) and (4) are reasonable inferences from the passage, but choice (3) is much closer to the main idea. The same is true of choice (5). It is a possible inference, but it is not related to the main idea, like choice (3).

4. Answer: (1)   The reason that you know this is the correct answer is because the other answers, which refer to empty hours, cleaning, loneliness and cooking, are all directly or indirectly mentioned in the passage as examples of the bogies of old people. Choice (1) may well be a bogie of old people too, but it is not one from the passage.

6. Answer: (5)   Keeping in mind that the main idea of the passage deals with the empty lives of old people, it is clear that only choice (5) has no relationship to the concerns of old people and is thus the correct answer. All the other choices are related to the concerns of old people on a cruise.

4 Fiction

In fiction, the author uses facts and details to make the main idea seem compelling. If the main idea were simply stated directly, the reader would probably not be as interested.

Sometimes you will be called upon to identify or restate particular facts or details from a passage. Usually these will be facts or details that support the main idea or contrast with it. When you read a passage, as you look for the main idea, you should also note the details that support it.

Read the following passage by Nadine Gordimer. As you read, look for the facts and details the author uses to support the main idea. Try to state the main idea and the supporting details in your own words. Use the Purpose Question above the passage to help you.

WHAT IS BEHIND THE CHAIN AND THE CURTAIN?

When I got home that same evening, the fellow wasn't there. He'd gone. Not a word, not a note; nothing. Every time I heard the lift rattling I thought, here he is. But he didn't come. When I was home on Saturday afternoon I couldn't stand it any longer
(5) and I went up to the Versfelds and asked the old lady if I couldn't sleep there a few days, I said my flat was being painted and the smell turned my stomach. I thought, if he comes to the garage, there are people around, at least there are the boys. I was smoking nearly as much as *he* used to and I couldn't sleep. I had to ask
(10) Mr. Levine to give me something. The slightest sound and I was in a cold sweat. At the end of the week I had to go back to the flat, and I bought a chain for the door and made a heavy curtain so's you couldn't see anyone standing there. I didn't go out, once I'd got in from work—not even to the early flicks—so I wouldn't have
(15) to come back into the building at night. You know how it is when you're nervous, the funniest things comfort you: I'd just tell myself, well, if I shouldn't turn up to work in the morning, the boy'd send someone to see.

Then slowly I was beginning to forget about it. I kept the cur-
(20) tain and the chain and I stayed at home, but when you get used to something, no matter what it is, you don't think about it all the time, any more, though you still believe you do. I hadn't been to Maison Claude for about two weeks and my hair was a sight. Claude advised a soft perm and so it happened that I took a cou-
(25) ple of hours off in the afternoon to get it done. The boss-boy Jack says to me when I come back, "He was here."

Strategies for READING

═ Restate Information ═

This skill involves identifying the main idea, topic sentence and supporting details in order to present information in another way. It can often help you better understand something you are reading or studying.

Often an author will say the same thing in a number of ways. It may not be obvious that the same thing is being said, because the author is using a variety of examples, with different details, but all making the same point.

This is particularly true about feelings. Instead of just saying how a character felt, the author will tell you things that the character did. The character may not even understand the significance of these acts, but these actions are the details that support the main idea. When you read these details, these examples, you will find that they make the main point clearer to you. Looking for the way in which the author restates a major idea by the use of supporting details will help you understand the passage.

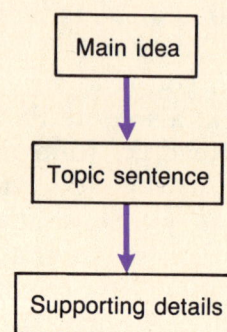

Main idea

↓

Topic sentence

↓

Supporting details

Examples

DIRECTIONS: Use the information on this page and the passage by Nadine Gordimer on the preceding page to choose the <u>one</u> best answer for each item below.

1. Which sentence below *best* restates the main idea of the passage?

   (1) The lady in the passage is a paranoid schizophrenic.
   (2) The lady in the passage does not like her apartment any longer.
   (3) The lady in the passage has really let herself go.
   (4) The lady is afraid of someone she knows.
   (5) The lady is very careful to maintain a secure apartment.

   Answer: (4) Choice (1) is incorrect. There is no indication that the lady is schizophrenic. There is no support for choice (2). Choices (3) and (5) are supported, but they do not restate the main idea.

2. Which sentence below does *not* in some way support the main idea of the passage?

   (1) The lady was smoking too much and could not sleep.
   (2) The slightest noise caused her to break into a cold sweat.
   (3) She did not want to come back into the building at night.
   (4) She worked at a garage with some boys.
   (5) She made a heavy curtain so no one could see into her apartment.

   Answer: (4) Choices (1), (2), (3) and (5) all are details that restate and support the main idea of the passage. Although choice (4) is true, it has nothing to do with the main idea of the passage.

Practice

HINT

Remember that an author may restate his or her main idea by giving contrasting details as well as by giving multiple examples of details that directly support the main idea.

DIRECTIONS: Choose the one best answer for each item below.

Items 1–8 refer to the following passage by Joyce Carol Oates.

DO CLOTHES MAKE THE MAN?

Tall and scarecrow-thin he was; but did not mind. Did not pay much attention to his appearance. Which was ironic, people had noted, since he paid such scrupulous attention to the appearance of others and of things . . . to a universe of detail, beautiful
(5) clamorous inexhaustible detail. He was in love with surfaces, he claimed. Meaning by surfaces everything there was: layer upon layer upon layer. But his own physical existence did not interest him. It was a means, a medium. A vehicle. At times a burden: because he could not trust it. Suddenly tired, so bone-weary he
(10) believed himself on the brink of utter extinction, he would laugh nervously and berate himself for being lazy or "out of condition." No, the physical being was untrustworthy, an inferior Siamese twin stuck to the soul, a clownish Doppelgänger one could not— unfortunately—do without. He clothed this creature in matching
(15) trousers and vests and coats, he shod its bunion-prone feet in custom-made shoes that soon became muddy and scuffed, he jammed a shapeless hat upon its head, and sometimes added fey decorative touches: an ascot tie of flamboyant purple, a marigold in his buttonhole, one or two or even three of his famous big
(20) rings. For the past several years he had worn a copper bracelet to ward off the evil spirits that bring rheumatism, and it gave to his bony wrist a certain dash he rather liked.

Daisy dressed carefully. Not quite with style but with care, elaborate care. It had begun as a game between them, years ago,
(25) that she would have to ask her father permission for various things, and have to stand inspection by him before going out; gradually it had become a ritual and though Bonham did not care what the girl wore, so long as it was decent and appropriate to the season, he was unable to extricate himself from the ritual
(30) without upsetting her. He had tried, he had tried. God knows. *He* knew. But once imprinted in Daisy's imagination, the clothing-inspection ritual, like a number of other rituals, had become a permanent feature of their life together.

GO ON TO THE NEXT PAGE.

1. What is the main idea of the passage?

   (1) The man was a clownish Doppel-gänger.
   (2) The man's own physical existence did not interest him.
   (3) The man was a flashy dresser.
   (4) The man was a mystic.
   (5) The man was embarrassed because he was out of condition.

2. Which detail below does *not* in some way support the main idea of the passage?

   (1) He did not mind being as tall and thin as a scarecrow.
   (2) He did not trust his own body.
   (3) His body was a means, a medium and a vehicle.
   (4) He did not pay much attention to his appearance.
   (5) He was prone to bunions.

3. From the context, it appears that "Dop-pelgänger" (line 13) means

   (1) a person who cares about surfaces
   (2) a German Siamese twin
   (3) a German clown
   (4) a very close companion
   (5) a clotheshorse

4. From the context, it appears that "fey" (line 17) means

   (1) conservative or drab
   (2) whimsical or fanciful
   (3) expensive
   (4) custom made
   (5) well matched

5. Which statement below *best* describes the main interest of the man in the passage?

   (1) He was chiefly interested in details and appearances.
   (2) He went to a lot of expense and trouble to avoid rheumatism.
   (3) The most important thing to him was having matching trousers and vests and coats.
   (4) He was concerned about getting into condition.
   (5) He collected big rings.

6. What details about the man's clothes restate the main idea of the passage?

   (1) He dressed in layers and layers like the surfaces of everything there was.
   (2) His copper bracelet had a certain dash which he rather liked.
   (3) His custom-made shoes were very elegant and expensive.
   (4) His hat was shapeless and his shoes were scuffed.
   (5) He always wore a flower in his buttonhole.

7. How does the man in the passage think his daughter ought to dress?

   (1) She should dress carefully.
   (2) She should make dressing into a ritual.
   (3) She should dress with style.
   (4) She should dress elaborately.
   (5) She should dress in clothes appropriate to the season.

8. How does the man in the passage feel about Daisy's ritual of dressing for inspection?

   (1) He is indifferent to Daisy's strange behavior.
   (2) He does not like Daisy's ritual, but he feels trapped by it.
   (3) He appreciates her asking his opinion about matters of taste and style.
   (4) He is glad Daisy's ritual about dressing is a permanent feature of their life together.
   (5) He finds her ritual about dressing an amusing game.

42   PRACTICE

Before you take the GED Mini-Test, check your answers on pages 44–45.

GED Mini-Test

4

TIP In your daily lives you are forced to schedule your time. Do the same thing when taking a test—manage your time so that you answer all the questions. You may want to first answer all the items that are easy for you. Then go back to the more difficult items.

DIRECTIONS: Choose the one best answer for each item below.

Items 1–6 refer to the following passage by Mary Renault.

WHO WERE THE BULL DANCERS?

I was getting to know the other dancers now, both men and girls. It was no soft fellowship, the company of the Bull Court. One knew one's own odds and everyone else's; daily one ate and talked and scuffled with people doomed to die; those who were bull-shy, those who had given up,
(5) or had a bad oracle from their gods. Gods of all the earth are worshipped in the Bull Court; which is why the altar outside the dancers' door of the ring is sacred to them all. And there were nearly as many ways of divining: with sand and pebbles, with water-droppings or with bees or slivers of ivory, with birds, like the Hellenes, or, as the
(10) Sauromantians do, with lizards. Those marked for death died and were remembered little, as a dropped stone leaves ripples in a pool according to its weight. Yet there were a few who had looked for death since their first dance, and had faced it certainly, and yet death held off from them.
One never knew. It was what gave spice to the Bull Court. It was
(15) said that if a dancer lived three years, the Goddess set him free. No one could remember anyone lasting half as long. Yet one could not tell one's fate. One said to oneself that there might be war, or some tumult we could get away in; or the Palace might burn down. Sometimes at night I would remember how the Labyrinth had no walls, and the seas round
(20) Crete are empty, with no neighbor islands to give warning of surprise.
It was a hard fellowship; but it was one without envy. Anything you were good for was good for all the rest. There was none of that jealousy one finds among warriors or bards or craftsmen. People would throw you to the bull if they did not trust you; but they would rather have you
(25) fit to trust, and would help you learn. Among the bull-leapers there was bound to be emulation, and they would not teach their show tricks; but I never knew them enemies, unless it was for love. As for the glory of our patrons, that was nothing to us. Our concern was first, like the victims in the ancient pit, to stay alive; and after that, to have honor
(30) among each other. Patrons and lovers and gamblers would send jewels to the dancers, who wore them all, for bull-dancers are showy and love finery. But no one could judge like us.

GO ON TO THE NEXT PAGE.

1. Which sentence *best* restates the main idea of the first paragraph (lines 1–13)?

   (1) In the Bull Court, death was a matter of fate.
   (2) Those who died left ripples like a stone in water.
   (3) All gods are worshipped in the Bull Court.
   (4) The dancers in the Bull Court were a rough lot.
   (5) Some dancers were looking for death.

2. Which statement below reflects a reasonable inference drawn from the context about the bull dancers?

   (1) The bull dancers fought a lot with each other.
   (2) All the bull dancers were looking for death with every dance.
   (3) The bull dancers came from many different places and backgrounds.
   (4) The bull dancers were highly paid professionals.
   (5) Many of the bull dancers worshipped bulls in the Bull Court.

3. Which sentence *best* restates the main idea of the second paragraph (lines 14–20)?

   (1) The bull dancers liked to live dangerously.
   (2) The bull dancers burned out quickly.
   (3) The bull dancers had a three-year contract.
   (4) The bull dancers had hope despite the odds.
   (5) The bull dancers were terrified of dying.

4. Which statement below reflects a reasonable conclusion from the passage?

   (1) The bull dancers liked spices.
   (2) The bull dancers were being held against their will.
   (3) Many of the bull dancers could not remember things well.
   (4) The bull dancers were fearful of surprise attacks.
   (5) The bull dancers lived in the Labyrinth for three years.

5. Which sentence *best* restates the main idea of the last paragraph (lines 21–32)?

   (1) The bull-leapers were a dog-eat-dog bunch.
   (2) The bull dancers would do anything for jewelry.
   (3) The dancers jealously guarded the tricks of their trade.
   (4) The bull dancers led hard lives.
   (5) The bull dancers cooperated to help each other stay alive.

6. The bull dancers *most* respected the opinions of

   (1) bull-leapers and other bull dancers
   (2) warriors and bards
   (3) patrons and lovers
   (4) lovers and gamblers
   (5) craftsmen and jewelers

Check your answers to the GED Mini-Test on page 45.

Answers and Explanations

Practice   *pp. 41–42*

1. **Answer:** (2)   Choices (1) and (5) each restate phrases from the passage, but each phrase is taken out of context and neither is the main idea. There is no support in the passage for choice (4). Choice (3) is also not supported in the passage, although it is a possible, but incorrect, inference.

2. **Answer:** (5)   Every other choice refers in some way to the attitude that the speaker has about his physical existence. And his attitude about his physical existence is the main idea of the passage. Choice (5) is only a detail about his body and it has nothing to do with his *attitude* about his body.

3. **Answer:** (4)   Choice (1) is a statement from the passage describing the speaker. It is not a statement that describes "Doppelgänger" as used in the context of the passage. Choices (2) and (3) use the word "German" and "Doppelgänger" is a German word, but the context does not support either choice. There is no support for choice (5). Thus choice (4) is correct.

5. **Answer:** (1)   Choice (2) is false, although rheumatism is mentioned in the passage. Choices (3), (4) and (5) are all details from the passage. But it is plain from reading the passage that these details are things that do not interest the speaker much at all.

7. **Answer:** (5)   This is the only choice that is directly supported by the information in the passage. Choice (2) is wrong; he thinks the opposite. Choices (1) and (4) are what she thinks, not what he thinks. Choice (3) may be true, but there is no direct support for it. Thus, by a process of elimination, choice (5) is the only right answer.

4. **Answer:** (2)   Choice (1) is wrong because although it may describe the man, it does not describe a "fey decorative touch." In the same manner, choices (3), (4) and (5) are all wrong. They are all details from the passage that are contrasted with the kinds of details that are described in the passage as "fey."

6. **Answer:** (4)   Choice (1) uses words from the passage, but nowhere in the passage is there support for what choice (1) says. Choice (5) is wrong because of the word "always." Choice (3) is true, but it does not restate the main idea. Choice (2) is also true, but choice (4) is closer to the main idea—that the man is not interested in his physical existence.

8. **Answer:** (2)   Choice (1) is clearly wrong, the man is not indifferent. Choices (3), (4) and (5) are also wrong; the man thinks the opposite. The passage says the man tried and tried to get Daisy to stop this ritual. Thus, it is reasonable to infer that he did not like the ritual, and that he felt trapped, since all his efforts to stop it had failed.

GED Mini-Test   *pp. 43–44*

1. **Answer:** (1)   There is no support in the passage for choice (2), although this choice sounds profound and may be true. Choices (3), (4) and (5) each restate details from the passage that relate to the main idea, but that do not restate the main idea. Choice (1) is thus the right answer because it is closest to the main idea.

3. **Answer:** (4)   There is no support in the passage for choice (1). Choice (3) is a possible inference, but not really supported. Choice (2) is also a possible inference, but since the main idea is that the bull dancers still had hope, choice (4) is a better answer. Choice (5) may be true of some bull dancers, but not all.

5. **Answer:** (5)   There is no support in the passage for choice (1). Choice (2) is wrong because although the bull dancers had jewelry there is no indication that they would "do anything" to get it. Choice (3) is partly true but not wholly true, since the passage says people "would help you learn." Choice (4) may be true, but the main idea of the passage is cooperation and trust.

2. **Answer:** (3)   Choice (2) is wrong because of the word "all." Not all the bull dancers were looking for death. Choice (1) is a possible inference from the passage, but not really supported by the passage. There is no support at all in the passage for choices (4) and (5), although choice (5) does restate details out of context.

4. **Answer:** (2)   There is no support in the passage for any of the other choices. Each of the other choices picks up some detail from the passage, like surprise attacks, or the period of three years, or some key word, like "spice." However, none of these other choices says anything that would be a reasonable conclusion.

6. **Answer:** (1)   All the other choices are false. There is no indication in the passage that the bull dancers paid any attention at all to the opinions of anyone else. Note that each of the other choices uses at least one key word from the passage. This shows you how important it is to read the question, as well as the passage, carefully.

5 Nonfiction

In **nonfiction** the author is describing the world or the people in it as they actually exist. But the reading skill of drawing conclusions—taking the information in a passage and making a judgment based on it—is important in both fiction and nonfiction.

The selections you will be reading in this lesson are nonfiction. They are from biographies or autobiographies. The author is not trying to create a world from imagination; the author is describing the real world. Selections from other types of nonfiction will be covered in a later lesson.

Read the following passage by James Huntington and Lawrence Elliott. Try to identify the main idea and absorb the major details. Then you will be able to draw the conclusions requested by the questions that follow the passage. Use the Purpose Question above the passage to help you.

WHERE IS THE EDGE OF NOWHERE?

"My mother was Athabascan, born around 1875 in a little village at the mouth of the Hogatza River, a long day's walk north of the Arctic Circle. The country was wild enough—blizzards and sixty-below cold all the winter months, and floods when the ice
(5) tore loose in spring, swamping the tundra with spongy muskegs so that a man might travel down the rivers, but could never make a summer portage of more than a mile or so between them.

And the people matched the land. From the earliest time in Alaska, there had been bad feeling between Indian and Eskimo,
(10) and here the two lived close together, forever stirring each other to anger and violence. If an Indian lost his bearings and tracked the caribou past the divide that separated the two hunting grounds, his people would soon be preparing a potlatch in his memory, for he was almost sure to be shot or ground-sluiced, and
(15) his broken body left for the buzzards. Naturally this worked both ways. Then, in the 1890's, prospectors found gold to the west, on the Seward Peninsula, and the white man came tearing through. Mostly he was mean as a wounded grizzly. He never thought twice about cheating or stealing from the native people, or even
(20) killing a whole family if he needed their dog team—anything to get to Nome and the gold on those beaches.

And once, through two winters and a summer, my mother, who looked like a child and weighed less than ninety pounds, walked a thousand miles across this desperate land to get back to
(25) her home and her two children."

Strategies for READING

Draw a Conclusion

This skill involves making a judgment about given information, using the information given and your own prior knowledge and reasoning skills to draw a conclusion. It is the same as making an inference.

When you draw **conclusions** from something you read, you take the information given and apply your reasoning skills to arrive at a judgment. In order to do this, you will need to use all the skills you have learned in the previous lessons. You will need to use the context to find the meaning of unfamiliar words and phrases. You will need to identify main ideas, whether explicit or implicit. You will also need to restate what you have read and understood. With what you know from the supporting details, you can draw a sound conclusion.

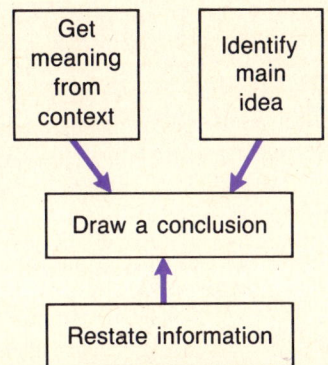

```
┌──────────┐        ┌──────────┐
│   Get    │        │ Identify │
│ meaning  │        │   main   │
│   from   │        │   idea   │
│ context  │        │          │
└────┬─────┘        └────┬─────┘
     │                   │
     ▼                   ▼
   ┌──────────────────────┐
   │  Draw a conclusion   │
   └──────────┬───────────┘
              ▲
   ┌──────────┴───────────┐
   │  Restate information  │
   └──────────────────────┘
```

Examples

DIRECTIONS: Use the information on this page and the passage by James Huntington and Lawrence Elliott on the preceding page to choose the <u>one</u> best answer for each item below.

1. Which of the following is the *most* accurate conclusion to draw about spring coming to Alaska?

    (1) The woman walked a thousand miles to get home.
    (2) The white man came tearing through.
    (3) There was flooding, and the tundra became swampy.
    (4) The weather got warmer.
    (5) The Indians and the Eskimos began fighting.

Answer: (3)   Choices (1), (2) and (5) are wrong because they describe events that have no connection with spring. Choice (4) is correct, but it is a less detailed conclusion.

2. What conclusion do you draw from the author's statement "And the people matched the land" (line 8)?

    (1) The white man never thought twice about cheating or stealing.
    (2) It was easy to get lost.
    (3) A man was almost sure to be shot.
    (4) The people were as wild as the land.
    (5) The people were a match for the winters.

Answer: (4)   Choices (1) and (3) have nothing to do with the land. Choice (2) is true, but does not answer the question. Choice (5) is wrong because it discusses the people and weather, not the land.

Remember when you read nonfiction that, although the author is describing people and events that are real, the author may color a description with his or her own feelings.

DIRECTIONS: Choose the one best answer for each item below.

Items 1–8 refer to the following passage by William O. Douglas.

HOW DOES A JUDGE MAKE A DECISION?

It was shortly after that episode that Hughes made a statement to me which at the time was shattering but which over the years turned out to be true: "Justice Douglas, you must remember one thing. At the constitutional level where we work, ninety per-
(5) cent of any decision is emotional. The rational part of us supplies the reasons for supporting our predilections."

I had thought of the law in the terms of Moses—principles chiseled in granite. I knew judges had predilections. I knew that their moods as well as their minds were ingredients of their deci-
(10) sions. But I had never been willing to admit to myself that the "gut" reaction of a judge at the level of constitutional adjudications, dealing with the vagaries of due process, freedom of speech, and the like, was the main ingredient of his decision. The admission of it destroyed in my mind some of the reverence for
(15) immutable principles. But they were supplied by Constitutions written by people in conventions, not by judges. Judges are, after all, not creative figures; they represent ideological schools of thought that are highly competitive. No judge at the level I speak of was neutral. The Constitution is not neutral. It was designed to
(20) take the government off the backs of people, and no wiser man than Hughes ever sat on our Court. I say that although his predilections, drawn from a different age, were not always mine. I never, for example, could envision Hughes in a boxcar filled with Wobblies (IWWs) roaring across the dusty plains of Washing-
(25) ton State at night, but it was not difficult to picture Hugo Black, Wiley Rutledge, Felix Frankfurter and Frank Murphy there. I could, however, imagine Hughes as an advocate pleading our cause or as a judge putting into imperishable words the tolerance which government must show even the most lowly of us.

GO ON TO THE NEXT PAGE.

1. From the context of the passage, what would you conclude that the word "predilections" in line 8 means?

   (1) rationalizations
   (2) immutable principles
   (3) "gut" reactions
   (4) due processes
   (5) legal training

2. From the context of the passage, what would you conclude the word "adjudications" in line 11 means?

   (1) emotions
   (2) vagaries
   (3) admissions
   (4) principles
   (5) decisions

3. What conclusion do you draw from lines 1–15 of the passage?

   (1) Sometimes the truth is shattering.
   (2) Judges are made, not born.
   (3) Judges are born, not made.
   (4) Judges decide cases based on emotion.
   (5) Judges have no reverence for immutable principles.

4. What has the author concluded from his experiences as a judge?

   (1) Important decisions are based principally on feelings.
   (2) The law is chiseled in granite.
   (3) Hughes was a great man.
   (4) Due process is the main ingredient of a decision.
   (5) His mind was destroyed.

5. What conclusion does the author draw about the Constitution?

   (1) It was written by people in a convention.
   (2) It is designed to protect the people from the government.
   (3) It is ideological and highly competitive.
   (4) It was not written by judges.
   (5) It was written for neutral judges.

6. What do you conclude about the author's attitude towards Hughes?

   (1) He might at first disagree with Hughes, but later realized the wisdom of what Hughes had said.
   (2) He thought Hughes was a creative man.
   (3) He thought Hughes was a harsh man.
   (4) Hughes and the author had violent arguments.
   (5) Hughes had no predilections.

7. What can you conclude about the Wobblies from this passage?

   (1) They lived in Washington State and traveled at night.
   (2) They were called Wobblies because they were unbalanced people.
   (3) They were poor and lowly people who rode in boxcars.
   (4) They rode on trains with famous people.
   (5) They would not have wanted to ride in the same boxcar with Hughes.

8. What can you conclude about the author's views from this passage?

   (1) He believed in competition.
   (2) He never wanted to learn anything.
   (3) He disliked the Wobblies.
   (4) He thought everyone was entitled to tolerance from the government.
   (5) He thought that Hugo Black, Wiley Rutledge, Felix Frankfurter and Frank Murphy were more formal in their behavior than Hughes.

Before you take the GED Mini-Test, check your answers on pages 51–52.

TIP

When you read a question, if you cannot find the right answer, reread all the choices to be sure you read them correctly the first time. There may be one key word that makes an answer choice wrong.

DIRECTIONS: Choose the <u>one</u> best answer for each item below.

Items 1–6 refer to the following passage by Robert A. Caro.

WHAT WAS LYNDON JOHNSON REALLY LIKE?

Whiteside was right. All the characteristics of Majority Leader and President Lyndon Baines Johnson that were so unique and vivid when unveiled on a national stage—the lapel-grabbing, the embracing, the manipulating of men, the "wheeling and dealing"—all these were charac-
(5) teristics that the students at San Marcos had seen. And the similarity extended to aspects of the man less public. The methods Lyndon Johnson used to attain power on Capitol Hill were the same ones he had used on College Hill, and the similarity went far beyond the stealing of an election. At San Marcos, power resided in the hands of a single older
(10) man. Johnson had begged that man for the opportunity to run his errands, had searched for more errands to run, had offered that man an audience when he felt talkative, companionship when he was lonely. And he had flattered him—flattered him with a flattery so extravagant and shameless (and skillful) that his peers had marveled at it. And the friend-
(15) ship of that one older man had armored him against the enmity of hosts of his peers, had given him enough power of his own so that it no longer mattered to him what others thought of him. In Washington, the names of his patrons—of older men who bestowed power on Lyndon Johnson—would be more famous: Rayburn, Russell, Roosevelt. But the technique
(20) would be the same.

So were techniques more complicated than reliance on a single, older individual. The penchant for vote-counting and vote-changing that, during Johnson's Majority Leadership, was to entrance a nation—that penchant was there at San Marcos. The passion for deception, the obses-
(25) sion with secrecy—they were there, too. Johnson's entire career, not just as a Congressman but as a Congressman's secretary, would be character-ized by his aversion to ideology or to issue, by an utter refusal to be backed into firm defense of any position or any principle. That charac-teristic was evident at San Marcos. And the same also, of course, was
(30) the talent that was beyond talent—the natural genius for politics—that animated all these techniques. . . .

1. The period in Lyndon Johnson's life that is the author's subject in this passage is

(1) just before his death
(2) when he was president
(3) when he was Majority Leader
(4) when he was in college
(5) when he was in high school

2. What did Lyndon's peers think of him?

(1) He was their hero.
(2) Many of his peers disliked Lyndon.
(3) They were flattered by his attentions.
(4) They tried to interfere with his success.
(5) They marveled at his greatness even then.

GO ON TO THE NEXT PAGE.

3. What was Lyndon Johnson's main technique for attaining power?

   (1) He sought out powerful men as patrons.
   (2) He wheeled and dealed.
   (3) He embraced people and made them feel loved.
   (4) He was a unique and vivid personality.
   (5) He ran errands.

4. What is the author's main point?

   (1) Lyndon Johnson was unpopular.
   (2) Lyndon Johnson was a lapel-grabber.
   (3) Lyndon Johnson changed totally after he came to Washington, D.C.
   (4) Powerful men just naturally liked Lyndon Johnson.
   (5) Lyndon Johnson's ways of manipulating people to get what he wanted were already developed before he came to Washington, D.C.

5. According to the passage, what was Lyndon Johnson's attitude toward matters of principle?

   (1) He believed that principles were the cornerstone of democracy.
   (2) It was impossible to get him to defend any principle.
   (3) He prided himself on being a man of high principles.
   (4) He was obsessed with secret principles.
   (5) Deception was his only principle.

6. According to the passage, Lyndon Johnson's talent beyond talent was

   (1) his natural genius for politics
   (2) his penchant for vote-counting and vote-changing
   (3) his passion for deception and for obsessive secrecy
   (4) his aversion to ideology
   (5) his skill for extravagant and shameless flattery

Check your answers to the GED Mini-Test on page 52.

Answers and Explanations

Practice   *pp. 48–49*

1. **Answer:** (3) It is plain from the passage that the word "predilections" is something close to emotions, and is not rational. Since choice (3) is the only choice close to something emotional, it is clearly the best answer.

2. **Answer:** (5) If you read the sentence where the word "adjudications" appears, you will note that it seems to be used in the same way as the word "decision." All the other choices appear in the passage, but none of them fits the context of the sentence.

3. **Answer:** (4) Choice (1) is a statement from the passage but not Justice Douglas' main idea. Choices (2) and (3) are interesting observations, but do not appear anywhere in the passage. Choice (5) is wrong because the passage mentions losing "some reverence" but nowhere does it say that judges have "no reverence."

4. **Answer:** (1) Choice (3) is also correct, but choice (1) is closer to the main idea and is, thus, a better answer. Choice (2) is also a statement from the passage, but it does not answer the question. You can eliminate choices (4) and (5) because there is no support for either of them anywhere in the passage.

5. **Answer:** (2) There is no support in the passage for choice (3). While choice (5) may be true, it is not addressed by the passage. Choices (1) and (4) are both true and are both specifically addressed in the passage. However, neither is a conclusion Justice Douglas draws about the Constitution. Both are just facts about the Constitution.

6. **Answer:** (1) Choices (2) and (5) are incorrect, as the passage says just the opposite. There is no support in the passage for choices (3) and (4).

7. Answer: (3)   There is no support in the passage for choice (2). Choice (4) is an incorrect inference. Douglas can imagine Frankfurter or Murphy riding with them, but he never says they did. Choice (5) is wrong because it was Hughes who would not want to ride with the Wobblies and not the other way around. Choice (1) may be partly true, but the passage does not say that the Wobblies lived in Washington.

8. Answer: (4)   There is no support for choices (1), (2) and (3). Choice (5) is also wrong because the opposite is implied. The author could imagine them in a boxcar with the Wobblies.

GED Mini-Test *pp. 50–51*

1. Answer: (4)   There is no support anywhere in the passage for choice (1). There really is no support for choice (5) either, but this choice would be close in time to the right answer. The passage specifically refers to time described in choices (2) and (3). But a careful reading of the passage makes it plain that college, the time referred to in choice (4), is the period of time that the author is writing about.

2. Answer: (2)   Choice (1) is false; the passage shows the opposite. Choice (3) is false because Johnson did not flatter his peers. Although choice (4) might be true, the passage does not support it. Choice (5) is wrong because it was his skill with flattery and not his greatness that made his peers marvel.

3. Answer: (1)   Choice (2) is true, but it was not his main technique. Choice (5) is also true and is closer to his main technique. Choice (5) really shows how Johnson manipulated and flattered powerful men. There is no support in the passage for choice (3). There is no support for choice (4) either. In fact, the passage shows just the opposite—Johnson made up with flattery what he lacked in charm.

4. Answer: (5)   Choice (4) may be true, but the passage indicates that Lyndon Johnson manipulated powerful men and not that they naturally liked him. Choice (3) is not an accurate conclusion from the passage. Choices (1) and (2) are merely details to support the main idea.

5. Answer: (2)   Choice (1) sounds like something a president would think, but it is not what this passage says. In the same way there is no support in the passage for choice (3) either. Choices (4) and (5) are both reasonable inferences from the passage, but neither of them is directly supported in the passage. Choice (2) is directly supported and for that reason it is the best possible answer.

6. Answer: (1)   All the other choices are mentioned in the passage, and all the other answers describe skills or gifts that Lyndon Johnson possessed. In this case, the dashes (—) are a tip-off that the material between them is a restatement of the material just before them. So choice (1) is the best answer, since it almost exactly reproduces the material between the dashes.

6 Fiction

Fiction writing often contains assumptions. **Assumptions** are facts or opinions that the author takes for granted but does not prove. The author may also create characters who make assumptions that the author does not share. The author records the assumptions the characters make as a way of showing what kind of people his characters are.

Read the following passage by E. L. Doctorow. Try to identify the speaker's assumptions. What are their implications? Use the Purpose Question to help you.

WHAT DO THE ASSEMBLY LINE AND MAMMALS HAVE IN COMMON?

Morgan let him take it all in. He puffed on his cigar. Finally he spoke. Ford, he said gruffly, I have no interest in acquiring your business or in sharing its profits. Nor am I associated with any of your competitors. Ford nodded. I have to allow that is
(5) good news, he said, giving off a sly glance. Nevertheless, his host continued, I admire what you have done, and while I must have qualms about a motorcar in the hands of every mongoloid who happens to have a few hundred dollars to spend, I recognize that the future is yours. You're still a young man—fifty years or
(10) thereabouts—and perhaps you understand as I cannot the need to separately mobilize the masses of men. I have spent my life in the coordination of capital resources and the harmonic combination of industries, but I have never considered the possibility that the employment of labor is in itself a harmonically unifying process
(15) apart from the enterprise in which it is enlisted. Let me ask you a question. Has it occurred to you that your assembly line is not merely a stroke of industrial genius but a projection of organic truth? After all, the interchangeability of parts is a rule of nature. Individuals participate in their species and in their genus. All
(20) mammals reproduce in the same way and share the same designs of self-nourishment, with digestive and circulatory systems that are recognizably the same, and they enjoy the same senses. Obviously this is not to say all mammals have interchangeable parts, as your automobiles. But shared design is what allows tax-
(25) onomists to classify mammals as mammals. And within a species—man, for example—the rules of nature operate so that our individual differences occur on the basis of our similarity. So that individuation may be compared to a pyramid in that it is only achieved by the placement of the top stone.

Identify an Implication

This skill identifies assumptions, facts or statements that are taken for granted (not proved), and that the author takes for granted.

In the same way that you sometimes have to infer the main idea of a paragraph (as in Lesson 3), you may have to infer the underlying assumptions. For example, if the author says that one character wanted to go to the best college in the land and also said that the character had applied only to Harvard, the **implication** you would draw from those two statements is that the best college in the land is Harvard. This may be what the author thinks or merely what the character thinks.

Examples

DIRECTIONS: Use the information on this page and the passage by E. L. Doctorow on the preceding page to choose the one best answer for each item below.

1. What is the implication of Morgan's statement that begins on line 7 with "qualms about . . ." and ends with " . . . dollars to spend"?

   (1) Morgan's statement shows that he does not like mongoloids.
   (2) Morgan's statement shows that he does not like motorcars.
   (3) Morgan's statement shows that he thinks that the average person is stupid.
   (4) Morgan's statement shows that he is a very nervous person.
   (5) Morgan's statement shows that he thinks a mongoloid can hold a motorcar in his hands.

Answer: (3) Choice (1) is partly true, but choice (3) is more precise. Choices (2) and (5) are incorrect. Choice (4) would be possible, but the context of the passage as a whole does not support it.

2. Which of the following statements *best* describes Morgan's assumptions as shown by the passage as a whole?

   (1) Morgan believes that all great men are like the top stone on a pyramid.
   (2) Morgan believes that industrial genius and organic truth are interchangeable parts.
   (3) Morgan believes that all mammals have interchangeable parts.
   (4) Morgan believes that life is an assembly line.
   (5) Morgan believes that there are fundamental similarities between mammals and automobiles.

Answer: (5) There is no support in the passage for choices (1) or (4). Choice (3) is almost a direct quote from the passage, but Morgan says the opposite. Choice (2) is a very good answer except for the last two words.

When you are looking for assumptions, look for what the characters or the author are *thinking*. You will probably not find assumptions in the author's or the characters' descriptions of the scene or other details.

DIRECTIONS: Choose the one best answer for each item below.

Items 1–4 refer to the following passage by Donald Thomas.

WHAT DOES THE FUTURE HOLD FOR GENERAL MOLTKE?

To a soldier of the Imperial Guard, the pale-grey carriage was as familiar as that of the German Emperor himself. It bore the tall, portly figure of the new Chief of the General Staff, Colonel-General Helmuth Von Moltke. True, he had yet to win a reputa-
(5) tion equal to that of his uncle, the great Moltke who had crushed the Austrians in 1866 and the French four years later. For all that, he would have time to prove himself in the great war that must one day come. And prove himself he would. It was in his blood. . . .

(10) Even as he looked out upon the scene, Moltke's attention was drawn to the reflection of his own face in the glass of the carriage-window. It bore the appearance of a tired stranger. The lines of the cheeks and jaw sagged not with age but with exhaustion.

(15) At moments like this he knew that he should have resisted more determinedly when he had been nominated as successor to Count von Schlieffen. His family name and the expectations of what he might do to justify it had doomed him to office.

"You will find that I lack the habit of rapid decision," he had
(20) said to Schlieffen, knowing the words would be repeated to the Emperor. "I am too reflective, too prone to second thoughts. In a sense I am more conscientious than a Chief of Staff should be. I am not a gambler who can risk everything on a single brilliant throw."

(25) The only consequence was that they turned even this self-criticism against him. It was merely the modesty expected in a hero of the second generation, the descendant of the great Moltke who had led the German armies to Paris and whose statue now stood among the trees of the Siegesallee, white marble lettered in
(30) gold.

GO ON TO THE NEXT PAGE.

1. Which of the following statements *best* reflects Moltke's assumptions about what would happen in the future?

   (1) Moltke was sure that he was doomed.
   (2) Moltke was certain that there would be a great war in the future.
   (3) Moltke feared that he would collapse from exhaustion.
   (4) Moltke felt that he would not perform well as Chief of Staff.
   (5) Moltke felt that greatness would not be his because he was not a gambler.

2. What do Moltke and the other people mentioned in the passage assume about heroism?

   (1) They assume that heroes are members of the Imperial Guard.
   (2) They assume that heroes are prone to self-criticism.
   (3) They assume that all heroes are warriors.
   (4) They assume that heroism runs in families.
   (5) They assume that heroes must be born into distinguished families.

3. Which statement *best* reflects Moltke's assumptions about what qualities a Chief of Staff ought to have?

   (1) A Chief of Staff ought to come from a good family.
   (2) A Chief of Staff ought to be reflective and conscientious.
   (3) A Chief of Staff ought to be a brilliant gambler.
   (4) A Chief of Staff ought to be someone who is young and energetic.
   (5) A Chief of Staff should have a name in gold letters on white marble.

4. What do the people in the passage assume about Moltke's statement to Schlieffen?

   (1) They do not assume anything but take the statement at face value.
   (2) They assume that Moltke is just trying to get out of serving as the new Chief of Staff.
   (3) They assume that Moltke is just being modest.
   (4) They assume that his statement shows that Moltke is exhausted.
   (5) They assume that Moltke statement's shows his false modesty.

Items 5–6 refer to the following passage by E. L. Doctorow.

WHAT WISDOM CAN TWO BITS BUY?

... And in this book, which cost me just twenty-five cents, I found everything I needed to set my mind at rest. Reincarnation is the only belief I hold, Mr. Morgan. I explain my genius this way—some of us have just lived more times than others. So you
(5) see, what you have spent on scholars and traveled around the world to find, I already knew. And I'll tell you something, in thanks for the eats, I'm going to lend that book to you. Why, you don't have to fuss with all these Latiny things, he said waving his arm, you don't have to pick the garbage pails of Europe and build
(10) steamboats to sail the Nile just to find out something you can get in the mail order for two bits!

5. The speaker assumes that his genius

   (1) results from his having lived before
   (2) is worth two bits
   (3) came from a two-bit book
   (4) means that he knows everything
   (5) results from his belief in reincarnation

6. The speaker assumes that studying European and ancient cultures

   (1) improves one's mind
   (2) involves examining garbage
   (3) is a waste of time
   (4) can only be done by scholars
   (5) leads to reincarnation

Before you take the GED Mini-Test, check your answers on page 59.

TIP

When you read a passage on the GED test, ask yourself how the author or the character knows what he or she thinks are facts. If there is no reason given in the passage, then they are probably assumptions.

DIRECTIONS: Choose the one best answer for each item below.

Items 1–6 refer to the following passage by Peter Taylor.

WHAT ARE THE VIEWS OF THE DEAN OF MEN?

I am not unsympathetic, Jack, to your views on the war. I am not unsympathetic to your views on the state of the world in general. From the way you wear your hair and from the way you dress I do find it difficult to decide whether you or that young girl you say you are about
(5) to marry is going to play the male role in your marriage—or the female role. But even that I don't find offensive. And I am not trying to make crude jokes at your expense. You must pardon me, though, if my remarks seem too personal. I confess I don't know you as well as a father *ought* to know his son, and I may seem to take liberties. . . .
(10) I don't honestly know when I decided to go into college teaching, Jack. I considered doing other things—a career in the army or navy. Yes, I might have gone to Annapolis or West Point. Those appointments were much to be desired in the Depression years, and my family did still have a few political connections. One thing was certain, though.
(15) Business was just as much out of the question for me as politics had been for my father. An honest man, I was to understand, had too much to suffer there. Yes, considering our family history, an ivory tower didn't sound like a bad thing at all for an honest man and a serious man. . . .
(20) After I had been dean of men for two years, I was made academic dean of the college. In two more years, I was president of the college. Even with as little time as you have spent with me through the years, Jack, you have seen what a successful marriage my second marriage has been, and what a happy, active life I have had. One sacrifices something.
(25) One sacrifices, for instance, the books one might have written after that first one. More important, one may sacrifice the love, even the acquaintance of one's children. One loses something of one's self even. But at least I am not tyrannizing over old women and small children. At least I don't sit gazing into space while my wife and perhaps some kindly neigh-
(30) bor woman waits patiently to see whether or not I will risk a two-heart bid. A man must somehow go on living among men, Jack. A part of him must. It is important to broaden one's humanity, but it is important to remain a mere man, too. But it is a strange world, Jack, in which an old man must tell a young man this.

GO ON TO THE NEXT PAGE.

1. What assumption does the speaker make about Jack?

   (1) He assumes that Jack is not a real man because of the way Jack wears his hair and the way he dresses.
   (2) He assumes that Jack is a member of the anti-war movement.
   (3) He assumes that Jack holds views about the world in general that differ from those he holds.
   (4) He assumes that Jack is not a dutiful son.
   (5) He assumes that marriage will be a cruel joke at Jack's expense.

2. What is the implication of the speaker's statement that appointments to Annapolis were desired in the Depression and that his family still had a few political connections?

   (1) The implication is that the speaker wanted a career in military service.
   (2) The implication is that the speaker decided to go into college teaching because he could not get into West Point.
   (3) The implication is that appointments to West Point and Annapolis were given to those with good political connections.
   (4) The implication is that the speaker's family lost their political power during the Depression.
   (5) The implication is that the speaker could not decide whether to go to Annapolis or West Point.

3. What assumption does the speaker make about the business world?

   (1) He assumes that it is identical to the world of the military.
   (2) He assumes that because his family was political, there was no room in the world of business for him.
   (3) He assumes that because of the Depression, there is no promise in the world of business.
   (4) He assumes that he is not serious enough for a business career.
   (5) He assumes that the world of business is crooked and no place for an honest man.

4. From the context, which statement below appears to *best* describe what the speaker means when he refers to the "ivory tower"?

   (1) the world of business
   (2) West Point and Annapolis
   (3) the world of politics
   (4) residence in the old family homeplace
   (5) the world of college teaching

5. Which statement *best* reflects the implications of lines 29–31 of the passage?

   (1) The speaker means that he cannot stand playing card games, particularly bridge.
   (2) The speaker cannot play cards very well, and it takes him a long time to make a bid.
   (3) The speaker has contempt for those who waste a lot of time in the world of women rather than moving in the world of men and action.
   (4) The speaker has much too much to do to permit himself the luxury of doing nothing.
   (5) The speaker does not like women because he thinks all they know how to do is play cards.

6. Which statement *best* reflects the implications drawn from the passage as a whole concerning the speaker's relationship with Jack?

   (1) The speaker's relationship with Jack has been a happy and active one.
   (2) He has sacrificed his relationship with Jack to achieve other goals.
   (3) He is sorry that he tyrannized over Jack as a young child.
   (4) He spurns having any relationship with Jack because Jack is not a real man.
   (5) He thinks Jack should make more sacrifices.

Check your answers to the GED Mini-Test on page 59.

Answers and Explanations

Practice   *pp. 55–56*

1. **Answer:** (2)   Choice (1) is clearly wrong. Choice (3) uses the word "exhaustion" from the passage, but it finds no other support in the passage. Choices (4) and (5) both reflect things Moltke might have thought; however, the only certain thing the passage says he thought about the future was choice (2).

2. **Answer:** (4)   There is no support in the passage for choice (1) or choice (2), although Moltke is prone to self-criticism. Choice (3) is a possible inference but not directly supported. Choice (5) is close; however, the notion is that heroism is a family trait, not a trait only of distinguished families.

3. **Answer:** (3)   There is no support for choice (5). Choice (1) is what others think, but not Moltke. Choice (2) is the opposite of Moltke's own statement. Choice (4) would be a good inference about what Moltke thinks, but choice (3) has direct support in the passage.

4. **Answer:** (3)   Choice (2) is wrong. If they believed this they would not have made Moltke Chief of Staff. Since Moltke's statements about himself were negative, choice (1) is wrong for the same reason. There is no support in the passage for choice (4). Choice (5) is very close to the correct answer, except for the word "false."

5. **Answer:** (1)   Choice (2) reflects the cost of the book and has nothing to do with his genius. Choice (3) is wrong because his genius came from his prior lives. Choice (5) is wrong because it is not his belief in reincarnation that is the source of genius but the assumed fact of reincarnation. There is no support in the passage for choice (4).

6. **Answer:** (3)   It is plain from the passage that choice (1) is false. There is no support in the passage for choice (5). Both choices (2) and (4) are inferences that could be drawn from the passage, but neither answers the question as well as choice (3).

GED Mini-Test   *pp. 57–58*

1. **Answer:** (1)   Choices (2) and (3) are wrong because the speaker does not assume these things, he knows Jack's views. There is no support for choice (4) at all. Choice (5) uses words from the passage and may be true, but it is not implied in the passage.

2. **Answer:** (3)   Choice (2) is wrong because the implication of the passage is that he could have gone into the military if he had wished. This also eliminates choice (1). Choice (5) has no support in the passage. Choice (4) is a possible implication, but it is not as clear an implication as choice (3).

3. **Answer:** (5)   There is no support at all in the passage for choice (1). Choice (2) is wrong because there is no connection in the passage between politics and business. Choice (3) is wrong for the same reason. Choice (4) is the opposite of the information in the passage.

4. **Answer:** (5)   The reason you know this is the right answer is the first sentence of the paragraph where "ivory tower" appears. The speaker begins by explaining why he went into college teaching and concludes by saying that his decision did not sound like a bad thing.

5. **Answer:** (3)   There is no support in the passage for choice (2). Choices (4) and (5) are possible inferences, but they are not directly supported. Choice (1) is also a possible inference; however, only choice (3) relates lines 29–31 to the main idea of the passage.

6. **Answer:** (2)   There is no support in the passage for choices (1), (3) and (5). Choice (4) is close to the correct answer, but a reading of the passage as a whole, with its focus on sacrifice, makes it plain that choice (2) is the right answer.

7 Fiction

When reading fiction or nonfiction, you will need to be able to recognize and understand consequences. **Consequences** are the results of actions. These results are sometimes also called "effects."

You have heard of cause and effect relationships. There are also *logical* consequences, which are effects produced by reasoning and not by action. Finding logical consequences is very similar to drawing conclusions, which you have studied in Lesson 5.

Often an author of fiction will not spell out cause and effect relationships. You will have to infer them from the context. Causes and effects are more likely to be specifically set forth in nonfiction writing.

Read the following passage by Nevil Shute. Look for causes and effects as you read. Use the Purpose Question above the passage to help you.

WHAT IS THE TRUTH ABOUT THE BOMBINGS?

John Osborne and the captain stared at him. "The Russians never bombed Washington," Dwight said. "They proved that in the end."

He stared back at them. "I mean, the very first attack of all."

(5) "That's right. The very first attack. They were Russian long-range bombers, II 626's, but they were Egyptian manned. They flew from Cairo."

"Are you sure that's true?"

"It's true enough. They got the one that landed at Puerto Rico
(10) on the way home. They only found out it was Egyptian after we'd bombed Leningrad and Odessa and the nuclear establishments at Kharkov, Kuibyshev, and Molotov. Things must have happened kind of quick that day."

"Do you mean to say, we bombed Russia by mistake?" It was
(15) so horrible a thought as to be incredible.

John Osborne said, "That's true, Peter. It's never been admitted publicly, but it's quite true. The first one was the bomb on Naples. That was the Albanians, of course. Then there was the bomb on Tel Aviv. Nobody knows who dropped that one, not that
(20) I've heard, anyway. Then the British and Americans intervened and made that demonstration flight over Cairo. Next day the Egyptians sent out all the serviceable bombers that they'd got, six to Washington and seven to London. One got through to Washington and two to London. After that there weren't many American
(25) or British statesmen left alive."

— **Understand a Consequence** —

This skill involves identifying cause and effect to find a consequence. A consequence is a conclusion reached through logic.

While reading the passage by Nevil Shute, you probably noticed how one idea led to another. The actions led to definite consequences.

To **understand a consequence,** ask two questions:

What has happened?   What will be the outcome(s)?

The answers identify the conclusion, or consequence, of the cause and effect relationship. Once you understand what the conclusion is, you have identified a consequence of this relationship.

Key Words

led to	due to
brought	resulted
about	from
caused	because of
produced	
by	
first	next
	last

Examples

DIRECTIONS: Use the information on this page and the passage by Nevil Shute on the preceding page to choose the one best answer for each item below.

1. Which statement does *not* describe a cause or effect in the chain of events that led up to the war of the passage?

   (1) The Albanians bombed Naples, and then somebody bombed Tel Aviv.
   (2) The Americans bombed Leningrad and Odessa and the nuclear facilities of the Russians at Kharkov.
   (3) The Russians bombed Cairo and London.
   (4) After the Tel Aviv bomb, the British and Americans sent in demonstration planes over Egypt.
   (5) The Egyptians bombed London and Washington.

Answer: (3) All the other choices are from somewhere in the passage and each is given as one of the causes in a series. Note that except for the Albanians each of the other causes is also an effect. Choice (3) could be a possible inference from the passage, but it is not given in the passage as a cause.

2. Which statement *best* describes the one basic consequence discussed in the passage?

   (1) Nobody knew who dropped the bomb on Tel Aviv, but the Americans thought that the Egyptians had.
   (2) The Russians should have never given airplanes to Egypt.
   (3) The war was caused by the deaths of most of the statesmen of Britain and America.
   (4) The war became a world war because of a whole series of mistakes and misunderstandings.
   (5) Things happened very quickly on the day the war started.

Answer: (4) Choice (5) is a true statement from the passage, but not the basic consequence. Choices (1) and (2) may be reasonable inferences, but they are not part of the chain of events described in the passage. Choice (3) is a reasonable answer, but choice (4) sums up the passage better.

Characters in fiction do not always seem
to understand causes and effects as well
as the author does. Sometimes their questions
and speculations reveal the cause and effect
relationships that the author wants you to infer.

DIRECTIONS: Choose the one best answer for each item below.

Items 1–6 refer to the following passage by Kate Wilhelm.

HOW DO IDENTICAL TWINS BEHAVE?

" . . . Anyhow, years ago Huysman got interested in the study
of monozygotic twins. Identical twins. He did some important
work, good research. There are anomalies in twin behavior that
have yet to be understood completely. If they are separated at
(5)   birth and raised separately, there are often similarities in their
lives that are hard to understand. For instance, say Carol and
Karen are born in New York and Karen is taken a few months
later to grow up in California. They both marry a man named
George on a June day in the same year at the same time. They
(10)   both have two sons born at the same time. They have the same illnesses and the same accidents. And so on. This is repeated over
and over. They don't know about each other, don't know they are
twins. In fact, when twins are raised together this pattern is less
likely to occur."

(15)   Drew felt at a loss. "There must be some reason. I mean, it
isn't just Carol and Karen. It's also the Georges and the people
driving the other cars involved with their accidents. Or not clearing snow off their sidewalks, whatever the accidents are. In fact,
it's like an infinite regression of what ifs. You know, the what if I
(20)   hadn't been on that corner at the time you came out, we'd never
have met. And so on, back through their entire lives."

"Very good," Florence said approvingly. "Exactly what Huysman asked: what's behind all this? Anyway, moving on. He then
got involved in a series of experiments on chimps. He did genetic
(25)   manipulations on them, and linked them in what he called singlet
fashion. We're back to the quantum mechanics area, by the way.
He was convinced that he could pair them in such a fashion, and
he accumulated tons of material that seem to bear out his claim.
Of course, these animals were all controlled in such a way that
(30)   they couldn't make choices the way twins can and do. He had to
introduce other factors. He stressed one of the paired chimps and
watched the other for the proper reactions. And he got them, over
and over."

GO ON TO THE NEXT PAGE.

1. Which of the statements below *best* describes the main idea of the passage?

   (1) Identical twins are the same thing as monozygotic twins.
   (2) Identical twins who grow up in California and New York marry people with the same first name.
   (3) Identical twins who are raised apart are more likely to have similar lives than are those who are raised together.
   (4) Identical twins who are raised together are more likely to have similar lives than are those who are raised apart.
   (5) There are similarities in the lives of identical twins that science does not completely understand.

2. What cause and effect relationship does the example about Carol and Karen in lines 6–12 show?

   (1) The example shows that they were trying to get back together all the time.
   (2) The example shows that twins seem to act from some shared impulse.
   (3) The example shows that people who are born in New York are special.
   (4) The example shows that twins need to spend a few months together for strange things to happen.
   (5) The example shows that scientists are very observant people.

3. Which of the statements below does *not* reflect Drew's thinking in lines 15–21?

   (1) Identical twins are very different from other people.
   (2) The similarities in the lives of identical twins are startling because they depend on other people's choices, too.
   (3) Drew does not know the reason why the lives of twins are similar.
   (4) There is something strange about people named Carol and George.
   (5) An infinite regression of what ifs is necessary to explain the lives of twins.

4. Which sentence below *best* defines the word "regression" as it is used in line 19 of the passage?

   (1) Regression means moving backward through time.
   (2) Regression means moving forward through time.
   (3) Regression does not have anything to do with time.
   (4) Regression means a task, like clearing snow off a sidewalk.
   (5) Regression is a word scientists use for infinity.

5. Which of the statements below *best* describes the cause and effect relationship Huysman's experiments showed?

   (1) His experiments showed that twin behavior is caused by genetics.
   (2) His experiments showed that twin behavior is caused by quantum mechanics.
   (3) His experiments did not show anything about the cause of twin behavior.
   (4) His experiments showed that twin behavior is caused by stress.
   (5) His experiments showed that chimps can learn quantum mechanics.

6. What is the significance of the last two sentences of the passage?

   (1) They show that chimps know how to react properly.
   (2) They show that chimps are very sensitive to stress.
   (3) They show that Huysman conducted his experiment over and over.
   (4) They show that when chimps are genetically paired, they behave like twins.
   (5) They show that everything can be explained by quantum mechanics.

Before you take the GED Mini-Test, check your answers on page 66.

TIP

To help you improve your memory and read for understanding, try to make up a picture in your mind of what you are reading. This helps in making inferences, such as identifying chronological order or getting the mood the author is trying to convey, and, thus, do better on the GED test.

DIRECTIONS: Choose the one best answer for each item below.

Items 1–8 refer to the following passage by Carl Sagan.

WHAT IS THE STORY OF ADNIX?

Years before, he had invented a module that, when a television commercial appeared, automatically muted the sound. It wasn't at first a context-recognition device. Instead, it simply monitored the amplitude of the carrier wave. TV advertisers had taken to running their ads louder
(5) and with less audio clutter than the programs that were their nominal vehicles. News of Hadden's module spread by word of mouth. People reported a sense of relief, the lifting of a great burden, even a feeling of joy at being freed from the advertising barrage for the six to eight hours out of every day that the average American spent in front of the televi-
(10) sion set. Before there could be any coordinated response from the television advertising industry, Adnix had become wildly popular. It forced advertisers and networks into new choices of carrier-wave strategy, each of which Hadden countered with a new invention. Sometimes he invented circuits to defeat strategies which the agencies and the net-
(15) works had not yet hit upon. He would say that he was saving them the trouble of making inventions, at great cost to their shareholders, which were at any rate doomed to failure. As his sales volume increased, he kept cutting prices. It was a kind of electronic warfare. And he was winning.
(20) They tried to sue him—something about a conspiracy in restraint of trade. They had sufficient political muscle that his motion for summary dismissal was denied, but insufficient influence to actually win the case. The trial had forced Hadden to investigate the relevant legal codes. Soon after, he applied, through a well-known Madison Avenue agency in which
(25) he was now a major silent partner, to advertise his own product on commercial television. After a few weeks of controversy his commercials were refused. He sued all three networks and in *this* trial was able to prove conspiracy in restraint of trade. He received a huge settlement, that was, at the time, a record for cases of this sort, and which con-
(30) tributed in its modest way to the demise of the original networks.

There had always been people who enjoyed the commercials, of course, and they had no need for Adnix. But they were a dwindling minority. Hadden made a great fortune by eviscerating broadcast advertising. He also made many enemies.

GO ON TO THE NEXT PAGE.

1. Which sentence below *best* describes the effect caused by the invention of Adnix?

    (1) Suddenly television news began to spread by word of mouth.
    (2) People were relieved to be freed from television advertising.
    (3) People began to watch television for six to eight hours out of every day.
    (4) TV advertisers began to run their ads louder and louder.
    (5) Adnix had been invented many years before the time of the passage.

2. Which sentence below does *not* describe a cause and effect relationship concerning Adnix and TV ads?

    (1) At first Adnix worked by recognizing the amplitude of the carrier wave.
    (2) Adnix could spot TV ads because they were broadcast louder than TV programs.
    (3) Adnix caused new strategies of carrier-wave strategy.
    (4) Adnix later worked by recognizing the context of TV ads.
    (5) Adnix increased audio clutter in TV ads.

3. What was the effect of the invention of Adnix on television advertisers?

    (1) They reported a sense of relief, the lifting of a great burden.
    (2) They tried to invent ways of delivering their programs in spite of Adnix.
    (3) Their shareholders were furious about how much Adnix was costing the networks.
    (4) They immediately and effectively coordinated their response.
    (5) They just gave up because they knew they were doomed to failure.

4. What caused Hadden to keep cutting the price of Adnix?

    (1) He wanted to undercut his competition.
    (2) He cut his prices because his sales were increasing.
    (3) He wanted to make Adnix available to people who were not wealthy.
    (4) He wanted people to watch television more than eight hours a day.
    (5) He was a poor businessman and did not know a good thing when he saw it.

5. What happened in the lawsuit filed by the advertisers against Hadden?

    (1) They used their political muscle to destroy his product.
    (2) They won their case because Hadden had insufficient evidence.
    (3) Hadden won by filing a motion for summary dismissal.
    (4) Hadden investigated all the relevant legal codes.
    (5) Hadden won because the advertisers failed to prove their case.

6. What caused Hadden to file a lawsuit against the networks?

    (1) He filed his lawsuit because they would not run ads for Adnix on TV.
    (2) He enjoyed suing people and investigating legal codes.
    (3) He filed his lawsuit because the advertisers had sued him.
    (4) He filed his suit because the politicians were on his side.
    (5) He filed his suit because he liked controversy.

7. What happened in the lawsuit filed by Hadden against the networks?

    (1) Hadden proved a conspiracy and won a huge settlement.
    (2) Hadden became the owner of all three networks.
    (3) Hadden lost the case.
    (4) Hadden entered the advertising business.
    (5) Hadden's motion for dismissal was denied.

8. What caused Hadden to make many enemies?

    (1) There were many people who enjoyed ads.
    (2) People were jealous of his wealth.
    (3) His invention helped to destroy the networks.
    (4) People resented his silent partnership in a Madison Avenue agency.
    (5) People realized too late that they had no need for Adnix.

Check your answers to the
GED Mini-Test on page 66.

Answers and Explanations

Practice   *pp. 62–63*

1. **Answer:** (5)   Choices (2) and (4) are false, although choice (2) is a possible inference. Choice (1) is true but not the main idea. Choice (3) is true and close to the main idea but it is really a detail that is included in choice (5).

2. **Answer:** (2)   There is no support for choices (1) and (5). Choices (3) and (4) are possible inferences, but they are not really supported by the passage. Thus, by a process of elimination, choice (2) is the only correct answer.

3. **Answer:** (4)   The other four choices do reflect Drew's thinking in lines 15–21.

4. **Answer:** (1)   The key to this answer is in the next sentences where you see that regression is about time and going backward.

5. **Answer:** (1)   There is no support for choices (4) and (5). Choice (3) states the opposite of the main idea of the passage. Choice (2) is a possible inference but since the passage as a whole concerns genetic manipulations, choice (1) is the best answer.

6. **Answer:** (4)   Choices (1) and (2) are possible inferences but they do not concern twin behavior, the subject of the experiments. Choice (3) is only a detail, a fact necessary to make the point. There is no support for choice (5).

GED Mini-Test   *pp. 64–65*

1. **Answer:** (2)   There is no support for choice (1). Choices (3) and (4) were clearly not caused by the invention of Adnix—they were true before it was invented. Choice (5) is a true statement but it was not an effect caused by the invention.

2. **Answer:** (5)   All the other choices are either statements from the passage about Adnix or they are inferences from other statements about Adnix. Only choice (5) does not appear anywhere in the passage as a consequence of Adnix.

3. **Answer:** (2)   Choice (1) is an effect of Adnix, but not on television advertisers. Choice (4) is the opposite of what the passage says. There is no support for choice (3). Choice (5) is partly true—they were doomed to failure—but they did not know it and they did not give up.

4. **Answer:** (2)   This choice is the only one that has direct support in the passage. There is no support for choices (4) and (5). Choices (1) and (3) are possible inferences, but since choice (2) has direct support, it is clearly the best answer.

5. **Answer:** (5)   Choices (1), (2) and (3) are all wrong, and each one is specifically disproved in the passage. Choice (4) is true, but it is plain that this answer relates to something that happened after the trial. Thus, choice (5) is best.

6. **Answer:** (1)   Choice (4) is false—the politicians were not on his side. There is no support in the passage for choices (2) and (5). Choice (3) is a good guess and might be true, but choice (1) has direct support and is the best answer.

7. **Answer:** (1)   Choice (3) is clearly wrong. Choice (4) is true, but it did not happen in the lawsuit filed by Hadden. Choice (5) is wrong because it relates to the lawsuit filed by the advertisers against Hadden. There is no support anywhere in the passage for choice (2).

8. **Answer:** (3)   Choice (5) is false. Choice (1) is a possible answer but Adnix would not directly affect these people. Choices (2) and (4) are both possible answers, but it is plain from the last two sentences that it was not Hadden's money but what he did to advertisers that made enemies.

8 Fiction

One thing that makes literature different from ordinary writing is that most authors of literature not only have something new to say, but also they find new ways to say it. In effect, they push the language to new extremes. There are many ways to do this. In this lesson you will learn about one, called **figurative language**.

All figurative language is concerned with comparisons. A figure of speech may be a direct comparison stating that one thing is like another—for example, "My love is like a red, red rose." A figure of speech may be an indirect comparison. This usually differs from a direct comparison by eliminating the word "like"—for example, "She was a millstone around his neck." Obviously, a person cannot actually be a millstone. An effect is created by joining things basically not alike.

Another figurative comparison is when exaggeration is employed. In this case the effect is created not because the things are really so dissimilar—although in many cases they may be—but because the scales involved are so different. For example, the figure of speech "quicker than Hell could fry a gnat" gets your attention because of the imbalance of a gnat and hellfire.

Finally, there is a special class of comparison that involves treating objects or non-human things as if they were human—for example, "The night has a thousand eyes." The effect comes from giving human qualities to things that are not human.

Read the following passage by Iris Murdoch. Try to use the figurative language to help you to understand what the author is saying. Use the Purpose Question above the passage to help you.

WHAT IS THE MATTER WITH EDWARD?

Edward was now in total darkness. The glow of the oil lamps through the high windows of the Atrium had been extinguished, wrapped up in an obscurity which was like some black velvet textile or soft inky stuff which filled space and touched Edward's
(5) face like ectoplasm. His feet, lacking confidence in this deprivation of sensory guidance, moved slowly and uncertainly, and he had lost his sense of direction. . . . The night sky, the arching trees, could as well have been the walls of a tiny black lightless room, an oubliette in the centre of which he was now standing.
(10) He reached out again but could touch nothing. Then suddenly something took him by the throat, a frightful sensation that made him stagger and gasp harshly. . . . The sensation which had suddenly felled him was fear, pure contentless fear such as he had never experienced before.

Identify Techniques (Figurative Language)

This skill involves learning how to recognize figurative language and to understand the effect it creates. Good figurative language is forceful and brief, and it has a sense of newness about it.

Usually the author uses **figurative language** to get your attention and to convey to you how the characters in the passage feel or to describe things. Whether it is feelings or things, the effect will be to catch you and to make you think.

For example, in describing a character the author could say he had white hair and was seven feet tall. How much more interesting it is if the author instead says that he was a skyscraper capped by a fluffy white cloud. As you read the passages in this lesson, ask yourself what the authors mean by their use of figurative language and also how they use it for effect.

Examples

DIRECTIONS: Use the information on this page and the passage by Iris Murdoch on the preceding page to choose the one best answer for each item below.

1. Which phrase below *best* describes what the author is trying to do when she says "something took him by the throat" (line 11)?

   (1) She is describing the dark night.
   (2) She is describing an oubliette.
   (3) She is describing fear as a person or an animal.
   (4) She is describing the smoke from the oil lamps.
   (5) She is trying to frighten the reader.

   Answer: (3) It is plain from the passage that the author is talking about fear in figurative language. So choices (1), (2) and (4) are all wrong. Choice (5) is better because it relates to fear; but the author wants to tell the reader how Edward felt.

2. Which phrase below *best* describes the effect of the phrase "an obscurity which was like some black velvet textile or soft inky stuff" (lines 3–4)?

   (1) It describes the feeling of terror.
   (2) It describes what cloth feels like.
   (3) It describes the smoke from the oil lamps.
   (4) It describes the way the darkness feels.
   (5) It describes ectoplasm.

   Answer: (4) Choice (1) is wrong. The feeling of fear comes later. Choices (2), (3) and (5) are wrong. There is no support for these answers.

Practice

HINT Before you analyze figurative language, be sure that you have read the passage correctly. Sometimes long sentences and phrases are hard to follow but are not figurative.

DIRECTIONS: Choose the one best answer for each item below.

Items 1–4 refer to the following passage by Rita Mae Brown.

WHAT INFECTED RICHMOND?

A carnival of hope infected Richmond. McClellan stayed at Harrison's Landing. He plopped there like a frog full of buckshot. He moved neither forward nor backward, but seemed imprisoned by his own weight. Richmond was saved. Churches offered up
(5) services, people shouted, "Gloria in Excelsis," and Lee, instead of being the goat, was now the hero.

While Lutie, like everyone around her, offered up prayers of thanksgiving to Almighty God, she thought of the weeks of battles as the slaughterhouse of heroes. The death lists were appalling.
(10) The best families of the South lost their husbands, sons, and brothers. Hardly anyone was untouched, especially since the upper classes led the regiments, brigades, and divisions. The leaders, the wealthy and the gifted, were cut down by the scythe of war no less than the small farmer, the shopkeeper, even the
(15) vagrant seeking to redeem himself by military service. They died alike, and Death, as always, impartially selected his victims. She used to think of Death as a personal force, the god of the underworld, Hades or Pluto. Odd, too, that Pluto was the god of riches. Each day you bargained with this god, but in the end he got the
(20) better of the deal. She put aside that embroidered, mythical notion. Death these days was a threshing machine. Someone started the blades whirling, and it wouldn't cut off.

1. What does the author mean when she says "like a frog full of buckshot" (line 2)?

(1) She means McClellan looked like a frog.
(2) She means McClellan was overweight.
(3) She means McClellan's army could not move.
(4) She means someone shot McClellan.
(5) She means McClellan's army was defeated.

2. What is the effect of the phrase "cut down by the scythe of war" (lines 13–14)?

(1) It shows that the dead were farmers.
(2) It shows that war was like a sweeping blade.
(3) It shows that they fought with scythes.
(4) It shows that war was bloody.
(5) It shows how the dead were appalled.

GO ON TO THE NEXT PAGE.

3. What is the author doing when she says "Death, as always, impartially selected his victims" (line 16)?

(1) She is showing that Death is final.
(2) She is showing that good and bad men as well as rich and poor men were killed.
(3) She is showing that Death is generous and brings its victims peace.
(4) She is showing how awful Death is.
(5) She is showing that Death is a threshing machine, or a sweeping scythe.

4. How does the author use figurative language to show how Lutie feels about the war?

(1) She describes the way that Lutie went to church.
(2) She shows how Lutie's idea of death changed from the idea of a god to the idea of a threshing machine.
(3) She describes how Lutie was worn down by the war.
(4) She describes the people who died.
(5) She describes Lutie as embroidering a shroud.

Items 5–6 refer to the following passage by John Updike.

HOW DOES THE WEATHER HAPPEN IN AN ELM?

The weather happens mostly in the elm, a vast elm not yet felled by the blight. Its branches overarch the corner. Its drooping twigs brush the roofs of the dark house, the young couple's house, and the Latroys'. Shaped like a river system, meandering
(5) tributaries thickening and flowing into the trunk, but three-dimensional, a solid set of streets where pigeons strut, meet, and mate, the tree's pattern of limbs fills the Blandys' bedroom windows and their eyes on awaking on all weathers: glistening and sullen in November rain, so one feels the awful weight the tree
(10) upholds, like a cast-iron cloud; airy tracery after a snow, or in the froth of gloom; in summer a curtain of green, with a lemon-yellow leaf, turned early, here and there like a random stitch. Lying bedridden in fever or in despair, each of the Blandys has concluded, separately, that though there was nothing to life but
(15) lying here looking at the elm forever, it would suffice—it would be, though just barely, enough.

5. Which of the following is *not* an example of figurative language?

(1) "shaped like a river system" (line 4)
(2) "meandering tributaries thickening and flowing" (lines 4–5)
(3) "a solid set of streets where pigeons strut, meet, and mate" (lines 6–7)
(4) "like a cast-iron cloud" (line 10)
(5) "lying bedridden in fever or in despair" (line 13)

6. What is the effect of the author's use of figurative language?

(1) The reader learns many scientific facts about trees.
(2) The author shows off how large a vocabulary he has.
(3) The reader learns many useful facts about river systems.
(4) The reader learns how to forecast the weather.
(5) The reader sees the tree through the eyes of the Blandys and gets a feel for what it means to them.

Before you take the GED Mini-Test, check your answers on pages 72–73.

GED
Mini-Test

8

TIP

You will do better on the GED exam if you are well rested on the day of the test. You will do better if you sleep well the night before than if you try to cram.

DIRECTIONS: Choose the one best answer for each item below.

Items 1–6 refer to the following passage by John Updike.

WHAT HAPPENED IN THE SNOW?

Away from the shelter of the shed, the wind was a high monotonous pitch of pain. His cheeks instantly ached, and the hinges linking the elements of his face seemed exposed. His septum tingled like glass—the rim of a glass being rubbed by a moist finger to produce a note. Drifts
(5) ribbed the trail, obscuring Becky's ski tracks seconds after she made them, and at each push through the heaped snow his scope of breathing narrowed. By the time he reached the first steep section, the left half of his back hurt as it did only in the panic of a full asthmatic attack, and his skis, ignored, too heavy to manage, spread and swept him toward a
(10) snowbank at the side of the trail. He was bent far forward but kept his balance; the snow kissed his face lightly, instantly, all over; he straightened up, refreshed by the shock, thankful not to have lost a ski. Down the slope Becky had halted and was staring upward at him, worried. A huge blowing feather, a partition of snow, came between them. The cold,
(15) unprecedented in his experience, shone through his clothes like furious light, and as he rummaged through his parka for the inhalator he seemed to be searching glass shelves backed by a black wall. He found it, its icy plastic the touch of life, a clumsy key to his insides. Gasping, he exhaled, put it into his mouth, and inhaled; the isoproterenol spray,
(20) chilled into drops, opened his lungs enough for him to call to his daughter, "Keep moving! I'll catch up!"

Solid on her skis, she swung down among the moguls and wind-bared ice, and became small, and again waited. The moderate slope seemed a cliff; if he fell and sprained anything, he would freeze. His
(25) entire body would become locked tight against air and light and thought. His legs trembled; his breath moved in and out of a narrow slot beneath the pain in his back. The cold and blowing snow all around him constituted an immense crowding, but there was no way out of this white cave but to slide downward toward the dark spot that was his
(30) daughter. He had forgotten his lessons. Leaning backward in an infant's tense snowplow, he floundered through alternating powder and ice.

"You O.K., Daddy?" Her stare was wide, its fright underlined by a pale patch on her cheek.

He used the inhalator again and gave himself breath to tell her, "I'm
(35) fine. Let's get down."

GO ON TO THE NEXT PAGE.

1. What is the author doing when he says "the wind was a high monotonous pitch of pain" (lines 1–2)?

    (1) He is describing the wind as a creature that is crying in pain.
    (2) He is describing the way the wind feels to the man in the passage.
    (3) He is trying to get across the idea that the man in the passage is bored to death.
    (4) He is trying to get across the point that the wind was pitched so high that people could not hear it, only feel it.
    (5) He is describing frostbite.

2. What is the author doing when he says "his septum tingled like glass—the rim of a glass being rubbed by a moist finger to produce a note" (lines 3–4)?

    (1) He is instructing the reader about playing a glass harmonica.
    (2) He is describing the sound of the wind.
    (3) He is comparing the man's ache to a single vibrating note.
    (4) He is showing that the man was thirsty and wanted a drink.
    (5) He is describing the music that the man carried in his heart.

3. What does the author mean when he says "its icy plastic the touch of life, a clumsy key to his insides" (line 18)?

    (1) He means that the man found the car keys that he lost in the snow.
    (2) He is describing a cup of coffee the man drank from a plastic cup.
    (3) He is describing the inhalator that the man uses to stop his asthma attack.
    (4) He is describing the man's skis.
    (5) He means that the man was not a very good skier.

4. What is the effect of the phrase "shone through his clothes like furious light" (lines 15–16)?

    (1) The author graphically illustrates the extreme nature of the cold.
    (2) The reader is impressed with the author's nice turn of phrase.
    (3) The author shows it was a bright day.
    (4) The author shows how angry the man was to be out skiing.
    (5) The author shows that the man's clothes were thin and almost worn out.

5. Why does the author say that "the moderate slope seemed a cliff" (lines 23–24)?

    (1) He wants to show that the man was skiing on a very dangerous mountain.
    (2) He wants to show that the slope was frozen into a solid wall of ice.
    (3) He wants to show that the man was in such distress that even a moderate slope seemed impossible to ski.
    (4) He wants to show that the man was a coward.
    (5) He wants to show that women are much better skiers than men.

6. What is the effect of the phrase "His breath moved in and out of a narrow slot beneath the pain in his back" (lines 26–27)?

    (1) It shows that the man was breathing through a crash helmet.
    (2) It shows that the man fell down and cut his back.
    (3) It shows that the man was having visions from the cold.
    (4) It shows how difficult it was for the man to breathe.
    (5) It shows that the man had blacked out and was unconscious.

Check your answers to the GED Mini-Test on page 73.

Answers and Explanations

Practice *pp. 69–70*

1. **Answer:** (3)   Choices (1) and (2) are literal interpretations. The next sentence reveals that McClellan was simply sitting. There is no support for choices (4) and (5). Also, the buckshot in the image is designed to show the frog could not jump.

2. **Answer:** (2)   Choice (3) is a literal interpretation. Choice (4) is a literal inference. There is no support for choice (5). Choice (1) is partly true—some of the dead were farmers, but not all. Thus, choice (2) is the one best answer.

3. Answer: (2) Although choice (1) is a factual statement about death, it is not what the author means. Choice (4) is wrong; the author is trying to show how death is impartial, not awful. Choice (5) has support later in the passage, but it is not what the author is trying to do with this statement. Choice (3), like choice (2), treats death as a person; however, the characteristics in choice (3) are not the ones the author intends. So choice (2) is best.

5. Answer: (5) Although this choice sounds almost figurative, it is really a literal statement. Choices (1) and (2) are both clearly examples of figurative language since they compare the tree to a river system. Choice (3) is also figurative, comparing the tree to a street and indirectly the pigeons to people. Choice (4) is obviously figurative language, comparing something as light as a cloud to something made of iron.

4. Answer: (2) There is no support for choices (3) or (5). The author does describe the people who died so there is some support for choice (4). But this description does not use figurative language to show Lutie's feelings. In the same way, there is support for choice (1), but it is not figurative language either. Choice (2) on the other hand discusses the way Lutie's figurative ideas of death change. These ideas are also the main images of the passage.

6. Answer: (5) Choices (1), (3) and (4) have no support in the passage, although each of these choices uses key words that relate to the figurative language in the passage. Choice (2) may be a true statement, but it is not an effect of the author's use of figurative language. The real purpose of the figurative language is to show the varied ways the tree is seen by the people in the passage.

GED Mini-Test   *pp. 71–72*

1. Answer: (2) The whole focus of the passage is the effect of the cold on the man. It is the man who feels the pain, not some creature, so choice (1) is wrong. There is no support for choice (3) except the word "monotonous." Choice (4) is wrong for the same reason. The wind has a high pitch, but the focus is the pain the man feels. Choice (5) is closer to how the man feels, but there is no indication in the passage that he has frostbite.

3. Answer: (3) There is no support for choice (1) except the word "key" and the author is not talking about car keys. There is no support for choices (2) or (4) except the word "plastic," and the author is talking about a plastic inhalator, and not skis or a cup of coffee. Choice (5) is probably a true statement, but it has nothing to do with the figurative language in the question. Choice (3) is the only answer that refers to asthma.

5. Answer: (3) There is no support for choice (1). The man's daughter skis the slope easily. The same is true of choice (2). The problem is not the slope, but the man. Just because the man has asthma or is a poor skier does not show that he is a coward, so choice (4) is wrong, too. Although the man's daughter skis better than he does, the author is not trying to show that women are better skiers. He is trying to show how the man feels.

2. Answer: (3) Choice (1) is wrong. The author is not trying to tell the reader how to make music from a glass, but how the man ached. Choice (2) is wrong because the author is not describing the wind, but the man's chest. There is no support in the passage for choice (4). Choice (5) is a possible inference from the key words "septum" and "note," but it is plain from the context that the man is not hearing music in his heart; he is feeling pain, as described in choice (3).

4. Answer: (1) Choice (2) may be true but it is not an effect the author intends, and so is not as good as choice (1). Choice (3) is a possible inference, but the author is talking about the cold as a light and not the kind of day it was. There is no support for choice (4). Choice (5) is another possible inference, but since the author is trying to show how extreme the cold was and not the condition of the man's clothes, choice (1) is better.

6. Answer: (4) Choices (1) and (2) take this language literally and make inferences from it. They are both wrong because the language is figurative. Choices (3) and (5) are both better inferences, but they both draw conclusions that go far beyond the information in the passage. There is really no support for the man having visions or being unconscious. All the passage supports is that it was hard for the man to breathe.

9 Fiction

When you read fiction, you are taking in the information the author has laid out for you. The author expects you to use this information to put yourself into the setting and to think like the characters. When you can do this, you will be able to transfer ideas to a new context. In other words, you will be able to use given information to predict events or behavior in new settings.

Before you can apply information in a new context, you must first be sure to correctly understand the information the author gives you. Your first step thus will be going through the process you have already studied in previous lessons. When you are certain you have understood this information correctly, you can apply it to new situations. About one question in six in the GED test will ask you to apply information in a new context.

Read the following passage by Winston Graham. Look for the main ideas as you read. Try to state them in your own words. This will prepare you to transfer these ideas to a new context. Use the Purpose Question above the passage to help you.

WHY DID GEORGE WARLEGGAN MARRY HIS FIRST WIFE?

... A cold young man to whom material possessions, material power and business acumen meant everything, he had coveted his beautiful first wife while she was still only affianced to Francis Poldark. He had known her to be unattainable on all counts, not
(5) merely because of her marriage but because he knew he meant less than nothing in her eyes. Through the years he had striven to mean something to her—and had succeeded on a material level. Then, less than a year after Francis's death, he had seized a sudden opportunity to put his fortunes to the test; and with a sense
(10) of incredulity he had heard her say yes.

Of course it was not as straightforward as that, and he knew it at the time. Long before Francis's death the Trenwith Poldarks had been poverty-stricken; but after his death everything had worsened, and Elizabeth had been left alone to try to keep a
(15) home together, with no money, little help, and four people, including her ailing parents, dependent on her. He did not pretend she had married him out of love: Her love, however much she might protest to the contrary, had always been directed towards Francis's cousin, Ross. But it was *him* she had married and no other:
(20) She had become Mrs. George Warleggan in name and in more than name, and the birth of a son to them had given him a new happiness, and new feeling of fulfillment, and a new stirring of deeper affection for her.

Transfer Concepts to a New Context

This skill involves taking information from a passage and using it in another situation.

Applying information in a new **context** means drawing conclusions about new facts based in part on what you have already learned from the passage. For example, if you read that a character always goes to work at exactly the same time every day, then you could infer that the character follows regular patterns in daily life. If you were then asked about what this character did on the weekend, you might conclude that weekends probably followed a regular pattern, also. However, there might be other—contrasting—facts about this character. If so, the inference about the weekends might not be correct. The key to applying information to a new context is to use *all* the information available to you.

Examples

DIRECTIONS: Use the information on this page and the passage by Winston Graham on the preceding page to choose the one best answer for each item below.

1. Which statement *best* describes an action George might take?

   (1) George Warleggan would personally pay for a hospital for the poor.
   (2) George Warleggan would welcome Ross into his and his wife's home.
   (3) George Warleggan would hesitate when opportunity knocked.
   (4) He would scorn a man who would sacrifice money for principle.
   (5) George Warleggan would challenge a man to a duel for no reason at all.

Answer: (4) Choices (1), (2) and (3) are all contradicted by the passage. George likes money too much to be charitable; he seems to be jealous of Ross; and he is not one to let opportunity slip by. Choice (5) has no support in the passage.

2. Which statement *best* describes an action Elizabeth might take?

   (1) Elizabeth would leave her husband and run off with Ross.
   (2) Elizabeth would urge any daughter of hers to marry for love.
   (3) Elizabeth would urge any daughter of hers to marry for money.
   (4) Elizabeth would fall in love with anyone richer than George.
   (5) Elizabeth would always tell the truth no matter who might be hurt by it.

Answer: (3) Choices (1) and (2) are false; Elizabeth did the opposite. Choice (5) is specifically contradicted by the passage—she would not admit to George that she loved Ross. Choice (4) goes too far. Elizabeth married for money out of necessity, not greed.

HINT

Remember when you read questions to ask yourself whether the questions relate to something directly or indirectly stated in the passage. If the questions do neither, then they are probably designed to have you apply information in a new context.

DIRECTIONS: Choose the one best answer for each item below.

Items 1–4 refer to the following passage by Olive Ann Burns.

WHAT WAS GRANDPA TWEEDY LIKE?

Then there was Grandpa Tweedy, my daddy's daddy out in Banks County. He talked hard times morning, noon, and night. Called himself a farmer, but you never saw him behind a plow or driving a team. Lazy, great goodness. Like the lilies of the field in
(5) the Bible, he toiled not, neither did he spend his own money. He was always asking Papa to help him out. All he ever did was sit on the porch and swat flies, and like I said, even had him a pet hen to peck them up.

When Papa left the farm at sixteen to go work for Grandpa
(10) Blakeslee, he made twenty dollars a month and had to send half of it home to pay the field hand who took his place. That was the custom. But even after Papa married at nineteen, making forty dollars a month, he still had to send Grandpa Tweedy ten of it, till the day he was twenty-one. My mother never said she didn't
(15) like her father-in-law, but I could tell she didn't, and that may of been why.

What started me hating him, he wouldn't let me fish on Sunday. Said it was a sin. I remember I put out some set hooks late one Saturday, thinking if I caught a fish, it wouldn't be a sin to
(20) take him off the hook next morning. End his suffering, you know. Early Sunday I ran down to the river and one of the lines was just a-jiggling! But when I ran up the hill and asked Grandpa's permission to get my fish off the hook, he said, "Hit'll still be thar t'morrer, Lord willin'. The Lord ain't willin', it'll be gone. Now git
(25) in the house and study yore catechism till time to leave for preachin'."

Of course the fish was gone Monday morning. But I got back at Grandpa Tweedy. I'd noticed a big hornet's nest in the privy, just under the tin roof, so I bided my time behind a tree till I saw
(30) him go in there. Giving him just long enough to get settled good, I let fly with a rock and it hit that tin roof like a gunshot. . . .

GO ON TO THE NEXT PAGE.

1. Which of the following actions would you expect Grandpa Tweedy to take?

   (1) He would be the first man to fix anything that needed fixing.
   (2) He would tend his lilies night and day just like in the Bible.
   (3) He would talk for hours on end about his incredible good fortune.
   (4) He would be glad to lend a helping hand to any of his children.
   (5) He would let a fence fall down before he would repair it.

2. Which statement reflects the *most* likely reason that Papa sent money home to Grandpa Tweedy?

   (1) Papa was paying back his father for money loaned to him for school.
   (2) Children have a moral obligation to support parents who cannot support themselves.
   (3) Papa felt guilty for having left the farm.
   (4) Papa felt guilty for not having brought his wife back to the farm to live.
   (5) As a matter of law, parents are entitled to some of the earnings of children who are not of legal age.

3. Grandpa Tweedy would be likely to

   (1) do his farm work on Sunday
   (2) insist on proper education of his grandchildren
   (3) take a day off and go fishing with his grandson
   (4) claim that what happens to people in life is predestined
   (5) believe in the importance of modern conveniences

4. Which of the following sentences *best* describes something you would expect the grandson in the passage to do?

   (1) He would break every one of the Ten Commandments.
   (2) He would study the Bible every chance he got.
   (3) He would be a hooligan and destroy property.
   (4) He would get even, not mad.
   (5) He would get mad, not even.

Items 5–6 refer to the following passage by Olive Ann Burns.

WHAT DID GRANDPA BLAKESLEE'S WILL SAY?

"Now I want my burying to remind folks that death aint always awful. God invented death. Its in God's plan for it to happen. So when my time comes I do not want no trip to Birdsong's Emporium or any other. Dressing somebody up to look alive don't make it so." . . .

"I dont want no casket. Its a waste of money. What I would really like is to be wrapped up in two or three feed sacks and laid right in the ground. But that would bother you all, so use the pine box upstairs at the store that Miss Mattie Lou's coffin come in. I been saving it. . . . "

5. You would expect Grandpa Blakeslee

   (1) to be conventional
   (2) to be very vain
   (3) to be mindful of what others expected
   (4) to not care what society thought
   (5) to be in the funeral business

6. You would expect Grandpa Blakeslee

   (1) to clean out his attic once a year
   (2) to have the first nickel he earned
   (3) to give his daughter a fancy wedding
   (4) to send his son to Harvard
   (5) to like organic gardening

Before you take the GED Mini-Test, check your answers on pages 79–80.

TIP

When answering GED test items, try to see in your mind the characters and scenes that you read about. Often this will help you to understand how they would think if they were in a different situation.

DIRECTIONS: Choose the one best answer for each item below.

Items 1–6 refer to the following passage by Rex Stout.

WHAT WAS SO SPECIAL ABOUT THE CORN?

When the doorbell rang that Tuesday evening in September and I stepped to the hall for a look and through the one-way glass saw Inspector Cramer on the stoop, bearing a fair-sized carton, I proceeded to the door, intending to open it a couple of inches and say through the crack,

(5) "Deliveries in the rear." He was uninvited and unexpected, we had no case and no client, and we owed him nothing, so why pretend he was welcome?

But by the time I reached the door I had changed my mind. Not because of him. He looked perfectly normal—big and burly, round red

(10) face with bushy gray eyebrows, broad heavy shoulders straining the sleeve seams of his coat. It was the carton. It was a used one, the right size, the cord around it was the kind McLeod used, and the NERO WOLFE on it in blue crayon was McLeod's style of printing. Having switched the stoop light on, I could observe those details as I approached, so I swung

(15) the door open and asked politely, "Where did you get the corn?"

I suppose I should explain a little. Usually Wolfe comes closest to being human after dinner, when we leave the dining room to cross the hall to the office, and he gets his bulk deposited in his favorite chair behind his desk, and Fritz brings coffee; and either Wolfe opens his cur-

(20) rent book or, if I have no date and am staying in, he starts a conversation. The topic may be anything from women's shoes to the importance of the new moon in Babylonian astrology. But that evening he had taken his cup and crossed to the big globe over by the bookshelves and stood twirling the globe, scowling at it, probably picking a place he would

(25) rather be.

For the corn hadn't come. By an arrangement with a farmer named Duncan McLeod up in Putnam County, every Tuesday from July 20 to October 5, sixteen ears of just-picked corn were delivered. They were roasted in the husk, and we did our own shucking as we ate—four ears

(30) for me, eight for Wolfe, and four in the kitchen for Fritz. The corn had to arrive no earlier than five-thirty and no later than six-thirty. That day it hadn't arrived at all; and Fritz had had to do some stuffed eggplant, so Wolfe was standing scowling at the globe when the doorbell rang.

GO ON TO THE NEXT PAGE.

1. What would you expect Nero Wolfe's attitude towards Inspector Cramer to be?

   (1) He would have loved him like a brother.
   (2) He would not have known who Inspector Cramer was.
   (3) He would have welcomed him only if they had some business.
   (4) He would have treated him just as he would treat McLeod.
   (5) He would not want to see him because he owed him money.

2. Which of the following sentences *best* describes the speaker?

   (1) He was an observant person with a sense of humor.
   (2) He was an observant person with no sense of humor.
   (3) He was not an observant person, but he had a sense of humor.
   (4) He was a smart aleck.
   (5) He was a person who could not make a decision.

3. If Nero Wolfe went out to dinner, where would he be likely to go?

   (1) He would go to a fast-food restaurant.
   (2) He would go to an expensive restaurant with excellent food and fine service.
   (3) He would go to a fancy restaurant where he might be noticed.
   (4) He would go to a family restaurant where everyone sat at the same table.
   (5) He would go to the oldest restaurant in the city.

4. Which sentence below *best* describes the kinds of things that Nero Wolfe might read?

   (1) He would read any book that was currently on the best-seller list.
   (2) He would read only books about food or cooking.
   (3) He would read books about women and women's clothing.
   (4) He would read books about ocean voyages.
   (5) He would read books on any subject at all.

5. Which sentence *best* describes behavior you would expect of Wolfe?

   (1) You would expect him to be absolutely on time for an appointment.
   (2) You would expect him to have many overdue library books.
   (3) You would expect him to adjust his schedule to any problem.
   (4) You would expect him to tolerate fruits and vegetables that were somewhat past their prime.
   (5) You would expect him to send a Christmas card to Inspector Cramer.

6. Why was Nero Wolfe twirling the globe and scowling?

   (1) He hated Inspector Cramer and did not wish to see him.
   (2) His readings in Babylonian astrology convinced him it would be a terrible day.
   (3) He had not had a vacation for months and just wanted to get away.
   (4) He had had to eat stuffed eggplant when he had planned to have fresh corn.
   (5) He had had trouble with McLeod before and this was the last straw.

Check your answers to the GED Mini-Test on page 80.

Answers and Explanations

Practice *pp. 76–77*

1. **Answer:** (5) There is no support for choice (2). Choices (3) and (4) are wrong; the passage indicates just the opposite. While there is no direct contradiction in the passage for choice (1), since laziness seems to be one of Grandpa's basic qualities, this choice is wrong.

2. **Answer:** (5) Choice (2) is wrong because the passage does not indicate that Grandpa could not support himself. Choice (1) is wrong because there is no indication Grandpa loaned anyone money. Choices (3) and (4) might be true, but since Papa had to send money until the day he was twenty-one, it was a legal obligation, not a moral one.

3. **Answer:** (4)   Choice (1) is directly contradicted by the passage since Grandpa will not permit his grandson to fish on Sunday. Choice (5) is contradicted by the fact that Grandpa has a privy. Choice (2) has no direct support in the passage. Choice (3) is not directly contradicted by the passage, but there is no support for it, either. Thus, choice (4) is the only inference that has support in the passage.

5. **Answer:** (4)   Choice (5) is contradicted by the fact that he does not want to be sent to Birdsong's Emporium. Choice (2) is contradicted by the passage as a whole, since his plans for his funeral are not at all vain. Choice (1) is contradicted for the same reason; his plans are hardly conventional. Choice (3) is contradicted because Grandpa is so unconventional. For this reason, choice (4) is the best possible answer.

4. **Answer:** (4)   Although there is some evidence in the passage that the grandson was not rigidly bound by God's law, there is no evidence that he would break any of the Commandments. There is also no evidence for choices (2) or (3), although choice (3) is a more likely inference than choice (2). Thus, the alternatives narrow down to choices (4) and (5). Choice (4) is better since he did get even but not mad.

6. **Answer:** (2)   Choice (3) is contradicted by the fact that he set so little store in ceremony. Anyone who would be buried in feed sacks is not likely to care for fancy weddings. His saving the pine box contradicts choice (1), and there is no support anywhere in the passage for choices (4) or (5). There is no direct support for choice (2) either, but there is much indirect support, since the whole passage is focused on what a waste of money he thinks a funeral is.

GED Mini-Test   *pp. 78–79*

1. **Answer:** (3)   Choice (5) is partly true—he probably did not want to see him—but there is no reason to think he owed him money. Choice (2) is false. It is plain that both Wolfe and the speaker know who Inspector Cramer is. There is no support in the passage for choices (1) and (4). Thus, choice (3) would be the right answer by a process of elimination even if there were no direct support for it.

3. **Answer:** (2)   It is plain from the passage that Wolfe likes excellent food, does not like common tastes and has plenty of money. It follows that he would not like fast food, he would not care to be noticed, he would not care to sit with people he did not know and he would not care how old a restaurant was. Since choice (2) has all the things you would expect Wolfe to like and none he would dislike, it is the only safe choice.

5. **Answer:** (1)   Although Wolfe knows Cramer there is no reason to conclude he would send him a Christmas card, so choice (5) is wrong. Choice (4) is contradicted by the whole passage. Clearly fresh vegetables are of the utmost importance to Wolfe. Choices (2) and (3) are both wrong because anyone who was so careful about schedules would not adjust them happily, nor keep library books beyond the time they were due.

2. **Answer:** (1)   Choice (4) is wrong because it is plain from the passage that the speaker may have a sense of humor but adjusts his conduct to the circumstances. Choice (2) is wrong because he does have a sense of humor. Choice (3) is wrong because he is clearly observant. Choice (5) is not supported by the passage. The speaker could change his mind but he made quick decisions. Thus, choice (1) is correct.

4. **Answer:** (5)   There is some support in the passage that Nero Wolfe might read the books described in all the other choices. This really is an example of a question where the correct answer is all of the above. Choice (5) includes all the other answers.

6. **Answer:** (4)   There is no support in the passage for choice (5). There may be some support for choice (1) since Wolfe did not seem to like Cramer, but there is no indication that he hated him. There is no support for choice (2) either, although there is some indication that Wolfe knew about astrology. There is no support for choice (3) at all. The fact that Wolfe wanted to get away was because he was displeased about the corn.

Mini-Review

In the preceding nine lessons, you have learned strategies for reading fiction and nonfiction. Most of these strategies focus on one goal—the goal of helping you fully understand what the author is saying. To understand what the author is saying, you have learned how to identify main ideas, both implicit and explicit. You have also learned how to look for implications and assumptions and how to restate what you have read. You have learned how to spot causes and effects and how to draw conclusions.

Other strategies you have studied are designed to teach you how to understand not only the author's point but also the techniques he or she uses to get that point across. Finally, you have learned to apply your understanding of ideas and techniques in a new context.

The following exercises are a review of these strategies. The questions that follow each passage may test whether you have accurately understood what you have read, or they may test whether you can apply what you have learned in another context. You may also be asked questions about the techniques the authors use and what the effects of those techniques are.

DIRECTIONS: Choose the <u>one</u> best answer for each item below.

Items 1–4 refer to the following passage by Maxine Hong Kingston.

WHO WAS THE WOMAN WHO INVENTED BOXING?

When we Chinese girls listened to the adults talking-story, we learned that we failed if we grew up to be but wives or slaves. We could be heroines, swordswomen. Even if she had to rage across all China, a swordswoman got even with anybody who hurt her family. Perhaps
(5) women were once so dangerous that they had to have their feet bound. It was a woman who invented white crane boxing only two hundred years ago. She was already an expert pole fighter, daughter of a teacher trained at the Shao-lin temple, where there lived an order of fighting monks. She was combing her hair one morning when a white crane
(10) alighted outside her window. She teased it with her pole, which it pushed aside with a soft brush of its wing. Amazed, she dashed outside and tried to knock the crane off its perch. It snapped her pole in two. Recognizing the presence of great power, she asked the spirit of the white crane if it would teach her to fight. It answered with a cry that
(15) white crane boxers imitate today. Later the bird returned as an old man, and he guided her boxing for many years. Thus she gave the world a new martial art.

GO ON TO THE NEXT PAGE.

1. Which of the following statements *best* describes the author's ideal Chinese woman?

   (1) The ideal Chinese woman should stay home and keep house.
   (2) The ideal Chinese woman should be educated in a Shao-lin temple.
   (3) The ideal Chinese woman should have bound feet.
   (4) The ideal Chinese woman should be a strong and heroic person.
   (5) The ideal Chinese woman should be beautiful and should spend a lot of time combing her hair.

2. Where did the author learn about white crane boxing?

   (1) She learned about it from a white crane two hundred years ago.
   (2) She learned about it from an old man who could transform himself into a crane.
   (3) She learned about it while she was studying at a Shao-lin temple.
   (4) She learned about it from a swordswoman who got even with everybody.
   (5) She learned about it while she was listening to the adults tell stories.

3. What technique does the author use to get across her view of the ideal Chinese woman?

   (1) She uses figurative language.
   (2) She uses a legend about a powerful Chinese woman.
   (3) She uses a true story of a famous heroine from the history books.
   (4) She tells the story of her own life.
   (5) She tells the story of a woman who failed.

4. Which of the following statements reflects a belief you would expect the author to have?

   (1) Cranes are important birds and should be protected.
   (2) The family is the most important thing in life to a swordswoman.
   (3) Everyone would benefit from a retreat at a Shao-lin temple.
   (4) Everyone should learn how to fight with a sword.
   (5) The best thing for a Chinese woman is being a wife.

Items 5–6 refer to the following passage by Allen Drury.

WHO WAS THE PIG IN A POKE?

It was not surprising at all that most of these trumpeters of the Vice-Presidential nominee really had only the haziest idea of what he was all about. It was not surprising that this sudden and overwhelming flood of praise should have come quite automatically, simply because he
(5) was the running mate of the man they wanted for President. It was not surprising that they should thus give this lavish and enormous buildup to a man who was, for many of them, a pig in a poke. He was their pig in their poke, and it was not the first time in American History that the self-same process had occurred. And this time, of course, he was on the
(10) Right Side of everything. That really made it perfect.

5. Which statement below reflects a cause and effect relationship contained in the passage?

   (1) The Vice-Presidential candidate is praised by the Presidential candidate's supporters just because he is the running mate of the man they want for President.
   (2) Ignorance causes bliss.
   (3) The Presidential candidate's supporters support the Vice-Presidential candidate because he is a pig in a poke.
   (4) Politics makes strange bedfellows.
   (5) History causes the choice of an unknown.

6. What does the context imply that "He was their pig in their poke" (lines 7–8) means?

   (1) Because the Vice-Presidential candidate was a member of "their" political party, he was obviously the man for the job.
   (2) The Vice-Presidential candidate was greedy and slow.
   (3) The Vice-Presidential candidate was a fine and outstanding gentleman.
   (4) The Vice-Presidential candidate was a trumpeter.
   (5) The Vice-Presidential candidate had long been well known in the political party.

GO ON TO THE NEXT PAGE.

WHAT IS A MAHLER ORCHESTRA?

She had never before seen a Mahler orchestra—nine French horns, wave on wave of violins and cellos, a whole long row of gleaming trumpets, brighter than welders' lights, another of trombones, two rows of basses, four harps. It was awesome, almost frightening. It filled the vast
(5) stage from wingtip to wingtip like some monstrous black creature too enormous to fly, guarding the ground with its head thrust forward—the light-drenched, empty podium. When the last of the enlarged orchestra was assembled and the newcomers had tuned, the houselights dimmed, and as if at some signal invisible to commoners, the people below her
(10) began to clap, then the people all around her. Now she too was clapping, her mother and father clapping loudly beside her, the roar of applause growing louder and deeper, drawing the conductor toward the light. He came like a panther, dignified yet jubilant, flashing his teeth in a smile, waving at the orchestra with both long arms. He shook hands with the
(15) concertmaster, bounded to the podium—light shot off his hair—turned to the audience and bowed with his arms stretched wide, then straightened, chin high, as if reveling in their pleasure and miraculous faith in him. Then he turned, threw open the score—the applause sank away—and for a moment studied it like a man reading dials and gauges of
(20) infinite complexity. He picked up his baton; they lifted their instruments. He threw back his shoulders, where he held them still, as if casting a spell on his army of musicians, all motionless as a crowd in suspended animation, the breathless dead of the whole world's history, awaiting the impossible.

7. What is the effect of the author's use of figurative language at the beginning of the passage?

(1) It frightens the reader.
(2) It shows that welders play musical instruments.
(3) It shows that nine is an important number.
(4) It shows how large the orchestra was.
(5) It shows how disorganized the orchestra was.

8. Why were the people in the audience clapping?

(1) They were clapping for the enormous black creature on the stage.
(2) They were clapping because the conductor was coming on stage.
(3) They were clapping because the orchestra had played beautifully.
(4) They were clapping because they wanted an intermission.
(5) They were clapping because they liked Mahler.

9. From the context, what would you infer that a "podium" (line 7) is?

(1) It is the spot where the conductor stands to direct the orchestra.
(2) It is the feeding station for a great black vulture.
(3) It is a type of foot problem.
(4) It is a place with dials and gauges of infinite complexity.
(5) It is a cage for a panther.

10. What is the effect of the phrase "the breathless dead of the whole world's history, awaiting the impossible" (lines 23–24)?

(1) It reminds you of the impossible dream.
(2) It shows how hard it is to play music.
(3) It shows how totally still the orchestra was waiting for the conductor to start.
(4) It shows that there are many old people in an orchestra.
(5) It shows that a lot of musicians have asthma.

10 Nonfiction Essay

One form of nonfiction writing you will encounter in the GED is the essay. An **essay** tells the reader about a subject that the reader often knows nothing about.

Some essays are formal. The writer is an expert in the field and writes in a logical and systematic style. Other essays are more informal. The writer sets forth his or her own personal feelings or views, often in a humorous or relaxed style. Whether an essay is formal or informal, the writer will try to make it easy for readers to understand and enjoy the subject. This is important because essays are short. Writers do not have much space in which to develop ideas. Style and structure are important tools used by authors to give readers a quick grasp of the points.

As you read the essays in this lesson, look for what the author is saying and also for how he or she is making it easy for you to understand.

Read the following passage by Helen Bevington. As you read look for ways the author is trying to make the subject both understandable and enjoyable. Use the Purpose Question above the passage to help you.

WHY WAS MRS. TROLLOPE OUTRAGED?

Dickens thought Americans spit too much. So did Sydney Smith. So did Harriet Martineau, Captain Frederick Marryat, and Oscar Wilde. So did Mrs. Francis Trollope, mother of Anthony, who came to this country with three children in 1827 to open a

(5) department store in Cincinnati for the selling of fancy goods and knickknacks. The enterprise, known as "Trollope's Folly," failed and left her penniless. She stayed in America three years, then flounced home to write that two-volume work *Domestic Manners of the Americans*, loudly deploring our native habit of chewing

(10) tobacco and spitting on the carpet. Mrs. Trollope was fifty-two years old, a bossy woman, launched with this outraged book upon a literary career. In his *Autobiography*, Anthony apologized for his mother's ire. "The Americans were to her rough, uncouth, and vulgar—and she told them so." . . .

(15) When the *Domestic Manners* became a best seller in both England and America (Southey and Wordsworth read and praised the book), it caused howls of resentment, indignation, and rage in this country, where for a time the author's name was a byword, a term of abuse. If a man happened to spit on the floor in a theater

(20) or put his feet up on the railing, he would hear catcalls of "A Trollope! A Trollope!" It served him right.

Identify Elements of Style and Structure

This skill involves identifying the characteristic ways in which an author uses language and organizes his or her material.

One structural element is **apposition.** When an author uses this technique, he or she uses a parallel, or repetitive, structure to restate, or tell you something additional about the subject—for example, "a byword, a term of abuse" in lines 18–19 on page 84. The phrase "a term of abuse" is in apposition. It tells about what a byword is. Several phrases may be used in sequence.

Writers use this technique to convey a lot of information in a brief space. When you learn to recognize it and to understand its effect, which is to repeat, or reinforce, the information that comes before it, you will grasp the meaning of a passage much more quickly. Commas or dashes may be clues to this technique.

Examples

DIRECTIONS: Use the information on this page and the passage by Helen Bevington on the preceding page to choose the one best answer for each item below.

1. Which of the following phrases does *not* tell you more about the material preceding it?

   (1) "mother of Anthony" (line 3)
   (2) "known as 'Trollope's Folly'" (line 6)
   (3) "If a man happened to spit" (line 19)
   (4) "a bossy woman" (line 11)
   (5) "a term of abuse" (lines 18–19)

2. Which sentence below *best* describes the effect of the author's use of repetitive structure?

   (1) It makes the passage a lot longer.
   (2) The reader becomes bored.
   (3) It confuses the reader.
   (4) The reader gets a lot of information in a very short space.
   (5) The reader can see that the author must have a college degree.

Answer: (3)   Choices (1) and (4) tell you more about Mrs. Trollope. Choice (2) follows the word "enterprise" and restates what the enterprise was called. Choice (5) is a phrase that follows "byword" but actually restates information about the author's name. Choice (3) does not have any information just before it.

Answer: (4)   Choice (1) is false. Choice (2) may be true in that a reader may become bored, but not because of a lack of creativity or because of the use of apposition. Choice (3) is false. The reader who uses the clues the author provides does not become confused. Choice (5) has no support in the passage. It does not require a degree.

Practice

HINT

Remember when you see a string of phrases set off by commas or dashes, the author may be restating or adding detail to what he or she has said before.

DIRECTIONS: Choose the one best answer for each item below.

Items 1–8 refer to the following passage by Lewis Thomas.

WHAT ARE THE HAZARDS OF SCIENCE?

It is hard to predict how science is going to turn out, and if it is really good science it is impossible to predict. This is the nature of the enterprise. If the things to be found are actually new, they are by definition unknown in advance, and there is no

(5) way of telling in advance where a really new line of inquiry will lead. You cannot make choices in this matter, selecting things you think you're going to like and shutting off the lines that make for discomfort. You either have science or you don't, and if you have it you are obliged to accept the surprising and disturbing pieces

(10) of information, even the overwhelming and upheaving ones, along with the neat and promptly useful bits. It is like that.

The only solid piece of scientific truth about which I feel totally confident is that we are profoundly ignorant about nature. Indeed, I regard this as the major discovery of the past hundred

(15) years in biology. It is, in its way, an illuminating piece of news. It would have amazed the brightest minds of the eighteenth-century Enlightenment to be told by any of us how little we know, and how bewildering seems the way ahead. It is this sudden confrontation with the depth and scope of ignorance that represents the

(20) most significant contribution of twentieth-century science to the human intellect. We are, at last, facing up to it. In earlier times, we either pretended to understand how things worked or ignored the problem, or simply made up stories to fill the gaps. Now that we have begun exploring in earnest, doing serious science, we are

(25) getting glimpses of how huge the questions are, and how far from being answered. Because of this, these are hard times for the human intellect, and it is no wonder that we are depressed. It is not so bad being ignorant if you are totally ignorant; the hard thing is knowing in some detail the reality of ignorance, the worst

(30) spots and here and there the not-so-bad spots, but no true light at the end of any tunnel nor even any tunnels that can yet be trusted. Hard times, indeed.

GO ON TO THE NEXT PAGE.

1. What does the author mean when he says "You either have science or you don't" (line 8)?

   (1) Science is a talent you must be born with—you cannot learn it.
   (2) Only a true genius can ever hope to be a good scientist.
   (3) A successful scientist must be selective.
   (4) A successful scientist must be prepared for surprises.
   (5) A successful scientist must be able to see where he is headed.

2. When the author says "even the overwhelming and upheaving ones" on line 10 of the passage he means

   (1) earthquakes and tidal waves
   (2) knowledge is power
   (3) some information is really useless and disrupts the laboratory
   (4) some information is disturbing
   (5) scientists are as powerful as gods

3. Which of the following sentences *best* describes the main idea of the passage?

   (1) The people of the eighteenth century were much smarter than the people of the twentieth century.
   (2) We realize today that we are still profoundly ignorant about nature.
   (3) We have lost the ability to make up stories to fill the gaps.
   (4) Twentieth-century tunnel engineers are not reliable.
   (5) Scientists are naturally depressed.

4. How does the author catch your attention *initially*?

   (1) He includes references to history.
   (2) He uses the image of a tunnel.
   (3) He uses a lot of repetition.
   (4) He uses a lot of big words that sound impressive.
   (5) He joins together in one sentence concepts that are natural opposites.

5. What does the author mean when he says "nor even any tunnels that can yet be trusted" (lines 31–32)?

   (1) Science is unsure where it is going or how it will get there.
   (2) True science has been driven underground.
   (3) He wants to display his skill with figurative langugage.
   (4) Twentieth-century science suffers from tunnel vision.
   (5) It takes a long time to trust a tunnel.

6. What does the author mean when he says "We are, at last, facing up to it" (line 21)?

   (1) We are finally trying to deal with how little we know.
   (2) We are on the verge of a major new development in science.
   (3) For the first time since the eighteenth century, we are ready to overcome ignorance.
   (4) We can finally see the light at the end of the tunnel.
   (5) We realize it is not so bad being ignorant.

7. When the author says "the worst spots and here and there the not-so-bad spots" (lines 29–30) he describes

   (1) details of the reality of ignorance
   (2) scientific tunnel vision
   (3) Enlightenment amazement
   (4) an illuminating piece of news
   (5) a major discovery in biology

8. Which statement reflects a belief you would expect the author to have?

   (1) Ignorance is better than knowledge.
   (2) A bird in the hand is better than two in the bush.
   (3) A stitch in time saves nine.
   (4) Doing serious science means exploring wherever the data leads.
   (5) People should avoid careers in science because it is depressing.

Before you take the GED Mini-Test, check your answers on pages 89–90.

PRACTICE 87

GED Mini-Test

10

TIP

Whenever you read a passage that seems to have many words you do not understand, slow down and see whether you can get clues from the context. You may also find clues in the questions. Sometimes you can figure out what a word does mean by eliminating incorrect choices.

DIRECTIONS: Choose the one best answer for each item below.

Items 1–6 refer to the following passage by E. B. White.

WHAT ARE THE THREE NEW YORKS?

There are roughly three New Yorks. There is, first, the New York of the man or woman who was born here, who takes the city for granted and accepts its size and its turbulence as natural and inevitable. Second, there is the New York of the commuter—the city that is devoured by

(5) locusts each day and spat out each night. Third, there is the New York of the person who was born somewhere else and came to New York in quest of something. Of these three trembling cities the greatest is the last—the city of final destination, the city that is a goal. It is this third city that accounts for New York's high-strung disposition, its poetical

(10) deportment, its dedication to the arts, and its incomparable achievements. Commuters give the city its tidal restlessness, natives give it solidity and continuity, but the settlers give it passion. And whether it is a farmer arriving from Italy to set up a small grocery store in a slum, or a young girl arriving from a small town in Mississippi to escape the

(15) indignity of being observed by her neighbors, or a boy arriving from the Corn Belt with a manuscript in his suitcase and a pain in his heart, it makes no difference: each embraces New York with the intense excitement of first love, each absorbs New York with the fresh eyes of an adventurer, each generates heat and light to dwarf the Consolidated Edi-

(20) son Company.

The commuter is the queerest bird of all. The suburb he inhabits has no essential vitality of its own and is a mere roost where he comes at day's end to go to sleep. Except in rare cases, the man who lives in Mamaroneck or Little Neck or Teaneck and works in New York, dis-

(25) covers nothing much about the city except the time of arrival and departure of trains and buses, and the path to a quick lunch. He is desk-bound, and has never, idly roaming in the gloaming, stumbled suddenly on Belvedere Tower in the Park, seen the ramparts rise sheer from the water of the pond, and the boys along the shore fishing for

(30) minnows, girls stretched out negligently on the shelves of the rocks; he has never come suddenly on anything at all in New York as a loiterer, because he has no time between trains. He has fished in Manhattan's wallet and dug out coins but has never listened to Manhattan's breathing, never awakened to its morning, never dropped off to sleep in its

(35) night. . . .

GO ON TO THE NEXT PAGE.

1. What does the author mean by the phrase "the city that is devoured by locusts each day and spat out each night" (lines 4–5)?

   (1) He means that the people of New York spit a lot.
   (2) He means that commuters take from the city but give nothing to it.
   (3) He means that New York has an insect problem.
   (4) He means that only locusts can live in New York.
   (5) He means there are many poor people in New York.

2. What is the effect of the author's use of the phrase "heat and light to dwarf the Consolidated Edison Company" (lines 19–20)?

   (1) He shows that the Consolidated Edison Company is run by dwarfs.
   (2) He shows that the newcomers have fevers.
   (3) He shows just how excited and enthusiastic the newcomers are.
   (4) He shows how weak the Consolidated Edison Company is.
   (5) He shows that he does not like commuters.

3. What does the author mean when he says "Of these three trembling cities the greatest is the last" (lines 7–8)?

   (1) He means that the last shall be first.
   (2) He means that there are many shaky people in New York.
   (3) He means that the New York of the commuter is the greatest of the three.
   (4) He means that the New York of the native is the greatest of the three.
   (5) He means that the New York of the settlers is the greatest of the three.

4. Which of the following techniques is *not* used by the author to describe New York?

   (1) He uses examples in groups of threes to focus attention on the three New Yorks.
   (2) He writes about the city as if it had feelings and interests.
   (3) He uses the image of New York as a train station connecting Italy and Mississippi.
   (4) He uses figurative language to restate his descriptions.
   (5) He uses the descriptive word "tidal" to suggest that the commuters go in and out like the tides.

5. What technique does the author use to paint a picture of the commuter?

   (1) He describes the commuter's neck in great detail.
   (2) He describes the commuter as a boy fishing for minnows.
   (3) He uses the image of a bird that returns to its roost each night.
   (4) He describes him as a loiterer.
   (5) He uses exaggeration.

6. What does the author mean when he says the commuter has "fished in Manhattan's wallet and dug out coins" (lines 32–33)?

   (1) The commuter has not fished in the Park with the boys at Belvedere Tower.
   (2) The commuter earns his living in Manhattan.
   (3) The commuter is a pickpocket.
   (4) The commuter fishes coins from the tracks while he is waiting for the train.
   (5) Commuters often find lost wallets while idly roaming in the gloaming.

Check your answers to the GED Mini-Test on page 90.

Answers and Explanations

Practice *pp. 86–87*

1. **Answer:** (4) Choices (3) and (5) may be true, but the focus of the passage is the unpredictability of good science. Only choice (4) relates to this main idea. Choices (1) and (2) both are general statements and are not supported by the passage.

2. **Answer:** (4) Choices (1) and (2) are wrong. There is no support for choice (5). Choice (3) is only restating the information in the previous phrase.

3. **Answer:** (2)   Choice (3) is false—it is not that we have lost the ability, we are simply no longer satisfied with stories. Choice (1) is also false—in the eighteenth century people believed they knew the answers, but they were simply wrong. There is no support in the passage for choices (4) and (5).

5. **Answer:** (1)   This is the only choice that ties the main idea of the passage to the tunnel image. Choice (3) is a possibility, for this is figurative language. But choice (3) is not what the author means. There is no support for choices (2), (4) or (5) in the passage. Choices (4) and (5) use key words, but they are plainly not what the author means.

7. **Answer:** (1)   Note that this phrase is used in apposition to restate the previous phrase about "the reality of ignorance." The commas are a clue. There is no support for any of the other answers, since none of them is concerned with ignorance except possibly choice (2); however, choice (1) is directly related to ignorance, and choice (2) is only indirectly related if at all.

4. **Answer:** (5)   The author contrasts positive words like "solid," "truth" and "confident" with "profound ignorance." Choices (3) and (4) are false. Choices (1) and (2) are things the author does, but not initially, and, thus, are not correct answers. The key word in this question is *initially*.

6. **Answer:** (1)   There is no support in the passage for choice (2)—the development is the recognition of ignorance. Choice (3) is wrong because we have a long way to overcome ignorance. Choice (4) is the opposite of what the passage says. Choice (5) is a true statement but it does not answer the question.

8. **Answer:** (4)   Choices (2) and (3) have no relationship to the passage at all. Choices (1) and (5) do relate to the passage, since they are concerned with ignorance and science. Choice (1) is not what the author believes—he finds the degree of ignorance a little frightening but he believes in knowledge. Choice (5) is wrong because the passage reveals nothing about how the author feels about the matter of career choice.

GED Mini-Test   *pp. 88–89*

1. **Answer:** (2)   There is no support for choice (1). Choices (3) and (4) would make sense only if the author were speaking literally. But he is speaking figuratively, more to describe the commuters than the city. There is also no support for choice (5), although there may be many poor people in New York. Only choice (2) fits the context.

3. **Answer:** (5)   Choice (1) has no support in the passage. Choice (2) is wrong because the author does not say the *people* are "trembling." Choice (4) is also wrong because the native New Yorker is the one who takes the city for granted. Only the settler sees the city as a goal, or gives it passion.

5. **Answer:** (3)   This image is used in the first two sentences. Choices (2) and (4) are wrong. The passage says the commuter never is these things. Choice (1) is wrong; the "necks" in the passage are the names of the towns. Choice (5) is wrong. Although the author does use exaggeration, he does not use it to describe the commuter.

2. **Answer:** (3)   Choice (4) is the opposite effect of the exaggeration, but the author is using this effect to describe the newcomers and not the electric company. There is no support for choice (1). Choice (2) makes sense only if the phrase is read literally, but it is figurative language. Choice (5) may be a true statement but has nothing to do with the question.

4. **Answer:** (3)   All the other choices are used by the author in the passage. Choice (3) is the right answer because this image is never used. A train station is used later in the passage, but not in the part to which the question refers. Italy and Mississippi also appear in the passage, but not in the context of a train station.

6. **Answer:** (2)   There is no support in the passage for choices (3), (4) and (5), although choice (5) does repeat a phrase from the passage. Choice (1) is wrong, although it is a true statement from the passage. It is clearly not the answer to the question. Only choice (2) provides an answer to the question that fits the context of the passage.

11 Poetry

The selections in this lesson and the next three lessons are **poetry.** As in fiction, the author is creating a world from imagination rather than describing the world or people as they actually exist. Poetry also differs from fiction in that almost all poetry is short. The poet tries to condense everything into a very small space. Fiction writers, on the other hand, write until they have finished the story.

Since the poet must work in a very small space, he or she employs various techniques to try to grab your attention and to condense the most meaning into a small space. Poets thus rely heavily on figurative language of the type you have already studied and on other techniques, for example, rhyme and rhythm. Poets also frequently are trying to push language to new extremes, to use it in ways that nobody else has thought of. Thus, some poetry may at first seem dense and difficult to understand.

Still, you can apply many of the skills you have already learned to read and understand poetry. The poet will have a main idea. He or she will give you clues in the context. And the poet will use the same kinds of devices you have already studied. So do not be afraid of poetry!

Read the following poem by Wendell Berry. Try to grasp the poet's main idea and the techniques he used to get that main idea across. Use the Purpose Question above the selection to help you.

WHOSE MEMORIES LIVE ON?

A Praise

His memories lived in the place
like fingers locked in the rock ledges
like roots. When he died
and his influence entered the air
(5)   I said, Let my mind be the earth
of his thought, let his kindness
go ahead of me. Though I do not escape
the history barbed in my flesh,
certain wise movements of his hands,
(10)   the turns of his speech
keep with me. His hope of peace
keeps with me in harsh days,
the shell of his breath dimming away
three summers in the earth.

Identify an Implication

This skill identifies assumptions, facts or statements that are taken for granted (not proved), and that the author takes for granted.

Implications will almost never be identified as such in poems. You will have to **infer** them from what the poets say and particularly from *how* they say it. The symbols, images and figurative language they use will all provide important clues.

Sometimes, however, the poet will write a poem from the point of view of a character. The assumptions in the poem may thus be what the *character* thinks.

You have already studied the skill of identifying implications in fiction in Lesson 6. The same basic process is involved in identifying implications in poetry.

Examples

DIRECTIONS: Use the information on this page and the poem by Wendell Berry on the preceding page to choose the one best answer for each item below.

1. Which of the following statements is a fair assumption you could draw from the poem?

   (1) The man the poet is writing about became a ghost when he died.
   (2) The man who died lived in a place where there were rock ledges.
   (3) The poet had suffered some physical injury at some point in his history.
   (4) The man who died was a pacifist.
   (5) The man the poet is writing about died three summers ago.

Answer: (5) When the poet says "the shell of his breath dimming away three summers in the earth" it is fair to assume that the man died three summers ago. All the other choices play off of key words in the poem, but are not fair assumptions.

2. Which of the following statements is a fair assumption about the kind of person the man who died was?

   (1) He was an outdoorsman and climbed rock ledges.
   (2) He was a wise, kind, peace-loving man.
   (3) He left the poet a lot of money.
   (4) He somehow put a barb in the poet's body at some point in the past.
   (5) He liked to talk a lot.

Answer: (2) Choice (1) is wrong, the poet is talking about memories of the man, and not the man himself, when the poet talks about rock ledges. There is no support at all for choices (3), (4) and (5). By contrast, there is support for every descriptive word in choice (2).

H I N T ▷ Remember that poets often write on more than one level at the same time. When you read a poem, try to find all the levels, literal and figurative, before you decide what the poem means.

DIRECTIONS: Choose the one best answer for each item below.

Items 1–4 refer to the following poem by Phil George.

WHAT HAPPENS IN THE SWEAT LODGE?

Old Man, The Sweat Lodge

"This small lodge is now alive,
The womb of our mother, Earth.
The blackness in which we sit,
The ignorance of our impure minds
(5)   These burning stones are
The coming of a new life."
Near my heart I place his words.

Naked, like an infant at birth, I crouch,
Cuddled upon fresh straw and boughs.
(10) Confessing, I recall all evil deeds.
For each sin I sprinkle water on fire-hot stones;
Their hissing is a special song and I know
The place from which Earth's seeds grow is alive.

Old Man, the Sweat Lodge heals the sick;
(15) Brings good fortune to one deserving
Sacred steam rises—vapor fill my very being—
My pores slime out their dross.
After chanting prayers to the Great Spirit,
I lift a blanket to the East;
(20) Through this door dawns wisdom.

Cleansed, I dive into icy waters.
Pure, I rinse away unworthy yesterday.
"My son, walk straight in this new life.
Youth I help to retain in you.
(25) Return soon. Visit an old one.
Now, think clean, feel clean, be happy."
I thank you, Old Man, the Sweat Lodge.

GO ON TO THE NEXT PAGE.

1. Which of the following statements *best* summarizes the main idea of the poem?

   (1) The Sweat Lodge is the Indian version of a public bathhouse.
   (2) There is an old man who is in charge of the Sweat Lodge.
   (3) Spiritual cleansing occurs in the Sweat Lodge.
   (4) The sauna was invented by Indians.
   (5) The Sweat Lodge is a good place to get warmed up.

2. What assumption is behind the speaker's statement that the Sweat Lodge heals the sick?

   (1) The Sweat Lodge is the Indian version of a hospital.
   (2) Naked infants benefit from being brought to the Sweat Lodge.
   (3) Everyone should have a steam bath at least once a week.
   (4) Most illnesses are caused by air that is too dry.
   (5) Sickness can be spiritual and can be cured by a ceremony of confession.

3. Which of the following statements is a fair assumption drawn from the poem about the speaker's beliefs?

   (1) He believes in civil rights for Indians.
   (2) He worships the Great Spirit and believes that Earth is alive.
   (3) He believes in the ancient wisdom of Eastern cultures.
   (4) He believes that swimming in icy water is good for your health.
   (5) He believes he is filled with slime.

4. How does the poet try to get across his main idea?

   (1) He speaks of birth and creation.
   (2) He uses a lot of words describing colors.
   (3) He uses gross exaggeration.
   (4) He speaks of dying and death.
   (5) He uses the same number of lines in each part of the poem.

Items 5–6 refer to the following poem by Phil George.

WHAT ARE THE MORNING BEADS?

Morning Beads

Into drops of crystal dew
Displayed upon a lily leaf,
I see tonight's desire.

One bead...another...
Trickles down, down;
Embellishing the camas stem.

With the Jeweler of the Dawn
Mother strings beads in sunrise hues
On Moccasins I will wear tonight.

5. By "Jeweler of the Dawn" the speaker *most* probably means

   (1) his mother
   (2) Nature, or the rising sun
   (3) another Indian who makes jewelry
   (4) a rainstorm
   (5) a bead maker

6. By "tonight's desire" the speaker *most* probably means

   (1) his girlfriend
   (2) a party
   (3) a long sleep
   (4) his new moccasins
   (5) some new jewelry

Before you take the GED Mini-Test, check your answers on pages 96–97.

DIRECTIONS: Choose the one best answer for each item below.

Items 1–6 refer to the following poem by Randall Jarrell.

WHAT GOES ON AT THE WASHINGTON ZOO?

The Woman at the Washington Zoo

The saris go by me from the embassies.

Cloth from the moon. Cloth from another planet.
They look back at the leopard like the leopard.

And I. . . .
(5)   this print of mine, that has kept its color.
Alive through so many cleanings; this dull null
Navy I wear to work, and wear from work, and so
To my bed, so to my grave, with no
Complaints, no comment: neither from my chief,
(10) The Deputy Chief Assistant, nor his chief—
Only I complain. . . . this serviceable
Body that no sunlight dyes, no hand suffuses
But, dome-shadowed, withering among columns,
Wavy beneath fountains—small, far-off, shining
(15) In the eyes of animals, these beings trapped
As I am trapped but not, themselves, the trap,
Aging, but without knowledge of their age,
Kept safe here, knowing not of death, for death—
Oh, bars of my own body, open, open!

(20) The world goes by my cage and never sees me.
And there come not to me, as come to these,
The wild beasts, sparrows pecking the llamas' grain,
Pigeons settling on the bears' bread, buzzards
Tearing the meat the flies have clouded. . . .
(25)   Vulture,
When you come for the white rat that the foxes left,
Take off the red helmet of your head, the black
Wings that have shadowed me, and step to me as man:
The wild brother at whose feet the white wolves fawn;
(30) To whose hand of power the great lioness
Stalks, purring . . . .
              You know what I was,
You see what I am: change me, change me!

GO ON TO THE NEXT PAGE.

1. What implication about the speaker's job status do you draw from the poem?

   (1) The speaker is a bureaucrat in Washington, D.C.
   (2) The speaker is an animal keeper at the Washington Zoo.
   (3) There is no information in the poem on which to base any assumptions about the speaker's job.
   (4) The speaker is retired.
   (5) The speaker works at an embassy.

2. Which of the following statements *best* describes the main idea of the poem?

   (1) The speaker is happy with her lot in life.
   (2) The speaker believes in the rights of animals.
   (3) The speaker feels that she is trapped like the animals in the zoo.
   (4) The speaker is sad because she does not have much money for bright clothes.
   (5) The speaker wants to be changed into a lion.

3. What does the speaker mean by the line "these beings trapped/As I am trapped but not, themselves, the trap" (lines 15–16)?

   (1) She means that she knows she is insane and all the animals are insane, too.
   (2) She means that she lives in a prison next door to the zoo.
   (3) She means that she was once caught in an animal trap by accident.
   (4) She means that the animals have been put behind bars while she is trapped within herself.
   (5) She means that she is as dangerous as an animal trap.

4. What does the speaker mean by the line "And there come not to me, as come to these,/The wild beasts" (lines 21–22)?

   (1) She means that she does not have the ability to talk to wild animals.
   (2) She means that wild animals are afraid of her.
   (3) She means that many wild animals break into the zoo.
   (4) She means that she throws bread to the pigeons but they will not get too close to her.
   (5) She means that there is no variety or adventure in her life.

5. From the context, it is reasonable to assume that "saris" (line 1) are

   (1) moonrocks
   (2) worthless people
   (3) leopard trainers
   (4) some sort of clothing
   (5) foreign cars used by embassies

6. "The wild brother at whose feet the white wolves fawn" (line 29) means

   (1) Little Richard
   (2) the Deputy Chief Assistant
   (3) the great lioness
   (4) untamed man
   (5) an Eskimo

Check your answers to the GED Mini-Test on page 97.

Answers and Explanations

Practice   *pp. 93–94*

1. **Answer:** (3)   Choice (1) may be true, but the main idea is the cleansing, and not the fact that the sweat lodge is public. Choice (2) is a possible inference, since it is not clear from the poem who the old man represents, but choice (2) is not the main idea. Choices (4) and (5) are not supported.

2. **Answer:** (5)   The focus of the passage is on spiritual cleansing and confession. None of the other choices focuses on either the spirit or confession. They all focus on sickness or health in a general way. Thus, choice (5) is the only real explanation.

3. **Answer:** (2) There is no support in the passage for choice (3). All the other choices may be true, but only choice (2) is related to the main idea of the passage, which is concern with life and nature and man's relationship to the Earth.

5. **Answer:** (2) It is plain from the passage that the speaker is talking literally about his mother and figuratively about the Jeweler. So choices (1), (3) and (5) are wrong. Choice (4) is a possibility, but choice (2) is supported by the word "dawn."

4. **Answer:** (1) Choice (5) is false. There is no support for choice (4). While the poet uses figurative language, there is no significant use of color-words or exaggeration. So choice (1) is the best answer.

6. **Answer:** (4) Although the poem uses figurative language, here the speaker is probably talking literally. Also, this is the only choice that fits the context and has support in the passage, which is focused upon the beads on moccasins.

GED Mini-Test *pp. 95–96*

1. **Answer:** (1) Choice (3) is false; there is substantial information in the poem about the woman's job and her dissatisfaction with it. There is no support for choice (4); it is contradicted by the line "I wear to work." Choice (5) is wrong—it is not the speaker who has any connection with an embassy, but the people who wear the saris. Choice (2) is a possible answer, but there is more support for choice (1) in the context.

3. **Answer:** (4) There is no support for choices (3) and (5); the poem has nothing to do with animal traps. There is no support for choice (1) either, although it is a possible inference. The same is true for choice (2). Only choice (4) fits the context of the poem, and has direct support in the poem. Thus, choice (4) is clearly the best answer.

5. **Answer:** (4) Choice (1) is wrong; the speaker is talking about cloth and not rocks from the moon. This is also the clue that supports choice (4). There is no support for choices (2) or (3). Choice (5) is a possible guess, but the clue about cloth makes choice (4) a better answer from the context.

2. **Answer:** (3) Choice (1) is false; the speaker is not happy. Choice (2) may be true, but it is not the main idea. There is some support in the passage for choice (4). However, the poet is using clothes as a detail and not as the main idea. Choice (5) is a possible inference from figurative language, but it does not fit the rest of the poem as well as choice (3).

4. **Answer:** (5) Clearly this is figurative language that you can assume to be related to the main idea. None of the other choices seems to be related to the main idea, and none of them has direct support in the poem.

6. **Answer:** (4) Choice (1) could be true only if this language were literal, and even then there is no direct support for it. There is no support for choices (2) or (5) in the poem. Choice (3) is also wrong. It is plain from the context that the great lioness is different from the wild brother. Thus, only choice (4) fits the context.

12 Poetry

Poetry, like music, frequently uses rhythm and rhyme. These are really attention-grabbers that focus your mind on key words or on the repetitive treatment of ideas.

Just like popular song, which is built around one or two really good lines, a poem using rhythm and rhyme will focus your attention on the most important lines or ideas. **Rhythm** is like the beat of music. Just as there are many kinds of beats in music—the polka does not have the same beat as punk rock—there are many kinds of beats or rhythms in poetry. Sometimes these rhythms are themselves part of the poet's point. For example, a poem about a cradle may have a rhythm like that of a cradle rocking.

Rhymes are words or parts of words that sound the same or nearly the same—for example, log and dog or gold and stole. Rhyme is not used nearly as often as rhythm by poets who are writing at this time, although songwriters still frequently use rhyme. If a poem sounds like a song it is probably because of the poet's use of rhyme as well as rhythm.

The following poem by Karl Shapiro has both rhythm and rhyme. Look for both as you read it. You may wish to try reading the poem aloud.

WHY IS THE POET CALLING THE CHILD?

Calling the Child

From the third floor I beckon to the child
Flying over the grass. As if by chance
My signal catches her and stops her dance
Under the lilac tree;
(5) And I have flung my net at something wild
And brought it down in all its loveliness.
She lifts her eyes to mine reluctantly,
Measuring in my look our twin distress.

Then from the garden she considers me
(10) And gathering joy, breaks from the closing net
And races off like one who would forget
That there are nets and snares.
But she returns and stands beneath the tree
With great solemnity, with legs apart,
(15) And wags her head at last and makes a start
And starts her humorous marching up the stairs.

Identify Elements of Style and Structure

This skill involves identifying the characteristic ways in which an author uses language and organizes his or her material.

In poetry, this involves identifying **rhythm,** the beat to a line, and **rhyme,** the repetition of sounds and their effects. Since both rhythm and rhyme involve patterns of repetition, either of a beat or of a sound, the effect is like music. The reason that a poet uses this effect is to focus your attention, as a reader, on the lines or thoughts that the poet wants to stress. In poems that have **stanzas,** or repetitious groups of lines, like verses of a song, it will often be the last line of a stanza that is the focus. But it could be anywhere. Another clue is when the poet changes the beat in a particular line, making it longer or shorter, or in some other way different. Poets usually do this to make you focus your attention on that particular line, or one just before it or after it.

As you read the poems in this lesson first look for obvious patterns of rhymes and the length of the lines. You should always look for the rhythm in poems, too, but the more obvious patterns will help you to find the rhythm. Also, you can sometimes find the rhythm by reading the poem aloud.

Examples

DIRECTIONS: Use the information on this page and the poem by Karl Shapiro on the preceding page to choose the <u>one</u> best answer for each item below.

1. Which statement *best* describes the effect of the rhyme in the poem?

   (1) It adds music, and it seems to connect the parts of the poem together.
   (2) It has no effect in this poem.
   (3) There is no rhyme in this poem.
   (4) It makes the poem sound childish.
   (5) It makes the poem sound important.

Answer: (1)   Choices (2) and (3) are false. There is rhyme, and the effect of the rhyme is choice (1). Choice (4) is false. There is no support for choice (5). Rhyme never makes a poem sound important.

2. What is the effect of the poet's use of the image of the net?

   (1) It shows the child's wild, free nature.
   (2) It shows that he is a skilled hunter.
   (3) It shows that parents trap their children.
   (4) It shows that the poet is heartless.
   (5) It shows that rhythm adds meaning to the poem.

Answer: (1)   Choices (2) and (4) would be right only if you take the image literally, but it is figurative language. Choice (3) is clearly not what the poet means. Choice (5) has nothing to do with the image of the net.

Practice

H I N T ▷

When you read rhymed poems, pay attention to the **rhyme scheme**, the pattern of the rhymes. The last line is often a key line.

DIRECTIONS: Choose the one best answer for each item below.

Items 1–2 refer to the following poem by Wendell Berry.

WHAT IS NECESSARY TO THE POET?

The Necessity of Faith

True harvests no mere intent may reap.
Finally we must lie down to sleep
And leave the world, all we desire
To darkness, malevolence, and fire.
(5) Who wakes and stands his shadow's mark
Has passed by mercy through the dark.
We save the good, lovely, and bright
By will in part, in part delight;
But they live through the night by grace
(10) That no intention can efface.

1. The mood of this poem can be *best* described as

(1) thoughtful
(2) joyous
(3) joking
(4) sarcastic
(5) fearful

2. Which statement below *best* describes the main idea of the poem?

(1) A careful farmer goes to bed early.
(2) It is dreams that keep people going.
(3) The poet suffers from nightmares.
(4) We survive by will and intent.
(5) We survive by grace and mercy.

Items 3–4 refer to the following poem by Langston Hughes.

WHAT IS A RAISIN IN THE SUN?

Harlem

What happens to a dream deferred?

Does it dry up
like a raisin in the sun?
Or fester like a sore—
(5) And then run?
Does it stink like rotten meat?
Or crust and sugar over
like a syrupy sweet?
Maybe it just sags
(10) like a heavy load.

Or does it explode?

GO ON TO THE NEXT PAGE.

3. What is the main idea of this poem?

   (1) Lots of dreams smell bad.
   (2) There is a graveyard of dreams like the graveyard of the elephants.
   (3) People suffer when dreams are deferred.
   (4) Dreams get better when they are deferred.
   (5) You do not have to pay for your dreams right away.

4. Which line is the *most* important line from the poem?

   (1) "like a raisin in the sun"
   (2) "What happens to a dream deferred?"
   (3) "like a syrupy sweet"
   (4) "Does it stink like rotten meat?"
   (5) "Maybe it just sags"

Items 5–6 refer to the following poem by John Updike.

WHERE DOES GAS COME FROM?

Energy: A Villanelle

The logs give back, in burning, solar fire
   green leaves imbibed and processed one by one;
nothing is lost, but still, the cost grows higher.

The ocean's tons of tide, to turn, require
(5)   no more than time and moon; it's cosmic fun.
The logs give back, in burning, solar fire.

All microorganisms must expire
   and quite a few became petroleum;
nothing is lost but, still, the cost grows higher.

(10)   The oil rigs in Bahrain imply a buyer
   who counts no cost, when all is said and done.
The logs give back, in burning, solar fire

but Good Gulf gives it faster; every tire
   is by the fiery heavens lightly spun.
Nothing is lost but, still, the cost grows higher.

(15)

So guzzle gas, the leaden night draws nigher
   when cinders mark where stood the blazing sun.
The logs give back, in burning, solar fire;
nothing is lost but, still, the cost grows higher.

5. According to the poem, what is the ultimate source of energy?

   (1) Energy comes from logs.
   (2) Energy comes from the sun.
   (3) Energy comes from the moon.
   (4) Energy comes from Bahrain.
   (5) Energy comes from the Gulf Oil Company.

6. What is the poet *most* concerned about?

   (1) the cost of gasoline
   (2) the ocean tides
   (3) ever-increasing pollution
   (4) Gulf Oil Company
   (5) buying oil rigs in Bahrain

Before you take the GED Mini-Test, check your answers on pages 103–104.

TIP You may have strong personal feelings about some passages in the GED test. Do not let these feelings get in the way of trying to understand the passage and answer the questions about it.

DIRECTIONS: Choose the one best answer for each item below.

Items 1–3 refer to the following poem by Loren Eiseley.

WHAT IS THIS STRANGE SEASON?

Strange Season

First go the birds, bound south and always south,
And then the fox, sly-faced, among the leaves
Sniffs the dark air; the fields released from drouth
Sigh in the night. The great orb spider weaves
(5) His low-hung calculations, lost in fear
That midnight might brew crystal in his veins.
This is the end of summer; the long year
Is settling toward November and the rains.

First go the birds—but stubborn is the heart
(10) Responsive still to unforgotten springs,
Hoarding its love while spinning leaves depart,
Hearing no sound of passing or of wings.
This is the heart's strange season—brave but lost
Under the cold blue pole star of the frost.

1. Which statement *best* summarizes the main idea of this poem?

   (1) The poet is depressed because winter is coming.
   (2) The poet is sad because he is a bird-watcher, and all the birds are flying south.
   (3) All the animals are getting ready to hibernate for winter.
   (4) Man is divorced from seasonal rhythms.
   (5) Winter is a bad time of year.

2. What is the meaning of the phrase "might brew crystal in his veins" (line 6)?

   (1) The spider is afraid that his blood will turn to sugar.
   (2) The spider is afraid that he will freeze.
   (3) The spider is afraid of the hands of the clock.
   (4) The spider is afraid that his blood will boil away.
   (5) The spider is afraid he will err in his low-hung calculations.

3. Which statement describes why the poet breaks his poem into two parts?

   (1) It makes the poem seem shorter than it really is.
   (2) It makes the poem seem longer than it really is.
   (3) It helps the poet to contrast the animals in the first part with the man in the second part.
   (4) It helps the poet to use different rhymes.
   (5) It helps the poet to focus upon the spider.

GO ON TO THE NEXT PAGE.

Items 4–6 refer to the following poem by Gwendolyn Brooks.

WHY FIRST FIGHT, THEN FIDDLE?

First Fight. Then Fiddle.

First fight. Then fiddle. Ply the slipping string
With feathery sorcery; muzzle the note
With hurting love; the music that they wrote
Bewitch, bewilder. Qualify to sing
(5)   Threadwise. Devise no salt, no hempen thing
For the dear instrument to bear. Devote
The bow to silks and honey. Be remote
A while from malice and from murdering.
But first to arms, to armor. Carry hate
(10)   In front of you and harmony behind.
Be deaf to music and to beauty blind.
Win war. Rise bloody, maybe not too late
For having first to civilise a space
Wherein to play your violin with grace.

4. Which statement below *best* summarizes the main idea of this poem?

   (1) The poet wants to spend her time bowing in silk and eating honey.
   (2) The poet is a witch.
   (3) The poet is a lady warrior.
   (4) The poet is the woman who invented white crane boxing.
   (5) The beautiful things in life come only from struggle.

5. Why does the poet use the image of the violin?

   (1) The violin stands for all the beautiful things in life.
   (2) A machine gun fits inside a violin case.
   (3) A violin is like a woman with a neck and a body.
   (4) The violin stands for war.
   (5) It was easier to use the image of a violin than it was the image of a harmonica.

6. Which statement *best* describes the effect of rhyme in this poem?

   (1) It shows that the poet does not know many words that rhyme.
   (2) It makes the poem flow very smoothly.
   (3) It shows that the poem is divided into two parts that say the same thing.
   (4) It makes the poem sound like the music of a violin.
   (5) It makes the poem sound like the sounds of a battlefield.

Check your answers to the GED Mini-Test on page 104.

Answers and Explanations

Practice   *pp. 100–101*

1. **Answer:** (1)   There is no support for the other choices.

2. **Answer:** (5)   There is no support for choice (1)—all the language that relates to farming is figurative language. Choice (2) is false; the poem is not about dreams, but the contrast between will and grace. There is no support for choice (3). Choice (4) is close to the main idea, but what the poet says is that grace, not will, is what keeps us going.

3. **Answer:** (3)   Choice (1) would be true only if the poet were speaking literally, and in any case, his concern is not with dreams themselves but with the deferral of dreams. There is no support for choice (2), although it is a possible inference. Choice (4) is contradicted by the context of the poem. The dreams seem to get worse, not better. There is no support for choice (5)—the poet is not talking about deferred payment.

5. **Answer:** (2)   All the other choices have some support in the poem because every other choice describes a source of energy. However, the question asks for the "ultimate" source of energy, and the poem makes it plain that the sun is the ultimate source of energy. The sun makes the trees grow and also makes the microorganisms grow. They, not the Gulf Oil Company or Bahrain, produce the logs and the oil.

4. **Answer:** (2)   The poem only makes sense if you focus on this line. The poet focuses on this line by placing it as the first line and to the left of all the other lines. All the other choices are descriptions of what may happen to a dream deferred; they are all answers to the poet's question. But in this poem none of these lines is as important as the first line.

6. **Answer:** (3)   Line 16 speaks of "the leaden night" where cinders, and not the sun, fill the sky, with the poet's conclusion that "the cost grows higher." The other choices only pick up details used in the poem.

GED Mini-Test   *pp. 102–103*

1. **Answer:** (4)   Choice (1) may be true, but choice (4) is better because it is concerned with the relationship of the man and the animals. The same is true of choice (3). There is no support for choice (2), although it is a possible inference; but, again, it is a less comprehensive answer than choice (4). Choice (5) is a very general statement but, like the other choices, it does not address the relationship between the man and the animals.

3. **Answer:** (3)   In this poem, the first part is about the way the animals are in harmony with the turning season and the second part is about the man being out of tune. The break reinforces this difference. Also, there is no support for any of the other choices, except possibly choice (5). But even if choice (5) is true, choice (3) is better because it is more universal.

5. **Answer:** (1)   Choices (2) and (3) may be true, but they have nothing to do with the main idea of the poem. Choice (4) is false because the violin does not stand for war; it stands for the opposite of war. There is no support for choice (5). Since choice (1) ties into the main idea, it is the best answer.

2. **Answer:** (2)   Choice (1) has little support in the poem, only the word "crystal," but the crystal the poet is talking about is ice, not sugar. Choice (4) has no support; the poet does not mean boil when he says brew. There is no support for choice (3) other than the word "midnight." Choice (5) restates key words from the poem, but they have nothing to do with the phrase and the question. So choice (2) is the only good answer.

4. **Answer:** (5)   In this poem, war and fighting are contrasted with music and playing a violin. The only choice that addresses both these things is choice (5), which refers to beautiful things and to struggle. Also, there is no support for any of the other choices.

6. **Answer:** (3)   The rhyme helps to separate the two parts just as the break in the previous poem helped to separate it. Choice (1) is not a reasonable inference from the rhymes used. Choices (2) and (4) are false; the poet intentionally breaks up the lines, and the rhymes do not sound like a violin. Choice (5) is closer to the truth, but not really supported either.

13 Poetry

Creating a picture in the mind of the reader by the use of figurative language enables the poet to avoid long, detailed, factual explanations.

In this lesson you will study the use of figurative language in poetry. Because the poet must express his or her points in a very small space, poets make frequent use of figurative language. The reader fills in details based on the mental picture the poet has suggested. Figurative language is also important to the emotional effect, or mood, created by the poem.

Poets also use figurative language to create **ambiguity,** or multiple levels of meaning. This is a way for the poet to make you think about the meaning and how things are meant. Try reading the poem several times and let your mind wander as you read, trying to see pictures of what the poet says. Also read the possible choices. Since one of the choices is right, it may give you insight into the poem.

Read the following poem by Joyce Carol Oates. What kind of mental picture do you begin to form? Use the Purpose Question above the passage to help you.

WHAT HAPPENED WHEN THE WIND WENT CRAZY?

Where the Wind Went Crazy

the tops of the palm trees are smashed
palm leaves hang down, shredded
limp and light as threads
the trunks like concrete
(5)   that never lived

mammoth towers
uninhabited

I feel the two of us grown to
mammoth towers
(10)   our heads dizzied by the height
time is piled beneath us
blocks pushing us up
there is motion of nerves between us
strung between us like wires

(15)   lovers, we need no hurricane
to make war upon each other
and each cell of our living tissue
is at peace

Identify Figurative Language

This skill involves learning how to recognize figurative language in poetry and to understand the effect it creates. Good figurative language has several important characteristics—it makes a point by being forceful and brief, and it has a sense of newness about it.

In Lesson 8 you learned that all **figurative language** is concerned with comparisons. Figurative language works best when the comparisons are unusual. In poetry figurative language is often extreme, almost bizarre. The reason a poet uses this kind of language is partly to get your attention but mainly to make you think. The poet wants you to look at the world or at feelings in a new way and to see how intricate simple things can be or how simple intricate ones can be.

Examples

DIRECTIONS: Use the information on this page and the poem by Joyce Carol Oates on the preceding page to choose the one best answer for each item below.

1. Why does the poet describe the palm trees?

   (1) The poet likes palm trees.
   (2) The poet is comparing palm trees and telephone poles.
   (3) The poet is comparing lovers to palm trees torn up by a hurricane.
   (4) The poet is comparing palm trees to a hurricane.
   (5) The poet is comparing palm trees to apartment buildings after a hurricane.

Answer: (3) Choice (1) may be true, but it is clearly not the reason why the poet is using the image of palm trees. Choice (2) is wrong because the poem as a whole is focused on the palm trees and the lovers. Choice (4) is false. Choice (5) is not as good an answer as choice (3), which focuses on the lovers.

2. Which statement below *best* describes what the poet means in lines 13–14?

   (1) She means that she feels like a palm tree.
   (2) She means that there is a sense of tension, like electricity, between the lovers.
   (3) She means that the hurricane makes her nervous.
   (4) She means that she feels like a tower.
   (5) She means that she is insane.

Answer: (2) Choices (1) and (4) are both ideas supported by the poem, but they are not supported by lines 13–14. There is no support for choice (5). Choice (3) is a possible inference from the word "nerves," but not a very strong one. Choice (2) is the best answer.

Practice

When you get questions on the GED about figurative language, try to eliminate the answers that are literal. This will narrow your choices down, and, if you guess, you will have a better chance of selecting the correct answer.

DIRECTIONS: Choose the one best answer for each item below.

Items 1–4 refer to the following poem by Anne Sexton.

HOW COLD IS REALLY COLD?

God's Backside

Cold
like Grandfather's icehouse,
ice forming like a vein
and the trees,
(5) rocks of frozen blood,
and me asking questions of the weather.
And me stupidly observing.
Me swallowing the stone of winter.
Three miles away cars push
(10) by on the highway.
Across the world
bombs drop
in their awful labor.
Ten miles away
(15) the city faints on its lights.
But here
there are only a few houses,
trees, rocks, telephone wires
and the cold punching the earth.
(20) Cold slicing the windowpane
like a razor blade
for God, it seems,
has turned his backside to us,
giving us the dark negative,
(25) the death wing,
until such time
as a flower breaks down the front door
and we cry "Father! Mother!"
and plan their wedding.

GO ON TO THE NEXT PAGE.

1. Which statement below *best* describes the mood created in lines 1–25?

   (1) The mood of the poem is upbeat and cheerful.
   (2) The mood of the poem is thoughtful and lighthearted.
   (3) The mood of the poem is gloomy and depressed.
   (4) The mood of the poem is romantic.
   (5) The mood of the poem is sarcastic.

2. What does the poet mean in lines 26–29?

   (1) The poet means that her parents were not yet married.
   (2) The poet means that flowers have extraordinary powers.
   (3) The poet means that flowers can break down doors.
   (4) The poet means that spring will follow the cold winter.
   (5) The poet means that her parents are planning to visit in the spring.

3. Which of the following phrases is *not* used by the poet to describe the cold?

   (1) "like Grandfather's icehouse"
   (2) "ice forming like a vein"
   (3) "rocks of frozen blood"
   (4) "bombs drop/in their awful labor"
   (5) "Cold slicing the windowpane/like a razor blade"

4. What topics would you expect this poet to be likely to write about?

   (1) baseball games and cocktail parties
   (2) deaths and suicides
   (3) babies and motherhood
   (4) patriotism and devotion
   (5) gardens and politics

Items 5–6 refer to the following poem by Wendell Berry.

WHERE DO YOU GO WHEN YOU TRAVEL AT HOME?

Traveling at Home

Even in a country you know by heart
it's hard to go the same way twice.
The life of the going changes.
The chances change and make a new way.
(5) Any tree or stone or bird
Can be the bud of a new direction. The
natural correction is to make intent
of accident. To get back before dark
is the art of going.

5. What does the poet mean by the phrase "Any tree or stone or bird/can be the bud of a new direction" (lines 5–6)?

   (1) Small things can change the direction of a person's life.
   (2) Stones, trees and birds are good guideposts.
   (3) Stones, trees and birds are unfriendly to travelers on life's road.
   (4) A person can read hidden meaning in the world of nature.
   (5) Like trees and birds, stones are alive.

6. Which statement below *best* reflects the main idea of this poem?

   (1) People who travel should always take maps to avoid getting lost.
   (2) Even the most experienced traveler will not be able to go exactly the same way every time.
   (3) The art of living involves shaping chance happenings to your own purposes.
   (4) People should be prepared not to reach their destinations before dark.
   (5) Travelers risk having motor vehicle accidents.

Before you take the GED Mini-Test, check your answers on pages 110–111.

GED Mini-Test

13

TIP

When you read a poem on the GED test, remember to use the skills you learned in studying fiction: look for an explicit main idea first and then an implicit main idea, and use context clues.

DIRECTIONS: Choose the one best answer for each item below.

Items 1–3 refer to the following poem by Marge Piercy.

WHO WANTS TO BE OF USE?

To be of use

The people I love the best
jump into work head first
without dallying in the shallows
and swim off with sure strokes almost out of sight.
(5) They seem to become natives of that element,
and black sleek heads of seals
bouncing like half-submerged balls.

I love people who harness themselves, an ox to a heavy cart,
who pull like water buffalo, with massive patience,
(10) who strain in the mud and the muck to move things forward,
who do what has to be done, again and again.

I want to be with people who submerge
in the task, who go into the fields to harvest
and work in a row and pass the bags along,
(15) who are not parlor generals and field deserters
but move in a common rhythm
when the food must come in or the fire be put out.

The work of the world is common as mud.
Botched, it smears the hands, crumbles to dust.
(20) But the thing worth doing well done
has a shape that satisfies, clean and evident.
Greek amphoras for wine or oil,
Hopi vases that held corn, are put in museums
but you know they were made to be used.
(25) The pitcher cries for water to carry
and the person for work that is real.

1. Which line from the poem *best* summarizes the main idea of the poem?

   (1) "They seem to become natives of that element"
   (2) "who are not parlor generals and field deserters"
   (3) "The work of the world is common as mud."
   (4) "Hopi vases that held corn, are put in museums/but you know they were made to be used."
   (5) "The pitcher cries for water to carry/and the person for work that is real."

GO ON TO THE NEXT PAGE.

2. From the context, the word "amphora" (line 22) probably means

(1) an animal like an ox or water buffalo
(2) parlor generals and field deserters
(3) some sort of container
(4) botched work
(5) a shapeless blob

3. What does the poet mean by the phrase "Botched, it smears the hands, crumbles to dust" (line 19)?

(1) People should not be afraid to get their hands dirty.
(2) People should not use cheap materials that will not stand the test of time.
(3) People should wear gloves when they work to cut down on messy hands.
(4) Work poorly done soils the worker and does not last.
(5) Work is a burden we all have to bear.

Items 4–5 refer to the following poem by Karl Shapiro.

WHAT IS MAN'S SHELL?

Man on Wheels

Cars are wicked, poets think.
Wrong as usual. Cars are part of man.
Cars are biological.
A man without a car is like a clam without a shell.
(5)   Granted, machinery is hell,
But carless man is careless and defenseless.
Ford is skin of present animal.
Automobile is shell.
You get yourself a shell or else.

4. What does the poet mean by the phrase "Ford is skin of present animal" (line 7)?

(1) He means that there is a new animal living today called a Ford.
(2) He means that cars are as much a part of man today as is man's own skin.
(3) He means that people should buy Fords, not GM cars.
(4) He means modern life is a hell of machinery.
(5) He means that if you cannot have a skin you need a shell.

5. What is the poet's basic attitude toward cars?

(1) He believes that cars are wicked.
(2) He believes that cars and other machines are hell.
(3) He believes that cars are a necessary part of modern life.
(4) He believes that clams should drive cars.
(5) He believes that a man without a car does not have a care in the world.

Check your answers to the GED Mini-Test on page 111.

Answers and Explanations

Practice *pp. 107–108*

1. **Answer:** (3) Choice (1) is wrong; the poem is filled with figurative language about the cold and death. The only hopeful part of the poem is the last three lines; still the overall mood of the poem is not upbeat or cheerful. Choice (2) is wrong; while the poem is thoughtful, it is not lighthearted. There is no support for either choice (4) or (5).

2. **Answer:** (4) The poet is speaking figuratively. The flower represents the springtime, and the power to break down the door is the power of spring, not some power of the flower itself. So choices (2) and (3) are both wrong because they are literal, as are choices (1) and (5).

3. **Answer:** (4) Actually, this answer is figurative language, like all the other choices. However, the figurative language about the bombs dropping is not used by the poet to describe the cold. She is describing something happening far away, across the world, and is contrasting that description with the description of the cold. Also, all the other choices are not only figurative language about the cold, but they describe the immediate scene as well.

5. **Answer:** (1) There is no support for choice (5). Choice (2) is a good choice, but the poem focuses on the accidental changes, and adjusting to them and not on finding a way by reading signs. There is no support for choice (3). Choice (4) is not as good as choice (1). Choice (1) is the only choice that focuses on changes that are not intentional.

4. **Answer:** (2) It is difficult to predict what a poet would think based on a single poem. But this poem is so dark and depressing, so filled with images of cold and gloom, that choice (2) is the only choice that fits. There is no support at all for choices (1) and (4). Choices (3) and (5) have some support, since the poem uses the words "Mother" and "flower" at the end. However, the poem has nothing to do with babies or politics, so these answers are also wrong, and only choice (2) really fits.

6. **Answer:** (3) As in the last question, there is only one choice that is focused on chance, or accidental, occurrences. Choices (1) and (5) are wrong because they are general observations about traveling, but not the sort of travel the poet means. Choice (4) is wrong because it is literal, and because it is not what the poet says. Choice (2) is a true statement, and is close to the main idea, but not as close as choice (3).

GED Mini-Test *pp. 109–110*

1. **Answer:** (5) The whole point of this poem is that the poet admires people who do real or useful work and that people need this kind of work to be satisfied. Choice (1) has nothing to do with this idea, and choice (2) simply describes the sort of people the poet is talking about. In the same way, choice (3) is a detail that supports the main idea. Choice (4) is closer to the main idea, but it also is a detail supporting the main idea and not the main idea itself.

3. **Answer:** (4) Choices (1) and (3) are possible inferences from the poem, but they do not address the key word "botched." The focus of the poet is on work that is botched and not work in general. Choice (2) is closer to the context, since the poet does use the test of time as a measure of good work; but, again, choice (2) does not focus on botching work. Choice (5) is a general statement that may be true, but it does not answer this question. Only choice (4) focuses on work poorly done.

2. **Answer:** (3) This is the right choice because amphoras are compared, at least indirectly, to pitchers and vases. Another clue is the line "for wine or oil," which implies that an amphora is a container for wine or oil. And in fact that is exactly what an amphora is. Also, none of the other choices makes any sense in the context of the poem; whereas choice (3) fits perfectly.

4. **Answer:** (2) Choice (1) is false; the poet is not talking about a new animal but the skin of the present animal, man. Choice (3) is wrong because it takes the language literally, and the poet is speaking figuratively. There is some support for choice (4), but the focus of the poem is that we cope by having cars and not that life is hell. Choice (5) restates key words from the poem, but it does not say what the poet means.

5. **Answer:** (3) Choice (5) is false; the poem says the opposite. Although the poem talks about clams and cars, it does not say that clams should drive, so choice (4) is wrong. There is some support for choice (2), but, as in the last question, the focus is on coping and not really on machines being hell. For the same reason, choice (1) is wrong. Only choice (3) reflects the real focus of the poem, which is that cars are necessary whether we like them or not.

14 Poetry

In addition to using rhythm and rhyme and figurative language, poets also use symbols and images to get your attention, to add layers of meaning to their poems and to help them say a lot in a little space.

A symbol is something that has more than one meaning. It means one thing on a literal level but also suggests other possible meanings. For example, seasons are frequently used as symbols. Winter symbolizes old age and death; spring symbolizes youth and love. Colors also are often symbolic. White is purity, and red is passion or war. Light itself is used as a symbol, usually standing for the good or wise. Poets often use symbols as a key method of getting a point across.

Images are words or phrases that appeal to the reader's senses. Images create pictures in the reader's mind or recreate sensations of taste, smell or hearing. For example, "rosy-fingered dawn" is an image. "The freight train pawed and snorted" is another. In poetry, images are often striking, but not always.

Read the following poem by Roderick Jellema. As you read, try to see what symbols the poet is using. Use the Purpose Question above the poem to help you.

WHO ARE THE MIGRANTS?

Migrants

Birds obeying migration maps etched in their brains
Never revised their Interstate routes.
Some of them still stop off in Washington, D.C.

This autumn evening as the lights of the Pentagon
(5)   Come on like the glare of urgent trouble through surgery
    skylights,
Come on like a far-off hope of control,

I watch a peaceful V-sign of Canada Geese
Lower their landing gear, slip to rest on the slicky Potomac,
(10) Break rank and huddle with the bobbing power boats.

Wings of jets beating the air, taking turns for the landing—
Pterodactyls circling the filled-in swamps under National Airport.
There is a great wild honking

Of traffic on the bridges—
(15) The daily homing of migrants with headlights dimmed
Who loop and bank by instinct along broken white lines.

Identify Effects of Techniques (Symbols and Images)

This skill involves identifying the characteristic ways in which an author uses language (poetic symbols and images) and understanding the effects this language creates.

When poets use **images** and **symbols,** they are making direct statements that imply more than they say. An image is created by the language used. The effect of that image is in the reader's mind rather than in the poet's. The reader brings to the poem the things that make the image work.

When poets use symbols, words or pictures that stand for two or more things at the same time, they create their own meanings and connections. The symbols can be obvious or not, depending upon the audience. The effect of these symbols is created by the poet. When looking for the effect, look for the most obvious connection first.

Examples

DIRECTIONS: Use the information on this page and the poem by Roderick Jellema on the preceding page to choose the one best answer for each item below.

1. Which statement *best* describes what the poet is doing in the poem?

   (1) He is comparing spring and fall.
   (2) He is comparing the river and the airport.
   (3) He is contrasting the boats and the jets.
   (4) He is contrasting the geese and the Interstate highway.
   (5) He is comparing and contrasting the commuters and the geese.

   Answer: (5) Choices (1), (2) and (3) are false. In choice (4) the poet uses the highway like the images in choices (2) and (3), as details to focus on the real comparison, the commuters and the geese.

2. Which statement *best* describes the way the poet feels about the commuters?

   (1) He thinks that they have maps etched on their brains.
   (2) He thinks they follow habits, like the geese.
   (3) He does not like them at all.
   (4) He thinks they want to fly away, like the geese.
   (5) He thinks they are confused, like the geese.

   Answer: (2) Choice (1) is wrong; it is the geese who have the maps in their brains. There is no support for choice (3). Choices (4) and (5) are wrong because the geese are not confused, and do not want to fly away.

When you read a difficult poem, try to understand it literally before you try to understand the meanings of symbols and images.

DIRECTIONS: Choose the one best answer for each item below.

Items 1–2 refer to the following poem by Wendell Berry.

FOR WHOM DOES THE WHEEL TURN?

The Wheel

At the first strokes of the fiddle bow
the dancers rise from their seats.
The dance begins to shape itself
in the crowd, as couples join,
(5) and couples join couples, their movement
together lightening their feet.
They move in the ancient circle
of the dance. The dance and the song
call each other into being. Soon
(10) they are one—rapt in a single
rapture, so that even the night
has its clarity, and time
is the wheel that brings it round.

In this rapture the dead return.
(15) Sorrow is gone from them.
They are light. They step
into the steps of the living
and turn with them in the dance
in the sweet enclosure
(20) of the song, and timeless
is the wheel that brings it round.

1. On the simplest level, what is the poet describing in this poem?

(1) He is describing a ferris wheel at a county fair.
(2) He is describing a church choir at a country church.
(3) He is describing a square dance or some similar sort of dance.
(4) He is describing the milky way.
(5) He is describing a funeral procession.

2. What is the mood of this poem?

(1) sarcastic
(2) joking
(3) thoughtful
(4) despairing
(5) angry

GO ON TO THE NEXT PAGE.

WHAT ARE THE FACES IN OUR FINGERS?

At Our Fingers' Tips There Are Small Faces

concise whorls of flesh
fine as hairs
circling one another in a puzzle of lines
that would describe us unmistakably
(5)　and eternally

we stare into the small faces
a universe of tiny flesh
if gouged inside-out they would reveal
a deep red richness of flesh
(10)　minute bleeding in the labyrinth of flesh
and all the secrets of the crevices
in our heads or in the rock of the earth—

but our fingertips are closed
secret and silent as ourselves
(15)　hidden as our eardrums
they touch lightly the winter air
and like the air they are barriers
protecting one world from another

3. Which statement *best* describes what the poet is talking about in lines 1–5?

(1) She is describing someone looking at a photograph.
(2) She is describing the lines that make up a fingerprint.
(3) She is describing an image in a mirror.
(4) She is describing lines written in a personal diary.
(5) She is describing a crossword puzzle.

4. Which statement *best* describes the main idea of the poem?

(1) Some people have little faces painted on their fingertips.
(2) We are all flesh and blood.
(3) Every person's fingerprints are unique.
(4) We are all locked in ourselves.
(5) The skin is a barrier against disease.

5. Based on the poem, which statement below would the poet probably agree with?

(1) People often do not communicate with each other.
(2) Life is a lot of fun.
(3) Time is like a wheel.
(4) People ought to keep their hands clean and their finger-nails short.
(5) Everyone ought to be fingerprinted.

DIRECTIONS: Choose the <u>one</u> best answer for each item below.

Items 1–4 refer to the following poem by Loren Eiseley.

WHO ARE THE DRAGONS?

Dragons We Are

Strange to find him here a hundred feet
                     above the lake shore waters,
not a land tortoise, but lying there on the grass
like a carven Chinese dragon
(5)   scarcely real
till the dog barked,
             a tiny remnant
dwarfed from reptile age, back plates and all.
                But why he trudged so slow
(10)   and painfully
up a hill crowded with sharp stones, he does not choose
to answer. Maybe he wanted to see,
              see for himself,
absorb within his wary horn-dense skull
(15)   what moved up here and flourished.
                I could have told him
he'd never keep that peaceful patch of lawn,
New monsters stirred, and I was one of them.
His shell had that fine chiseled touch as though
(20)   gods in some age just past had given him
unqualified attention. He was more beautiful
than much above the waters so I took him down
                   with care
and launched him, hoping he
(25)   would find some other place to drowse. Like him
                   I seek the sun
but then dogs yelp or people intervene.
Armor is best, the reptiles had that straight.
Dragons we are and better if not seen.

GO ON TO THE NEXT PAGE.

1. Which statement *best* describes what the poet is talking about in lines 1–8 of the poem?

   (1) The poet is talking about a carved Chinese dragon.
   (2) The poet is talking about an ancient land tortoise.
   (3) The poet is talking about a snake, emerging from an egg shell.
   (4) The poet is talking about a small turtle that lives in a lake.
   (5) The poet is talking about a fossil of a dinosaur, buried in a hillside.

2. When the poet says he "launched" (line 24) the animal, he probably means he

   (1) threw it into the air
   (2) dropped it from a hundred feet
   (3) carried it to the lake shore and carefully set it in the water's edge
   (4) built a raft
   (5) took the animal to the poet's launch

3. What does the poet mean when he says "a tiny remnant dwarfed from reptile age" in lines 7–8 of the poem?

   (1) He means that he found a little fossil piece of an ancient creature.
   (2) He means that the dog is a remnant of a reptile age.
   (3) He means that the little turtle is a direct link to the reptile age, and has hardly changed at all.
   (4) He means that the turtle is a dwarf turtle, no larger than a thumb.
   (5) He means that the turtle is an old turtle, who has climbed the hill to die.

4. Based on the poem as a whole, which statement describes what the poet believes?

   (1) He believes that the reptiles are about to take over the earth.
   (2) He believes that all living things are connected and have something in common.
   (3) He believes that dogs will inherit the earth.
   (4) He believes that the dinosaurs will soon return.
   (5) He believes that human beings will soon be extinct, like the dinosaurs.

Check your answers to the GED Mini-Test on page 118.

Answers and Explanations

Practice   *pp. 114–115*

1. **Answer:** (3)   You know that this is the right answer because the real focus of the whole poem is dancing, and this is the only choice that mentions a dance. Choice (3) fits all the parts of the poem, and is the only choice that does.

2. **Answer:** (3)   The poet is not sarcastic, joking or angry in this poem, which means that choices (1), (2) and (5) are not correct. Although the poem talks of death, it is not despairing, which means that choice (4) is also incorrect.

3. **Answer:** (2)   Of course, you have to read the whole poem to be sure, but the word "fingertips" in line 13 is a clue, just like the title. This shows how important it is to use all the clues, since all the other choices seem to fit if you do not read the poem carefully. If you read lines 1–5 again, trying to see how every word fits, you will see that they do, and that a fingerprint, or the end of a finger that makes the print, is the only choice that does.

4. **Answer:** (4)   The whole purpose of focusing on the fingertips is that they are filled with information that is closed, "secret and silent as ourselves." While choices (2), (3) and (5) are all true, they do not tie in to the last six lines of the poem. Choice (4) connects the idea of the fingertip with the last six lines, and so is the best answer. There is, of course, no support for choice (1).

5. **Answer:** (1)   Choice (2) has no support at all; the poem is not about fun. Choice (3) is from the previous poem, not this one. Choices (4) and (5) both pick up on details from the poem, but neither one addresses the feelings of the poet. Choice (1) reflects the main idea of the poem, which is that each person is closed up like a fingertip, filled with information that never comes out. It follows from this that the poet does not think people communicate much.

GED Mini-Test   *pp. 116–117*

1. **Answer:** (4)   You can eliminate choices (1) and (2) right away, because the poet says it was not a tortoise, and it was like a Chinese dragon, but not that it was a dragon. You have to read the whole poem to eliminate choices (3) and (5), since you then learn that the creature has a shell, and so is not a snake, and is a living creature, and so is not a fossil. Only choice (4) fits the whole poem.

2. **Answer:** (3)   He means that he "launched" the little turtle in the same way one launches a small boat, by setting it off from the edge of the water.

3. **Answer:** (3)   Once again you can eliminate choices (1) and (2) since what he is talking about is alive and since the "back plates" show that he is not talking about a dog. Choice (4) is close to the right answer, but the poem does not support the size of the turtle as no larger than a thumb. Choice (5) almost fits the context, too, but there is no indication that the turtle is about to die. Thus, only choice (3) fits the whole poem and has some support for every statement in it.

4. **Answer:** (2)   This question is really a give-away, since all the other choices are clearly wrong, and none of them has any support in the poem. In fact, after you answered this question, you should have realized any wrong choices you may have selected in the previous three questions and corrected them. This question shows how reading all the questions to a given poem can help you to understand the parts of the poem you are not sure about.

15 Drama

Drama is a form of writing that is meant to be acted out by performers and viewed by an audience.

Another word for drama is plays. A **play** is written by a **playwright** to communicate ideas and feelings or simply to tell a story. And although a play is not fully realized until it is performed, you can read plays in print and use the same reading skills that you use when you read fiction.

A playwright communicates ideas and feelings mainly through what each character says—to himself or herself, to the other characters or, sometimes, directly to the audience.

When you read a play, you will often read the **stage directions.** These directions usually appear in parentheses and in italics, and describe a character or setting or indicate what a character is doing. They help you visualize the play's action.

Read the following play excerpt by Lanford Wilson. See what information you can learn about the characters by reading what they say. Use the Purpose Question above the excerpt to help you.

HOW DO THIS MAN AND WOMAN FEEL ABOUT EACH OTHER?

MATT: . . . You do real work at the hospital. All the boys said they liked you best. All those other nurses, though, with their eyes they were saying: "Don't you go away, Matt, Sally is gonna come around."

(5) SALLY: They enjoyed the game.

MATT: Yes, me too. But they weren't telling me to go away.

SALLY: Well, then I'm telling you to go away; nothing will come from it, Matt—

MATT: See, they could tell that I was in love with you, and they

(10) were telling me you might be in love with me, and wouldn't that be a catastrophe.

SALLY: (*Beat*) I don't think I even know what that means; I don't know if you know what that—

MATT: Aside from that, though, you're afraid you might love me.

(15) SALLY: I don't think *that* is even a desirable state to be in—

MATT: Agreed, a hundred percent; all you have to say is, No, I am not.

SALLY: Why don't you just leave and make us all happier.

MATT: I don't know that leaving would make you happy. It

(20) wouldn't make me happier. It would be easier. See, I can take no for an answer; I can't take evasion, I can't take I'm scared, I can't take hiding in the kitchen.

SALLY: Just put it out of your mind, Matt. It's impossible.

═ Identify an Implication ═

This skill identifies assumptions, facts or statements that are taken for granted (not proved), and that the author takes for granted.

Imagine, for instance, that you are reading a play in which a main character says more than once that he or she needs to make a will or get his or her affairs in order. Although the character never says so you can **infer,** or figure out, from these statements that the character is about to die, or at least has been thinking about death. The character's words **imply** this idea about death, while you, the reader, **infer** it.

You usually cannot make an inference based upon one line or speech by a character. You must read a longer passage in order to generalize about a major idea of a play or draw an inference about a character.

Examples

DIRECTIONS: Use the information on this page and the excerpt by Lanford Wilson on the preceding page to choose the one best answer for each item below.

1. From the excerpt you can infer that Sally

   (1) thinks being in love with Matt would be desirable
   (2) is sure she does not love Matt
   (3) is unsure of her feelings for Matt
   (4) is sure she loves Matt
   (5) has hidden her feelings from her co-workers at the hospital.

Answer: (3) This is correct because if she were sure she could either ask him to leave or say she loves him. This uncertainty rules out choices (2) and (4). Choice (1) is the opposite of what Sally says in the passage, and choice (5) is contradicted by the material in the passage.

2. From the excerpt you can infer that Matt

   (1) respects Sally for evading her feelings
   (2) could accept Sally's honest rejection but not her uncertainty
   (3) is shy about expressing his feelings for Sally
   (4) wants Sally to be afraid of him
   (5) would be happier if Sally said no

Answer: (2) This is correct because of his words in lines 19–21, which rule out choice (1). Choice (3) is contradicted by his assertive behavior, and there is no support at all for choice (4). Choice (5) is tempting but wrong; Matt says he could *accept* an outright no, not that it would make him *happy.*

Practice

HINT ▷ Remember to read behind the characters' words in a play to see what is being implied. Also look closely at the stage directions. They often, though not always, give you more information about the characters and their ideas.

DIRECTIONS: Choose the one best answer for each item below.

Items 1–4 refer to the following excerpt by Joseph Stein.

HOW ARE PERCHIK AND MENDEL DIFFERENT?

(TEVYE *notices that* PERCHIK *is eying the cheese hungrily.*)
TEVYE: Here, have a piece.
PERCHIK: I have no money. And I am not a beggar.
TEVYE: Here—it's a blessing for me to give.
(5) PERCHIK: Very well—for your sake! (*He takes the cheese and devours it.*)
TEVYE: Thank you. You know, it's no crime to be poor.
PERCHIK: In this world, it's the rich who are the criminals. Some day their wealth will be ours.
(10) TEVYE: That would be nice. If they would agree, I would agree.
MENDEL: And who will make this miracle come to pass?
PERCHIK: People. Ordinary people.
MENDEL: Like you?
PERCHIK: Like me.
(15) MENDEL: Nonsense!
TEVYE: And until your golden day comes, Reb Perchik, how will you live?
PERCHIK: By giving lessons to children. Do you have children?
TEVYE: I have five daughters.
(20) PERCHIK: Five?
TEVYE: Daughters.
PERCHIK: Girls should learn too. Girls are people.
MENDEL: A radical!

1. Which of the following statements *best* describes Mendel's opinion of Perchik?

   (1) Perchik has sound ideas.
   (2) Perchik has ridiculous ideas.
   (3) Perchik is a good teacher.
   (4) Perchik can perform miracles.
   (5) Perchik is a beggar.

2. With which of the following statements is Mendel likely to agree?

   (1) The rich of the world are criminals.
   (2) Ordinary people can change history.
   (3) Men and women are equal.
   (4) The poor will continue to be poor.
   (5) Boys and girls should be educated.

GO ON TO THE NEXT PAGE.

3. The playwright has used the stage directions to show that

    (1) Perchik likes cheese better than anything else
    (2) Tevye has a lot of leftover cheese
    (3) Perchik has not eaten for a long time
    (4) Mendel is trying to see if Perchik will steal the cheese
    (5) Perchik likes to eat for free

4. From the passage you can infer that Tevye

    (1) is looking for a teacher for his daughters
    (2) has a very practical view of life
    (3) thinks Perchik is a fool
    (4) always sides with Perchik instead of Mendel
    (5) does not want any more money than he has

Items 5–6 refer to the following excerpt by Beth Henley.

HOW DO THESE WOMEN ACT WITH EACH OTHER?

CHICK: . . . Oh! Oh! Oh! I almost forgot. Here's a present for you. Happy birthday to Lenny, from the Buck Boyles! (*She takes a wrapped package from her bag and hands it to Lenny.*)
LENNY: Why, thank you, Chick. It's so nice to have you remember
(5)   my birthday every year like you do.
CHICK: (*modestly*) Oh, well, now, that's just the way I am, I suppose. That's just the way I was brought up to be. Well, why don't you go on and open up the present?
LENNY: All right. (*She starts to unwrap the gift.*)
(10) CHICK: It's a box of candy—assorted crèmes.
LENNY: Candy—that's always a nice gift.
CHICK: And you have a sweet tooth, don't you?
LENNY: I guess.
CHICK: Well, I'm glad you like it.
(15) LENNY: I do.
CHICK: Oh, speaking of which, remember that little polka-dot dress you got Peekay for her fifth birthday last month?
LENNY: The red-and-white one?
CHICK: Yes; well, the first time I put it in the washing machine, I
(20) mean the very first time, it fell all to pieces. Those little polka dots just dropped right off in the water.
LENNY: (*crushed*) Oh, no. Well, I'll get something else for her, then—a little toy.
CHICK: Oh, no, no, no, no, no! We wouldn't hear of it! I just
(25) wanted to let you know so you wouldn't go and waste any more of your hard-earned money on that make of dress. Those inexpensive brands just don't hold up. I'm sorry, but not in these modern washing machines.

5. From the passage you can infer that Lenny

    (1) has a mind of her own
    (2) likes to receive candy as a present
    (3) always says what others want her to say
    (4) always remembers Chick's birthdays
    (5) does not have much money

6. Chick mentions the polka-dot dress to

    (1) show off her knowledge of fashion
    (2) give Lenny a gift idea for Peekay
    (3) show how well brought up she is
    (4) make Lenny feel bad
    (5) show off her knowledge of washing machines

Before you take the GED Mini-Test, check your answers on page 125.

DIRECTIONS: Choose the <u>one</u> best answer for each item below.

Items 1–4 refer to the following excerpt by Paddy Chayefsky.

WHAT KIND OF LIVES DO MARTY AND ANGIE LEAD?

ANGIE: Well, what do you feel like doing tonight?

MARTY: I don't know. What do you feel like doing?

ANGIE: Well, we're back to that, huh? I say to you: "What do you feel like doing tonight?" And you say to me: "I don't know, what do you feel like
(5)   doing?" And then we wind up sitting around the house with a couple of cans of beer, watching Sid Caesar on television. Well, I tell you what I feel like doing. I feel like calling up Mary Feeney. She likes you. (*Marty looks up quickly at this.*)

MARTY: What makes you say that?

(10) ANGIE: I could see she likes you.

MARTY: Yeah, sure.

ANGIE: (*Half rising in his seat*) I'll call her up.

MARTY: You call her up for yourself, Angie. I don't feel like calling her up. (ANGIE *sits down again. They both return to reading the paper for a*
(15) *moment. Then* ANGIE *looks up again.*)

ANGIE: Boy, you're getting to be a real drag, you know that?

MARTY: Angie, I'm thirty-six years old. I been looking for a girl every Saturday night of my life. I'm a little, short, fat fellow, and girls don't go for me, that's all. I'm not like you. I mean, you joke
(20) around, and they laugh at you, and you get along fine. I just stand around like a bug. What's the sense of kidding myself? Everybody's always telling me to get married. Get married. Get married. Don't you think I wanna get married? I wanna get married. They drive me crazy. Now, I don't wanna wreck your Saturday night for you, Angie. You
(25) wanna go somewhere, you go ahead. I don't wanna go.

ANGIE: Boy, they drive me crazy too. My old lady, every word outta her mouth, when you gonna get married?

MARTY: My mother, boy, she drives me crazy.

1. The things Marty and Angie say imply that they both

   (1) spend a lot of evenings calling up women for dates
   (2) want to get married
   (3) spend a lot of evenings sitting around
   (4) are under pressure from each other to get married
   (5) believe they will be married soon

2. In the first stage directions the playwright's purpose is to show that Marty

   (1) is content to sit around
   (2) is not interested in what Mary Feeney thinks of him
   (3) is angry about what Angie has said
   (4) wants to change the subject
   (5) is interested in what Mary Feeney thinks of him

GO ON TO THE NEXT PAGE.

3. From the passage you can infer that Marty

(1) thinks he is attractive to women
(2) is jealous of Angie
(3) does not want to get married
(4) thinks he is unattractive to women
(5) is able to joke and make women laugh

4. According to the passage

(1) both men have met Mary Feeney
(2) only Marty has met Mary Feeney
(3) only Angie has met Mary Feeney
(4) the men have been given Mary's number by a friend
(5) Mary Feeney does not like either man

Items 5–6 refer to the following excerpt by William Gibson.

HOW CAN ANNIE AND HELEN WORK TOGETHER?

ANNIE: It's hopeless here. I can't teach a child who runs away.

KELLER: (*nonplussed*) Then—do I understand you—propose—

ANNIE: Well, if we all agree it's hopeless, the next question is what—

KATE: Miss Annie. I am not agreed. I think perhaps you—underestimate

(5) Helen.

ANNIE: I think everybody else here does.

KATE: She did fold her napkin. She learns, she learns, do you know she began talking when she was six months old? She could say "water." Not really—"wahwah." "Wahwah," but she meant water, she knew what it

(10) meant, and only six months old, I never saw a child so—bright, or outgoing— It's still in her, somewhere, isn't it? You should have seen her before her illness, such a good-tempered child—

ANNIE: (*agreeably*) She's changed.

KATE: Miss Annie, put up with it. And with us.

(15) KELLER: Us!

KATE: Please? Like the lost lamb in the parable, I love her all the more.

ANNIE: Mrs. Keller, I don't think Helen's worst handicap is deafness or blindness. I think it's your love. And pity.

KELLER: Now what does that mean?

(20) ANNIE: All of you here are so sorry for her you've kept her—like a pet, why, even a dog you housebreak. No wonder she won't let me come near her. It's useless for me to try to teach her language or anything else here. I might as well—

KATE: (*cuts in*) Miss Annie, before you came we spoke of putting her in

(25) an asylum.

5. Which of the following *best* describes Annie's position in this passage?

(1) She does not have the skills to teach Helen.
(2) She cannot teach Helen if her family spoils her.
(3) She does not like students who run away.
(4) She has successfully taught Helen to fold her napkin.
(5) She liked Helen better before her illness.

6. With which of these statements about handicapped children would Annie agree?

(1) Handicapped children cannot be taught language.
(2) Handicapped children should be given everything they want.
(3) Handicapped children must be taught and not pitied.
(4) Handicapped children are better off in an asylum.
(5) Handicapped children should be treated like pets.

Check your answers to the GED Mini-Test on page 125.

Answers and Explanations

Practice   pp. 121–122

1. **Answer:** (2) This is correct because of Mendel's responses to Perchik's statements. And, since Mendel thinks so little of Perchik, choices (3) and (4) must also be ruled out. Choice (5) may be true, but there is no evidence to support it.

2. **Answer:** (4) This is correct because of Mendel's response to Perchik's suggestion of eventual wealth. Choices (1), (2) and (5) are the ideas of Perchik, not those of Mendel, and choice (3) is an extension of the ideas in choice (5).

3. **Answer:** (3) This is correct because Perchik's behavior implies severe hunger. Choices (1), (2) and (5) are not supported by the passage. Although choice (4) may very well be true, there is no evidence one way or the other in the passage.

4. **Answer:** (2) This is correct because he concerns himself with day-to-day reality. Choices (1) and (3) are not supported by the passage and, since Tevye takes no sides, choice (4) is ruled out. Choice (5) is the opposite of what Tevye suggests.

5. **Answer:** (3) This is correct since Lenny usually echoes what Chick has already said. Choice (1) is the opposite of choice (3). Lenny says that candy is a nice gift, not that she *likes* it, ruling out choice (2). Choice (4) is not supported by the passage. And Chick remarks only on Lenny's hard-earned money, not the *amount*, making choice (5) incorrect.

6. **Answer:** (4) This is correct because Chick shows that she is not looking for a new present for Peekay, but is judging Lenny's original present, which also rules out choice (2). Choices (1) and (5) are not supported by the passage. Choice (3) is incorrect because Chick's behavior is the opposite of what well-brought-up people do.

GED Mini-Test   pp. 123–124

1. **Answer:** (3) This is correct because of Angie's second speech, which also rules out choice (1). Choice (2) is incorrect because only Marty says he wants to get married. Choice (4) is not supported by the passage. Choice (5) is unlikely in their present situation.

2. **Answer:** (5) This is correct because the quick response indicates interest, which would also rule out choice (2). Choice (1) is the opposite of what the passage suggests. Choice (3) is not supported. Choice (4) is incorrect because Marty's response does not suggest a wish to change the subject.

3. **Answer:** (4) This is correct because Marty's description of himself suggests that women do not "go for him" because of his looks, which also rules out choice (1). Choice (3) is contradicted by the passage. Choice (2) is ruled out because Marty implies an admiration for Angie, also indicated in choice (5).

4. **Answer:** (1) This is correct because of Angie's third speech. This would also make choices (2) and (3) incorrect. The men have Mary's phone number, but there is no support for choice (4). Since there is a suggestion that Mary likes Marty, choice (5) must be ruled out.

5. **Answer:** (2) This is correct because Annie talks about how the Kellers' treatment of Helen keeps Annie from reaching her. Choice (1) is the opposite of what Annie believes, and, since she merely says she cannot *teach* students who run away, choice (3) must be ruled out. Neither choice (4) nor choice (5) is supported by information in the passage.

6. **Answer:** (3) This is correct because Annie cites pity as a major block to teaching Helen. Choice (1) is untrue for her or she would not be a teacher of a blind and deaf child. Choices (2) and (5) are the opposite of what she has said she believes in the passage, and choice (4) is obviously something they are all trying to avoid.

16 Drama

Both *dialogue* and *monologue* come from Greek words meaning "speak" or "words." In addition, *dia* means "among" or "between," while *mono* means "single" or "one." So you can see how the words *dialogue* and *monologue* describe the number of people who are speaking.

When you read a drama, or play, you get much of your information about the **setting**, where a scene takes place, the **characters** and the **plot**, or story, from the **dialogue**. In general, a dialogue in literature is any conversation among two or more characters. In a play, the words of each character are identified by the characters' names, which are usually printed along the left-hand side of each page, before each change of speaker.

A **monologue** is a second way of presenting information in a play. A monologue is a long speech given by one character. Sometimes a monologue is delivered to another character or characters on stage. At other times a character will break out of the ongoing action on stage to direct his or her monologue to the audience.

When you read either a dialogue or a monologue you must use your imagination to see the characters who are speaking. If you were seeing a play in production, the set and the actors would do most of the work for you. But when you *read* a play, much of the responsibility for visualizing a description, a character or an action on stage is up to you.

Read the following monologue by Robert Anderson. See what you can learn by visualizing the character and the place he describes as he speaks. Use the Purpose Question above the passage to help you.

HOW DOES THIS MAN FEEL ABOUT HIS FATHER'S HOME?

GENE: My father's house was in a suburb of New York City, up in Westchester County. It had been a quiet town with elms and chestnut trees, lawns and old sprawling houses with a certain nondescript elegance. My father had been mayor of
(5) this town, a long time ago . . . Most of the elms and chestnut trees had gone, and the only elegance left was in the pretentious names of the developments and ugly apartment houses . . . Parkview Meadows Estates . . . only there was no meadow, and no park, and no view except of the neon signs
(10) of the chain stores. Some old houses remained, like slightly frowzy dowagers. The lawns were not well kept, and the houses were not painted as often as they should have been, but they remained. My father's house was one of these.

Identify Elements of Style and Structure

This skill involves identifying the characteristic ways in which an author uses language and organizes his or her material.

The **language** in plays is either dialogue or monologue. This language gives you information about the setting, the characters or character relationships and the plot of a play.

The **organization** of a play consists of the form it takes on the printed page. Remember that the characters' names are set off in capital letters. Character emotions may often be in parentheses. Stage directions are usually set off from dialogue and are also in parentheses.

The language of the portion of the play on page 126 is a monologue. The character, Gene, tells the reader about the setting, Westchester County, and the plot, and he infers a mood.

Examples

DIRECTIONS: Use the information on this page and the passage by Robert Anderson on the preceding page to choose the <u>one</u> best answer for each item below.

1. This monologue basically describes

   (1) a mayoral election
   (2) the changes in a town over time
   (3) the houses and lawns of a town
   (4) the speaker's father
   (5) the location of a town

Answer: (2) This is correct because the speaker describes how the town has changed. Although the houses, lawns and location of the town are mentioned, they support the basic description, ruling out choices (3) and (5). Choice (1) is incorrect, as no mayoral election is mentioned, and the speaker's father is only mentioned, not described, ruling out choice (4).

2. From the monologue you can infer that

   (1) the speaker's father dislikes his home
   (2) the developments are well named
   (3) the town has changed for the worse
   (4) the speaker wishes his father would live with him
   (5) the speaker is in the paint business

Answer: (3) This is correct because all of the present-day descriptions are negative. The father's opinion about his house is not mentioned, ruling out choice (1). Choice (2) contradicts material in the passage, and there is no support for choice (4) or (5).

Practice

HINT

Remember that stage directions may give you helpful information about setting or characters.

DIRECTIONS: Choose the <u>one</u> best answer for each item below.

Items 1–5 refer to the following passage by Elizabeth Diggs.

WHAT PROBLEM DOES THIS FAMILY NEED TO FACE?

JOSEPHINE: Good morning, dear. (EVELYN *turns on stove to heat coffee,* THAYER *takes a large mixing bowl and pours cornflakes in it, then adds milk and sugar*) What do you think I did? I overslept! Haven't slept past six-thirty in I don't know how long.

(5) EVELYN: You were up late.

JOSEPHINE: Oh, I usually am. I go to bed with a good book and I can't stop for hours. Funny, isn't it? Puts most people to sleep. Your grandfather couldn't turn two pages before his eyes would close. But not me. I get wide awake with excitement—even books

(10) I've read before—isn't that the limit?

EVELYN: Did you see any shooting stars?

JOSEPHINE: Don't recall any. (THAYER *exits to porch with his bowl of cornflakes*)

EVELYN: I saw four or five on the way up here Friday night. I

(15) stopped to look.

JOSEPHINE: My, that's a lot of wishes! I guess I'm too old for wishes. I haven't looked for a shooting star in many years.

EVELYN: You did last night.

JOSEPHINE: Oh no. (*shakes her head as if the idea is absurd*)

(20) EVELYN: (*puzzled, can't really believe that* JOSEPHINE *doesn't remember*) We all stayed in here talking, and you went outside. You said you were looking for shooting stars.

JOSEPHINE: (*confused*) Is that right?

EVELYN: You don't remember, do you?

(25) JOSEPHINE: You know, I don't.

EVELYN: You were telling us about how Grandfather used to rehearse his arguments and everybody'd get in on it. (JOSEPHINE *chuckles*) You remember that, don't you?

JOSEPHINE: I can't say that I do.

EVELYN: Oh.

---

1. This scene takes place in a

   (1) cafeteria
   (2) dining room
   (3) kitchen
   (4) living room
   (5) porch

2. You can tell from the passage that

   (1) Josephine and Evelyn are sisters
   (2) Josephine is Evelyn's mother
   (3) Josephine is Evelyn's granddaughter
   (4) Evelyn is Josephine's nurse
   (5) Evelyn is Josephine's granddaughter

GO ON TO THE NEXT PAGE.

3. The main plot action you can infer from this dialogue is that

    (1) Josephine and Evelyn do not get along
    (2) Josephine is beginning to forget things in the present
    (3) Josephine is getting up earlier
    (4) Evelyn is developing an interest in shooting stars
    (5) Josephine is sick of cooking breakfast for everyone

4. The main thing you learn about the characters in this passage is that

    (1) Josephine is more concerned about her memory loss than Evelyn is
    (2) neither character is concerned about Josephine's memory loss
    (3) Josephine enjoys reminiscing about her husband
    (4) Evelyn is more concerned about Josephine's memory loss than Josephine is
    (5) Evelyn enjoys listening to her grandmother talk about her grandfather

5. The stage directions on lines 19–23 tell you that

    (1) both characters are confused
    (2) both characters are angry
    (3) Evelyn is confused and Josephine is angry
    (4) Evelyn often cooks breakfast for Josephine
    (5) Josephine dislikes shooting stars

Items 6–7 refer to the following monologue by Edgar Lee Masters.

WHAT WENT WRONG IN THE LIFE OF THIS CHARACTER?

BENJAMIN PANTIER: Together in this grave lie Benjamin Pantier, Attorney at Law
And Nig, his dog, constant companion, solace and friend.
Down the gray road, friends, children, men and women,
(5)   Passing one by one out of life, left me till I was alone
With Nig for partner, bed-fellow, comrade in drink.
In the morning of life I knew aspiration and saw glory.
Then she, who survives me, snared my soul
With a snare which bled me to death.
(10)   Till I, once strong of will, lay broken, indifferent,
Living with Nig in a room back of a dingy office.

6. From the monologue you can infer that the scene takes place in

    (1) Benjamin Pantier's law office
    (2) the cemetery where Benjamin Pantier is buried
    (3) Benjamin Pantier's bedroom
    (4) a hospital room
    (5) Benjamin Pantier's house

7. You can infer that Benjamin Pantier believes the major problem in his life was

    (1) insufficient study in law school
    (2) too much drinking
    (3) an unattractive law office
    (4) a woman who destroyed his dreams
    (5) his attachment to animals

Before you take the GED Mini-Test, check your answers on page 132.

GED Mini-Test

16

DIRECTIONS: Choose the one best answer for each item below.

Items 1–4 refer to the following passage by Jane Martin.

WHY DOES THE SPEAKER'S MOTHER BEHAVE THIS WAY?

LAURIE: The day my mother found out she was dying she asked me to go out and buy her these clear glass marbles. Dad and I hadn't even known she was ill which was nothing new. Whenever you asked my mother if she was ill she would throw things at you, sesame buns,
(5) the editorial page, a handful of hair ribbons. 'Do not,' she would say, 'suggest things to suggestible people.' Anyway, I brought her the marbles and she counted ninety of them out and put them in this old cut-glass bowl which had been the sum total of great Aunt Helena's estate. Apparently, the doctor had given her three months
(10) and she set great store by doctors. She said she always believed them because they were the nearest thing to the Old Testament we had. 'I wouldn't give you two bits for these young smiley guys,' she'd say, 'I go for a good, stern-furrowed physician.' She wouldn't even have her teeth cleaned by a dentist under fifty. So she counted out
(15) ninety clear glass marbles and set them in the bowl on her bedside table. Then she went out and spent twelve hundred dollars on night-gowns. She said, 'In my family you are only dying when you take to your bed, and that, my darlings, is where I am going.' And she did. . . .

1. The main thing described in this monologue is

(1) the appearance of Laurie's mother
(2) the preparation for death made by Laurie's mother
(3) Laurie's feelings about her mother
(4) the purchases made by Laurie's mother
(5) Laurie's actions on behalf of her mother

2. You can infer that Laurie's mother chose ninety marbles because

(1) she wanted something pretty to look at
(2) she had a glass bowl to fill
(3) the doctors had told her that keeping busy would help her recover
(4) she wanted to look at her reflection
(5) the doctors had told her that she had three months to live

3. When Laurie's mother said 'Do not suggest things to suggestible people,' she meant:

(1) Do not make any suggestions at all.
(2) Do not buy me hair ribbons.
(3) Do not ask me if I'm ill or I'll probably get sick.
(4) Do not make stupid suggestions or I'll throw things at you.
(5) Do not give me any unasked-for advice.

4. From the monologue you can infer that the *best* doctor for Laurie's mother would be

(1) a younger, well-educated woman
(2) an older, serious man
(3) a religious man
(4) a younger, joke-cracking man
(5) an older, well-educated woman

GO ON TO THE NEXT PAGE.

Items 5–6 refer to the following passage by Charlie L. Russell.

WHAT DECISION HAS MRS. BROOKS MADE AND WHY?

MRS. BROOKS: But, girl, this morning I made up my mind, I'm leaving Mr. Brooks.

RUBY: Gladys, it's not that bad, is it? Remember it ain't the easiest thing in the world to leave a man after all these years.

(5)   MRS. BROOKS: Humph. Telling me I couldn't buy a new dress for Gail's wedding; that was the last straw.

RUBY: You know, Gladys, there is such a thing as going from the refrigerator into the frying pan.

MRS. BROOKS: Oh, Ruby, be serious.

(10)   RUBY: I am just as serious as cancer. I mean, it's not as though the man won't work. Everybody knows that he ain't known to mess up a piece of money.

MRS. BROOKS: A lot of good it does me. Everything in the house is in his name. My name don't appear on nothing except the income tax

(15)   deductions.

RUBY: Oh, girl.

MRS. BROOKS: Oh, and the way that man courted me before we got married! Such sweet names he called me. And the day after we got married

he started calling me Mrs. Brooks. And now he's got me keeping that old

(20)   appointment book so he'll know what I'm doing every minute of the day. The only thing I don't have to put in it is when I cough or go to the bathroom.

RUBY: Ah, child.

MRS. BROOKS: And don't let me even look like I want to disagree with

(25)   him. He rants and raves up a storm, acting like he's going to thunder and lightning for forty days and forty nights.

RUBY: If ever there was a man who knows how to get mad, it's Mr. Brooks.

MRS. BROOKS: Last week I overspent buying groceries, and talking

(30)   about a man carrying on! You'd have thought that seventeen cents was going to cause a panic down on Wall Street.

RUBY: Now, Gladys, you know sometimes he does have good intentions.

MRS. BROOKS: My granny always said that the road to hell is paved with good intentions.

5. Which of the following *best* describes Mrs. Brooks' position in this passage?

(1) She appreciates the fact that Mr. Brooks has good intentions.
(2) She no longer has any patience with Mr. Brooks' behavior.
(3) She has decided to leave Mr. Brooks on the spur of the moment.
(4) She is willing to give Mr. Brooks one more chance.
(5) She likes joking with Ruby about leaving Mr. Brooks.

6. According to the passage, which of the following statements does *not* describe Mr. Brooks?

(1) He has a bad temper and gets angry easily and often.
(2) He controls the way Mrs. Brooks spends the household money.
(3) He makes Mrs. Brooks account for the way she spends her time.
(4) He does not work hard to support the Brooks family.
(5) He is very formal with Mrs. Brooks.

Check your answers to the GED Mini-Test on page 132.

Answers and Explanations

Practice *pp. 128–129*

1. **Answer:** (3) This is correct because of the stove and food preparations. The stove rules out choices (2) and (4), and the homey atmosphere rules out choice (1). One of the characters exits *to* the porch, ruling out choice (5).

2. **Answer:** (5) This is correct because of Josephine's references to her husband as "your grandfather" when she talks to Evelyn, ruling out choices (1), (2) and (3). Choice (4) is a possibility since Evelyn could be nursing her grandmother, but it is not supported by the passage.

3. **Answer:** (2) This is correct because Josephine has forgotten several things recently. Choices (3) and (4) make true statements, but they are not major plot developments. There is no evidence to support either choice (1) or (5).

4. **Answer:** (4) This is correct because Josephine acts very matter-of-fact about her memory loss, while Evelyn keeps talking about it, ruling out choices (1) and (2). Choices (3) and (5) make true statements, but neither is the main thing you learn about these characters.

5. **Answer:** (1) This is correct because the directions suggest that the characters are confused and puzzled, not angry, ruling out choices (2) and (3). The content of choices (4) and (5) is not mentioned at all in the stage directions.

6. **Answer:** (2) This is correct since the first line refers to his grave. Choices (1), (3), (4) and (5) must all be ruled out because they refer to places that Pantier may reasonably have been only during his life.

7. **Answer:** (4) This is correct because Pantier suggests that his dreams were broken by a woman. Choice (1) is not supported, and choice (2) is probably true, but is not his main problem. Choices (3) and (5) are the results of his lost dreams, not the causes.

GED Mini-Test *pp. 130–131*

1. **Answer:** (2) This is correct because the complete passage supports this main idea. Choices (1) and (3) must be ruled out because neither Laurie's mother nor Laurie's feelings for her are described. Choices (4) and (5) support the main idea.

2. **Answer:** (5) This is correct because ninety marbles represent ninety days, or three months. Choices (1), (2) and (4) may be true, but they are not supported by the passage; there is no evidence for choice (3).

3. **Answer:** (3) This is correct because the statement reflects her belief that talking about something bad can make it happen. Choices (1), (4) and (5) are all things Laurie's mother may have said, but they do not reflect the meaning of the statement. There is no support for choice (2).

4. **Answer:** (2) This is correct because her mother disapproves of "young smiley guys" and wants someone "stern-furrowed," which rules out choice (4). Choice (3) is tempting because of the reference to the Old Testament, but does not include an age. Since women are not mentioned at all, choices (1) and (5) must also be ruled out.

5. **Answer:** (2) This is correct because this is consistent with her decision to leave him. Choices (1) and (4) are contradicted by the passage. Choice (3) is not supported, and only Ruby makes jokes, which also rules out choice (5).

6. **Answer:** (4) This is correct because, according to Ruby, everyone knows Mr. Brooks is a hard worker. All of the other choices *do* reflect descriptions of Mr. Brooks taken from the passage.

17 Drama

When you read a play, you learn most of what you need to know from the character's words. Not surprisingly much of this information is about the characters themselves.

As in fiction, plays provide ways for you to learn about characters. First, you can learn about a character through his or her own words and actions. Second, you can learn about a character by what others say about him or her. You have to be careful here, though. Character A may talk about character B, but you find that you really learn more about character A. For example, suppose that Karen talks about her sister Pam, a successful businesswoman. According to Karen, Pam's success is due to her having had good breaks and having married a wealthy man. These words really tell you more about Karen—that she is jealous or resentful of Pam's success.

Unlike fiction, plays have few places in which you can learn about characters by what the author says about them. The stage directions and character descriptions may give you some information. And, once in a while, a play has a character who serves as the narrator, or the voice of the playwright, but this is rare.

Read the following excerpt from Charles Aidman's stage version of Edgar Lee Masters' *Spoon River Anthology* to learn about the character. Use the Purpose Question to help you.

WHAT DOES THIS CHARACTER WANT AND WHY?

JUDGE SELAH LIVELY: Suppose you stood just five feet two,
And had worked your way as a grocery clerk,
Studying law by candlelight
Until you became an attorney at law?
(5) And then suppose through your diligence,
And regular church attendance,
You became attorney for Thomas Rhodes,
Collecting notes and mortgages,
And representing all the widows
(10) In the Probate Court? And through it all
They jeered at your size, and laughed at your clothes
And your polished boots? And then suppose
You became the County Judge?
And Jefferson Howard and Kinsey Keene,
(15) And Harmon Whitney, and all the giants
Who had sneered at you, were forced to stand
Before the bar and say "Your Honor"—
Well, don't you think it was natural
That I made it hard for them?

Identify Techniques (Characterization)

This skill involves recognizing the ways in which we learn about characters and drawing conclusions about them.

Characterization uses a character's words or actions to indicate **motivation,** or *why* he or she says or does something.

A simple way to find motivation in many plays is to ask yourself this question: **What does Character A *want* in this scene? Is it the same or different from what the other character or characters want?** A single scene does not usually tell you whether a character succeeds or fails in his or her purpose, but it will give you an idea of what the purpose is.

Motivation is also often a question of cause and effect. A character acts in a certain way or says something because of what other characters have said or done. If you are having trouble figuring out a character's motivation, try forming a "Character A does such and such because . . ." sentence and see if this helps.

Examples

DIRECTIONS: Use the information on this page and the excerpt from the stage version of Edgar Lee Masters' *Spoon River Anthology* on the preceding page to choose the <u>one</u> best answer for each item below.

1. You can infer from the monologue that the judge basically wanted to

   (1) be a good lawyer
   (2) get revenge on people who laughed at him
   (3) stop representing widows in probate
   (4) give up his judgeship
   (5) put Jefferson Howard and all his friends in jail

Answer: (2) This is correct because the entire monologue supports this position. Choices (1) and (3) are wrong because he obviously has already done these things. Choice (4) would not give him the power to do choice (2) and choice (5) is not supported by the passage.

2. You can infer that the townspeople laughed at the judge *mainly* because of

   (1) his poor skill as a lawyer
   (2) his job as a grocery clerk
   (3) his attitude
   (4) his size
   (5) his choice of law school

Answer: (4) This is correct because this is mentioned most often. Choice (1) is contradicted by the passage. Choice (2) is something he may feel ashamed of, but it is not a cause for laughter; choice (3) is mentioned only in addition to his size. Choice (5) is not supported by the passage.

Practice

H
I
N
T

Remember that you can learn two basic things about characters by what they say and do. You can learn what they want, and you can learn why they do or say the things they do. Often, though not always, the two are connected.

DIRECTIONS: Choose the one best answer for each item below.

Items 1–2 refer to the following excerpt by Tina Howe.

DO MAGS AND FANNY VIEW GARDNER IN THE SAME WAY?

FANNY: (*pulling* MAGS *next to her onto the sofa*) I'm so glad you're finally here, Mags. I'm very worried about Daddy.
MAGS: Mummy, please, I just got here.
FANNY: He's getting quite gaga.
(5) MAGS: Mummy . . . !
FANNY: You haven't seen him in almost a year. Two weeks ago he walked through the front door of the Codman's house, kissed Emily on the cheek and settled down in the maid's room, thinking he was home!
(10) MAGS: Oh come on, you're exaggerating.
FANNY: He's as mad as a hatter and getting worse every day! It's this damned new book of his. He works on it around the clock. I've read some of it, and it doesn't make one word of sense, it's all at 6s and 7s . . .
(15) GARDNER: (*poking his head back in the room, spies some of his papers on a table and grabs them*) Ahhh, here they are. (*and exits*)
FANNY: (*voice lowered*) Ever since this dry spell with his poetry, he's been frantic, absolutely . . . frantic!
MAGS: I hate it when you do this.
(20) FANNY: I'm just trying to get you to face the facts around here.
MAGS: There's nothing wrong with him! He's just as sane as the next man. Even saner, if you ask me.
FANNY: You know what he's doing now? You couldn't guess in a million years! . . . He's writing criticism! Daddy! (*She laughs.*) Can
(25) you believe it? The man doesn't have one analytic bone in his body. His mind is a complete jumble and always has been!

1. Fanny shows by her words that she wants to

(1) impress Mags with Gardner's book
(2) leave Gardner in someone else's care
(3) convince Mags that Gardner needs help
(4) get Mags to leave again soon
(5) get out more socially with Gardner

2. Mags shows by her words that she wants to

(1) deny Fanny's worries about Gardner
(2) read Gardner's poetry
(3) have a long talk with Fanny
(4) move back home
(5) believe Fanny about Gardner

GO ON TO THE NEXT PAGE.

Items 3–6 refer to the following excerpt by Tennessee Williams.

HOW DOES ALMA MAKE THESE PEOPLE REVEAL THEMSELVES?

MRS. BUCHANAN: You mustn't misunderstand me about Miss Alma. Naturally I feel sorry for her, too. But, precious, precious! In every Southern town there's a girl or two like that. People feel sorry for them, they're kind to them, but, darling, they keep at a

(5) distance, they don't get involved with them. Especially not in a sentimental way.

JOHN: I don't know what you mean about Miss Alma. She's a little bit—quaint, she's very excitable, but—there's nothing *wrong* with her.

(10) MRS. BUCHANAN: Precious, can't you see. Miss Alma is an *eccentric*!

JOHN: You mean she isn't like all the other girls in Glorious Hill?

MRS. BUCHANAN: There's always at least one like her in every Southern town, sometimes, like Miss Alma, rather sweet, sometimes even gifted, and I think that Miss Alma *does* have a rather

(15) appealing voice when she doesn't become too carried away by her singing. Sometimes, but not often, pretty. I have seen Miss Alma when she was almost pretty. But never, never *quite*.

JOHN: There are moments when she has beauty.

MRS. BUCHANAN: Those moments haven't occurred when *I* looked at

(20) her! Such a wide mouth she has, like the mouth of a clown! And she distorts her face with all those false expressions. However, Miss Alma's looks are beside the point.

JOHN: Her, her eyes are fascinating!

MRS. BUCHANAN: Goodness, yes, disturbing!

(25) JOHN: No, quite lovely, I think. They're never the same for two seconds. The light keeps changing in them like, like—a running stream of clear water. . . .

MRS. BUCHANAN: They have a demented look!

JOHN: She's not demented, Mother.

3. Mrs. Buchanan *mainly* wants to

(1) get everyone to feel sorry for Alma
(2) show John how much she knows about Southern towns
(3) demonstrate her musical knowledge
(4) keep John from getting involved with Alma
(5) prove how much she likes Alma

4. Mrs. Buchanan says the things she does because she

(1) admires beauty
(2) feels sorry for Alma
(3) likes talking about Alma
(4) is sentimental and indulges John
(5) is critical and a snob

5. John probably does *not* want to

(1) disagree politely with his mother
(2) express his own opinion of Alma
(3) talk about Alma's eyes
(4) avoid seeing Alma again
(5) see Alma again

6. John says the things he does because he

(1) fears Alma has designs on him
(2) does not think Alma is demented
(3) respects Alma for her differences
(4) does not pay much attention to Alma
(5) judges Alma harshly

Before you take the GED Mini-Test, check your answers on page 139.

17

DIRECTIONS: Choose the <u>one</u> best answer for each item below.

Items 1–4 refer to the following excerpt by James Baldwin.

WHAT DO DAVID AND LUKE HAVE IN COMMON?

LUKE: You play piano like I dreamed you would.

DAVID: I been finding out lately you was pretty good. Mama never let us keep a phonograph. I just didn't never hear any of your records—until here lately. You was right up there with the best, Jellyroll Morton and

(5) Louis Armstrong and cats like that.

LUKE: You fixing to be a musician?

DAVID: No.

LUKE: Well, it ain't much of a profession for making money, that's the truth.

(10) DAVID: There were guys who did.

LUKE: There were guys who didn't.

DAVID: You never come to look for us. Why?

LUKE: I started to. I wanted to. I thought of it lots of times.

DAVID: Why didn't you never do it? Did you think it was good riddance

(15) we was gone?

LUKE: I was hoping you wouldn't never think that, never.

DAVID: I wonder what you expected me to think. I remembered you, but couldn't never talk about you. I use to hear about you sometime, but I couldn't never say, That's my daddy. I was too ashamed. I remembered

(20) how you used to play for me sometimes. That was why I started playing the piano. I used to go to sleep dreaming about the way we'd play together one day, me with my piano and you with your trombone.

LUKE: David. David.

DAVID: You never come. You never come when you could do us some

(25) good. You come now, now when you can't do nobody any good. Every time I think about it, think about *you*, I want to break down and cry like a baby. You make me—ah! You make me feel so bad.

LUKE: Son—don't try to get away from the things that hurt you. The things that hurt you—sometimes that's all you got. You got to learn to

(30) live with those things—and—use them . . . .

1. You can infer that David *mainly* wants to

  (1) be a musician and leave his family
  (2) forget about his father for good
  (3) be a better musician than his father
  (4) find out what his father thinks of him
  (5) understand why his father has been gone

2. You can infer that Luke wants to

  (1) show David that he can live with pain
  (2) brag about his musical success
  (3) pretend David's pain does not exist
  (4) encourage David to be a musician
  (5) tell David what a good pianist he is

GO ON TO THE NEXT PAGE.

3. One main idea you can infer from the passage is that

    (1) Luke's success as a musician has made David jealous
    (2) Luke's absence has made David feel bad about himself
    (3) David wants to be as good as Louis Armstrong
    (4) Luke and David have different ideas about how much money musicians make
    (5) David wants Luke to leave

4. David started to play the piano originally because

    (1) he heard a record of his father playing the trombone
    (2) he heard his father play in a night club
    (3) he wanted to make a lot of money
    (4) he remembered his father playing the trombone for him
    (5) he wanted to tell people that he was a musician like his father

Items 5–6 refer to the following excerpt by Lanford Wilson.

WHAT DOES SHIRLEY DO TO ENTERTAIN HERSELF?

JOHN: You better watch that one. She's gettin' a little big for her pants, ain't you? How old are you now? How old are you?

JUNE: You wouldn't know, of course.

SHIRLEY: Age is the most irrelevant judge of character or maturity that—

(5) JOHN: Yeah, yeah, how old are you?

JUNE: She's thirteen.

SHIRLEY: I am nineteen and I will be twenty next month.

JUNE: She's thirteen.

SHIRLEY: I am eighteen years old, and it is none of your business . . .

(10) JUNE: She's thirteen.

SHIRLEY: I'm seventeen. If you must know.

JUNE: You are not seventeen, you cretin.

SHIRLEY: I will be seventeen in less than twenty-five days. I will!

JUNE: She's thirteen.

(15) SHIRLEY: I am fifteen years old!

JUNE: She's fourteen. (JOHN *picks* SHIRLEY *up and carries her over his shoulder to the porch and slams the door on her. All through this, she is screaming: "Put me down, put me down, Rhett Butler, put me down"*)

JOHN: (*Smiles, turns back to the bedroom*) Yeah? You better watch that

(20) one. (*Exits to his bedroom*)

SHIRLEY: (*Comes back in, follows him to steps*) I happen to, am going to be an artist, and an artist has no age. . . .

5. You can infer that which of the following is *not* true?

    (1) Shirley is annoyed that June keeps insisting that Shirley is thirteen.
    (2) Shirley may become an artist.
    (3) John is Shirley's brother.
    (4) June enjoys teasing Shirley.
    (5) Shirley likes a good argument.

6. Shirley acts the way she does in order to

    (1) antagonize everyone
    (2) get experience to use as an artist
    (3) dramatize herself and get attention
    (4) force others to keep track of her birthday
    (5) make people see that age is not important

Check your answers to the GED Mini-Test on page 139.

Answers and Explanations

Practice   pp. 135–136

1. **Answer:** (3) This is correct because she uses words such as "gaga" and "mad as a hatter." Choice (2) is not supported, although Fanny does seem to think Mags should spend more time at home, which also rules out choice (4). Choice (5) is an unlikely motivation, as she would not want him to be seen in his condition.

2. **Answer:** (1) This is correct because she makes light of Fanny's worries, which rules out choice (5). Choice (2) is not supported, and choice (3) is contradicted by the passage. Choice (4) might be Fanny's wish, but Mags does not show any motivation for such a move.

3. **Answer:** (4) This is correct because she senses John's admiration for Alma and works against it. Choice (1) is wrong because she only pretends to feel sorry for Alma, and choice (5) is clearly contradicted by the passage. Choice (2) is true but a minor point, and choice (3) is irrelevant.

4. **Answer:** (5) This is correct because her every word is judgmental and proud. Choice (1) may be true but is not relevant, and choice (2) is only a pretense. Choice (3) is wrong because she talks about Alma only to try to turn John from Alma. Choice (4) is contradicted by the passage.

5. **Answer:** (4) There is nothing in the scene to support the idea that John does not wish to see Alma again. The other choices are all supported by what John says, and how he says it.

6. **Answer:** (3) This is correct because of his obvious admiration of Alma's qualities, which rules out choice (5). Choice (1) is not supported, and choice (2) is a true statement but not a main idea. Choice (4) is contradicted by the amount of time John spends talking about Alma.

GED Mini-Test   pp. 137–138

1. **Answer:** (5) This is correct because of David's frequent questions along these lines. Choice (1) is unsupported; choice (2) is tempting because his father has caused him pain, but is also not supported. Choice (3) may be true but there is no evidence for it. Choice (4) offers support for the main idea.

2. **Answer:** (1) This is correct because he has learned this himself and hopes to pass it on, which rules out choice (3). Choice (2) is contradicted by the passage; choice (4), from what he says about musicians, is not one Luke would make for David. Choice (5) is a true statement, but not a major motivation.

3. **Answer:** (2) This is correct because he says he feels bad as he talks about Luke's absence. Choice (1) is contradicted by the passage, and choice (3) states the way he thinks about Luke, not himself. Choice (4) is true, but not a main idea; though the two men have a troubled history, choice (5) is unsupported.

4. **Answer:** (4) This is correct because he states this in lines 19–21. Choice (1) is contradicted by the passage, and choice (2) is not supported. There is no evidence one way or the other for choice (3), and choice (5) is incorrect because David says he never felt he could talk to people about Luke.

5. **Answer:** (3) Choice (1) is obviously true, because Shirley stops inflating her age as soon as June admits that Shirley is 14. There is nothing to support that choice (2) is false. Choices (4) and (5) are shown to be true throughout this scene.

6. **Answer:** (3) This is correct because her actions are those of someone seeking attention. Choice (1) is too strong. Though she may become an artist, her concerns are really with the present moment, ruling out choice (2). Choice (4) is unsupported, and choice (5) is also wrong because her motivation is simply to stir up excitement.

18 Drama

There are two main kinds of popular drama. A **comedy** is a play in which the playwright communicates his or her ideas mainly by making you, the audience, laugh. A **drama**, on the other hand, is a play in which the playwright communicates his or her ideas mostly by making you think or feel strongly about something.

The line between comedy and drama is often blurred, especially today. Many comedies are about serious subjects, and many dramas contain comic characters or extended comic scenes.

Read the following passage from a comedy by Woody Allen. See what subject matter you find in the passage and notice what makes you laugh. Use the Purpose Question above the passage to help you.

WHAT DOES THIS SCENE MAKE FUN OF?

AMBASSADOR: . . . Axel, most fathers start their sons in the mail room and let them work their way up. I started you on top and you worked your way to the mail room. This Embassy is a clean start for you. If it's not run letter perfect, I'll fire you and if your
(5) own father fires you—it's the end of the line. Goodbye. (*Exits.*)
MAGEE: Have a good flight, Dad. (*Crosses to door and calls.*) Mr. Kilroy!
KILROY: (*Entering.*) You called?
MAGEE: For the next two weeks I am in charge of this Embassy.
(10) Business will go on as usual and it would mean a great deal to me to have your full cooperation.
KILROY: Your father should have known better than to leave in charge a man who was asked to leave Africa.
MAGEE: That's not fair. Some of the best men in the foreign ser-
(15) vice have at one time or another been recalled from a country.
KILROY: Africa is a continent. You've been recalled from an entire continent. And what about Japan, you never mention that, or the Soviet Union—you managed to cover that up, too.
MAGEE: You know I've had some bad breaks careerwise.
(20) KILROY: (*Accusatory.*) And you were hung in effigy in Panama!
MAGEE: I admitted I was!
KILROY: Yes, but you didn't say it was by our own Embassy!
(*Phone rings.* KILROY *lets* MAGEE *get it.*)
MAGEE: (*Into phone.*) Yes? Yes, this is the American Embassy . . .

— Identify Elements of Style and Structure (Theme) =

This skill involves identifying the characteristic ways in which an author uses language and organizes his or her material.

A **theme** is the basic subject of a literary work. A play may have one or more themes, each illustrated in different scenes. A theme is always phrased in general terms; it does not include a reference to any character, plot action or other specific element of a scene or play. Many themes are not stated outright, and you must infer them, or figure them out. You can do this by reading what the characters say and looking for the main ideas.

As you may have guessed from your own reading and TV watching, comedies and dramas may use the same themes. The difference is in the approach. One play may present an argument between children and parents in a comic way. Another play may let you see the sadness in such a conflict.

Examples

DIRECTIONS: Use the information on this page and the excerpt by Woody Allen on the preceding page to choose the one best answer for each item below.

1. The theme of this scene is

   (1) the conflict between Magee and Kilroy
   (2) U.S. embassy etiquette
   (3) the difference between countries and continents
   (4) the inefficiency of the U.S. foreign service
   (5) the efficiency of the U.S. foreign service

Answer: (4) This is correct because most of the content treats Magee's obvious lack of competence, which rules out choice (5). Choice (1) describes a relationship between characters, which is too specific for a theme, and choice (2) is unsupported. Choice (3) is a minor point mentioned by Kilroy, not a theme.

2. The element *most* likely to cause laughter in this scene is

   (1) Kilroy's comments on other countries
   (2) other characters' comments on Magee's professional history
   (3) the character of Magee
   (4) the character of the Ambassador
   (5) the possibility of Magee's being hung in effigy

Answer: (2) This is correct because, according to them, Magee's behavior has been the opposite of that of a good foreign diplomat. Choice (1) does not involve comic material, and you do not learn enough about either Magee or the Ambassador to justify choices (3) or (4). Choice (5) states something that has already taken place.

Practice

Remember that a theme deals with a large and very general idea or subject. When you read a scene in a play, look beyond the specific characters and plot to find the theme.

DIRECTIONS: Choose the <u>one</u> best answer for each item below.

Items 1–6 refer to the following passage by Elizabeth Diggs.

WHAT ARE EVELYN AND JOSEPHINE ARGUING ABOUT?

JOSEPHINE: I was once courted by a young man from Harvard—before I met your grandfather. Dashing fellow. Had a Pierce-Arrow with lavender trim. There was an automobile! It was only my Yankee practicality that kept me from marrying him.

(5) EVELYN: Were you in love with him?

JOSEPHINE: Not profoundly, but that's hard to know at twenty, and he had a rather handsome inheritance. Fortunately I had the sense to ask him how much, and he told me. Well, I did some calculations and figured he'd run through it in ten years' time. And

(10) he did! Ruined himself before the crash!

EVELYN: (*teasing but genuinely shocked*) Grandmother! How could you be so cold-blooded? Maybe you broke his heart!

JOSEPHINE: Never marry for money, girls. Ambition is better security.

(15) EVELYN: Come on—you didn't marry for security.

JOSEPHINE: Of course I did. Love is just a fancy name for it.

EVELYN: Well, marriage is no longer a functional institution. I have a theory, based on personal observation: whatever you get married for, you'll get the opposite—if it's security, your husband

(20) will be unfaithful; if it's money, he'll lose it; if it's love, he'll end up despising you, or you'll despise him. It fits every married couple I know.

JOSEPHINE: You must know a sorry group of people! You kids are romantics. You think you're *supposed* to be happy, and you start

(25) fussing and fuming if someone doesn't come and hand it to you . . .

1. The theme of this dramatic scene is

   (1) the disagreement between Evelyn and Josephine
   (2) Josephine's Yankee upbringing
   (3) the nature of marriage
   (4) the romance of marriage
   (5) the ambition of women

2. The word "handsome" in line 7 means

   (1) invested
   (2) good-looking
   (3) available
   (4) sizable
   (5) tall and dark

GO ON TO THE NEXT PAGE.

3. In terms of how they view marriage

  (1) Evelyn is more practical than Josephine
  (2) the women have equally romantic views
  (3) Josephine is more romantic than Evelyn
  (4) Josephine is more practical than Evelyn
  (5) both women believe marriage is supposed to make one happy

5. With which of the following statements is Evelyn *most* likely to agree?

  (1) It is best to marry for security.
  (2) Marriage is an extremely functional institution.
  (3) Whatever people expect of marriage, they will be disappointed.
  (4) Bad marriages run in families.
  (5) All husbands are unfaithful.

4. With which of the statements below is Josephine *most* likely to agree?

  (1) Love can include a wish for material security.
  (2) One should have many boyfriends before marrying.
  (3) Only men with money and expensive cars are worth marrying.
  (4) If you marry for money, you will end up poor.
  (5) One should only marry for love.

6. After seeing or reading this scene, an audience might be likely to

  (1) invest their money wisely
  (2) decide to marry only for love
  (3) think about what they want out of marriage
  (4) collect data on their friends' marriages
  (5) find the idea of marriage comical

Items 7–8 refer to the following monologue by Edgar Lee Masters.

WHAT SOUNDS DOES THIS CHARACTER HEAR?

FIDDLER JONES: The earth keeps some vibration going
There in your heart, and that is you.
And if the people find you can fiddle,
Why, fiddle you must, for all your life.
(5)   How could I till my forty acres
Not to speak of getting more,
With a medley of horns, bassoons and piccolos
Stirred in my brain by crows and robins
And the creak of a wind-mill—only these?
(10) And I never started to plow in my life
That some one did not stop in the road
And take me away to a dance or picnic.
I ended up with forty acres;
I ended up with a broken fiddle—
(15) And a broken laugh and a thousand memories,
And not a single regret.

7. The theme of this dramatic monologue is

  (1) living life on 40 acres
  (2) living life on your own terms
  (3) the nature of memories
  (4) living life as a farmer
  (5) the disappointments of life

8. You can infer that the speaker

  (1) became a fiddler because farming bored him
  (2) regrets the life he chose
  (3) played the fiddle because of something inside him
  (4) inherited forty acres of land
  (5) had earthquakes on his land

Before you take the GED Mini-Test, check your answers on page 146.

TIP

When you consider the possible answers to a question, try to rule out the ones that are obviously wrong first. Then go on to consider the remaining choices.

DIRECTIONS: Choose the one best answer for each item below.

Items 1–2 refer to the following excerpt by Joseph Heller.

WHAT DOES YOSSARIAN LEARN IN THIS SCENE?

YOSSARIAN: Can't you ground someone who's crazy?

DANEEKA: Oh, sure. There's a rule saying I *have* to ground anyone who's crazy.

YOSSARIAN: There is?

(5) DANEEKA: Sure. (*Reads thermometer.*) I don't feel so good. See? My temperature is low.

YOSSARIAN: Then why don't you ground me? I'm crazy.

DANEEKA: Why don't you ask me to? (*Hands* YOSSARIAN *the air ball of blood pressure gauge.*) Squeeze this.

(10) YOSSARIAN: (*Squeezing the air ball.*) I have to ask?

DANEEKA: That's what the rule says. (*Reads blood pressure and shakes his head.*) First you have to ask. Look into my ears.

YOSSARIAN: (*Looking into one of his ears.*) That's all I have to do?

DANEEKA: That's all. Just ask. The other ear too.

(15) YOSSARIAN: And then you can ground me? (DANEEKA *has the stethoscope in his ears and shrugs to indicate he doesn't hear. Shouting:*) Then you can ground me?

DANEEKA: (*Removes stethoscope and hands it to* YOSSARIAN.) No. Then I can't ground you. Now listen to my heart.

(20) YOSSARIAN: (*Taking the stethoscope and listening.*) You mean there's a catch.

DANEEKA: Sure there's a catch. Catch-22. Anyone who wants to get out of combat duty isn't really crazy.

YOSSARIAN: Wow. I think I'm starting to get it. I'm crazy and can be

(25) grounded. All I have to do is ask, right?

DANEEKA: Tap my chest. Lower.

YOSSARIAN: (*More and more rapidly.*) But as soon as I do ask, I will no longer be crazy and will have to fly more missions. I'll be *crazy* to fly more missions, and sane if I don't. But if I'm sane I have to fly them.

(30) DANEEKA: (*Turning around.*) Now tap my back.

YOSSARIAN: If I fly them, I'm crazy and don't have to, but if I don't want to I'm sane and—wow! That's some catch, that Catch-22.

DANEEKA: It's the best there is.

1. The theme of this comedy scene is

   (1) a clash between the military and civilians
   (2) Yossarian's growing confusion
   (3) the horror of combat missions
   (4) the insanity of military rules
   (5) the nature of medicine

2. You can infer that Catch-22 was created to

   (1) keep pilots flying more missions
   (2) stop pilots from flying missions
   (3) give military doctors more work
   (4) teach pilots how to be doctors
   (5) keep all doctors grounded

GO ON TO THE NEXT PAGE.

WHAT CAUSES THE CONFLICT BETWEEN MERIDIAN AND PARNELL?

PARNELL: Meridian—when I asked for mercy a moment ago—I meant—please—please try to understand that it is not so easy to leap over fences, to give things up—all right, to surrender privilege! But if you were among the privileged you would know what I mean. It's not a mat-

(5) ter of trying to hold *on*; the things, the privilege—are part of you, are *who* you are. It's in the *gut*.

MERIDIAN: Then where's the point of this struggle, where's the hope? If Mister Charlie can't change—

PARNELL: Who's Mister Charlie?

(10) MERIDIAN: You're Mister Charlie. *All* white men are Mister Charlie!

PARNELL: You sound more and more like your son, do you know that? A lot of the colored people here didn't approve of him, but he said things they longed to say—said right out loud, for all the world to hear, how much he despised white people!

(15) MERIDIAN: He didn't say things I longed to say. Maybe it was because he was my son. I didn't care *what* he felt about white people. I just wanted him to live, to have his own life. There's something you don't understand about being black, Parnell. If you're a black man, with a black son, you have to forget all about white people and concentrate on trying to save

(20) your child. That's why I let him stay up North. I was wrong, I failed, I failed. Lyle walked him up the road and killed him.

PARNELL: We don't *know* Lyle killed him. And Lyle denies it.

MERIDIAN: Of course, he denies it—what do you mean, we don't *know* Lyle killed him?

(25) PARNELL: We *don't* know—all we can say is that it looks that way. And circumstantial evidence is a tricky thing.

MERIDIAN: *When* it involves a white man killing a black man . . .

3. The theme of this passage is

(1) the nature of pain
(2) the conflict between Meridian and Parnell
(3) racism and justice
(4) circumstantial evidence
(5) the nature of fatherhood

5. When Meridian says "All white men are Mr. Charlie," he means

(1) blacks have trouble remembering individual white names
(2) Mr. Charlie is a name blacks use for white people
(3) all white men are named Charles
(4) all white men have nicknames
(5) all white people are incapable of change

4. You can infer that Parnell would find it hard to give up

(1) his friendship with Meridian
(2) his privileges as a white person
(3) his standing in the community
(4) his belief in Lyle's innocence
(5) his dislike of black people

6. With which of the following statements would Meridian *most* likely agree?

(1) Blacks want all whites to move up North.
(2) Blacks and whites can work out their differences.
(3) Blacks want to live their lives without having to worry about whites.
(4) Blacks want power over whites.
(5) Blacks want to win every trial that involves a black person.

Answers and Explanations

Practice   *pp. 142–143*

1. **Answer:** (3)   This is correct because marriage is the subject of discussion. Choice (1) refers to specific characters and is not a theme, and choice (2) is a minor background element. Choices (4) and (5) are points in the women's discussion, not themes.

2. **Answer:** (4)   This is correct because the inheritance is discussed in terms of its amount. Choice (1) is not a synonym for handsome. Choice (2) is not supported. Choice (3) is the wrong meaning, and choice (5) is not used to describe money.

3. **Answer:** (4)   This is correct because she believes in marrying for security while still calling it love. This view shocks Evelyn, ruling out choice (1). Because the women are different, choices (2) and (5) are false. As for choice (3), Josephine is *not* romantic.

4. **Answer:** (1)   This is correct because she claims to have married for both. Nothing she says indicates she would agree with choices (2) or (3), though she did have a monied boyfriend. Choice (4) is Evelyn's viewpoint, and choice (5) is not supported.

5. **Answer:** (3)   This is correct because she says that people get the opposite of what they want from marriage. Choice (1) is not supported, and choice (2) is contradicted by her own words. There is no evidence for choice (4), and she does not say *anything* about *all* husbands, ruling out choice (5).

6. **Answer:** (3)   This is correct since the focus of the scene is on what people want and get out of marriage. Choice (1) is not supported, and choice (2) is a decision only *some* audience members might make. Choice (4) is unlikely, and the scene's seriousness rules out choice (5).

7. **Answer:** (2)   This is correct because Jones' monologue describes his decisions and living with them. Choices (1) and (4) describe specific elements, and are not themes. Jones talks about his life, not his memories, ruling out choice (3). Choice (5) is not supported.

8. **Answer:** (3)   This is correct because of his words in lines 1–4. Choice (1) is tempting, but Jones never says farming bored him, only that fiddling was more important. Choice (2) is contradicted by the passage, and choices (4) and (5) are not supported.

GED Mini-Test   *pp. 144–145*

1. **Answer:** (4)   This is correct because the scene describes the craziness of rule Catch-22. Choice (1) is not supported, and choice (2), though an emotional element of the scene, is not a theme, nor is choice (3). Choice (5) is unsupported.

2. **Answer:** (1)   This is correct because this is what Yossarian learns, which rules out choice (2). Catch-22 may *lead* to choice (3), but this is not the reason for its creation. Choice (4) is not supported, nor is choice (5).

3. **Answer:** (3)   This is correct because the conflict between the two men centers on different justice for blacks and whites. Choice (1) is not supported, though both men are in pain. Choices (2) and (4) are specific elements, not themes, and choice (5) is not the main theme.

4. **Answer:** (2)   This is correct because he is white and admits it would be hard to surrender his privileges. Choices (1) and (3) are not stated as possibilities. We do not know here whether Parnell believes Lyle to be innocent, ruling out choice (4). Choice (5) is unsupported.

5. **Answer:** (2)   This is correct because of his own words. Choice (1) is obviously incorrect, and choices (3) and (4) lack seriousness and can be ruled out. Meridian may believe the ideas in choice (5), but this is not connected with the quotation about Mr. Charlie.

6. **Answer:** (3)   This is correct because of his words in lines 16–20. Choice (1) is not supported. Choice (2) is unlikely in this situation. Choice (4) is unsupported, and choice (5) is too general to be reasonable; Meridian simply wants justice to be done in each case.

In the preceding lessons you have learned strategies for reading fiction and nonfiction, poetry and drama. You have read and analyzed passages that cover the full range of popular literature. What you have studied is representative of the passages and questions that will appear on the GED exam. By doing the Practices and the GED Mini-Tests you have shown yourself that you can perform well on the GED exam.

The following is a final review of all the reading strategies you have studied. The questions that follow each passage may test whether you have accurately understood what you have read, or they may test whether you can apply what you have learned in another context. You may also be asked questions about the techniques the authors use and what the effects of those techniques are.

As you do this review, keep in mind one basic point: Authors—whether poets, dramatists or writers of fiction or nonfiction—are writing because they want to communicate with you. First, last and always, your goal should be to understand what the author is trying to say.

DIRECTIONS: Choose the <u>one</u> best answer for each item below.

Items 1–4 refer to the following poem by Daniel Mark Epstein.

WHO WAS AFRAID OF FLYING?

Miami

After years of stock-car racing, running
rifles to Cuba, money from Rio, high
diving from helicopters into the Gulf;
after a life at gunpoint, on a dare,
(5)   my father can't make the flight out of Miami.

Turbojets roar and sing, the ground crew
scatters out of the shadow of the plane.
My father undoes his seat belt, makes his way
up the aisle, dead-white and sweating,
(10)   ducks out of the hatchway, mumbling
luggage was left at the dock, his watch
in the diner. Head down
he lurches through the accordion boarding tube,
strides the shining wing of the airport, past
(15)   windows full of planes and sky, past bars,
candy machines and posters for Broadway shows.
Gasping in the stratosphere of terror, he
bursts through the glass doors and runs
to a little garden near the rental cars.
(20)   He sits among the oleanders and palms.

GO ON TO THE NEXT PAGE.

It started with the Bay Bridge.
He couldn't take that steel vault into the blue
above the blue, so much horizon!
Then it was the road itself, the rise and fall,
(25)   the continual blind curve.
He hired a chauffeur, he took the train.
Then it was hotels, so many rooms
the same, he had to sleep with the light on.
His courage has shrunk to the size of a windowbox.

(30)   Father who scared the witches and vampires
from my childhood closets, father
who walked before me like a hero's shield
through neighborhoods where hoodlums honed their knives
on concrete, where nerve was law,
(35)   who will drive you home from Miami?
You're broke and I'm a thousand miles away
with frightened children of my own.
Who will rescue you from the garden
where jets flash like swords above your head?

1. Which statement *best* describes what is happening in lines 1–20 of the poem?

(1) The man has arrived at the airport too late to catch his flight.
(2) At the last minute the man realizes that he has gotten on the wrong flight.
(3) The poet is describing the memory of a terrible plane crash.
(4) The man is too frightened to fly on an airplane.
(5) The poet is describing an airplane landing at the Miami airport.

2. Which statement *best* describes what lines 21–29 of the poem are saying?

(1) The poet is describing a trip to San Francisco.
(2) The poet is describing the memory of an automobile accident.
(3) The poet is describing the progress of his father's fear.
(4) The poet is describing a visit to an insane asylum where his father lives.
(5) The poet is saying that his father was always a coward.

3. Which statement *best* describes what the poet is saying in lines 30–39 of the poem?

(1) The poet is saying that he is ashamed that his father is a coward.
(2) The poet is saying that he is sorry that he cannot help his father.
(3) The poet is saying that his father has gotten what he deserved.
(4) The poet is saying that he is proud of his father.
(5) The poet is saying that his father was a hoodlum.

4. Which statement *best* describes how the man in the poem probably feels about life?

(1) He loves excitement and taking chances.
(2) Almost everything in life frightens him now.
(3) He is afraid of flying, but otherwise he is a very brave man.
(4) He is a coward, and he has always been a coward.
(5) He is very angry with his son because the son will not help him.

GO ON TO THE NEXT PAGE.

WHO ARE THE LITTLE GENERALS?

Rite of Passage

As the guests arrive at my son's party
they gather in the living room—
short men, men in first grade
with smooth jaws and chins.
(5)   Hands in pockets, they stand around
jostling, jockeying for place, small fights
breaking out and calming. One says to another
How old are you? Six. I'm seven. So?
They eye each other, seeing themselves
(10)   tiny in the other's pupils. They clear their
throats a lot, a room of small bankers,
they fold their arms and frown. *I could beat you*
up, a seven says to a six,
the dark cake, round and heavy as a
(15)   turret, behind them on the table. My son,
freckles like specks of nutmeg on his cheeks,
chest narrow as the balsa keel of a
model boat, long hands
cool and thin as the day they guided him
(20)   out of me, speaks up as a host
for the sake of the group.
We could easily kill a two year old,
he says in his clear voice. The other
men agree, they clear their throats
(25)   like Generals, they relax and get down to
playing war, celebrating my son's life.

---

5. Which of the following techniques does the poet *not* use?

(1) She compares the children in the poem to bankers.
(2) She compares the children in the poem to generals.
(3) She compares her son to a boat.
(4) She describes the children's clothes.
(5) She creates an atmosphere of tension in the poem.

6. Which statement below *best* describes the main idea of the poem?

(1) Children should be seen and not heard.
(2) There is a lot of difference between a child of six and a child of seven.
(3) Little boys start to act like men at an early age.
(4) Children watch too much TV.
(5) Children require constant supervision by adults.

7. What is the poet describing in this poem?

(1) She is describing a convention of bankers.
(2) She is describing a bunch of soldiers during war games.
(3) She is describing a memory from her own childhood.
(4) She is describing a little boy's birthday party.
(5) She is describing her son's school play.

8. Which of the following statements would the poet probably agree with?

(1) Children are just one burden after another.
(2) Children are vicious little beasts.
(3) Children are sweet little angels.
(4) Men seem to enjoy making war.
(5) Bankers should use throat lozenges.

GO ON TO THE NEXT PAGE.

Items 9–12 refer to the following passage by James Michener.

WHAT DID THE GIANT RATTLESNAKE DO?

(5)

(10)

(15)

(20)

(25)

(30)

(35)

The Quimpers were less lucky with another event caused by the flood, and this too would be remembered. The excessive waters disturbed many animals, causing them to venture into new areas and adopt new habits, and one of those most seriously displaced was a huge rattlesnake eight feet three inches long from the tip of his rattle and as big around as a small tree. He was really a monstrous creature, with a head as big as a soup plate and fangs so huge and powerful, they could discharge a dreadful injection. Veteran of many struggles, master of the sudden ambush, he had subdued baby pigs and fawns and rabbits and a multitude of rats and mice. His traditional home had been sixteen miles up the Brazos in a rocky ledge that gave him excellent protection and a steady supply of victims, but the floods had dislodged him and sent him tumbling down the river along with deer and alligators and javelinas. During the height of the flood each animal was so preoccupied with its own salvation that it ignored friends and enemies alike, but as the waters receded, each resumed its habits, and the snake found itself far downstream, lodged in unfamiliar rocks and with a most uncertain food supply. . . .

This great beast at Quimper's ferry, longer than any hitherto seen along the Brazos, did not seek contact with human beings; it did its best to avoid them, but if any threatened the quiet of its domain, it could strike with terrifying force. It would not have come into contact with the Quimpers had not Yancey gone probing along the farther bank, not doing any serious work or accomplishing much, but merely poking into holes with a stick to see what might be happening. As he approached where the snake lay hidden, he heard but did not recognize the warning rattle. Thinking it to be a bird or some noisy insect, he probed further, and found himself staring at the huge coiled snake not ten feet away.

'Mom!' he screamed, and Mattie, working at the ferry, grabbed the gun she kept aboard for protection against wandering Karankawa, and ran to help, but when she reached Yancey she found him immobilized, pointing at the coiled snake whose rattles echoed. 'Do something!' he pleaded.

Infuriated by his craven behavior and terrified of the snake, she pushed her son aside, and with her heart beating at a rate which must soon cause her to faint, she raised the gun. Not firing blindly, because she knew she had only one chance, she took aim as the snake prepared for its deadly thrust, and pulled the trigger. She felt the shock against her shoulder; she felt the snake brush against her knee; and she fainted.

9. From the context, what is it likely the Brazos is?

   (1) a river
   (2) a county
   (3) a ferry boat
   (4) a snake farm
   (5) a homestead

10. Which of the following statements describes an action Yancey Quimper would probably take?

   (1) He would keep his head under fire.
   (2) He would work from dawn to dusk.
   (3) He would go far in the world on true grit and character.
   (4) He would be unable to act in a time of crisis.
   (5) He would make his living as a traveling salesman.

GO ON TO THE NEXT PAGE.

11. The author states that the snake's food supply was *most* uncertain because

(1) many of the snake's victims had died in a great drought
(2) the snake was too old to get around
(3) the flood had left the snake in a new place where he could not hunt easily
(4) the Quimpers had killed most of the rats
(5) the snake's prey had gone south

12. The rattlesnake was about to strike at Yancey because

(1) it was hungry
(2) rattlers are by nature vicious
(3) Yancey had acted in a way the snake found threatening
(4) the snake had been stalking Yancey for days
(5) the snake was crazed by the flood

Items 13–16 refer to the following excerpt by Neil Simon.

DO THESE ROOMMATES AGREE ABOUT MOST THINGS?

FELIX: . . . (*Gets down on his knees, picks up chips and puts them into box.*) Don't forget I cook and clean and take care of this house. I save us a lot of money, don't I?

OSCAR: Yeah, but then you keep me up all night counting it.

(5) FELIX: (*Goes to table and sweeps chips and cards into box.*) Now wait a minute. We're not always going at each other. We have some fun too, don't we?

OSCAR: (*Crosses to couch.*) *Fun*? Felix, getting a clear picture on Channel Two isn't my idea of whoopee.

(10) FELIX: What are you talking about?

OSCAR: All right, what do you and I do every night? (*Takes off sneakers, dropping them on floor.*)

FELIX: What do we do? You mean after dinner?

OSCAR: That's right. After we've had your halibut steak and the dishes

(15) are done and the sink has been Brillo'd and the pans have been S.O.S.'d and the leftovers have been Saran-wrapped—what do we do?

FELIX: (*Finishes clearing table and puts everything on top of bookcase.*) Well, we read . . . we talk . . .

OSCAR: (*Takes off pants and throws them on floor.*) No, no. *I* read and

(20) *you* talk! . . . I try to work and you talk. . . . I take a bath and you talk. . . . I go to sleep and you talk. We've got your life arranged pretty good but I'm still looking for a little entertainment.

FELIX: (*Pulling upstage kitchen chairs away from table.*) What are you saying? That I talk too much?

(25) OSCAR: (*Sits on couch.*) No, no. I'm not complaining. You have a lot to say. What's worrying me is that I'm beginning to listen. . . .

13. Oscar and Felix disagree *mainly* about

(1) the amount of money they spend
(2) which TV programs to watch
(3) what to talk about
(4) what is fun and what is not
(5) what kind of food to eat

14. From the stage directions, you can infer that Felix

(1) cooks a lot
(2) plays a lot of poker
(3) cleans and straightens a lot
(4) shops a lot
(5) counts and banks money a lot

15. According to Oscar, Felix's main after-dinner activity is

(1) working
(2) reading
(3) sleeping
(4) cooking
(5) talking

16. You can infer from the passage that

(1) Felix is messier than Oscar
(2) Oscar is messier than Felix
(3) Felix makes more money than Oscar
(4) Felix has more fun than Oscar
(5) Oscar has more fun than Felix

GO ON TO THE NEXT PAGE.

Items 17–20 refer to the following excerpt by Robert Anderson.

WHAT ARE GENE'S MOTHER AND FATHER LIKE?

GENE: . . . Pennsylvania Station, New York, a few years ago. My mother and father were returning from Florida. They were both bored in Florida, but they had been going each winter for a number of years. If they didn't go, my father came down with pneumonia and my
(5) mother's joints stiffened cruelly with arthritis. My mother read a great deal, liked to play bridge and chatter and laugh gaily with "the girls" . . . make her eyes sparkle in a way she had and pretend that she had not had two operations for cancer, three heart attacks and painful arthritis . . . She used to say, "Old age takes courage." She
(10) had it. My father, though he had never been in the service, had the air of a retired brigadier general. He read the newspapers, all editions, presumably to help him make decisions about his investments. He watched westerns on television and told anyone who would listen the story of his life. I loved my mother . . . I wanted to love my
(15) father . . .

17. The *main* thing you learn about Gene's mother from Gene's words is that

(1) she has had three heart attacks
(2) she goes to Florida each winter
(3) she likes to play bridge
(4) she has cancer
(5) she has courage

18. The *main* thing you learn about Gene from his words is that he

(1) loved his parents equally
(2) loved his mother but not his father
(3) felt unloved by his parents
(4) loved his father but not his mother
(5) cared little for either parent

19. The *main* thing you learn about Gene's father from Gene's words is that

(1) he makes sound business decisions
(2) he acts in a self-important way
(3) he reads a lot of newspapers
(4) he wants to go back to the military
(5) he is a wild west expert

20. Gene's parents go to Florida each year because

(1) they are bored in New York
(2) their health is better in Florida
(3) Gene's mother likes to play bridge
(4) Gene's father makes investments
(5) they want to get away from Gene

Items 21–26 refer to the following excerpt by Michael Wilson.

FOR WHAT IS ESPERANZA SEARCHING?

ESPERANZA: Ramón . . . we're not getting weaker. We're stronger than ever before. (*He snorts with disgust.*) *They're* getting weaker. They thought they could break our picket line. And they failed. And now they can't win unless they pull off something big, and pull it off fast.
(5) RAMÓN: Like what?
ESPERANZA: I don't know. But I can feel it coming. It's like . . . like a lull before the storm. Charley Vidal says. . .
RAMÓN: (*exploding*) Charley Vidal says! Don't throw Charley Vidal up to me!
(10) ESPERANZA: Charley's my friend. I need friends. (*She looks at him strangely.*) Why are you afraid to have me as your friend?
RAMÓN: I don't know what you're talking about.
ESPERANZA: No, you don't. Have you learned nothing from this strike?

GO ON TO THE NEXT PAGE.

(15) Why are you afraid to have me at your side? Do you still think you can have dignity only if I have none?

RAMÓN: You talk of dignity? After what you've been doing?

ESPERANZA: Yes. I talk of dignity. The Anglo bosses look down on you, and you hate them for it. "Stay in your place, you dirty Mexican"—that's what they tell you. But why must you say to me, "Stay in *your* place"?

(20) Do you feel better having someone lower than you?

RAMÓN: Shut up, you're talking crazy.

(*But Esperanza moves right up to him, speaking now with great passion.*)

ESPERANZA: Whose neck shall I stand on, to make me feel superior? And what will I get out of it? I don't want anything lower than I am. I'm low

(25) enough already. I want to rise. And push everything up with me as I go . . .

RAMÓN: (*fiercely*) Will you be still?

ESPERANZA: (*shouting*) And if you can't understand this you're a fool—because you can't win this strike without me! You can't win *anything*

(30) without me!

(*He seizes her shoulder with one hand, half raises the other to slap her. ESPERANZA's body goes rigid. She stares straight at him, defiant and unflinching. RAMÓN drops his hand.*)

ESPERANZA: That would be the old way. Never try it on me again—never.

21. The theme of this passage is

(1) the nature of human dignity
(2) the coming of war
(3) the correct way to run a strike
(4) the nature of winning
(5) the conflict between Ramón and Esperanza

22. Esperanza compares the way Ramón has been treating her to the way

(1) adults treat children
(2) the workers treat the bosses
(3) the Anglos treat the Mexicans
(4) humans treat animals
(5) the Mexicans treat the Anglos

23. You can infer from this passage that Ramón believes that

(1) no one should go on strike
(2) workers and bosses are allies
(3) friendship is not possible between men and women
(4) women should be allowed to express themselves
(5) men and women together will win the strike

24. With which of the following statements would Esperanza *most* likely agree?

(1) It is important to succeed no matter whom you hurt.
(2) It is important to grow without pushing anyone else down.
(3) It is important for one person in a marriage to be stronger than the other.
(4) It is important to stay in your place and avoid conflict.
(5) It is important to struggle alone and without friends.

25. You can infer that Esperanza identifies dignity with

(1) having friends
(2) walking a picket line
(3) having self-respect
(4) being independent
(5) being more powerful than others

26. In lines 32–34 Esperanza makes the decision that she will

(1) leave Ramón soon
(2) not be involved in the strike
(3) urge the strikers to end the strike
(4) not allow Ramón to hit her again
(5) become Ramón's friend

Check your answers to the Review on pages 288–290.

Opening night celebrating a new, 18th century theater in Siena, Italy.

In the first section of this book you learned and applied various reading strategies to popular fiction, nonfiction, poetry and drama. In the next section you will continue studying reading strategies and literary forms, but this time in the realm of classical literature.

Classical literature includes literary works whose acknowledged quality has won them a permanent place in literary history. To merit such a place, a literary work has to prove itself over a long period of time. For this reason the term "classical literature" tends to refer to works written more (sometimes much more) than 25 years ago. Works of classical literature do not, of course, reflect up-to-the-minute trends and tastes. But it is exciting and reassuring to discover how accurately they express the continuing passions and anxieties of human experience. Their success in doing so is just one of the reasons why they have lasted so long.

Over the next ten lessons you will be reviewing and practicing a number of basic skills as they apply to classical fiction, nonfiction, poetry and drama.

Lesson 19 is the first of four lessons devoted to fiction. In it you will sharpen your skill at locating the main idea, or most important point, of a paragraph or passage. Then you will review cause and effect, the way in which one event leads to another. You will next interpret implications, the ideas and information that writers express indirectly, rather than directly. Lesson 22 deals with point of view, the observation point from which a writer tells a story. The passages in this lesson are taken from **autobiographies** and **biographies.**

In Lesson 23 you will study elements of style and structure in fiction. Style is the distinctive, recognizable way in which a writer uses words and descriptive word-pictures, or images. The underlying organization of a whole work or passage within it is called its structure.

Lesson 24 is devoted to another form of nonfiction, the **essay.** You will practice your ability to recognize **supporting details** and draw **inferences** as you read selections from both types of essay.

In Lessons 25 and 26 you will study poetry. The first of these lessons gives you practice in identifying the main idea of a poem. The second lesson is about interpreting a poem's **mood** and the ways in which a poet conveys particular emotions.

Lessons 27 and 28 are both about drama. The first deals with characterization, the ways in which playwrights tell us about the character and personalities of the people in a play. The second of these two lessons discusses mood in drama and gives you practice in recognizing the way the playwright's **stage directions** and the characters' own speeches convey the underlying emotions of a play.

autobiography
a person's life story as told by that person
biography
a person's life story as told by another person
essay
a literary composition written on a certain subject
supporting details
information that confirms main ideas or implications
inference
a conclusion drawn from an implication
mood
prevailing feeling, or atmosphere, of a literary work; its emotional impact
stage directions
instructions given throughout a play, describing characters' gestures and appearance

19 Fiction

Fiction is a form of writing that tells a story. The story may be inspired by real people, places or events, but the finished work is the author's own invention.

The characters and plot used by the author express serious or humorous truths about life and human nature. These general truths are the **main ideas** of a work of fiction. They are stated and restated in different ways throughout the story.

Read the following passage by D. H. Lawrence. Look for the main idea as you read. Try to state it in your own words. Use the Purpose Question above the passage to help you.

WHAT DO THIS WOMAN AND HER CHILDREN KNOW?

There was a woman who was beautiful, who started with all the advantages, yet she had no luck. She married for love, and the love turned to dust. She had bonny children, yet she felt they had been thrust upon her, and she could not love them. They looked

(5) at her coldly, as if they were finding fault with her. And hurriedly she felt she must cover up some fault in herself. Yet what it was that she must cover up she never knew. Nevertheless, when her children were present, she always felt the center of her heart go hard. This troubled her, and in her manner she was all the more

(10) gentle and anxious for her children, as if she loved them very much. Only she herself knew that at the center of her heart was a hard little place that could not feel love, no, not for anybody. Everybody else said of her: "She is such a good mother. She adores her children." Only she herself, and her children them-

(15) selves, knew it was not so. They read it in each other's eyes.

Identify an Unstated Main Idea

This skill identifies the most important point an author is trying to make. An unstated main idea is hinted at. It is implied.

The **main idea** of a paragraph may be one of the general truths the author wants to express. Or it may be something more specific—a comment or a piece of information the author wants you to have at this point. But whether it is general or specific, a paragraph's main idea is the most important, or overall, idea in that paragraph—its organizing principle.

Sometimes a main idea is stated directly in the **topic sentence,** which contains the most important, or overall, point of the paragraph. The topic sentence often begins or ends a paragraph. Occasionally it is in the middle, surrounded by supporting details.

Sometimes, however, a main idea is stated only by implication. When this is the case, the author makes the point indirectly, using examples and descriptive details to express and support the idea.

The passage on page 156 has an implied main idea. A supporting detail such as the one found on lines 7–8 helps identify it. The Purpose Question above the passage supplies additional main idea clues.

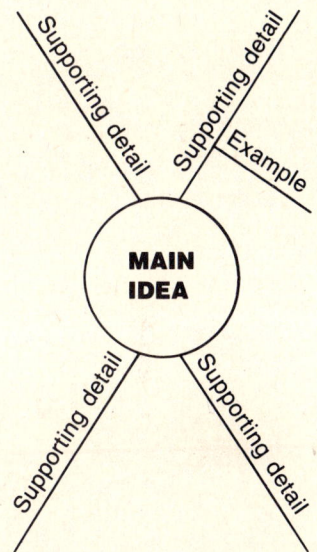

Examples

DIRECTIONS: Use the information on this page and the passage by D. H. Lawrence on the preceding page to choose the one best answer for each item below.

1. Which of the following states the main idea about the woman in the story?

   (1) She had beauty and advantages.
   (2) She had attractive children.
   (3) She was gentle with her children.
   (4) She was considered a good mother.
   (5) She did not love her children.

Answer: (5) Choices (1) and (2) give reasons for her to have been more loving. Choices (3) and (4) point up the difference between appearance and reality.

2. Which one of these statements does *not* support the main idea about the woman?

   (1) She was not really very lucky.
   (2) Her marriage was a happy one.
   (3) Her inner feelings troubled her.
   (4) Her children looked at her coldly.
   (5) She felt she had something to hide.

Answer: (2) This is correct because it is untrue. Choices (1), (3), (4) and (5) all provide details that support the main point of the passage.

Practice

HINT

Remember that the main idea of a paragraph is not always stated directly. If the main idea is not clear to you right away, re-read the paragraph. Then close your eyes and think how you would tell someone else the meaning of the paragraph in your own words.

DIRECTIONS: Choose the one best answer for each item below.

Items 1–3 refer to the following passage by Willa Cather.

WHAT DOES IT TAKE TO BE A PIONEER?

For the first three years after John Bergson's death, the affairs of his family prospered. Then came the hard times that brought everyone on the Divide to the brink of despair; three years of drought and failure, the last struggle of a wild soil
(5) against the encroaching plowshare. The first of these fruitless summers the Bergson boys bore courageously. The lure of the corn crop made labor cheap. Lou and Oscar hired two men and put in bigger crops than ever before. They lost everything they spent. The whole country was discouraged. Farmers who were
(10) already in debt had to give up their land. A few foreclosures demoralized the county. The settlers sat about on wooden sidewalks in the little town and told each other that the country was never meant for men to live in; the thing to do was to get back to Iowa, to Illinois, to any place that had proved hospitable. The
(15) Bergson boys, certainly, would have been happier with their uncle Otto, in the bakery shop in Chicago. Like most of their neighbors, they were meant to follow in paths already marked out for them, not to break trails in a new country. A steady job, a few holidays, nothing to think about, and they would have been very happy. . . .

1. Which of the following *most* nearly states the main idea of the passage?

(1) Drought caused crop failures.
(2) The soil was hard to farm.
(3) Foreclosures upset the county.
(4) People talked of going home.
(5) Few people had pioneer spirit.

2. The Bergsons' neighbors talked of going back to a place that was

(1) challenging
(2) boring
(3) uncomfortable
(4) livable
(5) exciting

3. Like most people, the Bergson boys

(1) enjoyed breaking new trails
(3) liked steady jobs and holidays
(5) preferred unmarked paths

(2) preferred ideas to things
(4) had lots of imagination

GO ON TO THE NEXT PAGE.

Items 4–9 refer to the following passage by Herman Melville.

WHAT IS TO BE DONE WITH AN EMPLOYEE WHO WILL NOT WORK AND WILL NOT LEAVE?

"I have given up copying," he answered, and slid aside.

He remained as ever, a fixture in my chamber. Nay—if that were possible—he became still more of a fixture than before. What was to be done? He would do nothing in the office; why

(5) should he stay there? In plain fact, he had now become a millstone to me, not only useless as a necklace, but afflictive to bear. Yet I was sorry for him. I speak less than truth when I say that, on his own account, he occasioned me uneasiness. If he would but have named a single relative or friend, I would instantly have

(10) written, and urged their taking the poor fellow away to some convenient retreat. But he seemed alone, absolutely alone in the universe. A bit of a wreck in the mid-Atlantic. At length, necessities connected with my business tyrannized over all other considerations. Decently as I could, I told Bartleby that in six days'

(15) time he must unconditionally leave the office. I warned him to take measures, in the interval, for procuring some other abode. I offered to assist him in this endeavor, if he himself would but take the first step towards a removal. "And when you finally quit me, Bartleby," added I, "I shall see that you go not away entirely

(20) unprovided. Six days from this hour, remember."

4. Which of the following *most* nearly states the main idea of the passage?

(1) Bartleby was an office fixture.
(2) Bartleby had to leave in six days.
(3) Bartleby had no friend or relative.
(4) Bartleby was hard to get rid of.
(5) Bartleby refused to do his work.

5. Which one of the following supports the main idea of the passage?

(1) Bartleby was looking for work.
(2) Bartleby was sailing the Atlantic.
(3) Bartleby's boss was sorry for him.
(4) Bartleby was a valuable asset.
(5) Bartleby was independently wealthy.

6. In line 16, "procuring some other abode" means

(1) taking a new lease on life
(2) finding another job
(3) locating a new apartment
(4) finding other people to bother
(5) developing a new office skill

7. In this passage, Bartleby's boss reveals himself to be

(1) demanding and tyrannical
(2) unconcerned and good humored
(3) frustrated and concerned
(4) self-absorbed and harried
(5) stingy and unforgiving

8. As used in line 5, the word "millstone" means

(1) a piece of jewelry
(2) a turn-of-the-century office machine
(3) a great burden
(4) a grinding stone
(5) a term of endearment

9. Judging from the passage, Bartleby's personality could be considered

(1) bubbly and upbeat
(2) suave and mysterious
(3) warm and understanding
(4) troubled and reclusive
(5) shy and sweet

Before you take the GED Mini-Test,
check your answers on pages 161–162.

TIP

Remember to skim the passage first, then reread it more slowly. Look for the main idea in each paragraph. Notice how the main idea of one paragraph serves as a building block for the next paragraph.

DIRECTIONS: Choose the <u>one</u> best answer for each item below.

Items 1–6 refer to the following passage by F. Scott Fitzgerald.

HOW DOES THIS MAN RELATE HIS IDENTITY TO THE PLACE HE CALLS HOME?

One of my most vivid memories is of coming back West from prep school and later from college at Christmas time. Those who went farther than Chicago would gather in the old dim Union Station at six o'clock of a December evening, with a few Chicago friends, already caught up in

(5) their own holiday gayeties, to bid them a hasty good-by. I remember the fur coats of the girls returning from Miss This-or-That's and the chatter of frozen breath and the hands waving overhead as we caught sight of old acquaintances, and the matchings of invitations: "Are you going to the Ordways'? the Herseys'? the Schultzes'?" and the long green tickets

(10) clasped tight in our gloved hands. And last the murky yellow cars of the Chicago, Milwaukee, & St. Paul railroad looking cheerful as Christmas itself on the tracks beside the gate.

When we pulled out into the winter night and the real snow, our snow, began to stretch out beside us and twinkle against the windows,

(15) and the dim lights of small Wisconsin stations moved by, a sharp wild brace came suddenly into the air. We drew in deep breaths of it as we walked back from dinner through the cold vestibules, unutterably aware of our identity with this country for one strange hour, before we melted indistinguishably into it again.

(20) That's my Middle West—not the wheat or the prairies or the lost Swede towns, but the thrilling returning trains of my youth, and the street lamps and sleigh bells in the frosty dark and the shadows on the snow. I am part of that, a little solemn with the feel of those long winters, a little complacent from growing up in the Carraway house in a

(25) city where dwellings are still called through decades by a family's name. I see now that this has been a story of the West, after all—Tom and Gatsby, Daisy and Jordan and I, were all Westerners, and perhaps we possessed some deficiency in common which made us subtly unadaptable to Eastern life.

1. Which one of the following is *not* a supporting detail in this paragraph?

   (1) The students waved to each other.
   (2) Everyone clutched red tickets.
   (3) The girls wore fur coats.
   (4) People discussed invitations.
   (5) The railroad cars looked cheerful.

2. In this passage, "unutterably" on line 17 means

   (1) unspeakably
   (2) sorrowfully
   (3) defiantly
   (4) indescribably
   (5) painfully

GO ON TO THE NEXT PAGE.

3. The main point of the first paragraph can be summed up as

   (1) the author's sadness at no longer being young and hopeful
   (2) the fun of taking a train home on vacation, instead of a plane
   (3) the author's happy memories of returning West from school
   (4) the excitement of meeting old friends on the way home
   (5) the importance of attending the best schools in the East

5. Which of the following *best* sums up the main idea of the paragraph?

   (1) The story has been about the Middle West.
   (2) The journeys home at Christmas changed the author's life.
   (3) The author's later life has been sad and disappointing.
   (4) The author and his friends were all from the Middle West.
   (5) Westerners are somehow unadaptable to life in the East.

4. Which of the following *best* states the main point about the trip?

   (1) It was a difficult and disturbing journey.
   (2) It was a chance to learn about the Middle West.
   (3) It was the start of everyone's Christmas vacation.
   (4) It was an exciting way to travel in midwinter.
   (5) It made people aware of their regional identity.

6. Which one of the following does *not* symbolize the author's Middle West?

   (1) street lamps and sleigh bells
   (2) shadows of holly wreaths
   (3) wheat fields and prairies
   (4) long snowy winters
   (5) houses called by family names

Check your answers to the GED Mini-Test on page 162.

Answers and Explanations

Practice   *pp. 158–159*

1. **Answer:** (5)   Choice (5) is the correct answer because the passage implies this on lines 15–19. This is an example of an unstated main idea found at the end of a passage. Remember, when answering an item asking for a main idea, to look for details that support your choice. If you cannot find any, then rethink the main idea.

3. **Answer:** (3)   This choice is supported in the passage on lines 18–19. Choices (1), (2), (4) and (5) are not details supported in the passage.

5. **Answer:** (3)   The main idea is supported in the passage with the statements "I offered to assist him in this endeavor" (line 17), and "I shall see that you go not away entirely unprovided" (lines 19–20).

2. **Answer:** (4)   Another word for "livable" is "hospitable." The notion of going back to a place that was livable can be found in the sentence beginning on line 11 and ending on line 14. This item is asking you to find a supporting detail. None of the other choices can be correct as they do not provide a detail supporting the idea of a livable place.

4. **Answer:** (4)   Choices (1), (2), (3), and (5) are true, but secondary to the main point. The Purpose Question gives you a clue that supports choice (4) with the words "will not work and will not leave."

6. **Answer:** (2)   Since the passage is about Bartleby's job, "abode" refers to a job, and not to a place to live. As such, choices (1), (3), (4) and (5) are incorrect.

7. Answer: (3) The details that support this choice can be found on line 4 (he was frustrated) and lines 11–12 (he was concerned). No other choices supply the boss's feelings.

8. Answer: (3) He is called a "millstone"—"useless" and "afflictive." Choice (4) is a literal definition of the word, but does not make sense in context. When trying to get meaning from context, one way is to eliminate the choices that are incorrect. Use each choice in the sentence in place of "millstone" to see which is the best substitute. Choices (1), (2) and (5) are wrong.

9. Answer: (4) Although Bartleby might be considered mysterious, choice (2), or even shy, choice (5), he does not show the traits mentioned in the other choices.

GED Mini-Test *pp. 160–161*

1. Answer: (2) The tickets were green (line 9). Choices (1), (3), (4) and (5) are all supporting details.

2. Answer: (4) Again, when trying to determine the meaning of a word in context, insert the choices in the sentence to see which one is a synonym, a word that means nearly the same thing as the given word. Eliminate the choices you know are incorrect first.

3. Answer: (3) This answer is correct, as it is a paraphrase of what is written in the first, or topic, sentence in this paragraph. ("One of my most vivid memories is of coming back West from prep school . . . ") There is no evidence for choices (1), (2) and (5) in the paragraph. Choice (4) is simply a supporting detail.

4. Answer: (5) There is no evidence for choices (1) and (2) in the paragraph. Choices (3) and (4) are supporting details.

5. Answer: (5) Choices (1) and (4) are true but secondary to the main point. There is no evidence for choices (2) and (3) in the paragraph.

6. Answer: (3) Remember that the item asks you to determine which choice does *not* reflect the author's Middle West. Choices (1), (4) and (5) are details that can be found in the passage. Choice (1) appears on line 22, choice (4) on line 23 and choice (5) on line 25. Choice (2) is not mentioned at all.

20 Fiction

The **plot** of a story is what happens to the characters in that story. It is an unfolding series of events. The way in which one event or development leads to another is called **cause and effect.** Recognizing the relationship between causes and effects in a paragraph or full-length work of fiction is called **understanding consequences.**

Read the following passage by James Joyce. As you read, trace the unfolding series of causes and effects that make up the story. Look for supporting details and events that signal cause and effect relationships. Use the Purpose Question above the passage to help you.

WHY DID MICHAEL FUREY DIE?

—Poor fellow, she said. He was very fond of me and he was such a gentle boy. We used to go out together, walking, you know, Gabriel, like the way they do in the country. He was going to study singing only for his health. He had a very good voice, poor
(5) Michael Furey.
—Well; and then? asked Gabriel.
—And then when it came to the time for me to leave Galway and come up to the convent he was much worse and I wouldn't be let see him, so I wrote a letter saying I was going up to Dublin
(10) and would be back in the summer and hoping he would be better then.
She paused for a moment to get her voice under control and then went on:
—Then the night before I left I was in my grandmother's
(15) house in Nun's Island, packing up, and heard gravel thrown up against the window. The window was so wet I couldn't see so I ran downstairs as I was and there was the poor fellow at the end of the garden, shivering.
—And did you not tell him to go back? asked Gabriel.
(20) —I implored of him to go home at once and told him he would get his death in the rain. But he said he did not want to live. I can see his eyes as well as well! He was standing at the end of the wall where there was a tree.
—And did he go home? asked Gabriel.
(25) —Yes, he went home. And when I was only a week in the convent he died and he was buried at Oughterard where his people came from. O, the day that I heard that, that he was dead!
She stopped, choking with sobs, and, overcome by emotion, flung herself face downward on the bed, sobbing in the quilt.

Identify Cause and Effect Relationships

A cause and effect relationship indicates how one thing affects another. A cause is what makes something happen. An effect is what happens as a result.

A **cause** is an initial action—a thought, word or deed that makes something else happen. An **effect** is the consequence, or result, of that action. Sometimes the relationship between cause and effect is stated directly, as, for example, when the author uses words and phrases like "because," "led to," "brought about" or "due to." More often, however, fiction writers let events speak for themselves. You will not find the word "because" anywhere in the passage on page 163, for example. Nevertheless, the tragic effect of one character's words and actions on the other is probably very clear to you.

It is important to remember that minor actions as well as major ones are connected by cause and effect. As in real life, what happens in a work of fiction involves a series of events, both large and small. If you look closely at the passage on page 163, you will see the whole chain of actions and reactions leading to Michael Furey's death.

> **Cause**
> What happened first?
>
> **Effect**
> What was the consequence or result?
>
> **Hint:**
> Sometimes putting events in chronological order helps identify a cause and effect relationship.

Examples

DIRECTIONS: Use the information on this page and the passage by James Joyce on the preceding page to choose the <u>one</u> best answer for each item below.

1. The immediate cause of Michael Furey's death was that he

   (1) had been in ill health
   (2) was hit by lightning
   (3) swam out to Nun's Island
   (4) stayed out in the rain
   (5) walked all the way to Dublin

Answer: (4) Choice (1), while true, was not the immediate cause of his death. Choices (2), (3) and (5) are not true.

2. The underlying cause of Michael Furey's death was that he

   (1) had failed to become a singer
   (2) had been rejected by his girl
   (3) did not want to live without love
   (4) wanted to get back at the world
   (5) suffered from a fatal disease

Answer: (3) Choices (1), (2) and (4) are untrue. Choice (5) might be a contributing factor, but the girl's story makes it clear that he lost his will to live when she went away.

Practice

HINT

Remember that cause and effect applies to small actions and reactions, as well as to big ones. If the relationship between cause and effect in a paragraph or conversation is not clear to you right away, reread it, then try to restate it in your own words.

DIRECTIONS: Choose the one best answer for each item below.

Items 1–4 refer to the following passage by Doris Lessing.

WILL THE LOCUSTS LEAVE ANYTHING BEHIND?

She went out to join the old man, stepping carefully among the insects. They stood and watched. Overhead the sky was blue, blue and clear.

"Pretty," said old Stephen with satisfaction.

(5) Well, thought Margaret, we may be ruined, we may be bankrupt, but not everyone has seen an army of locusts fanning their wings at dawn.

Over the slopes, in the distance, a faint red smear showed in the sky, thickened and spread. "There they go," said old Stephen.
(10) "There goes the main army, off South."

And from the trees, from the earth all round them, the locusts were taking wing. They were like small aircraft, maneuvering for the take-off, trying their wings to see if they were dry enough. Off they went. A reddish brown steam was rising off the
(15) miles of bush, off the lands, the earth. Again the sunlight darkened.

And as the clotted branches lifted, the weight on them lightening, there was nothing but the black spines of branches, trees. No green left, nothing. All morning they watched, the three of
(20) them, as the brown crust thinned and broke and dissolved, flying up to mass with the main army, now a brownish-red smear in the Southern sky. The lands which had been filmed with green, the new tender mealie plants, were stark and bare. All the trees stripped. A devastated landscape. No green, no green anywhere.

1. Most farmers would regard the appearance of a swarm of locusts as

   (1) a thrilling event
   (2) an upsetting event
   (3) a once in a lifetime occurrence
   (4) a yearly occurrence
   (5) a colorful display

2. As a result of the locust attack, Margaret and her family are probably

   (1) bankrupt
   (2) thankful
   (3) better off
   (4) unmoved
   (5) defeated

GO ON TO THE NEXT PAGE.

3. To Margaret and old Stephen, the sight of the locusts taking off is

(1) faintly amusing
(2) strangely beautiful
(3) sad and mournful
(4) deeply disturbing
(5) dull and boring

4. Throughout history, locusts have been regarded as

(1) the farmer's best friend
(2) a mixed blessing
(3) the farmer's unbeatable enemy
(4) a cause for rejoicing
(5) a minor inconvenience

Items 5–8 refer to the following passage by Joseph Conrad.

IS ELOPING WITH DIAMELEN WORTH ANY SACRIFICE?

We ran down to the water. I saw a low hut above the black mud, and a small canoe hauled up. I heard another shot behind me. I thought, 'That is his last charge.' We rushed down to the canoe; a man came running from the hut, but I leaped on him,

(5) and we rolled together in the mud. Then I got up, and he lay still at my feet. I don't know whether I had killed him or not. I and Diamelen pushed the canoe afloat. I heard yells behind me, and I saw my brother run across the glade. Many men were bounding after him. I took her in my arms and threw her into the boat,

(10) then leaped in myself. When I looked back I saw that my brother had fallen. He fell and was up again, but the men were closing round him. He shouted, 'I am coming!' The men were close to him. I looked. Many men. Then I looked at her. Tuan, I pushed the canoe! I pushed it into deep water. She was kneeling forward,

(15) looking at me, and I said, 'Take your paddle,' while I struck the water with mine. Tuan, I heard him cry. I heard him cry my name twice; and I heard voices shouting, 'Kill! Strike!' I never turned back. I heard him calling my name again with a great shriek, as when life is going out together with the voice—and I

(20) never turned my head. My own name! . . . My brother! Three times he called—but I was not afraid of life. Was she not there in that canoe? And could I not with her find a country where death is forgotten—where death is unknown?

5. The narrator let his brother be killed because the narrator

(1) relied on others to save him
(2) valued his own life more
(3) did not realize he was in trouble
(4) wanted to get him out of the way
(5) did not really care about him

6. Letting his brother die has made the narrator feel

(1) secretly glad
(2) self-justified
(3) guilt-ridden
(4) nonchalant
(5) resentful

7. The brother dies while helping the narrator

(1) escape from enemy prison
(2) rescue a maiden in distress
(3) carry out a personal vendetta
(4) complete a spying mission
(5) run away with his beloved

8. The narrator now believes he was wrong to think that

(1) he could get away with murder
(2) he could move to another place
(3) Diamelen really loved him
(4) love was worth any sacrifice
(5) he would not forget his brother

Before you take the GED Mini-Test, check your answers on pages 168–169.

GED Mini-Test

20

TIP

Remember to read questions twice. Reread the questions and the answers you have chosen before marking your answer sheet. When looking for causes, ask yourself *why* something happened.

DIRECTIONS: Choose the <u>one</u> best answer for each item below.

Items 1–7 refer to the following passage by Sherwood Anderson.

COULD THIS BE LOVE?

On the veranda of Banker White's house Helen was restless and distraught. The instructor sat between the mother and daughter. His talk wearied the girl. Although he had also been raised in an Ohio town, the instructor began to put on the airs of the city. He wanted to appear cos-

(5) mopolitan. "I like the chance you have given me to study the background out of which most of our girls come," he declared. "It was good of you, Mrs. White, to have me down for the day." He turned to Helen and laughed. "Your life is still bound up with the life of this town?" he asked. "There are people here in whom you are interested?" To the girl,

(10) his voice sounded pompous and heavy.

Helen arose and went into the house. At the door leading to a garden at the back she stopped and stood listening. Her mother began to talk. "There is no one here fit to associate with a girl of Helen's breeding," she said.

(15) Helen ran down a flight of stairs at the back of the house and into the garden. In the darkness she stopped and stood trembling. It seemed to her that the world was full of meaningless people saying words. Afire with eagerness she ran through a garden gate and, turning a corner by the banker's barn, went into a little side street. "George! Where are you,

(20) George?" she cried, filled with nervous excitement. She stopped running, and leaned against a tree to laugh hysterically. Along the dark little street came George Willard, still saying words. "I'm going to walk right into her house. I'll go right in and sit down," he declared as he came up to her. He stopped and stared stupidly. "Come on," he said and took hold

(25) of her hand. With hanging heads they walked away along the street under the trees. Dry leaves rustled under foot. Now that he had found her George wondered what he had better do and say.

1. Helen's overall impression of the instructor is one of

  (1) awe for his knowledge
  (2) fear of his power
  (3) boredom with his phoniness
  (4) jealousy because he has her mother's attention
  (5) interest because he lives in a city

2. Which of the following does *not* explain why Helen runs into the garden?

  (1) She is restless and distraught.
  (2) The instructor is a bore.
  (3) She is furious with her mother.
  (4) She is hoping to meet George.
  (5) She is looking for excitement.

GO ON TO THE NEXT PAGE.

3. We know that George is thinking about Helen because

(1) we can read his thoughts
(2) he is talking to himself about her
(3) the author tells us so
(4) he is telling a friend about her
(5) he is writing her a poem

4. We suspect that George and Helen are falling in love because they

(1) declare their feelings
(2) are both very calm and relaxed
(3) are the right age for romance
(4) are thinking about each other
(5) have broken up with other people

5. The instructor's impression of himself is that he is

(1) more sophisticated than his peers
(2) a good friend
(3) amusing but shy
(4) kind and helpful
(5) selfish and proud

6. Helen's hysterical laughter showed that she is

(1) emotionally unstable
(2) about to go berserk
(3) a borderline psychotic
(4) in need of a rest
(5) keyed-up and excited

7. From the evidence in the passage, it appears that Mrs. White would probably respond to Helen's falling in love with George Willard with

(1) indifference
(2) opposition
(3) encouragement
(4) joy
(5) relief

Check your answers to the GED Mini-Test on page 169.

Answers and Explanations

Practice *pp. 165–166*

1. **Answer:** (2)   This is correct because it is upsetting that locusts leave the land barren. Choices (1) and (5) might convey one aspect of a locust attack, but not the overall impact. There is no indication in the passage (or in nature) about the timing of a swarm of locusts, so choices (3) and (4) are incorrect.

2. **Answer:** (1)   There is nothing in the passage to suggest that Margaret and her family are choice (2), thankful, choice (3), better off, choice (4), unmoved, or choice (5), defeated, as a result of the locust attack.

3. **Answer:** (2)   Old Stephen actually calls the sight of the locusts fanning their wings at dawn "pretty." Margaret's thoughts show us that she thinks the sight is some compensation for the ruin brought by the locusts.

4. **Answer:** (3)   From the effects of the locust attack on the mealie crop, we can conclude that locusts mean nothing but ruin and trouble for farmers. Thus, choices (1) and (4) are incorrect because they are the opposite of the truth. Choices (2) and (5) indicate merely a neutral position, and thus are wrong, also.

5. **Answer:** (2)   There is no evidence in the passage for choices (1), (3) or (4). The passion with which he speaks about his brother makes choice (5) impossible.

6. **Answer:** (3)   Though the narrator does not come right out and say so, the narrator's feeling of guilt is made clear in the line, "My own name! . . . My brother!" There is no support, direct or implied, in the passage for choices (1), (2), (4) and (5).

7. **Answer:** (5) Choices (1), (3) and (4) are clearly wrong. Choice (2) may also be true, but there is no evidence for it in the passage.

8. **Answer:** (4) Because of the narrator's feelings for his brother, we know that choice (1) is untrue. Choice (2) is a misreading of the narrator's final statement. There is no evidence for choice (3). Choice (5) is the reverse of the narrator's feelings.

GED Mini-Test *pp. 167–168*

1. **Answer:** (3) This is correct because of the comment in line 10, "To the girl, his voice sounded pompous and heavy." There is no support in the passage for choices (1), (2), (4) and (5).

2. **Answer:** (3) This is correct because there is no evidence in the passage that Helen is furious with her mother. The question requires a choice that has no evidence in the passage. Choices (1), (2), (4) and (5) are all true as they are statements that can be supported in the passage, but—for that reason—they are *not* the answer to this question.

3. **Answer:** (2) The evidence that choice (2) is correct is in lines 22–23 in the passage. Choice (1) is also true, but choice (2) is a much clearer demonstration of his concentration on Helen. Choices (3), (4) and (5) are untrue.

4. **Answer:** (4) The support for choice (4) is in lines 18–20 and lines 22–23. Choices (1), (2) and (3) are untrue. Choice (3) may also be true, but it is not as important as choice (4).

5. **Answer:** (1) The support for choice (1) is in lines 3–5, especially "the airs of the city" and "wanted to appear cosmopolitan." Choices (2), (3) and (4) may be true, but they are not supported by the passage, as it is evident that the instructor has a good opinion of himself.

6. **Answer:** (5) Throughout the passage, Helen is depicted as being excited because she is young and in love. There is no evidence to suggest that she is choice (1), unstable, choices (2) and (3), insane, or choice (4), in need of rest.

7. **Answer:** (2) Line 13 indicates that Mrs. White thinks that there is no one in town good enough to associate with "a girl of Helen's breeding." There is no support, explicit or implicit, in the passage for choices (1), (3), (4) and (5).

21 Fiction

Most fiction writers make use of **implications,** or indirect statements, to tell us things. Guided by these implications, the reader arrives at conclusions about characters and situations. The process of interpreting implications is called **drawing inferences.**

Read the following passage by Conrad Aiken. Keep in mind that the experience is presented from the boy's perspective. Use the Purpose Question above the passage to help you.

WHAT IS HAPPENING TO THIS BOY?

All this time, of course (while he lay in bed), he had kept his eyes closed, listening to the nearer progress of the postman, the muffled footsteps thumping and slipping on the snow-sheathed cobbles; and all the other sounds—the double knocks, a frosty far-

(5) off voice or two, a bell ringing thinly and softly as if under a sheet of ice—had the same slightly abstracted quality, as if removed by one degree from actuality—as if everything in the world had been insulated by snow. But when at last, pleased, he opened his eyes, and turned them towards the window, to see

(10) himself this long-desired and now so clearly imagined miracle—what he saw instead was brilliant sunlight on a roof; and when, astonished, he jumped out of bed and stared down into the street, expecting to see the cobbles obliterated by the snow, he saw nothing but the bare bright cobbles themselves.

(15) Queer, the effect this extraordinary surprise had had upon him—all the following morning he had kept with him a sense of snow falling about him, a secret screen of new snow between himself and the world. If he had not dreamed such a thing—and how could he have dreamed it while awake?—how else could one

(20) explain it? In any case, the delusion had been so vivid as to affect his entire behavior. He could not now remember whether it was on the first or the second morning—or was it the third?—that his mother had drawn attention to some oddness in his manner.

"But my darling"—she had said at the breakfast table—"what

(25) has come over you? You don't seem to be listening . . ."

And how often that very thing had happened since!

Identify an Implication

This skill identifies assumptions, facts or statements that are taken for granted (not proved), and that the author takes for granted.

When information is not stated, it is **implied.** You must read between the lines to determine what you should understand. This will let you draw a conclusion.

Not everything an author wants us to know in a work of fiction is stated directly. If it were, we would miss half the pleasure and excitement of reading. In the passage by Conrad Aiken you have just read, for example, the author tells us a lot about the boy's odd perceptions, but does not give us any explanation for them. In fact, because Aiken is telling the story from the boy's point of view, he cannot come right out and explain them, any more than the boy himself can. Aiken can, however, **imply,** or indicate, what is going on by giving us a clear understanding of what the boy is hearing, feeling and thinking. This information becomes the evidence from which we then draw an **inference,** or conclusion, about the meaning of the boy's experiences.

Examples

DIRECTIONS: Choose the one best answer for each item below.

1. What inference does the author want us to draw about the boy's perceptions and behavior?

   (1) He is slowly going deaf.
   (2) He is under a magic spell.
   (3) He is playing games.
   (4) He is being disobedient.
   (5) He is slowly going mad.

Answer: (5) There is no evidence for choices (1), (2), (3) or (4), while the contrast between reality and his perceptions, the barrier the snow creates between himself and the world and the change in his behavior all suggest that a form of mental illness is beginning.

2. Which of the following does *not* serve as evidence of the boy's problem?

   (1) His mother notes a change in him.
   (2) He seems to enjoy this odd new sensation.
   (3) What he hears begins to terrify him.
   (4) The experience has begun to occur often.
   (5) The "snow" cuts him off from the world.

Answer: (3) There is no sign in the passage that the boy is frightened by what is happening to him. Choices (1), (2), (4) and (5) all support the idea that the boy is developing a mental problem.

Practice

HINT

By putting a passage into your own words, you will find yourself drawing some conclusions. Look for the supporting evidence that led you to those conclusions.

DIRECTIONS: Choose the <u>one</u> best answer for each item below.

Items 1–2 refer to the following passage by Ambrose Bierce.

WHAT IS THE SIGNIFICANCE OF CARTER DRUSE'S DECISION?

The sleeping sentinel in the clump of laurel was a young Virginian named Carter Druse. He was the son of wealthy parents, an only child, and had known such ease and cultivation and high living as wealth and taste were able to command in the mountain

(5) country of western Virginia. His home was but a few miles from where he now lay. One morning he had risen from the breakfast-table and said, quietly but gravely: "Father, a Union regiment has arrived at Grafton. I am going to join it."

The father lifted his leonine head, looked at the son a moment

(10) in silence, and replied: "Well, go, sir, and whatever may occur do what you conceive to be your duty. Virginia, to which you are a traitor, must get on without you. Should we both live to the end of the war, we will speak further of the matter. Your mother, as the physician has informed you, is in a most critical condition; at

(15) the best she cannot be with us longer than a few weeks, but that time is precious. It would be better not to disturb her."

So Carter Druse, bowing reverently to his father, who returned the salute with a stately courtesy that masked a breaking heart, left the home of his childhood to go soldiering. By con-

(20) science and courage, by deeds of devotion and daring, he soon commended himself to his fellows and his officers; and it was to these qualities and to some knowledge of the country that he owed his selection for his present perilous duty at the extreme outpost.

1. From his father's reaction to his decision, we can conclude that Carter's father

   (1) is sure his boy will be killed in the war
   (2) is too worried about his wife's health to care
   (3) never cared much for his son anyway
   (4) is committed to the other side in the war
   (5) has no understanding of his son's decision

2. Which of the following would be *unlikely* to be true of a civil war?

   (1) Close relatives end up fighting on opposite sides.
   (2) More than one member of a family is killed.
   (3) All differences are automatically forgotten afterwards.
   (4) Several members of one family fight in the same battle.
   (5) Choosing sides divides families as well as nations.

GO ON TO THE NEXT PAGE.

ARE THESE TWO SISTERS HAVING THE SAME LUCK AT LOVE?

As soon as they were gone, Elizabeth walked out to recover her spirits; or in other words, to dwell without interruption on those subjects that must deaden them more. Mr. Darcy's behavior astonished and vexed her.

(5) "Why, if he came only to be silent, grave, and indifferent," said she, "did he come at all?"

She could settle it in no way that gave her pleasure.

"He could be still amiable, still pleasing, to my uncle and aunt, when he was in town; and why not to me? If he fears me,

(10) why come hither? If he no longer cares for me, why silent? Teasing, teasing, man! I will think no more about him."

Her resolution was for a short time involuntarily kept by the approach of her sister, who joined her with a cheerful look, which showed her better satisfied with their visitors, than Elizabeth.

(15) "Now," said she, "that this first meeting is over, I feel perfectly easy. I know my own strength, and I shall never be embarrassed again by his coming. I am glad he dines here on Tuesday. It will then be publicly seen, that on both sides, we meet only as common and indifferent acquaintance."

(20) "Yes, very indifferent indeed," said Elizabeth, laughingly. "Oh, Jane, take care."

"My dear Lizzy, you cannot think me so weak, as to be in danger now."

"I think you are in very great danger of making him as much

(25) in love with you as ever."

3. In this passage, two sisters, Elizabeth and Jane, are

   (1) congratulating themselves on being good hostesses
   (2) discovering that they are in love with the same man
   (3) acting more friendly than either girl really feels
   (4) reacting to the visit of two men they are interested in
   (5) sharing their disappointment over their relationships

4. Mr. Darcy would please Elizabeth more if he were

   (1) taller and better looking
   (2) more serious and reserved
   (3) nicer to her relatives
   (4) more witty and charming
   (5) more attentive to her

5. Jane's visitor has left her feeling

   (1) more sure of herself
   (2) indifferent to him
   (3) superior to him
   (4) overwhelmed by emotion
   (5) shy and awkward

6. Even without a direct statement from the author, we know that

   (1) Elizabeth is hard to please
   (2) Jane is self-important
   (3) both girls are in love
   (4) both girls are headed for disappointment
   (5) both girls care too much about success in love

GED Mini-Test

21

TIP
You are not penalized for a wrong answer on the GED test. So, if you do not know an answer, *guess*.

DIRECTIONS: Choose the <u>one</u> best answer for each item below.

Items 1–7 refer to the following passage by E. M. Forster.

IS THIS THE WAY PEOPLE MIGHT LIVE IN THE FUTURE?

Imagine, if you can, a small room, hexagonal in shape, like the cell of a bee. It is lighted neither by window nor by lamp, yet it is filled with a soft radiance. There are no apertures for ventilation, yet the air is fresh. There are no musical instruments, and yet, at the moment that
(5) my meditation opens, this room is throbbing with melodious sounds. An arm-chair is in the center, by its side a reading-desk—that is all the furniture. And in the arm-chair there sits a swaddled lump of flesh—a woman, about five feet high, with a face as white as a fungus. It is to her that the little room belongs.
(10) An electric bell rang.
The woman touched a switch and the music was silent.
"I suppose I must see who it is," she thought, and set her chair in motion. The chair, like the music, was worked by machinery, and it rolled her to the other side of the room, where the bell still rang impor-
(15) tunately.
"Who is it?" she called. Her voice was irritable, for she had been interrupted often since the music began. She knew several thousand people; in certain directions human intercourse had advanced enormously.
But when she listened into the receiver, her white face wrinkled into
(20) smiles, and she said:
"Very well. Let us talk, I will isolate myself. I do not expect anything important will happen for the next five minutes—for I can give you fully five minutes, Kuno. Then I must deliver my lecture on 'Music during the Australian Period.'"
(25) She touched the isolation now, so that no one else could speak to her. Then she touched the lighting apparatus, and the little room was plunged into darkness.
"Be quick!" she called, her irritation returning. "Be quick, Kuno; here I am in the dark, wasting my time."
(30) But it was fully fifteen seconds before the round plate that she held in her hands began to glow. A faint blue light shot across it, darkening to purple, and presently she could see the image of her son, who lived on the other side of the earth, and he could see her.

1. From the various statements made about the woman, it is clear that she is

   (1) hostile and neurotic
   (2) patient and easy-going
   (3) witty and entertaining
   (4) selfish and self-absorbed
   (5) loving and warm-hearted

2. How do you think the author wants us to feel about the lifestyle described in this passage?

   (1) amused
   (2) amazed
   (3) horrified
   (4) intrigued
   (5) envious

3. This story was written 60 years ago. If the author were revising it today, he would probably

   (1) change the woman but leave everything else the same
   (2) add even more futuristic science fiction elements
   (3) turn it into a comedy
   (4) make the central character a man
   (5) leave it exactly as it is

4. The woman is a "swaddled lump of flesh" because she

   (1) is suffering from a wasting disease
   (2) does not eat proper food
   (3) does not get any exercise
   (4) is not really a human being
   (5) does not get enough sun

5. Though the woman is perfectly happy with her environment, the author suggests that

   (1) machines could do even more for people
   (2) she is not grateful enough for all that is done for her
   (3) she should spend more time talking with her son
   (4) machines can go out of control at any moment
   (5) people lose something by depending a lot on machines

6. The author implies that the woman knows thousands of people

   (1) intimately
   (2) only slightly
   (3) quite well
   (4) through letters
   (5) very unlike herself

7. Which of the following details does *not* suggest that the story is set in some future time?

   (1) the room's lighting and ventilation systems
   (2) the woman's fungus-like appearance
   (3) the woman's acquaintance with thousands of people
   (4) the woman's reliance on machines to move her
   (5) the glowing plate through which the woman communicates

Check your answers to the GED Mini-Test on page 176.

Answers and Explanations

Practice   *pp. 172–173*

1. **Answer:** (4)   The father's "breaking heart" (line 18) shows choices (2), (3) and (5) to be false. He mentions the possibility of death (line 12), but that is not his main sorrow. He grieves because his son has turned traitor by joining the other side (lines 11–12).

2. **Answer:** (3)   As this story suggests, choices (1), (2), (4) and (5) could all be true during a civil war. Only choice (3) seems unlikely (see lines 12–13, for example).

3. **Answer:** (4)   There is no evidence in the passage for choices (1), (2) or (3). As to choice (5), only Elizabeth, not Jane, is disappointed, and she does not share that feeling with Jane. Thus, choice (5) is only partly true, and is therefore incorrect.

5. **Answer:** (1)   Refer to lines 15–17. There is no evidence for choices (2), (3), (4) or (5) in the passage.

4. **Answer:** (5)   There is no evidence in the passage for choices (1) and (4). As for choices (2) and (3), he already is too quiet and serious (line 5) and very nice to her aunt and uncle (line 8).

6. **Answer:** (3)   Elizabeth may be a little hard to please and Jane a little self-congratulatory, but a more important fact about each girl is that she is in love (see lines 5–11 and 15–17). There is no evidence for choices (4) and (5) in the passage.

GED Mini-Test   *pp. 174–175*

1. **Answer:** (4)   While the woman does not appear to be hostile and neurotic, choice (1), it is quite clear that she is too wrapped up in her own concerns to be very patient or loving toward her son, and there is no evidence that she is witty.

3. **Answer:** (2)   Given the point the author seems to be making, he would leave the woman as she is, but add more futuristic elements to the lifestyle he is depicting.

5. **Answer:** (5)   There is no evidence in the passage for choices (1), (2) or (4). It is probably true that she should spend more time with her son, choice (3), but far more important is the idea that she—and those who live like her—have given up something precious by relying so much on machines.

7. **Answer:** (2)   Choices (1), (3), (4) and (5) all suggest a future world.

2. **Answer:** (3)   From the author's description of the woman's white, inert body, we can conclude that he finds her way of life horrifying, rather than amusing, amazing, intriguing or enviable.

4. **Answer:** (3)   There is no evidence in the passage for choices (1), (2) or (4). The woman's fungus-like white skin is explained by lack of sun, but her fleshy weakness is due to lack of exercise.

6. **Answer:** (2)   This is correct because her knowing "several thousand people" intimately—choice (1), through letters—choice (4), or quite well—choice (3), is not supported by any evidence in the passage. It is, however, probable that these people are very like her, and, therefore, choice (5) is also wrong.

22 Nonfiction Biography and Autobiography

Both biographies and autobiographies are concerned with real people and events. They differ in the **point of view** from which they are told.

In an autobiography a person uses the first person to tell his or her own story. In a biography one person tells another person's story.

Read the following selection by Catherine Drinker Bowen. As you read, take note of the author's point of view. Use the Purpose Question to help you.

HOW DOES JOHN ADAMS' NOMINATION OF WASHINGTON SURPRISE HANCOCK?

John worked hard. By the middle of June, he decided the moment was ripe. On a dull, muggy morning, he walked alone to Congress, determined to nominate Washington before the noon bell sounded from the tower. As soon as the members were
(5) seated, John rose and spoke briefly for the establishment of a Continental army, outlining the present dangers, chief of which was that the forces at Cambridge might dissolve entirely. What was to prevent the British from profiting by this delay, marching out of Boston and "spreading desolation as far as they could go"?
(10) For commander-in-chief of a Grand American Army he would like, John finished, to suggest *"a gentleman whose skill as an officer, whose independent fortune, great talents and universal character would command the respect of America and unite the full exertions of the Colonies better than any other person alive."*

(15) All the time he was speaking, Hancock wore a look of pleased, even radiant, expectancy. Facing the room in his chair behind the President's table, he was plainly visible to everyone, including John, who stood near the front. No one loved glory more than Hancock; he had the vanity of a child, open and vulner-
(20) able. John saw his face and hastened on, raising his voice a little: "A gentleman *from Virginia*, who is among us here, and well known to all."

Hancock shrank as at a blow. ("I never," John wrote later, "remarked a more sudden and striking change of countenance.
(25) Mortification and resentment were expressed as forcibly as his face could exhibit them.") Washington, who was on the south side of the room, left his seat at the word *Virginia* and slipped quietly out the door before his name was pronounced.

Identify Techniques (Point of View)

This skill involves identifying and distinguishing whose thoughts and feelings are being revealed. The point of view expressed is the author's but this viewpoint may be seen through the eyes of a character and, therefore, be hard to distinguish.

Point of view is the observation point from which a story is told. Told in the first person, an autobiography is likely to have a special quality of immediacy and emotional truth. No one else knows as much about that person's thoughts, feelings and experiences as the "I" who is telling the story. Biographies, which are told in the third person ("he" or "she"), naturally lack some of the intimacy and immediacy of autobiographies. But they can be just as exciting and dramatic.

In some cases the biographer has actually known or interviewed the person whose life story is being told. In other cases, where the subject of the biography is a historical figure, the biographer may bring the story to life with imagined details based on careful research of the people and the period. The author of the passage on page 177 lived 150 years after the subject. But notice how she brings the scene to life with descriptive details about the weather, the physical setting and the actions of both Hancock and Washington.

Examples

DIRECTIONS: Use the information on this page and the passage by Catherine Drinker Bowen on the preceding page to choose the one best answer for each item below.

1. The incident in this passage is described

   (1) from Hancock's viewpoint
   (2) in the third person
   (3) from Washington's viewpoint
   (4) in the first person
   (5) in the interviewer's words

Answer: (2)   The biographer describes the incident from Adams' viewpoint. Since it is someone else other than Adams telling the story, we know that it is told from the third-person point of view.

2. What tells us how Hancock's face looked in response to the nomination?

   (1) Adams' own words
   (2) Washington's memoirs
   (3) a newspaper account
   (4) a painting of the event
   (5) the biographer's imagination

Answer: (1)   Adams' own words are quoted about the look on Hancock's face (lines 23–26). There is no evidence for choices (2) to (5).

Practice

HINT ▷ Remember that an autobiography is told from the first-person point of view. A biography—one person's story told by another—is told from the third-person point of view.

DIRECTIONS: Choose the <u>one</u> best answer for each item below.

Items 1–4 refer to the following passage by Booker T. Washington.

WHAT WAS IT LIKE TO BE A SLAVE DURING THE CIVIL WAR?

I had no schooling whatever while I was a slave, though I remember on several occasions I went as far as the schoolhouse door with one of my young mistresses to carry her books. The picture of several dozen boys and girls in a schoolroom engaged

(5) in study made a deep impression upon me, and I had the feeling that to get into a schoolhouse and study in this way would be about the same as getting into paradise.

So far as I can now recall, the first knowledge that I got of the fact that we were slaves, and that freedom of the slaves was

(10) being discussed, was early one morning before day, when I was awakened by my mother kneeling over her children and fervently praying that Lincoln and his armies might be successful, and that one day she and her children might be free. In this connection I have never been able to understand how the slaves throughout

(15) the South, completely ignorant as were the masses so far as books or newspapers were concerned, were able to keep themselves so accurately and completely informed about the great National questions that were agitating the country. From the time that Garrison, Lovejoy, and others began to agitate for freedom,

(20) the slaves throughout the South kept in close touch with the progress of the movement. Though I was a mere child during the preparation for the Civil War and during the war itself, I now recall the many late-at-night whispered discussions that I heard my mother and the other slaves on the plantation indulge in.

(25) These discussions showed that they understood the situation, and that they kept themselves informed of events by what was termed the "grape-vine" telegraph.

1. During the Civil War, the author was

   (1) starting school
   (2) an old man
   (3) a soldier
   (4) a young man
   (5) still a child

2. The author remains impressed by

   (1) his mother's piousness
   (2) how kind his masters were
   (3) his schooling as a slave
   (4) how hard slaves had to work
   (5) how well-informed slaves were

GO ON TO THE NEXT PAGE.

3. This passage is told

   (1) by a biographer
   (2) in the present tense
   (3) in the first person
   (4) by a newspaper reporter
   (5) in the third person

4. The author thought of school as

   (1) a form of slavery
   (2) a terrifying challenge
   (3) the gateway to society
   (4) a kind of heaven
   (5) an arena for protest

Items 5–6 refer to the following passage by Lytton Strachey.

WHAT DID YOUNG FLORENCE WANT TO BECOME?

As the years passed, a restlessness began to grow upon her. She was unhappy, and at last she knew it. Mrs. Nightingale, too, began to notice that there was something wrong. It was very odd; what could be the matter with dear Flo? Mr. Nightingale sug-

(5) gested that a husband might be advisable; but the curious thing was that she seemed to take no interest in husbands. And with her attractions, and her accomplishments, too! There was nothing in the world to prevent her making a really brilliant match. But no! She would think of nothing but how to satisfy that singular

(10) craving of hers to be *doing* something. As if there was not plenty to do in any case, in the ordinary way, at home. There was china to look after, and there was her father to be read to after dinner. Mrs. Nightingale could not understand it; and then one day her perplexity was changed to consternation and alarm. Florence

(15) pronounced an extreme desire to go to Salisbury Hospital as a nurse; and she confessed to some visionary plan of eventually setting up a house of her own in a neighbouring village, and there founding "something like a Protestant Sisterhood, without vows, for women of educated feelings." The whole scheme was sum-

(20) marily brushed aside as preposterous; and Mrs. Nightingale, after the first shock of terror, was able to settle down again more or less comfortably to her embroidery. But Florence, who was now twenty-five and felt that the dream of her life had been shattered, came near to desperation.

(25) And, indeed, the difficulties in her path were great. For not only was it an almost unimaginable thing in those days for a woman of means to make her own way in the world and to live in independence, but the particular profession for which Florence was clearly marked out both by her instincts and her capacities

(30) was at that time a peculiarly disreputable one. . . .

5. By "a woman of means" (line 27), the author means

   (1) a woman of the streets
   (2) a wealthy woman
   (3) a mean-spirited woman
   (4) an intelligent woman
   (5) a marriageable woman

6. Florence's career hopes were

   (1) supported by her parents
   (2) considered very admirable
   (3) built around husband-hunting
   (4) greeted with shock and alarm
   (5) shared by all her friends

Before you take the GED Mini-Test, check your answers on page 182.

DIRECTIONS: Choose the <u>one</u> best answer for each item below.

Items 1–6 refer to the following passage by Colette.

WAS THIS CHILDHOOD A HAPPY ONE?

At half-past three everything slumbered still in a primal blue, blurred and dewy, and as I went down the sandy road the mist, grounded by its own weight, bathed first my legs, then my well-built lit-
(5) tle body, reaching at last to my mouth and ears, and finally to that most sensitive part of all, my nostrils. I went alone, for there were no dangers in that free-thinking countryside. It was on that road and at that hour that I first became aware of my own self, experienced an inexpressible state of grace, and felt one with the first breath of air that stirred, the first bird, and the sun so newly born that it still looked not quite round.

(10) "Beauty" my mother would call me, and "Jewel-of-pure-gold"; then she would let me go, watching her creation—her masterpiece, as she said—grow smaller as I ran down the slope. I may have been pretty; my mother and the pictures of me at that period do not always agree. But what made me pretty at that moment was my youth and the dawn, my
(15) blue eyes deepened by the greenery all round me, my fair locks that would only be brushed smooth on my return, and my pride at being awake when other children were asleep.

I came back when the bell rang for the first Mass. But not before I had eaten my fill, not before I had described a great circle in the woods,
(20) like a dog out hunting on its own, and tasted the water of the two hidden springs which I worshipped. One of them bubbled out of the ground with a crystalline spurt and a sort of sob, and then carved its own sandy bed. But it was no sooner born than it lost confidence and plunged underground again. The other spring, almost invisible, brushed over the
(25) grass like a snake, and spread itself out secretly in the middle of a meadow where the narcissus, flowering in a ring, alone bore witness to its presence. The first spring tasted of oak-leaves, the second of iron and hyacinth stalks. The mere mention of them makes me hope that their savour may fill my mouth when my time comes, and that I may carry
(30) hence with me that imagined draught.

1. When the author got up and went for a walk,

   (1) she was the only one awake
   (2) it was mid-afternoon
   (3) her mother was up, too
   (4) she went to Mass first
   (5) it was scary on the road

2. The tone of this passage is

   (1) poetic and happy
   (2) sad and sorrowful
   (3) sorry and regretful
   (4) nervous and anxious
   (5) witty and whimsical

GO ON TO THE NEXT PAGE.

3. The passage is written

    (1) as if in the child's words
    (2) from the mother's viewpoint
    (3) in the third person
    (4) in the form of a diary
    (5) in the first person

4. By "described a great circle" (line 19), the author means that she

    (1) drew a circle on the ground
    (2) told someone about her route
    (3) went hunting for a circle
    (4) followed a circular route
    (5) found a ring-like garden

5. As a child, the author was

    (1) rebellious
    (2) very pretty
    (3) independent
    (4) nervous and frail
    (5) shy and retiring

6. Both of the springs visited by the author as a child

    (1) were deep and dangerous
    (2) seemed magical to her
    (3) were noisy and bubbling
    (4) tasted of oak-leaves
    (5) held undrinkable water

Check your answers to the GED Mini-Test on page 183.

Answers and Explanations

Practice *pp. 179–180*

1. **Answer:** (5) See lines 21–22, in which the author describes himself as "a mere child" during the war.

2. **Answer:** (5) There is no evidence for choices (2) to (4). Although he undoubtedly was impressed by his mother's piousness, choice (1), the main point he makes here is how amazing it was that the slaves managed to keep themselves informed.

3. **Answer:** (3) As is clear from the author's use of "I," the passage is told in the first person, rather than in the third, by a biographer. The author uses the past, rather than the present, tense. We do not know if he is a reporter.

4. **Answer:** (4) In lines 6–7 the author says that going to school would be like "getting into paradise." There is no evidence for choices (1) to (3) or (5).

5. **Answer:** (2) The fact that all Florence was expected to do was look after the china, read to her father and find a husband indicates how well off the family was. From this we conclude that "a woman of means" means "a wealthy woman."

6. **Answer:** (4) It is made clear in lines 13–14 and 19–20 that the response to Florence's ambitions was shock and alarm, rather than support or admiration, choices (1) and (2). Lines 5–6 make it clear that she didn't want a husband, choice (3). Lines 25–30 show how unusual her career hopes were, choice (5).

GED Mini-Test

1. **Answer:** (3)   Lines 10–12 make clear that her mother was up to watch her set off on her early-morning jaunts. There is no evidence for choices (1), (2), (4) and (5) in the passage.

2. **Answer:** (1)   There is nothing sad, regretful, anxious or witty about this passage. It is a poetic and happy memory of the past.

3. **Answer:** (5)   This account of her childhood by the author herself is told in the first person, from an adult point of view. It is not a diary, because it was not written at the time it was happening.

4. **Answer:** (4)   We know that the author means "followed a circular route" because of her comparison of herself to a dog out hunting. She does mention a ring of flowers, but only later.

5. **Answer:** (3)   The author's early morning walks by herself—with her mother's blessing—show her to have been an energetic, adventurous, independent child with no need to rebel. Whether or not she was really pretty is left in doubt.

6. **Answer:** (2)   The clue here is "both." From her description, we know that the child regarded both as very special; only one was noisy, and only one tasted of oak-leaves. We know that the author drank from both, and that both were too small to be deep or dangerous.

23 **Fiction**

A writer's **style** is the distinctive, recognizable way that she or he uses words and images to create characters, setting, mood and action. **Structure** is the way a writer chooses to organize the plot of a story and shape the individual passages and sentences within it.

Read the following passage by Ernest Hemingway. Pay special attention to the way he develops the scene and tells us about the characters. Use the Purpose Question above the passage to help you.

WHAT IS THE BOY'S SECRET FEAR?

"Don't think," I said. "Just take it easy."

"I'm taking it easy," he said and looked straight ahead. He was evidently holding tight onto himself about something.

"Take this with water."

(5) "Do you think it will do any good?"

"Of course it will."

I sat down and opened the *Pirate* book and commenced to read, but I could see he was not following, so I stopped.

"About what time do you think I'm going to die?" he asked.

(10) "What?"

"About how long will it be before I die?"

"You aren't going to die. What's the matter with you?"

"Oh, yes, I am. I heard him say a hundred and two."

"People don't die with a fever of one hundred and two. That's (15) a silly way to talk."

"I know they do. At school in France the boys told me you can't live with forty-four degrees. I've got a hundred and two."

He had been waiting to die all day, ever since nine o'clock in the morning.

(20) "You poor Schatz," I said. "Poor old Schatz. It's like miles and kilometers. You aren't going to die. That's a different thermometer. On that thermometer thirty-seven is normal. On this kind it's ninety-eight."

"Are you sure?"

(25) "Absolutely," I said. "It's like miles and kilometers. You know, like how many kilometers we make when we do seventy miles in the car?"

"Oh," he said.

But his gaze at the foot of the bed relaxed slowly. The hold (30) over himself relaxed too, and the next day it was very slack and he cried easily at little things that were of no importance.

Identify Elements of Style and Structure

This skill involves identifying the characteristic ways in which an author uses language and organizes his or her material.

Each writer uses **language** differently to create characters, describe scenes and convey moods and feelings. Some writers, like Ernest Hemingway, use very few descriptive words and phrases. The effect they strive for is a clean, spare, unemotional style. Other writers make use of many descriptive words and images, or word pictures, to make their scenes and characters vivid.

Writers **structure** their works in characteristically different ways. Some tell a story in a very simple and straightforward manner. Others use a more elaborate and roundabout way. Some tell you exactly what their characters are thinking and feeling. Others let their characters' words and actions speak for themselves.

When reading for **style** and **structure**, ask yourself how you would read the passage out loud to someone. Sadly? Excitedly? Matter-of-factly? Humorously? Then look for clues that tell you how to read it. These clues—the descriptive words in the passage (or the absence of them) and the way the passage builds to a conclusion—are the elements of style and structure within it.

Examples

DIRECTIONS: Choose the one best answer for each item below.

1. The absence of descriptive images in this passage gives it

   (1) a cold, scientific effect
   (2) a dull, ho-hum feeling
   (3) a hardhitting, factual impact
   (4) a dry, scholarly quality
   (5) a dreamy, poetic aura

Answer: (3) Because we have little more than dialogue to go on, the revelation of the boy's secret fear comes as a shock. The tense and down-to-earth nature of the scene rules out choices (1), (2), (4) and (5).

2. Like the boy's fear, the passage

   (1) remains mysterious throughout
   (2) fails to reach a climax
   (3) awakens little sympathy
   (4) is about something trivial
   (5) builds up and subsides

Answer: (5) The underlying structure of the passage matches the build-up and resolution of the boy's fear, step for step. Choices (1), (2), (3) and (4) are wrong because the fear is explained (line 18); reaches a climax (lines 16–17); is clearly not trivial; and awakens our sympathy.

When reading a passage for style and structure, remember to ask yourself what feeling it conveys. Then look to see how the author structures the passages and uses (or does not use) descriptive words and images to create the mood.

DIRECTIONS: Choose the <u>one</u> best answer for each item below.

Items 1–2 refer to the following passage by Katherine Anne Porter.

WHAT KIND OF PERSON IS GRANNY WETHERALL?

Doctor Harry spread a warm paw like a cushion on her forehead where the forked green vein danced and made her eyelids twitch. "Now, now, be a good girl, and we'll have you up in no time."

(5)   "That's no way to speak to a woman nearly eighty years old just because she's down. I'd have you respect your elders, young man."

"Well, Missy, excuse me." Doctor Harry patted her cheek. "But I've got to warn you, haven't I? You're a marvel, but you must be

(10)   careful or you're going to be good and sorry."

"Don't tell me what I'm going to be. I'm on my feet now, morally speaking. It's Cornelia. I had to go to bed to get rid of her."

Her bones felt loose, and floated around in her skin, and Doc-

(15)   tor Harry floated like a balloon around the foot of the bed. He floated and pulled down his waistcoat and swung his glasses on a cord. "Well, stay where you are, it certainly can't hurt you."

"Get along and doctor your sick," said Granny Wetherall. Leave a well woman alone. I'll call for you when I want

(20)   you. . . . Where were you forty years ago when I pulled through milk-leg and double pneumonia? You weren't even born. Don't let Cornelia lead you on," she shouted, because Doctor Harry appeared to float up to the ceiling and out. "I pay my own bills, and I don't throw money away on nonsense!"

1. This story is about a woman who is

(1) losing her mind
(2) a charity case
(3) hard of hearing
(4) on her deathbed
(5) easy to deal with

2. "I'm on my feet now, morally speaking," means that Granny

(1) is financially independent
(2) feels morally superior
(3) can make her own decisions
(4) can stand up without help
(5) does not want medical care

GO ON TO THE NEXT PAGE.

WHAT DOES SCROOGE SEE AND HEAR AT THE CHRISTMAS PARTY?

There was first a game of blind-man's buff. And I no more believe Topper was really blinded than I believe he had eyes in his boots. Because the way in which he went after that plump sis- ter in the lace tucker was an outrage on the credulity of human

(5) nature. Knocking down the fire-irons, tumbling over the chairs, bumping up against the piano, smothering himself among the cur- tains, wherever she went, there went he. He always knew where the plump sister was. He wouldn't catch anybody else. If you had fallen up against him, as some of them did, he would have made a

(10) feint of endeavoring to seize you, which would have been an affront to your understanding; and would instantly have sidled off in the direction of the plump sister.

"Here is a new game," said Scrooge. "One half hour, Spirit, only one!"

(15) It was a Game called Yes and No, where Scrooge's nephew had to think of something, and the rest must find out what; he only answering to their questions yes or no as the case was. The fire of questioning to which he was exposed, elicited from him that he was thinking of an animal, rather a disagreeable animal, a

(20) savage animal, an animal that growled and grunted sometimes, and talked sometimes, and lived in London, and walked about the streets, and wasn't made a show of, and wasn't led by anybody, and didn't live in a menagerie, and was never killed in a market, and was not a horse, or an ass, or a cow, or a bull, or a tiger, or

(25) a dog, or a pig, or a cat, or a bear. At every new question put to him, this nephew burst into a fresh roar of laughter; and was so inexpressibly tickled, that he was obliged to get up off the sofa and stamp. At last the plump sister cried out:

"I have found it out! I know what it is, Fred! I know what it

(30) is!"

"What is it?" cried Fred.

"It's your uncle Scro-o-o-oge!"

Which it certainly was.

3. The mood of the passage is

(1) peaceful, calm and serene
(2) high-spirited and festive
(3) high-strung and overwrought
(4) highbrow and snobbish
(5) nervous, tense and anxious

4. The passage's structure does *not*

(1) mirror the games at the party
(2) reveal Scrooge's thoughts
(3) build up to a climax
(4) rapidly gather momentum
(5) lead up to a punchline

5. This author's style is

(1) simple and direct
(2) dry and scholarly
(3) wordy but lively
(4) solemn but profound
(5) flat and unemotional

6. In line 23, the word "menagerie" means

(1) birdcage
(2) den of iniquity
(3) merry-go-round
(4) stable
(5) zoo

Before you take the GED Mini-Test, check your answers on pages 189–190.

GED Mini-Test

23

TIP Skim a passage on the GED exam first for mood and meaning. But do not let your feelings about what you are reading get in the way. Read again for details.

DIRECTIONS: Choose the one best answer for each item below.

Items 1–6 refer to the following passage by Mark Twain.

WHAT DOES HUCK LEARN ABOUT THE MEANING OF "FEUD"?

One day Buck and me was away out in the woods, hunting, and heard a horse coming. We was crossing the road. Buck says:

"Quick! Jump for the woods!"

We done it, and then peeped down the woods through the leaves.

(5) Pretty soon a splendid young man come galloping down the road, setting his horse easy and looking like a soldier. He had his gun across his pommel. I had seen him before. It was young Harney Shepherdson. I heard Buck's gun go off at my ear, and Harney's hat tumbled off from his head. He grabbed his gun and rode straight to the place where we was

(10) hid. But we didn't wait. We started through the woods on a run. The woods warn't thick, so I looked over my shoulder, to dodge the bullet, and twice I seen Harney cover Buck with his gun; and then he rode away the way he come—to get his hat, I reckon, but I couldn't see. We never stopped running till we got home. The old gentleman's eyes blazed

(15) a minute—'twas pleasure, mainly, I judged—then his face sort of smoothed down, and he says, kind of gentle:

"I don't like that shooting from behind a bush. Why didn't you step into the road, my boy?"

"The Shepherdsons don't, father. They always take advantage."

(20) Miss Charlotte she held her head up like a queen while Buck was telling his tale, and her nostrils spread and her eyes snapped. The two young men looked dark, but never said nothing. Miss Sophia she turned pale, but the color come back when she found the man warn't hurt.

Soon as I could get Buck down by the corncribs under the trees by

(25) ourselves, I says:

"Did you want to kill him, Buck?"

"Well, I bet I did."

"What did he do to you?"

"Him? He never done nothing to me."

(30) "Well, then, what did you want to kill him for?"

"Why, nothing—only it's on account of the feud."

"What's a feud?"

"Why, where was you raised? Don't you know what a feud is?"

"Never heard of it before—tell me about it."

(35) "Well," says Buck, "a feud is this way. A man has a quarrel with another man, and kills him; then that other man's brother kills *him*; then the other brothers, on both sides, goes for one another; then the *cousins* chip in—and by-and-by everybody's killed off, and there ain't no more feud. But it's kind of slow, and takes a long time."

GO ON TO THE NEXT PAGE.

1. The two boys are pursued by

   (1) an older brother of Buck's
   (2) the son of a rival family
   (3) the old gentleman
   (4) an underage soldier
   (5) the local sheriff

2. From Sophia's reaction, it is clear that she

   (1) is in love with Harney
   (2) wishes Harney dead
   (3) finds the feud boring
   (4) wishes she were a boy
   (5) admires her brother

3. How do the events of the first half of the passage relate to the ideas in the second half?

   (1) as a commentary on them
   (2) as a contradiction to them
   (3) as an argument against them
   (4) as an introduction to them
   (5) as a distraction from them

4. In talking about feuds, the author could just as easily be talking about the origins of

   (1) disease
   (2) love
   (3) war
   (4) sin
   (5) poverty

5. No direct value judgment is made about feuds. How do you think the author regards them?

   (1) as too bad but necessary
   (2) as a test of family honor
   (3) as an exercise in manhood
   (4) as proof of family loyalty
   (5) as foolish and wasteful

6. The author's approach to style and structure does *not*

   (1) create recognizable stereotypes
   (2) make a complex plot seem simple
   (3) show his skill at writing dialogue
   (4) entertain and amuse the reader
   (5) carry a serious message

Check your answers to the GED Mini-Test on page 190.

Answers and Explanations

Practice *pp. 186–187*

1. **Answer:** (4)   Granny may be cranky, but there is no evidence to show that she is choice (1), losing her mind. Her own remarks in line 23 show that she is not a charity case. She has no trouble hearing the doctor's replies, ruling out choice (3). The doctor's presence and her own age and weakness make choice (4) the best answer.

2. **Answer:** (3)   Since Granny is bedridden, the answer is clearly not choice (4). She *is* financially independent, feels superior and does not want the doctor's help. But the meaning of her statement is that she does not want to be bossed around and told what to do—she can make her own decisions.

3. **Answer:** (2)   There is no evidence for any of the other answers in the passage; everyone at the party is not only excited but happy and at ease.

4. **Answer:** (2)   Scrooge's thoughts are not revealed. The passage *does* choice (1), mirror the party games; choice (3), build to a climax; choice (4), gather momentum; and choice (5), have a punchline.

5. Answer: (3) While wordy by today's standards, the style is full of life and feeling. It is not choice (1), simple, nor is it choice (2), dry, choice (4), solemn, or choice (5), flat.

6. Answer: (5) As a menagerie is a place wild animals are kept, choice (5) is correct. Choice (1) is incorrect. As the "animal" in question can growl and grunt, it is not a bird in a birdcage. Since the subject of the game is a live animal, choice (3) is also wrong. Line 24 specifically states "not a horse," thus choice (4) cannot be correct. And choice (2) is not supported by any evidence in the passage.

GED Mini-Test *pp. 188–189*

1. Answer: (2) Though he *looks* like a soldier, we know it is a young local civilian because the boys know his name (line 7).

2. Answer: (1) Sophia turns pale (line 23) when she thinks Harney might have been hurt, telling us that she cares for him. There is no evidence for choices (2), (3), (4) or (5) in the passage.

3. Answer: (4) The incident in the woods is both an example of and an introduction to the ideas in the final paragraph. Choices (1), (2), (3) and (5) do not describe this relationship.

4. Answer: (3) Because the subject is violence, vengeance and winning, the answer cannot be choice (1), disease, choice (2), love, choice (4), sin, or choice (5), poverty.

5. Answer: (5) Though Buck's family would agree with choices (1), (2), (3) and (4), Buck's own description of the meaning of "feuds" (lines 35–39) reveals how foolish and wasteful the author thinks them.

6. Answer: (1) Choices (2), (3), (4) and (5) all describe what the author's approach to style and structure *does* accomplish.

24 Nonfiction Essay

An essay is usually devoted to a single topic. The style of the essay depends on the topic's seriousness and on the personality of the writer.

Formal essays are often used to discuss abstract principles and issues. Informal essays often tell personal stories and include many colorful details drawn from life. The passage below, by Robert Frost, is an example of an informal essay. Reading it is almost like having a conversation with the man himself.

As you read the following selection, ask yourself what points are being implied. Use the Purpose Question to help you.

HOW DOES A TEACHER AND POET DECIDE HOW TO GRADE HIS STUDENTS?

. . . There are two ways of coming close to poetry. One is by writing poetry. And some people think I want people to write poetry, but I don't; that is, I don't necessarily. I only want people to write poetry if they want to write poetry. I have never

(5) encouraged anybody to write poetry that did not want to write it, and I have not always encouraged those who did want to write it. That ought to be one's own funeral. It is a hard, hard life, as they say.

(I have just been to a city in the West, a city full of poets, a

(10) city they have made safe for poets. The whole city is so lovely that you do not have to write it up to make it poetry; it is ready-made for you. But, I don't know—the poetry written in that city might not seem like poetry if read outside the city. It would be like the jokes made when you were drunk; you have to get drunk

(15) again to appreciate them.)

But as I say, there is another way to come close to poetry, fortunately, and that is in the reading of it, not as linguistics, not as history, not as anything but poetry. It is one of the hard things for a teacher to know how close a man has come in reading

(20) poetry. How do I know whether a man has come close to Keats in reading Keats? It is hard for me to know. I have lived with some boys a whole year over some of the poets and I have not felt sure whether they have come near what it was all about. One remark sometimes told me. One remark was their mark for the year; had

(25) to be—it was all I got that told me what I wanted to know. And that is enough, if it was the right remark, if it came close enough. I think a man might make twenty fool remarks if he made one good one some time in the year. His mark would depend on that good remark.

Identify an Implication and Draw a Conclusion

This skill identifies assumptions, facts or statements that are taken for granted (not proved) and that the author takes for granted. Using these implications you can form logical conclusions.

When reading an essay, look first for the ideas that are stated directly. Then look for other, equally important ideas that are **implied.** Frost tells us directly how he grades his students, for instance. But, indirectly, he also tells us something about the abstract nature of poetry. This is implied in his use of the phrase "coming close to" (line 1) and in his description of the inexact way he arrives at a mark for his students.

A writer's **conclusion** can usually be found:
At the beginning. (in the first sentence or paragraph) If this is the case the writer gives examples or explanations to indicate how this conclusion was reached.
At the end. Some writers end with a statement that summarizes the examples or explanations given throughout the piece.
At the beginning *and* the end. Some writers begin *and* end with a conclusion. This is true of the Frost essay on page 191.

Examples

DIRECTIONS: Use the information on this page and the passage by Robert Frost on the preceding page to choose the <u>one</u> best answer for each item below.

1. When Frost talks about "coming close to poetry" he means

   (1) being able to write it
   (2) leading a poetic life
   (3) being able to recite it
   (4) understanding its meaning
   (5) doing a translation of it

Answer: (4) For Frost "coming close to poetry" means understanding what it is all about (lines 16–17). While writing poetry may help one to understand it, choice 1, it is not the same as understanding it. There is no evidence for choices (2), (3) or (5).

2. We can conclude that, for Frost, both teaching and understanding poetry

   (1) are inexact and unscientific
   (2) require historical knowledge
   (3) benefit from religious faith
   (4) are a waste of time
   (5) are a subject for linguists

Answer: (1) The fact that, for Frost, the best indication of a student's grasp of poetry is a "right remark" (line 26) shows how inexact and unscientific both teaching it and understanding it are. There is no evidence for choices (2) to (5).

Practice

H I N T

When reading for implications, remember to look for ideas that are stated indirectly, as well as ideas that are stated directly. When you draw conclusions from information that is only implied, you are really "reading between the lines."

DIRECTIONS: Choose the one best answer for each item below.

Items 1–2 refer to the following passage by Virginia Woolf.

CAN ALL OF LIFE BE SYMBOLIZED BY A SINGLE MOTH?

The same energy which inspired the rooks, the ploughmen, the horses, and even, it seemed, the lean bare-backed downs, sent the moth fluttering from side to side of his square of the window-pane. One could not help watching him. One was, indeed, con-

(5) scious of a queer feeling of pity for him. The possibilities of pleasure seemed that morning so enormous and so various that to have only a moth's part in life, and a day moth's at that, appeared a hard fate, and his zest in enjoying his meager opportunities to the full, pathetic. He flew vigorously to one corner of his com-

(10) partment, and, after waiting there a second, flew across to the other. What remained for him but to fly to a third corner and then to a fourth? That was all he could do, in spite of the size of the downs, the width of the sky, the far-off smoke of houses, and the romantic voice, now and then, of a steamer out at sea. What

(15) he could do he did. Watching him, it seemed as if a fiber, very thin but pure, of the enormous energy of the world had been thrust into his frail and diminutive body. As often as he crossed the pane, I could fancy that a thread of vital light became visible. He was little or nothing but life.

(20) Yet, because he was so small, and so simple a form of the energy that was rolling in at the open window and driving its way through so many narrow and intricate corridors in my own brain and in those of other human beings, there was something marvelous as well as pathetic about him. It was as if someone had

(25) taken a tiny bead of pure life and decking it as lightly as possible with down and feathers, had set it dancing and zigzagging to show us the true nature of life. . . .

1. The author's attitude toward the moth is one of

(1) pity
(2) annoyance
(3) amusement
(4) wonder
(5) curiosity

2. By "a day moth" (line 7) the author means that the moth

(1) is active only during the day
(2) belongs to a unique species
(3) only lives for a day
(4) will become a butterfly
(5) must mate in the daytime

GO ON TO THE NEXT PAGE.

Items 3–4 refer to the following passage by William Faulkner.

WHAT MUST WRITERS DIRECT THEIR ENERGIES TOWARD?

Our tragedy today is a general and universal physical fear so long sustained by now that we can even bear it. There are no longer problems of the spirit. There is only the question: When will I be blown up? Because of this, the young man or woman
(5) writing today has forgotten the problems of the human heart in conflict with itself which alone can make good writing because only that is worth writing about, worth the agony and the sweat.

He must learn them again. He must teach himself that the basest of all things is to be afraid; and, teaching himself that, for-
(10) get it forever, leaving no room in his workshop for anything but the old verities and truths of the heart, the old universal truths lacking which any story is ephemeral and doomed—love and honor and pity and pride and compassion and sacrifice. Until he does so, he labors under a curse. He writes not of love but of
(15) lust, of defeats in which nobody loses anything of value, of victories without hope and, worst of all, without pity or compassion. His griefs grieve on no universal bones, leaving no scars. He writes not of the heart but of the glands.

Until he relearns these things, he will write as though he
(20) stood among and watched the end of man. I decline to accept the end of man. It is easy enough to say that man is immortal simply because he will endure: that when the last ding-dong of doom has clanged and faded from the last worthless rock hanging tideless in the last red and dying evening, that even then there will still be
(25) one more sound: that of his puny inexhaustible voice, still talking. I refuse to accept this. I believe that man will not only endure: he will prevail. He is immortal, not because he alone among creatures has an inexhaustible voice, but because he has a soul, a spirit capable of compassion and sacrifice and endurance. The
(30) poet's, the writer's, duty is to write about these things. . . .

3. The main idea stated directly in this passage is that

   (1) human beings are immortal because they have souls
   (2) the only thing worse than fear is lust
   (3) the world is bound to end in a nuclear war
   (4) writers must return to writing about universal truths
   (5) mankind will undoubtedly endure and prevail

4. A conclusion we can draw from the passage is that the author

   (1) enjoys telling other writers what to do
   (2) is obsessed with the idea of nuclear war
   (3) is concerned about the effects of fear on writers' work
   (4) actually holds out no hope for the future of mankind
   (5) is basically old fashioned and out of date in his views

Before you take the GED Mini-Test, check your answers on page 196.

DIRECTIONS: Choose the one best answer for each item below.

Items 1–6 refer to the following passage by E. B. White.

IS IT POSSIBLE TO RECAPTURE THE PLEASURES OF THE PAST?

One summer, along about 1904, my father rented a camp on a lake in Maine and took us all there for the month of August. We all got ring-worm from some kittens and had to rub Pond's Extract on our arms and legs night and morning, and my father rolled over in a canoe with all

(5) his clothes on; but outside of that the vacation was a success and from then on none of us ever thought there was any place in the world like that lake in Maine. We returned summer after summer—always on August 1st for one month. I have since become a salt-water man, but sometimes in summer there are days when the restlessness of the tides

(10) and the fearful cold of the sea water and the incessant wind which blows across the afternoon and into the evening make me wish for the placidity of a lake in the woods. A few weeks ago this feeling got so strong I bought myself a couple of bass hooks and a spinner and returned to the lake where we used to go, for a week's fishing and to

(15) revisit old haunts.

I took along my son, who had never had any fresh water up his nose and who had seen lily pads only from train windows. On the journey over to the lake I began to wonder what it would be like. I wondered how time would have marred this unique, this holy spot—the coves and

(20) streams, the hills that the sun set behind, the camps and paths behind the camps. I was sure the tarred road would have found it out and I wondered in what other ways it would be desolated. It is strange how much you can remember about places like that once you allow your mind to return into the grooves which lead back. You remember one

(25) thing, and that suddenly reminds you of another thing. I guess I remem-bered clearest of all the early mornings, when the lake was cool and motionless, remembered how the bedroom smelled of the lumber it was made of and of the wet woods whose scent entered through the screen. The partitions in the camp were thin and did not extend clear to the top

(30) of the rooms, and as I was always the first up I would dress softly so as not to wake the others, and sneak out into the sweet outdoors and start out in the canoe, keeping close along the shore in the long shadows of the pines. I remembered being very careful never to rub my paddle against the gunwale for fear of disturbing the stillness of the cathedral.

GO ON TO THE NEXT PAGE.

1. We know that this passage is from an informal essay because it

   (1) is very serious and dignified
   (2) reads like a scientific report
   (3) deals with abstract principles
   (4) has an easy-going, chatty style
   (5) takes a cool, impersonal tone

2. The author decided to return to the lake in order to

   (1) visit his elderly father
   (2) enjoy some salt-water fishing
   (3) visit the cathedral there
   (4) teach his son canoeing
   (5) re-experience its peacefulness

3. Before going to the lake, the author was afraid "the tarred road would have found it out" (line 21). By this he means he feared that

   (1) the road would no longer be there
   (2) the dirt road would have become a highway
   (3) a tar factory would have been started there
   (4) there would have been little change there
   (5) there would be a shopping mall there

4. Which of the following details was *not* part of the author's memories of the lakeside camp?

   (1) fishing for bass
   (2) going bareback riding
   (3) the scent of the pine woods
   (4) the stillness of the lake
   (5) getting up very early

5. By "incessant wind" (line 10), the author means that the wind

   (1) never stopped blowing
   (2) was just a slight breeze
   (3) brought thunderstorms
   (4) blew in gale-force gusts
   (5) could not be counted on

6. What the author does not state directly, but implies, is his

   (1) almost religious feeling about nature
   (2) disapproval of all signs of "progress"
   (3) longing to recapture the joys of youth
   (4) disillusionment with vacations by the sea
   (5) passion for fresh-water fishing

Check your answers to the GED Mini-Test on page 197.

Answers and Explanations

Practice   *pp. 193–194*

1. **Answer:** (4)   Though the author's interest in the moth includes pity and curiosity, it is mainly a feeling of wonder (lines 15–17). There is no evidence of annoyance or amusement.

2. **Answer:** (3)   The author's statement that being a day moth appeared "a hard fate" (line 8) supports the idea that the moth's life is only one day long. There is no evidence for choices (1) and (2) or (4) and (5).

3. **Answer:** (4)   Though the author does refer to our being "blown up," and does say that mankind will prevail and that our souls make us immortal, the main thrust of his argument is that writers must write about universal truths (lines 5–7, 10–14 and 27–30).

4. **Answer:** (3)   Several times the author speaks of his concern regarding the effect of fear on writers. There is no evidence for choices (1) and (2) or (4) and (5).

GED Mini-Test   *pp. 195–196*

1. **Answer:** (4)   The author's chatty, conversational style is typical of an informal essay. There is no evidence for choices (1) to (3) or choice (5).

2. **Answer:** (5)   In lines 9–12 the author states his reason for going back to the lake. Though he might also wish to teach his son canoeing, choice (4), that is not his main reason. There is no evidence for choices (1) to (3).

3. **Answer:** (2)   In this case "found it out" means "found its way there." There is no evidence in the passage for choices (1) or (3) to (5).

4. **Answer:** (2)   This is correct because there is no mention of riding of any kind. All the other details are mentioned.

5. **Answer:** (1)   "Incessant" means constant.

6. **Answer:** (3)   In line 15 the author refers to revisiting old haunts. In lines 17–34 he reviews memories obviously dear to him and wonders wistfully if things will still be the same. His fear that things may have changed suggests how much he wants to recapture his youth. There is some evidence for each of the other answers, but only choice (3) expresses the main implication.

25 Poetry

Of all the different forms of writing, **poetry** is the most compressed and imaginative. To express thoughts and feelings powerfully in a limited space, poets make use of rhythm, rhyme and vivid language. Like other writers they also make use of implications and supportive details to tell stories and put across main ideas.

Read the following poem by Archibald MacLeish. As you read, look for its main idea. Use the Purpose Question to help you.

WHAT SHOULD A POEM DO?

Ars Poetica

A poem should be palpable and mute
As a globed fruit

Dumb
As old medallions to the thumb

(5)　Silent as the sleeve-worn stone
Of casement ledges where the moss has grown—

A poem should be wordless
As the flight of birds

A poem should be motionless in time
(10)　As the moon climbs

Leaving, as the moon releases
Twig by twig the night-entangled trees,

Leaving, as the moon behind the winter leaves
Memory by memory the mind—

(15)　A poem should be motionless in time
As the moon climbs

A poem should be equal to:
Not true

For all the history of grief
(20)　An empty doorway and a maple leaf

For love
The leaning grasses and two lights above the sea—

A poem should not mean
But be.

Identify Figurative Language

This skill involves learning how to recognize figurative language and to understand the effect it creates. Good figurative language has several important characteristics—it makes a point by being forceful and brief, and it has a sense of newness about it.

Sometimes the very qualities that make a poem powerful—its density and its images—can make it seem hard to understand at first. Why can the poet not just come right out and say what she or he means? Why is **figurative language,** words or phrases that "paint a picture," used? In the poem you have just read, the poet *does* come right out and say what he means, but not until the end: "A poem should not mean/But be." By the time you read that, the poet has already given you several examples of what he means, in the form of seven images, or word-pictures. Each of the scenes and objects he describes is *mute*—without speech to explain itself. Yet each has the power to move us by its mere existence. From this we can conclude—as the poet states at the end—that he would rather have us be directly moved by poetry than go looking for its meanings.

It may help if you remember to read a poem slowly. Pause to let the poet's images take shape in your mind. Note the way the poet uses images to make implications and to provide details that support the main idea.

Examples

DIRECTIONS: Use the information on this page and the poem by Archibald MacLeish on the preceding page to choose the one best answer for each item below.

1. According to the poet, a poem should pass through the reader's mind like

   (1) a flock of birds in the sky
   (2) old medals through fingers
   (3) a sleeve through a window
   (4) leaves falling in winter
   (5) the moon behind a tree

Answer: (5) Though birds, medals, sleeves and leaves are all mentioned, the image used to describe the ideal poem is of the moon behind a tree in winter (lines 9–16).

2. If there were one more image at the end of the poem, beginning with "For hope," it might read

   (1) "a child's favorite toy"
   (2) "a speeding train"
   (3) "an open grave"
   (4) "a newly planted field"
   (5) "a highly polished table"

Answer: (4) Like the two preceding images, this one would have to represent an emotion. "Hope" is best represented by a form of new life—"a newly planted field."

Practice

HINT

When reading a poem, remember to take your time and let the poem's word-pictures build up in your mind.

DIRECTIONS: Choose the <u>one</u> best answer for each item below.

Items 1–4 refer to the following poem by Emily Dickinson.

WHY DOES THIS ANIMAL EVOKE STRONG REACTIONS?

The Snake

A narrow fellow in the grass
Occasionally rides;
You may have met him,—did you not?
His notice sudden is.

(5) The grass divides as with a comb,
A spotted shaft is seen;
And then it closes at your feet
And opens further on.

He likes a boggy acre,
(10) A floor too cool for corn.
Yet when a child, and barefoot,
I more than once, at morn,

Have passed, I thought, a whip-lash
Unbraiding in the sun,—
(15) When, stooping to secure it,
It wrinkled and was gone.

Several of nature's people
I know, and they know me;
I feel for them a transport
(20) Of cordiality;

But never met this fellow,
Attended or alone,
Without a tighter breathing,
And zero at the bone.

1. The *main* reason the poet uses a series of unusual images in the poem is to

   (1) make the idea of a snake more appealing
   (2) describe experiences of her childhood
   (3) share her special way of viewing snakes
   (4) practice creating word-pictures
   (5) refute popular beliefs about snakes

2. Which of these images does the poet use in the poem?

   (1) a mine-shaft
   (2) a wrinkled face
   (3) a cool barn floor
   (4) a braided whip
   (5) a barefoot child

3. By "several of nature's people" the poet means

   (1) poets who write about nature
   (2) scientists who study nature
   (3) neighborhood farmers
   (4) naturally good people
   (5) other types of animals

4. The phrases "zero at the bone" describes which of the following?

   (1) amusement and delight
   (2) fear and alarm
   (3) awe and wonder
   (4) scientific curiosity
   (5) relief and thankfulness

GO ON TO THE NEXT PAGE.

WHAT IS THE POET ASKING HIS FATHER TO DO?

Do Not Go Gentle into That Good Night

Do not go gentle into that good night
Old age should burn and rave at close of day;
Rage, rage, against the dying of the light.

(5) Though wise men at their end know dark is right,
Because their words had forked no lightning they
Do not go gentle into that good night.

Good men, the last wave by, crying how bright
Their frail deeds might have danced in a green bay,
Rage, rage, against the dying of the light.

(10) Grave men, near death, who see with blinding sight
Blind eyes could blaze like meteors and be gay,
Rage, rage, against the dying of the light.

And you, my father, there on the sad height,
Curse, bless, me now with your fierce tears, I pray.
(15) Do not go gentle into that good night.
Rage, rage, against the dying of the light.

---

5. The poet is asking his father to

(1) get angry at him
(2) be brave as he goes blind
(3) accept what fate has in store
(4) allow himself to cry
(5) fight the onset of death

6. Which of the following emotions does the poem convey *most* strongly?

(1) pity
(2) love
(3) fury
(4) contempt
(5) admiration

7. The phrase "their words had forked no lightning" (line 5) means that

(1) nothing had come of what they said or wrote
(2) no one had listened to them
(3) they had had nothing new to say to the world
(4) they had failed to address the real issues of the day
(5) they had preferred to keep silent about what they knew

8. Which of the following types of men does the poet *not* hold up as an example to his father?

(1) men who have gained wisdom
(2) men who have done good deeds
(3) men who have gone blind
(4) men in the prime of life
(5) men at the end of life

Before you take the GED Mini-Test,
check your answers on pages 203–204.

GED Mini-Test

25

TIP Do not panic just because you are reading poetry. Pay attention to details as you would in a story you were overhearing.

DIRECTIONS: Choose the one best answer for each item below.

Items 1–6 refer to the following poem by Ezra Pound.

HOW DOES THIS YOUNG WIFE IN CHINA FEEL?

The River-Merchant's Wife: A Letter

While my hair was still cut straight across my forehead
I played about the front gate, pulling flowers.
You came by on bamboo stilts, playing horse,
You walked about my seat, playing with blue plums.
(5) And we went on living in the village of Chokan:
Two small people, without dislike or suspicion.

At fourteen I married My Lord you.
I never laughed, being bashful.
Lowering my head, I looked at the wall.
(10) Called to, a thousand times, I never looked back.

At fifteen I stopped scowling.
I desired my dust to be mingled with yours
Forever and forever and forever.
Why should I climb the look out?

(15) At sixteen you departed,
You went into far Ku-to-yen, by the river of swirling eddies,
And you have been gone five months.
The monkeys make sorrowful noise overhead.

You dragged your feet when you went out.
(20) By the gate now, the moss is grown, the different mosses,
Too deep to clear them away!
The leaves fall early this autumn, in wind.

The paired butterflies are already yellow with August
Over the grass in the West garden;
(25) They hurt me. I grow older.
If you are coming down through the narrows of the river Kiang,
Please let me know beforehand,
And I will come out to meet you
          As far as Cho-fu-Sa.

(by Rihaku)

1. The couple in the poem knew each other as children. They were

    (1) schoolmates
    (2) enemies
    (3) sweethearts
    (4) rivals
    (5) playmates

2. The overall mood created by the poem is one of

    (1) wistful longing
    (2) passionate love
    (3) quiet despair
    (4) businesslike restraint
    (5) suppressed anxiety

GO ON TO THE NEXT PAGE.

3. By saying "Why should I climb the look out?" (line 14) the girl means

    (1) "It is hopeless for me to try to escape."
    (2) "Being happy, why should I look elsewhere?"
    (3) "My husband is not coming home, so why look for him?"
    (4) "My life is over. Why torture myself by looking outside?"
    (5) "Why should I have to man the watchtower?"

5. The falling leaves and pairs of yellowing butterflies "hurt" the girl because they remind her that

    (1) winter is on its way
    (2) her husband may be in danger
    (3) her happy childhood is over
    (4) life is short and she is alone
    (5) she has no children

4. The gathering moss at the front gate suggests that

    (1) the girl is actually dead and speaking from the grave
    (2) the husband has abandoned his young wife
    (3) the girl is a prisoner in her own home
    (4) the servants refuse to work in the husband's absence
    (5) the woman is leading a lonely and isolated life

6. How did the couple's youthful marriage come about?

    (1) They fell in love with each other at age fourteen.
    (2) The girl was already her husband's servant.
    (3) The marriage was arranged by their families.
    (4) A local ruler commanded that they get married.
    (5) They had to marry because the girl was pregnant.

Check your answers to the GED Mini-Test on page 204.

Answers and Explanations

Practice *pp. 200–201*

1. **Answer:** (3) The poet's chief aim is to share her own ways of seeing with the reader. She has no interest in making snakes more appealing or in refuting others beliefs, choices (1) and (5). She mentions a childhood experience, choice (2); and clearly enjoys creating word-pictures, choice (4); but these are not her *main* reasons.

3. **Answer:** (5) Since the poet has referred to the snake in human terms (as a "fellow"), we can assume that when she speaks of "several of nature's people," she is again referring to animals, rather than actual people.

5. **Answer:** (5) Though tears and blindness are mentioned in the poem, and though the poet does ask his father to curse as well as bless him, the main point of the poem is that his father should struggle against dying, rather than merely accept it.

2. **Answer:** (4) A barn floor and a barefoot child are mentioned, but not used as images. The "shaft" in the poem is a rod, not a mine-opening. The word "wrinkled" appears, but not with the word "face." In lines 13–14, the snake is compared to a "whip-lash unbraiding."

4. **Answer:** (2) The phrase "a tighter breathing" in line 23—and the fact that the poem is about a snake—tell us that "zero at the bone" describes a feeling of fear and alarm.

6. **Answer:** (2) If the poet did not love his father so much, he would not be begging him to fight so hard against death.

7. Answer: (1)   The phrase "their words had forked into lightning" suggests that, although the wise men had had something important to say, their words had not had much effect on the world.

8. Answer: (4)   The poet uses wise, good, blinded and dying men as examples of people who have fought against the onset of death.

GED Mini-Test   *pp. 202–203*

1. Answer: (5)   Lines 2–6 describe their happy, friendly relationship as childhood playmates. School is not mentioned, so choice (1) is incorrect. They were evidently neither enemies, choice (2), nor rivals, choice (4), as they played happily together. Nor were they sweethearts, choice (3).

2. Answer: (1)   The letter, while expressing her love, is neither passionate, despairing nor anxious; it is obviously not businesslike. Its references to their past happiness and to the passing season give it a sense of wistful longing.

3. Answer: (2)   Lines 11–13 tell us that at fifteen the girl fell in love with her husband. Her evident happiness with him rules out choices (1), (4) and (5). There is no evidence for choice (3).

4. Answer: (5)   The gathering moss at the gate suggests that, in her husband's absence, the girl neither goes out nor receives visitors; she is, therefore, very isolated and lonely. There is no evidence for choices (1), (2), (3) or (4) in the poem.

5. Answer: (4)   There is no evidence to suggest that she is worried about her husband's safety or about not having children. She does not seem to miss her childhood. The fact that the butterflies are in pairs and the season is passing remind her that life is short and her husband is away.

6. Answer: (3)   There is no evidence that she was his servant or that she was pregnant. A ruler's command would be too dramatic to leave unmentioned. We do know that they were not in love when they married, yet accepted the situation. We conclude that the marriage was arranged by their families.

26 Poetry

Poetry is concerned with emotions and feelings. A poet expresses these feelings in a limited space.

When we speak of the **mood** of a poem, we are talking about the feelings the poet seeks to express. To convey different states of emotion, poets make creative use of imagery, rhythm and word sounds.

Read the following poem by Elinor Wylie. As you read ask yourself what feeling, or mood, the poet is seeking to express. Use the Purpose Question above the poem to help you.

DOES THIS REMIND YOU OF A WINTER DAY?

Velvet Shoes

Let us walk in the white snow
   In a soundless space;
With footsteps quiet and slow,
   At a tranquil pace,
(5)   Under veils of white lace.

I shall go shod in silk,
   And you in wool,
White as a white cow's milk,
   More beautiful
(10)   Than the breast of a gull.

We shall walk through the still town
   In a windless peace;
We shall step upon white down,
   Upon silver fleece,
(15)   Upon softer than these.

We shall walk in velvet shoes:
   Wherever we go
Silence will fall like dews
   On white silence below.
(20)   We shall walk in the snow.

Identify Techniques (Mood)

This skill involves identifying the mood of a poem and the technique used by the poet to create that mood.

A poem gives creative shape to the poet's inner thoughts and feelings, and serves as a means to share them with others. If a poem is successful, it will touch a responsive chord in you—perhaps by reminding you of similar feelings you have had, or simply by creating a convincing **mood,** or atmosphere.

The poet's most effective tool in creating mood is **imagery**—word-pictures that bring a scene vividly to life. "Velvet Shoes" is about a walk in the snow. Each of the poem's images helps to share that experience with us by appealing to our senses of sight, touch and sound.

Other important elements in creating mood are **word sounds** and **rhythm.** Closely related, they convey emotion in much the same way that the notes and rhythm of a piece of music do.

To become more aware of a poem's rhythm and word sounds:
Read it aloud quietly. Do the lines hurry along breathlessly, or do they make you pause as you read them? Are there many words containing short vowel sounds—words like giggle, tickle, funny, whistle? Or are there many words that make you slow down as you pronounce them—words like moan, cold, sad, sighing?
Trust your own responses. Sometimes a poem's mood comes across more clearly than its meaning—especially on first reading.

Examples

DIRECTIONS: Choose the <u>one</u> best answer for each item below.

1. The mood expressed in the poem is one of

   (1) creeping terror
   (2) deep depression
   (3) repressed anxiety
   (4) wild jubilation
   (5) quiet delight

Answer: (5) The underlying emotion in the poem is pleasure; the poet is expressing her sense of hushed delight in the new-fallen snow.

2. All the images used in the poem share a common theme. It is

   (1) deafness and blindness
   (2) the innocence of animals
   (3) softness, whiteness, silence
   (4) the first signs of winter
   (5) the feel of various textures

Answer: (3) The poem's images are all designed to underscore the snow's essential softness and whiteness, as well as the silence it creates.

Practice

HINT ▷ Read a poem aloud quietly to discover its mood. Listen to the kind of "music" it makes— its rhythm and word sounds. Review the images in the poem to help you identify the mood.

DIRECTIONS: Choose the <u>one</u> best answer for each item below.

Items 1–4 refer to the following poem by Alfred, Lord Tennyson.

WHAT HAS HAPPENED TO MAKE THE POET FEEL THIS WAY?

Break, Break, Break

Break, break, break,
 On thy cold gray stones, O Sea!
And I would that my tongue could utter
 The thoughts that arise in me.

(5) O well for the fisherman's boy,
 That he shouts with his sister at play!
O well for the sailor lad,
 That he sings in his boat on the bay!

And the stately ships go on
(10) To their haven under the hill;
But O for the touch of a vanished hand,
 And the sound of a voice that is still!

Break, break, break,
 At the foot of thy crags, O Sea!
(15) But the tender grace of a day that is dead
 Will never come back to me.

1. Music for this poem should be

 (1) soft and romantic
 (2) fast and joyful
 (3) slow and triumphant
 (4) sad and mournful
 (5) harsh and discordant

2. The poet is longing for

 (1) the days of his childhood
 (2) his youth as a fisherman
 (3) his home by the sea
 (4) his lost skills as a writer
 (5) a loved one who has died

3. The words "cold gray stones" suggest

 (1) angry frustration
 (2) hopeless sadness
 (3) a kinship with nature
 (4) a mind in trouble
 (5) gentle resignation

4. The boy and girl and the sailor

 (1) remind the poet of life's joys
 (2) remind the poet of his boyhood
 (3) are a contrast to the poet's sorrow
 (4) are like the poet's sad story
 (5) are a frustrating distraction

GO ON TO THE NEXT PAGE.

Items 5–8 refer to the following poem by Theodore Roethke.

WAS THE POET'S CHILDHOOD A HAPPY ONE?

My Papa's Waltz

The whiskey on your breath
Could make a small boy dizzy;
But I hung on like death:
Such waltzing was not easy.

(5) We romped until the pans
Slid from the kitchen shelf;
My mother's countenance
Could not unfrown itself.

The hand that held my wrist
(10) Was battered on one knuckle;
At every step you missed
My right ear scraped a buckle.

You beat time on my head
With a palm caked hard by dirt,
(15) Then waltzed me off to bed
Still clinging to your shirt.

5. When read aloud, the rhythm of this poem is

(1) smooth and gliding
(2) sad and slow
(3) gentle and dreamy
(4) sweeping and exalted
(5) abrupt and jerky

6. The scene depicted in the poem

(1) illustrates how not to bring up a child
(2) describes a bittersweet childhood memory
(3) generates a happy mood of nostalgia
(4) contains nothing "poetic" enough to merit a poem
(5) is the poet's way of getting back at his parents

7. The father danced with the boy

(1) when he was drunk
(2) to celebrate a new job
(3) after a fight with his wife
(4) to annoy the neighbors
(5) after an accident at work

8. The poem shows

(1) why the poet is now so angry at his father
(2) how much of a problem the father really was
(3) how much the boy loved his father
(4) how unhappy the boy's mother was
(5) how amusing the poet now finds his father's behavior

Before you take the GED Mini-Test, check your answers on pages 210–211.

GED Mini-Test

26

TIP

When reading poetry on the GED exam, relax. Trust your first response to the mood of the poem. Then go back to confirm your reaction with supportive details.

DIRECTIONS: Choose the <u>one</u> best answer for each item below.

Items 1–6 refer to the following lines from a poem by Edgar Allan Poe.

HAVE YOU EVER HEARD BELLS THAT SOUND LIKE THIS?

The Bells, Stanza III

Hear the loud alarum bells—
Brazen bells!
What a tale of terror, now, their turbulency tells!
In the startled ear of night
(5)   How they scream out their affright!
Too much horrified to speak,
They can only shriek, shriek,
Out of tune,
In a clamorous appealing to the mercy of the fire,
(10)   In a mad expostulation with the deaf and frantic fire,
Leaping higher, higher, higher,
With a desperate desire,
And a resolute endeavor
Now—now to sit, or never,
(15)   By the side of the pale-faced moon.
Oh, the bells, bells, bells!
What a tale their terror tells
Of despair!
How they clang, and clash, and roar!
(20)   What a horror they outpour
On the bosom of the palpitating air!
Yet the ear it fully knows
By the twanging,
And the clanging,
(25)   How the danger ebbs and flows;
Yet the ear distinctly tells,
In the jangling,
And the wrangling,
How the danger sinks and swells,
(30)   By the sinking and the swelling in the anger of the bells—
Of the bells—
Of the bells, bells, bells, bells,
Bells, bells, bells—
In the clamor and the clangor of the bells!

GO ON TO THE NEXT PAGE.

1. These lines convey a mood of

    (1) giddy happiness
    (2) peaceful harmony
    (3) mournful sadness
    (4) vengeful triumph
    (5) desperate alarm

2. The bells are ringing this way because

    (1) a madman is in the belfry
    (2) the rector has been fired
    (3) a victory has been won
    (4) there is a fire somewhere
    (5) the town is under attack

3. The emotions described in the poem are

    (1) the poet's fear of all bells
    (2) what most people feel when the bells ring this way
    (3) actually a description of insanity
    (4) a figment of the poet's overactive imagination
    (5) more amusing than alarming

4. The rhythm of the poem would also be appropriate for a poem about

    (1) a sailboat
    (2) grazing sheep
    (3) a train locomotive
    (4) a school library
    (5) a sleeping baby

5. The words twanging, clanging, jangling, wrangling, clash and roar are effective because they

    (1) imitate the bells' sounds
    (2) rhyme with each other
    (3) are easy to understand
    (4) express the poem's mood
    (5) have a gentle sound

6. On which of the following occasions might some kind of bells *not* be rung?

    (1) a wedding
    (2) a funeral
    (3) an important victory
    (4) a chess tournament
    (5) a Sunday

Check your answers to the GED Mini-Test on page 211.

Answers and Explanations

Practice   *pp. 207–208*

1. **Answer:** (4)   Since the mood of the poem is one of mournful sadness, music that is romantic, joyful, triumphant or harsh would be inappropriate.

2. **Answer:** (5)   Though the poet mentions a boy and girl, a sailor and the sea, it is clear from lines 11–12 that he has lost someone he loved. There is no evidence for choice (3) or choice (4) in the poem.

3. **Answer:** (2)   The long-drawn-out "o" sounds of these words, plus the bleak image they conjure up, suggest hopeless sadness. There is scant evidence for choices (1), (3), (4) or (5) in the poem.

4. **Answer:** (3)   Though these sights and sounds may remind the poet of days gone by, and remind us that life holds pleasures, too, they mainly serve as a contrast to the poet's own sorrow. There is no evidence for choice (4) or choice (5) in the poem.

5. **Answer:** (5)   The rhythm of the poem has a driving, jerky beat, much like the motion of the drunken father as he "waltzed" his son around the kitchen. For this reason, music that was smooth, slow, gentle or exalted would be inappropriate.

6. **Answer:** (2)   The scene described—and the father in it—are both rough and loving, scary and tender. The combination makes for a memory that is both sweet and bitter. The mood is neither nostalgic nor critical, ruling out choices (1), (3) and (5). The poem shows that any subject is worthy of a poem.

7. Answer: (1)   We know from the first two lines that the father was drunk when he danced with his son. Whatever other reasons he may have had for dancing are neither stated nor implied.

8. Answer: (3)   Though the poem suggests that the father may have been a problem, and that the boy's mother may have been unhappy, there is no evidence that the poet now regards his father with anger or amusement. Rather, as the last line makes clear, the poem expresses the love that the boy felt for his father.

GED Mini-Test   *pp. 209–210*

1. Answer: (5)   Almost every line of the poem expresses frantic alarm. There is no evidence of sadness, peace, joy or triumph in the poem.

2. Answer: (4)   Lines 9–10 tell us that the occasion for the bells being rung is a fire. There is no evidence for choices (1), (2), (3) or (5) in the poem.

3. Answer: (2)   Sometimes, as in this case, a poem conveys emotions other than the poet's own private feelings. The poem is describing the effect that bells rung in this way have on everyone. There is no evidence for choice (3). The poet's imagination is indeed vivid, but persuasive; the poem is not funny; it conveys a sense of great alarm.

4. Answer: (3)   Read aloud, the poem's driving rhythm becomes clear. It would work as well in a poem about the sound of a train's wheels turning. It would be quite inappropriate for a poem about anything as peaceful as a sailboat, a library, sheep or a sleeping baby.

5. Answer: (1). Although several of these words rhyme, and all express the poem's mood and are easy to understand, the reason why they are effective is that they actually imitate the sounds made by the bells.

6. Answer: (4)   Obviously, bells are rung on Sundays, and sometimes also for weddings, funerals and important victories. It is fairly unlikely that bells would be rung in connection with a chess tournament.

27 Drama

Characterization is the means used by writers to tell us what their characters are like. In a play we learn about a character through that character's own words and actions, through other characters' reactions to him or her and through the stage directions, which describe the character's appearance, gestures and actions.

Read the following excerpt from a play by Lorraine Hansberry. As you read watch for the characterization of Walter. Use the Purpose Question to help you.

IS THIS MAN ACTING LIKE AN ADULT?

WALTER: I'm going out!

RUTH: Where?

WALTER: Just out of this house somewhere—

RUTH: (*Getting her coat*) I'll come too.

(5) WALTER: I don't want you to come!

RUTH: I got something to talk to you about, Walter.

WALTER: That's too bad.

MAMA: (*Still quietly*) Walter Lee— (*She waits and he finally turns and looks at her*) Sit down.

(10) WALTER: I'm a grown man, Mama.

MAMA: Ain't nobody said you wasn't grown. But you still in my house and my presence. And as long as you are—you'll talk to your wife civil. Now sit down.

RUTH: (*Suddenly*) Oh, let him go on out and drink himself to

(15) death! He makes me sick to my stomach! (*She flings her coat against him*)

WALTER: (*Violently*) And you turn mine too, baby! (RUTH *goes into their bedroom and slams the door behind her*) That was my greatest mistake—

(20) MAMA: (*Still quietly*) Walter, what is the matter with you?

WALTER: Matter with me? Ain't nothing the matter with *me*!

MAMA: Yes there is. Something eating you up like a crazy man. Something more than me not giving you this money. The past few years I been watching it happen to you. You get all nervous act-

(25) ing and kind of wild in the eyes— (WALTER *jumps up impatiently at her words*) I said sit there now, I'm talking to you!

WALTER: Mama—I don't need no nagging at me today.

MAMA: Seem like you getting to a place where you always tied up in some kind of knot about something. But if anybody ask you

(30) 'bout it you just yell at 'em and bust out the house and go out and drink somewheres. Walter Lee, people can't live with that. . . .

Identify Techniques (Characterization)

This skill involves recognizing the ways in which we learn about characters and drawing conclusions about them.

We get to know the characters in a play as we get to know people in real life—through their own words and actions, which is known as **characterization**. What they themselves actually say and do tells us a lot about how they feel about themselves.

We also learn about them through the words and actions of other characters. How the different characters in a play feel about each other, talk about each other and respond to each other reveal almost as much about them as their own words and actions do.

Stage directions also help. They are usually printed in italics throughout the play and often provide important clues about the characters' inner selves by describing their appearance, gestures and actions. For example: (WALTER *jumps up impatiently at her words*) (lines 25–26) on the preceding page, tells you his actions. You know he is angry and upset.

We learn about Walter in two ways:

Directly, *through his mother's description of his behavior.*
Indirectly, *through his words and the stage directions.*

Ask yourself how you would play Walter. Then go back and look for clues in *all* the characters' speeches that help you determine what kind of person he is.

Examples

DIRECTIONS: Choose the <u>one</u> best answer for each item below.

1. As portrayed in this scene, Walter is

    (1) cagey and secretive
    (2) criminally insane
    (3) lazy and cowardly
    (4) angry and defensive
    (5) depressed and withdrawn

Answer: (4) Walter's anger shows in the way he treats his wife and his defensiveness in his response to his mother.

2. Walter's mother comes across as

    (1) patient and long-suffering
    (2) hard and domineering
    (3) passive and easygoing
    (4) whiney and complaining
    (5) strong and caring

Answer: (5) Mama's concern for her son and his wife comes through in the strong stand she takes about his behavior.

Practice

H
I
N
T

Remember that characterization is the way writers tell us what their characters are like. After reading a passage from a play, ask yourself how you would play the different characters. Look for the clues, perhaps words in parentheses, that tell you about the characters.

DIRECTIONS: Choose the <u>one</u> best answer for each item below.

Items 1–2 refer to the following excerpt from a play by Tennessee Williams.

IS AMANDA REALLY CONCERNED ABOUT HER DAUGHTER'S FEELINGS?

AMANDA: I thought that you were an adult; it seems that I was mistaken. (*She crosses slowly to the sofa and sinks down and stares at* LAURA.)

LAURA: Please don't stare at me, Mother.

(5) (AMANDA *closes her eyes and lowers her head. Count ten.*)

AMANDA: What are we going to do, what is going to become of us, what is the future?

LAURA: Has something happened, Mother? (AMANDA *draws a long breath and takes out the handkerchief again. Dabbing process.*)

(10) Mother, has—something happened?

AMANDA: I'll be all right in a minute, I'm just bewildered— (*Count five.*)—by life. . . .

LAURA: Mother, I wish that you would tell me what's happened!

AMANDA: As you know, I was supposed to be inducted into my

(15) office at the D.A.R.* this afternoon. But I stopped off at Rubicam's business college to speak to your teachers about your having a cold and ask them what progress they thought you were making down there.

LAURA: Oh. . . .

(20) AMANDA: I went to the typing instructor and introduced myself as your mother. She didn't know who you were. "Wingfield," she said. "We don't have any such student enrolled at the school!"

I assured her she did, that you had been going to classes since early in January.

(25) "I wonder," she said, "if you could be talking about that terribly shy little girl who dropped out of school after only a few days' attendance?" . . .

*Daughters of the American Revolution: Patriotic society

GO ON TO THE NEXT PAGE.

1. The typing instructor has told Amanda that Laura dropped out of school. Laura *most* probably did it

(1) to embarrass her mother
(2) because she really is shy
(3) because she loves school
(4) to go dancing instead
(5) to make Amanda angry

2. If Amanda were a schoolteacher, she would *most* probably excel at

(1) coaching slow students
(2) training cheerleaders
(3) punishing troublemakers
(4) teaching mathematics
(5) running the library

Items 3–4 refer to the following excerpt from a play by Henrik Ibsen.

WHAT HAS NORA DONE FOR HER HUSBAND?

MRS. LINDE: Well, a wife can't borrow without her husband's consent.
NORA: (*tossing her head*) Ah, but when it happens to be a wife with a bit of a sense of business . . . a wife who knows her way
(5) about things, then. . . .
MRS. LINDE: But, Nora, I just don't understand. . . .
NORA: You don't have to. I haven't said I did borrow the money. I might have got it some other way. (*Throws herself back on the sofa.*) I might even have got it from some admirer. Anyone as
(10) reasonably attractive as I am. . . .
MRS. LINDE: Don't be so silly!
NORA: Now you must be dying of curiosity, Kristine.
MRS. LINDE: Listen to me now, Nora dear—you haven't done anything rash, have you?
(15) NORA: (*sitting up again*) Is it rash to save your husband's life?
MRS. LINDE: I think it was rash to do anything without telling him. . . .
NORA: But the whole point was that he mustn't know anything. Good heavens, can't you see! He wasn't even supposed to know
(20) how desperately ill he was. It was me the doctors came and told his life was in danger, that the only way to save him was to go South for a while. Do you think I didn't try talking him into it first? I began dropping hints about how nice it would be if I could be taken on a little trip abroad, like other young wives. I
(25) wept, I pleaded, I told him he ought to show some consideration for my condition, and let me have a bit of my own way. And then I suggested he might take out a loan. But at that he nearly lost his temper, Kristine. He said I was being frivolous, that it was his duty as a husband not to give in to all these whims and fancies of
(30) mine—as I do believe he called them. All right, I thought, somehow you've got to be saved. And it was then I found a way. . . .

3. From the speeches in this scene, Nora could be described as

(1) humble and obedient
(2) hysterical and panicky
(3) arrogant and evil
(4) resourceful and determined
(5) childish and impulsive

4. When Nora's husband called her "frivolous" (line 28), he meant she was

(1) the life of the party
(2) impractical
(3) scatterbrained
(4) hard to say "no" to
(5) flirtatious

Before you take the GED Mini-Test, check your answers on pages 217–218.

DIRECTIONS: Choose the one best answer for each item below.

Items 1–6 refer to the following excerpt from a play by Lillian Hellman.

CAN THIS CHILD BE TRUSTED?

MARY: I *did* pick the flowers near Conway's. You never believe me. You believe everybody but me. It's always like that. Everything I say you fuss at me about. Everything I do is wrong.

KAREN: You know that isn't true. (*Goes to* MARY, *puts her arm around*
(5) *her, waits until the sobbing has stopped*) Look, Mary, look at me. (*Raises* MARY's *face with her hand*) Let's try to understand each other. If you feel that you *have* to take a walk, or that you just *can't* come to class, or that you'd like to go into the village by yourself, come and tell me—I'll try to understand. I don't say that I'll always agree that you should do exactly
(10) what you want to do, but I've had feelings like that, too—everybody has—and I won't be unreasonable about yours. But this way, this kind of lying you do, makes everything wrong.

MARY: (*looking steadily at* KAREN) I got the flowers near Conway's cornfield.

(15) KAREN: (*looks at* MARY, *sighs, moves back toward desk and stands there for a moment*) Well, there doesn't seem to be any other way with you; you'll have to be punished. Take your recreation periods alone for the next two weeks. No horseback riding and no hockey. Don't leave the school grounds for any reason whatsoever. Is that clear?

(20) MARY: (*carefully*) Saturday, too?

KAREN: Yes.

MARY: But you said I could go to the boat races.

KAREN: I'm sorry, but you can't go.

MARY: I'll tell my grandmother. I'll tell her how everybody treats me
(25) here and the way I get punished for every little thing I do. I'll tell her. I'll—

MRS. MORTAR: Why, I'd slap her hands!

KAREN: (*turning back from door, ignoring* MRS. MORTAR's *speech. To* MARY) Go upstairs, Mary.

(30) MARY: I don't feel well.

KAREN: (*wearily*) Go upstairs now.

MARY: I've got a pain. I've had it all morning. It hurts right here. (*Pointing vaguely in the direction of her heart*) Really it does.

KAREN: Ask Miss Dobie to give you some hot water and bicarbonate of
(35) soda.

MARY: It's a bad pain. I've never had it before. My heart! It's my heart! It's stopped or something. I can't breathe.

GO ON TO THE NEXT PAGE.

1. Which of the following phrases *best* describes Karen?

   (1) prim and proper
   (2) harsh and demanding
   (3) kindly and forgiving
   (4) reasonable and firm
   (5) easily intimidated

2. Which of the following phrases *best* describes Mary?

   (1) lonely and misunderstood
   (2) pathetic and victimized
   (3) friendly and open
   (4) slow witted and dull
   (5) sneaky and uncooperative

3. Which of the following is Mary *most* capable of?

   (1) admitting mistakes
   (2) helping others
   (3) getting her own way
   (4) accepting punishment
   (5) obeying orders

4. The passage creates a sense of

   (1) harmony
   (2) suspense
   (3) conflict
   (4) sorrow
   (5) amusement

5. Karen, as the teacher, is responsible for Mary. This fact

   (1) makes it easy for Karen to control Mary's behavior
   (2) explains why Mary is being so difficult
   (3) makes the whole conflict of wills unnecessary
   (4) makes it easy for Mary to manipulate Karen's responses
   (5) makes Karen's job seem carefree and appealing

6. Given what we know about Mary, we can anticipate that later in the play she will

   (1) experience a change of heart
   (2) take revenge on Karen
   (3) become class president
   (4) become an honors student
   (5) become best friends with Karen

Check your answers to the GED Mini-Test on page 218.

Answers and Explanations

Practice   *pp. 214–215*

1. **Answer:** (2) A painful scene like this one is clearly not what Laura had in mind; her timidity in this scene makes it unlikely that she would have quit to do something as social as dancing. If she loved school, she would not have quit; therefore, she probably left because of shyness.

2. **Answer:** (3) Amanda's clear enjoyment of the role of punishing mother makes it unlikely that she would enjoy anything so helpful and positive as coaching slow learners or training cheerleaders. Her pleasure in playing a part makes it unlikely that she would enjoy a relatively quiet job teaching math or running a library.

3. **Answer:** (4) While Nora may have an impulsive streak, she is clearly not humble and obedient, hysterical or evil.

4. **Answer:** (2) When Nora's husband called her frivolous, he meant that she was being silly and impractical. There is no evidence for choices (1) or (3) to (5).

GED Mini-Test *pp. 216–217*

1. **Answer:** (4) Karen does her best to reason with Mary, but she is also firm with her. She is neither prim nor harsh, easily intimidated nor overly forgiving, toward the girl.

2. **Answer:** (5) Mary's tears and tantrums, threats and steady refusal to tell the truth tell us that she is manipulative and uncooperative. She may be lonely and misunderstood as well, choice (1), but those are not her chief traits. There is no evidence for choices (2), (3) or (4).

3. **Answer:** (3) Mary has proved that she can get her own way; she has also proved that she cannot accept punishment, obey orders or admit mistakes. There is no evidence that she would be good at helping others.

4. **Answer:** (3) The clash of wills between Mary and Karen makes this a scene full of conflict. There is no evidence for choices (1), (2), (4) or (5).

5. **Answer:** (4) Karen's responsibility for Mary makes her vulnerable to Mary's accusations and phony heart attack; Karen must ask herself if she is being unfair or unfeeling, at the same time that she is trying to discipline Mary. This makes the conflict between them both real and unavoidable.

6. **Answer:** (2) What we already know about Mary does not suggest the possibility of her changing very much. It is far more likely that Mary will find a way to get revenge on Karen.

28 Drama

When we speak of the **mood** of a play, we are talking about the emotional impact it has on the viewer or reader. In drama, mood is created by the characters' circumstances and by their response to those circumstances and to each other.

Read the following excerpt from a play by Carson McCullers. As you read ask yourself what the overall mood of the scene is. Use the Purpose Question to help you.

HAS BERENICE FORGOTTEN HOW SHE FELT WHEN HER HUSBAND DIED?

BERENICE: (*squaring her shoulders*) Now I am here to tell you I was happy. There was no human woman in all the world more happy than I was in them days. And that includes everybody. You listening to me, John Henry? It includes all the queens and mil-
(5) lionaires and first ladies of the land. And I mean it includes people of all color. You hear me, Frankie? No human woman in all the world was happier than Berenice Sadie Brown.

FRANKIE: The five years you were married to Ludie.

BERENICE: From that autumn morning when I first met him on the
(10) road in front of Campbell's Filling Station until the very night he died, November, the year 1933.

FRANKIE: The very year and the very month I was born.

BERENICE: The coldest November I ever seen. Every morning there was frost and puddles were crusted with ice. The sunshine was
(15) pale yellow like it is in winter time. Sounds carried far away, and I remember a hound dog that used to howl toward sundown. And everything I seen came to me as a kind of sign.

FRANKIE: I think it is a kind of sign I was born the same year and the same month he died.

(20) BERENICE: And it was a Thursday towards six o'clock. About this time of day. Only November. I remember I went to the passage and opened the front door. Dark was coming on; the old hound was howling far away. And I go back in the room and lay down on Ludie's bed. I lay myself down over Ludie with my arms
(25) spread out and my face on his face. And I pray that the Lord would contage my strength to him. And I ask the Lord to let it be anybody, but not let it be Ludie. And I lay there and pray for a long time. Until night.

JOHN HENRY: How? (*In a higher, wailing voice*) How, Berenice?

(30) BERENICE: That night he died. I tell you he died. Ludie! Ludie Freeman! Ludie Maxwell Freeman died! (*She hums.*)

Identify Effects of Techniques (Mood Shift)

This skill involves identifying the shifting mood of a play and recognizing the means by which mood is conveyed.

As in a real-life situation, the **mood** of a play can change from moment to moment and from scene to scene. The difference is that the mood of a real-life situation can go on changing, while the mood of a play builds to a climax and then ends as the curtain comes down. If the play is a comedy, whatever difficulties the characters have had will be resolved and the play will end on an upbeat note. If the play is a tragedy, the characters' problems and conflicts will overwhelm them and the play will end on a sad and serious note. Whether comedy or tragedy, however, the play will have undergone several major mood changes.

A playwright conveys this shifting mood in different ways:

Lighting, sets, sound effects and costumes can be used to signal and enhance a change of mood when a play is performed.

The stage directions may provide important clues to the mood when a play is read.

The most important force in changing and creating mood is the characters themselves.

In the scene you have just read, for example, notice how the mood changes from Berenice's first speech to her last. Pay special attention to the descriptive details she mentions about the day Ludie died. What mood do these details help create?

Examples

DIRECTIONS: Choose the one best answer for each item below.

1. The scene ends with a mood of

   (1) panic and hysteria
   (2) wistful nostalgia
   (3) hopeless despair
   (4) grief and mourning
   (5) angry protest

Answer: (4)   As Berenice recalls her love for her husband, and his death, the mood of the scene mounts to a climax of grief and mourning.

2. Which of these details does *not* contribute to the mood?

   (1) the meeting at Campbell's
   (2) the paleness of the sunshine
   (3) the coldness of the day
   (4) the howling of the dog
   (5) the onset of darkness

Answer: (1)   The mention of the filling station where Berenice met Ludie does not contribute to the mood; all the other details add to the mood of loss as a life ebbs away.

Practice

HINT

Remember that in drama, mood is created chiefly through the characters' speeches—what they say to and about each other. In some cases the stage directions may also help by describing the characters' facial expressions, gestures and actions.

DIRECTIONS: Choose the one best answer for each item below.

Items 1–2 refer to the following excerpt from a play by Oscar Wilde.

WHAT IS UNUSUAL ABOUT JACK WORTHING'S BEGINNINGS?

JACK: I have lost both my parents.
LADY BRACKNELL: To lose one parent, Mr. Worthing, may be regarded as a misfortune; to lose both looks like carelessness. Who was your father? He was evidently a man of some wealth.
(5) Was he born in what the Radical papers call the purple of commerce, or did he rise from the ranks of the aristocracy?
JACK: I am afraid I really don't know. The fact is, Lady Bracknell, I said I had lost my parents. It would be nearer the truth to say that my parents seem to have lost me. . . . I don't actually know
(10) who I am by birth. I was . . . well, I was found.
LADY BRACKNELL: Found!
JACK: The late Mr. Thomas Cardew, an old gentleman of a very charitable and kindly disposition, found me, and gave me the name of Worthing, because he happened to have a first-class
(15) ticket for Worthing in his pocket at the time. Worthing is a place in Sussex. It is a seaside resort.
LADY BRACKNELL: Where did the charitable gentleman who had a first-class ticket for this seaside resort find you?
JACK: (*Gravely.*) In a hand-bag.
(20) LADY BRACKNELL: A hand-bag?
JACK: (*Very seriously.*) Yes, Lady Bracknell. I was in a hand-bag—a somewhat large, black leather hand-bag, with handles to it—an ordinary hand-bag in fact.

1. The mood of this scene is

(1) dreamy and romantic
(2) pathetic and pitiful
(3) absurd and comical
(4) tense and suspenseful
(5) tragic and sorrowful

2. As characterized in this scene, Jack appears to be

(1) easily embarrassed
(2) sneaky and two-faced
(3) bored and sophisticated
(4) kind and saintly
(5) open and witty

GO ON TO THE NEXT PAGE.

Items 3–6 refer to the following excerpt from a play by Eugene O'Neill.

WHAT TROUBLE IS BREWING ABOARD CAPTAIN KEENEY'S SHIP?

KEENEY: (*Sharply*) Annie!

MRS. KEENEY: (*Dully*) Yes, David.

KEENEY: Me and Mr. Slocum has business to discuss—ship's business.

(5) MRS. KEENEY: Very well, David. (*She goes slowly out, rear, and leaves the door three-quarters shut behind her*)

KEENEY: Best not have her on deck if they's goin'·to be any trouble.

MATE: Yes, sir.

(10) KEENEY: And trouble they's goin' to be. I feel it in my bones. (*Takes a revolver from his coat pocket and examines it*) Got your'n?

MATE: Yes, sir.

KEENEY: Not that we'll have to use 'em—not if I know their breed

(15) of dog—jest to frighten 'em up a bit. (*Grimly.*) I ain't never been forced to use one yit; and trouble I've had by land and by sea s'long as I kin remember, and will have till my dyin' day, I reckon.

MATE: (*Hesitatingly*) Then you ain't goin'—to turn back?

KEENEY: Turn back? Mr. Slocum, did you ever hear o' me pointin'

(20) s'uth for home with only a measly four hundred barrel of ile in the hold?

MATE: (*Hastily*) No, sir—but the grub's gittin' low.

KEENEY: They's enough to last a long time yit, if they're careful with it; and they's plenty o' water.

(25) MATE: They say it's not fit to eat—what's left; and the two years they signed on fur is up today. They might make trouble for you in the courts when we git home.

KEENEY: Let them make what law trouble they kin! I've got to git the ile! . . .

3. The mood created in this scene is one of

(1) tension and danger
(2) serenity and calm
(3) sorrow and regret
(4) panic and hysteria
(5) rage and fury

4. Captain Keeney could be *best* described as

(1) sensitive and kind
(2) generous and open
(3) greedy and determined
(4) weak and indecisive
(5) cautious and suspicious

5. The "ile" (line 20) the captain speaks of is actually

(1) eels
(2) oil
(3) ale
(4) tiles
(5) sails

6. The trouble brewing aboard the captain's ship is

(1) starvation
(2) sickness
(3) court martial
(4) rebellion
(5) house arrest

Before you take the GED Mini-Test, check your answers on pages 224–225.

GED Mini-Test

28

DIRECTIONS: Choose the one best answer for each item below.

Items 1–6 refer to the following excerpt from a play by Anton Chekhov.

HOW DO THESE PEOPLE FEEL ABOUT LEAVING THEIR HOME?

ANYA: Good-bye, house! Good-bye, old life!

TROFIMOV: Hail to the new life! (*Goes out with* ANYA.)

(VARYA *looks around the room and slowly goes out.* YASHA *and* CHARLOTTA *with her dog go out.*)

(5) LOPAKHIN: And so, till spring. Come along, my friends. . . . Till we meet! (*Goes out.*)

(LYUBOV ANDREYEVNA *and* GAYEV *are left alone. As though they had been waiting for this, they fall onto each other's necks and break into quiet, restrained sobs, afraid of being heard.*)

(10) GAYEV: (*in despair*) My sister, my sister. . . .

LYUBOV ANDREYEVNA: Oh, my dear, sweet, lovely orchard! My life, my youth, my happiness, good-bye! . . . Good-bye!

ANYA'S VOICE: (*Gaily calling*) Mama!

TROFIMOV'S VOICE: (*Gay and excited*) Aa-oo!

(15) LYUBOV ANDREYEVNA: One last look at these walls, these windows. . . . Mother loved to walk about in this room. . . .

GAYEV: My sister, my sister!

ANYA'S VOICE: Mama!

TROFIMOV'S VOICE: Aa-oo!

(20) LYUBOV ANDREYEVNA: We're coming! (*They go out.*)

(*The stage is empty. There is the sound of doors being locked, then of the carriages driving away. It grows quiet. In the stillness there is the dull thud of an ax on a tree, a forlorn, melancholy sound. Footsteps are heard. From the door on the right* FIRS *appears. He is dressed as always*

(25) *in a jacket and white waistcoat, and wears slippers. He is ill.*)

FIRS: (*Goes to the door and tries the handle*) Locked. They have gone. . . . (*Sits down on the sofa.*) They've forgotten me. . . . Never mind . . . I'll sit here awhile. . . . I expect Leonid Andreich hasn't put on his fur coat and has gone off in his overcoat. (*Sighs anxiously.*) And I

(30) didn't see to it. . . . When they're young, they're green! (*Mumbles something which cannot be understood.*) I'll lie down awhile. . . . There's no strength left in you, nothing's left, nothing. . . . Ach, you . . . addlepate! (*Lies motionless.*)

(*A distant sound is heard that seems to come from the sky, the sound of*

(35) *a snapped string mournfully dying away. A stillness falls, and nothing is heard but the thud of the ax on a tree far away in the orchard.*)

GO ON TO THE NEXT PAGE.

1. The mood created in this scene is one of

    (1) gaiety and anticipation
    (2) sadness and regret
    (3) tension and anxiety
    (4) fear and horror
    (5) rage and hostility

2. The character called Firs is

    (1) a cousin of Gayev's
    (2) a timber merchant
    (3) an old family servant
    (4) Anya's father
    (5) a woodcutter

3. Gayev's sister feels that, in leaving the house, she is also saying goodbye to

    (1) a chance at riches
    (2) the sins of the past
    (3) painful memories
    (4) her youthful hopes
    (5) her unhappiness

4. When Firs says, "When they're young, they're green" (line 30) he is referring to

    (1) his young master
    (2) trees in the orchard
    (3) the new owners
    (4) young lovers
    (5) his own grandchildren

5. The sound of the ax in the orchard as the family leaves implies that

    (1) the family has been murdered
    (2) the property has been sold to land developers
    (3) the family has rented the orchard to tenant-farmers
    (4) the property is being taken over illegally
    (5) there is an attempt to stop a fire in the orchard

6. The stage directions call for "the sound of a snapped string mournfully dying away" (lines 34–35). This sound is meant to symbolize the

    (1) death of Firs
    (2) departure of the family
    (3) start of a tragic romance
    (4) greed of the developers
    (5) end of a way of life

Check your answers to the GED Mini-Test on page 225.

Answers and Explanations

Practice *pp. 221–222*

1. **Answer:** (3)   However sad it may be to have lost one's parents, being found in a hand-bag has its silly side. Nothing in the scene contributes to a dreamy, pathetic, tense or tragic mood.

2. **Answer:** (5)   Jack is very straightforward about his beginnings; he does not hide anything. There is no evidence in the passage for choices (1) to (4).

3. **Answer:** (1)   The mood in this scene is one of mounting tension and approaching danger. Keeney, by refusing to return home when his crew's two-year stint is up, is asking for trouble. There is no evidence for choices (2) to (5).

4. **Answer:** (3)   Keeney's determination to stay out until he gets what he came for—despite the rights of his crew and the state of the remaining food on board—marks him as a tough, greedy man. He is certainly not weak, kind, generous or cautious.

5. Answer: (2)   The "ile" the captain speaks of is oil. It is spelled oddly because he pronounces it that way. We know he means oil and not ale, because he is so greedy and determined to get it; only something as precious as oil would be worth risking his crew's anger for.

6. Answer: (4)   Though the food on board is hardly fit to eat, the crew is not likely to starve, choice (1). But their two-year stint is up and they want to go home. We know there is going to be trouble; Keeney has already armed himself in readiness for the first signs of a mutiny, or rebellion, on board. There is no evidence for choices (2), (3) or (5).

GED Mini-Test   *pp. 223–224*

1. Answer: (2)   The tears of Gayev and his sister and the words "despair," "forlorn" and "melancholy" in the stage directions—as well as the situation itself—all tell us that the mood is one of sadness, rather than tension, fear or rage. Only the two young people, Anya and Trofimov, greet the change in their lives happily.

2. Answer: (3)   We are not told exactly who Firs is, but we can assume that he is not a family member, or he would not have been left behind. He is clearly attached to the house (so he is not a merchant or a woodcutter), and worries about someone's going off without his coat on. From these clues we can conclude that he has been a family servant.

3. Answer: (4)   Gayev's sister, Lyubov Andreyevna, is heart-broken at leaving her home, which she sees as representing her whole life, her youth and her happiness (lines 11–12). She does not associate the house with past sins, unhappiness, or riches.

4. Answer: (1)   Firs has just mentioned that he should have made sure Leonid Andreich wore his fur coat. We know that he is a servant, rather than a family member, so we can conclude that he is referring to his master, choice (1). There is no evidence for choices (2) to (5).

5. Answer: (2)   Firs hears the sound of the ax without alarm; this tells us that there is nothing unexpected about the cutting down of the orchard. The family is obviously leaving for good; this tells us that they have not rented the property. The only conclusion we can draw is that the land has been sold to land developers, whose first step is to cut down the orchard.

6. Answer: (5)   There is no evidence for choices (3) to (4), and, although the mournful sound of the snapped string probably announces the death of Firs *and* comments on the departure of the family, choices (1) and (2), it really symbolizes the end of something larger, a whole way of life that Firs and the family were once a part of.

In this section you have studied fiction, drama, biography, autobiography, poetry and essays. You have learned to recognize main ideas, implications, consequences and supporting details. You have learned to identify elements of style and structure, mood, characterization and point of view. And you have practiced these skills by reading the passages and answering the questions that accompanied them.

The following exercises give you an additional opportunity to review some of the literary forms you have been learning about and a chance to continue practicing the reading strategies you have studied.

DIRECTIONS: Choose the one best answer for each item below.

Items 1–4 refer to the following passage by Jack London.

WHAT HAS THIS NEWCOMER OVERLOOKED?

The man flung a look back along the way he had come. The Yukon lay a mile wide and hidden under three feet of ice. On top of this ice were as many feet of snow. It was all pure white, rolling in gentle undulations where the ice jams of the freeze-up had formed. North and south,

(5) as far as his eye could see, it was unbroken white, save for a dark hairline that curved and twisted from around the spruce-covered island to the south, and that curved and twisted away into the north, where it disappeared behind another spruce-covered island. The dark hairline was the trail—the main trail—that led south five hundred miles to the

(10) Chilkoot Pass, Dyea, and salt water; and that led north seventy miles to Dawson, and still on to the north a thousand miles to Nulato, and finally to St. Michael on Bering Sea, a thousand miles and half a thousand more.

But all this—the mysterious, far-reaching hairline trail, the absence

(15) of sun from the sky, the tremendous cold, and the strangeness and weirdness of it all—made no impression on the man. It was not because he was long used to it. He was a newcomer in the land, a *chechaquo*, and this was his first winter. The trouble with him was that he was without imagination. He was quick and alert in the things of life, but

(20) only in the things, and not in the significances. Fifty degrees below zero meant eighty-odd degrees of frost. Such fact impressed him as being cold and uncomfortable, and that was all. It did not lead him to meditate upon his frailty as a creature of temperature, and upon man's frailty in general, able only to live within certain narrow limits of heat

(25) and cold; and from there on it did not lead him to the conjectural field of immortality and man's place in the universe. Fifty degrees below zero stood for a bite of frost that hurt and that must be guarded against by the use of mittens, earflaps, warm moccasins, and thick socks. Fifty degrees below zero was to him just precisely fifty degrees below zero.

(30) That there should be anything more to it than that was a thought that never entered his head.

GO ON TO THE NEXT PAGE.

1. The writing style of this author could be described as

   (1) graceful and delicate
   (2) witty and amusing
   (3) ornate and elaborate
   (4) restrained and factual
   (5) hysterical and overwrought

2. From the evidence in the text, we can conclude that this story is taking place

   (1) in the Soviet Union
   (2) in the far north
   (3) in the man's imagination
   (4) in prehistoric times
   (5) on some other planet

3. The overall mood of this passage is

   (1) grim and full of foreboding
   (2) exciting and suspenseful
   (3) mournful and meditative
   (4) tense and full of anxiety
   (5) nasty and sarcastic

4. In this passage the phrase "man's frailty" (lines 23–24) means human

   (1) vulnerability
   (2) toughness
   (3) individuality
   (4) stamina
   (5) endurance

Items 5–6 refer to the following passage by John Steinbeck.

WOULD YOU BUY A USED CAR FROM THIS MAN?

A stout, slow man sat in an office waiting. His face was fatherly and benign, and his eyes twinkled with friendship. He was a caller of good mornings, a ceremonious shaker of hands, a jolly man who knew all jokes and yet who hovered close to sadness, for in the midst of a laugh

(5) he could remember the death of your aunt, and his eyes could become wet with sorrow for your loss. This morning he had placed a flower in a vase on his desk, a single scarlet hibiscus, and the vase sat beside the black, velvet-lined pearl tray in front of him. He was shaved close to the blue roots of his beard, and his hands were clean and his nails polished.

(10) His door stood open to the morning, and he hummed under his breath while his right hand practiced legerdemain. He rolled a coin back and forth over his knuckles and made it appear and disappear, made it spin and sparkle. The coin winked into sight and as quickly slipped out of sight, and the man did not even watch his own performance. The fingers

(15) did it all mechanically, precisely, while the man hummed to himself and peered out the door. Then he heard the tramp of feet of the approaching crowd, and the fingers of his right hand worked faster and faster until, as the figure of Kino filled the doorway, the coin flashed and disappeared.

(20) "Good morning, my friend," the stout man said. "What can I do for you?"

Kino stared into the dimness of the little office, for his eyes were squeezed from the outside glare. But the buyer's eyes had become as steady and cruel and unwinking as a hawk's eyes, while the rest of his

(25) face smiled in greeting. And secretly, behind his desk, his right hand practiced with the coin.

"I have a pearl," said Kino. And Juan Tomás stood beside him and snorted a little at the understatement. The neighbors peered around the doorway, and a line of little boys clambered on the window bars and

(30) looked through. Several little boys, on their hands and knees, watched the scene around Kino's legs.

GO ON TO THE NEXT PAGE.

"You have a pearl," the dealer said. "Sometimes a man brings in a dozen. Well, let us see your pearl. We will value it and give you the best price." And his fingers worked furiously with the coin.

5. At the beginning of the passage, what kind of man do we think the dealer is?

(1) greedy and secretive
(2) shy and timid
(3) two-faced and tricky
(4) serious and scholarly
(5) soft-hearted and genial

6. Halfway through the passage, we begin to see the man differently. What tips us off?

(1) the way he hums to himself
(2) the arrival of Kino
(3) the flower on his desk
(4) the way he handles the coin
(5) his highly polished nails

Items 7–8 refer to the following poem by Walt Whitman.

WHAT IS MIRACULOUS ABOUT THE ORDINARY THINGS OF LIFE?

Miracles

Why, who makes much of a miracle?
As to me I know of nothing else but miracles,
Whether I walk the streets of Manhattan,
Or dart my sight over the roofs of houses toward the sky,
(5) Or wade with naked feet along the beach just in the edge of the water,
Or stand under the trees in the woods,
Or talk by day with any one I love,
Or sit at table at dinner with the rest,
Or look at strangers opposite me riding in the car,
(10) Or watch honeybees busy around the hive of a summer forenoon,
Or animals feeding in the fields,
Or birds, or the wonderfulness of insects in the air,
Or the wonderfulness of the sundown, or of stars shining so quiet
    and bright,
(15) Or the exquisite delicate thin curve of the new moon in spring;
These with the rest, one and all, are to me miracles,
The whole referring, yet each distinct and in its place.
To me every hour of the light and dark is a miracle,
Every cubic inch of space is a miracle,
(20) Every square yard of the surface of the earth is spread with the same,
Every foot of the interior swarms with the same.

To me the sea is a continual miracle,
The fishes that swim—the rocks—the motion of the waves—the ships
    with men in them,
(25) What stranger miracles are there?

7. The mood of the poem is

(1) quiet and mournful
(2) whimsical and jokey
(3) glad and exultant
(4) fearful and pessimistic
(5) giddy and hysterical

8. Which of the following does the poet *not* list as a miracle?

(1) walking barefoot on the beach
(2) sharing a dinner table
(3) the hours of day and night
(4) walking along city streets
(5) the sound of train whistles

GO ON TO THE NEXT PAGE.

Items 9–12 refer to the following excerpt by George Bernard Shaw.

HOW DO THESE THREE WOMEN REVEAL THEIR CHARACTERS?

MRS. DUDGEON: . . . Oh, it's you, is it, Mrs. Anderson?

JUDITH: (*very politely—almost patronizingly*) Yes. Can I do anything for you, Mrs. Dudgeon? Can I help to get the place ready before they come to read the will?

(5) MRS. DUDGEON: (*stiffly*) Thank you, Mrs. Anderson, my house is always ready for anyone to come into.

JUDITH: (*with complacent amiability*) Yes, indeed it is. Perhaps you had rather I did not intrude on you just now.

MRS. DUDGEON: Oh, one more or less will make no difference this morn-

(10) ing, Mrs. Anderson. Now that you're here, you'd better stay. If you wouldn't mind shutting that door! (JUDITH *smiles, implying "How stupid of me!" and shuts it with an exasperating air of doing something pretty and becoming.*) That's better. I must go and tidy myself a bit. I suppose you don't mind stopping here to receive anyone that comes until I'm

(15) ready.

JUDITH: (*graciously giving her leave*) Oh yes, certainly. Leave that to me, Mrs. Dudgeon; and take your time. (*She hangs up her cloak and bonnet.*)

MRS. DUDGEON: (*half sneering*) I thought that would be more in your way than getting the house ready. (ESSIE *comes back*) Oh, here you are! Come

(20) here: let me see you. (ESSIE *timidly goes to her.* MRS. DUDGEON *takes her roughly by the arm and pulls her round to inspect the results of her attempt to clean and tidy herself—results which show little practice and less conviction*) Mm! That's what you call doing your hair properly, I suppose. It's easy to see what you are, and how you were brought up.

(25) (*She throws her arm away, and goes on, peremptorily*) Now you listen to me and do as you're told. You sit down there in the corner by the fire; and when the company comes don't dare to speak until you're spoken to. (ESSIE *creeps away to the fireplace*) Your father's people had better see you and know you're there: they're as much bound to keep you from

(30) starvation as I am. At any rate they might help. But let me have no chattering and making free with them, as if you were their equal. Do you hear?

ESSIE: Yes.

9. Mrs. Dudgeon's words and actions in this scene show her to be

   (1) patient and long-suffering
   (2) gentle and easy-going
   (3) pure and high-minded
   (4) stingy and tight-fisted
   (5) cruel and hard-hearted

10. As described in the stage directions, Judith's looks and actions tells us that she is

    (1) sweet and self-sacrificing
    (2) smug and self-satisfied
    (3) high-strung and sensitive
    (4) depressed and withdrawn
    (5) angry and defensive

11. Essie utters only one word in this scene, but from what is said and done to her, we know she is

    (1) cagey and secretive
    (2) proud and arrogant
    (3) frisky and high-spirited
    (4) defeated and downtrodden
    (5) strong and domineering

12. From Mrs. Dudgeon's remarks to Essie, we gather that the girl is

    (1) the family servant
    (2) a neighbor's child
    (3) an honored guest
    (4) a poor relation
    (5) Judith's sister

GO ON TO THE NEXT PAGE.

WHAT SPECIAL RULES APPLY TO AN "INNER CIRCLE"?

In the passage I have just read from Tolstoi, the young second lieu-
tenant Boris Dubretskoi discovers that there exist in the army two
different systems or hierarchies. The one is printed in some little red
book and anyone can easily read it up. It also remains constant. A
(5) general is always superior to a colonel and a colonel to a captain. The
other is not printed anywhere. Nor is it even a formally organized secret
society with officers and rules which you would be told after you had
been admitted. You are never formally and explicitly admitted by anyone. You discover gradually, in almost indefinable ways, that it exists
(10) and that you are outside it; and then later, perhaps, that you are inside
it. There are what correspond to pass words, but they too are spontaneous and informal. A particular slang, the use of particular nicknames,
an allusive manner of conversation, are the marks. But it is not constant. It is not easy, even at a given moment, to say who is inside and
(15) who is outside. Some people are obviously in and some are obviously
out, but there are always several on the border-line. And if you come
back to the same Divisional Headquarters, or Brigade Headquarters, or
the same regiment or even the same company, after six weeks' absence,
you may find this second hierarchy quite altered. There are no formal
(20) admissions or expulsions. People think they are in it after they have in
fact been pushed out of it, or before they have been allowed in: this provides great amusement for those who are really inside. It has no fixed
name. The only certain rule is that the insiders and outsiders call it by
different names. From inside it may be designated, in simple cases, by
(25) mere enumeration: it may be called "You and Tony and me." When it is
very secure and comparatively stable in membership it calls itself "we."
When it has to be suddenly expanded to meet a particular emergency it
calls itself "All the sensible people at this place." From outside, if you
have despaired of getting into it, you call it "That gang" or "They" or "So-
(30) and-so and his set" or "the Caucus" or "the Inner Ring." If you are a candidate for admission you probably don't call it anything. To discuss it
with the other outsiders would make you feel outside yourself. And to
mention it in talking to the man who is inside, and who may help you in
if this present conversation goes well, would be madness.

13. The "Inner Ring" the author talks about is

    (1) found only in the army
    (2) a figment of imagination
    (3) an occult society
    (4) a name for the "in crowd"
    (5) a name for organized crime

14. The author's basic attitude toward inner circles is that he

    (1) heartily approves of them
    (2) heartily disapproves of them
    (3) finds them very funny
    (4) thinks they are evil
    (5) enjoys membership in them

GO ON TO THE NEXT PAGE.

WOULD THIS AUTHOR CHOOSE TO CONTINUE HIS SCHOOLING?

The morning came, without any warning, when my sisters surrounded me, wrapped me in scarves, tied up my bootlaces, thrust a cap on my head, and stuffed a baked potato in my pocket.

'What's this?' I said.

(5) 'You're starting school today.'

'I ain't. I'm stopping 'ome.'

'Now, come on, Loll. You're a big boy now.'

'I ain't.'

'You are.'

(10) 'Boo-hoo.'

They picked me up bodily, kicking and bawling, and carried me up to the road.

'Boys who don't go to school get put into boxes, and turn into rabbits, and get chopped up Sundays.'

(15) I felt this was overdoing it rather, but I said no more after that. I arrived at the school just three feet tall and fatly wrapped in my scarves. The playground roared like a rodeo, and the potato burned through my thigh. Old boots, ragged stockings, torn trousers and skirts, went skating and skidding around me. The rabble closed in; I was encir-

(20) cled; grit flew in my face like shrapnel. Tall girls with frizzled hair, and huge boys with sharp elbows, began to prod me with hideous interest. They plucked at my scarves, spun me round like a top, screwed my nose, and stole my potato.

I was rescued at last by a gracious lady—the sixteen-year-old junior-

(25) teacher—who boxed a few ears and dried my face and led me off to The Infants. I spent that first day picking holes in paper, then went home in a smouldering temper.

'What's the matter, Loll? Didn't he like it at school, then?'

'They never gave me the present!'

(30) 'Present? What present?'

'They said they'd give me a present.'

'Well, now, I'm sure they didn't.'

"They did! They said: 'You're Laurie Lee, ain't you? Well, just you sit here for the present.' I sat there all day but I never got it. I ain't going

(35) back there again!"

But after a week I felt like a veteran and grew as ruthless as anyone else. Somebody had stolen my baked potato, so I swiped somebody else's apple. . . . This tiny, white-washed Infants' room was a brief but cosy anarchy. In that short time allowed us we played and wept, broke

(40) things, fell asleep, cheeked the teacher, discovered the things we could do to each other, and exhaled our last guiltless days.

15. The main idea of this passage is

(1) school is dreadful
(2) school is wonderful
(3) schooling should not be forced
(4) people adapt to new situations
(5) young teachers are understanding

16. The author regards his early schooling with

(1) fear and distaste
(2) anger and disbelief
(3) fond amusement
(4) reluctant admiration
(5) bitter resentment

Check your answers to the Review on pages 290–291.

Sportscasters commenting on a play-by-play of a minor league baseball game.

review
critical writing that comments on a creative work

Another name for commentary is **review**, or criticism. A review is a personal essay written in an informal, relaxed and sometimes humorous style.

The main purpose of a review is to assist the reader by providing information about new creative works—books, films and so forth. It tells the reader what the work is about, who created it, who appears in it if it is performed and what the critic feels about its worth. In this way a reader can decide if the work is interesting.

A review's secondary purpose is to entertain the reader. The writing style may be unusual, even clever. It is not uncommon for reviews to be amusing and make readers chuckle, sometimes at the expense of the person who created the work being reviewed.

In this section you will read criticism of fiction, poetry, theater, television, film, music, dance and art. The reviews appeared in newspapers, magazines and books.

In the first lesson of the commentary section you will find reviews of fiction. In your reading you will learn strategies for understanding consequences. A **consequence** is the necessary effect of any action or decision.

The second lesson covers poetry and theater. You will discover that reviewers carefully choose words and details to show how they feel about a work. Loaded words cause an emotional response in readers. When the writer's attitude toward a subject is revealed by loaded words and phrases, the technique is called **tone**.

In the third lesson excerpts from television reviews are used to illustrate how writers present information from which they draw conclusions. A reader, however, is not obliged to accept the reviewer's conclusion. In fact, readers may form an entirely different conclusion.

The fourth lesson uses film reviews as examples to show how critics make assumptions about their subject. When information is not stated in a passage but left for readers to figure out, it is necessary to identify **implications.**

Music reviews in the fifth lesson will help you to recognize an author's **point of view.** Unlike fictional writing, commentary always speaks directly to the reader and reveals the author's personal viewpoint.

Reviews contain both **fact** and **opinion.** In the sixth lesson the selections taken from dance criticism show how to tell the difference. Unless you read carefully and sort out facts from opinions, a review can be misleading.

In the last lesson commentary on artists and their works can help you understand **cause and effect.** Sometimes clue words appear as a signal when a cause and effect relationship is being presented.

consequence
a necessary effect of an action or decision
tone
words and details revealing a writer's attitude
implication
idea that the writer takes for granted
point of view
the author's viewpoint
fact
a statement that can be proved true or false
opinion
personal feelings, which may or may not be supported by facts
cause and effect
an action that leads to an outcome, or result

29 Commentary Fiction

When reading reviews on fiction or on an author who wrote fiction, you are reading the reviewer's *opinion* about the person or the work.

Below is a *Time* magazine review about the life (and death) of a famous author of fiction. Use the Purpose Question above the passage to help you understand *what* has happened.

WHY DID SUCCESS SPOIL ERNEST HEMINGWAY?

In 1928 Hemingway's mother mailed him a chocolate cake. Along with it she sent the .32-cal. Smith & Wesson revolver with which Hemingway's father had just killed himself. Hemingway dropped the pistol into a deep lake in Wyoming "and saw it go

(5) down making bubbles until it was just as big as a watch charm in that clear water, and then it was out of sight."

The story is minutely savage in its details and haunting in its outcome: perfect Hemingway. And of course, there is the water.
. . .—lake water and trout stream and Gulf Stream and the rains

(10) after Caporetto and the endless washes of alcohol refracting in his brain. His style was a stream with the stones of nouns in it and a surface of prepositional ripples. . . .

. . . Ernest Hemingway's books are easier to know, and love, than his life. He wrote, at his early best, a prose of powerful and

(15) brilliant simplicity. But his character was not simple. In one of his stories, he wrote: "The most complicated subject that I know, since I am a man, is a man's life." The most complicated subject that he knew was Ernest Hemingway.

. . . His life belonged as much to the history of publicity as to

(20) the history of literature. He was a splendid writer who became his own worst creation, a hoax and a bore. He ended by being one of the most famous men in the world, white-bearded Mr. Papa. He stopped observing and started performing. . . .

Still, a long mythic fiesta between two explosions may not be

(25) a bad way to have a life. The first explosion came in Fossalta di Piave in northeastern Italy at midnight on July 8, 1918. A shell from an Austrian trench mortar punctured Hemingway with 200-odd pieces of shrapnel. . . . The second explosion came 25 years ago this summer. Early one morning in Ketchum, Idaho,

(30) Hemingway (suffering from diabetes, nephritis, alcoholism, severe depression, hepatitis, hypertension, impotence and paranoid delusions, his memory all but ruined by electroshock treatments) slid two shells into his double-barreled Boss shotgun. . . the last creature Hemingway brought down was himself.

(35) Hemingway was mourned mostly as a great celebrity, his worst side, and not as a great writer, which he was.

═ **Understand a Consequence** ═

This skill involves identifying cause and effect to find a consequence. A consequence is an effect of an action or decision.

While reading the passage on Ernest Hemingway, notice how some of the ideas connect to each other and how one idea seems to lead to another. His actions led to definite **consequences.**

Ask: What has happened? Sometimes a review will give a result. You must piece together events and figure out the reasons why it happened. Success seemed to destroy Hemingway. He acted like a fool instead of the superior writer that he actually was. Why? When he died, people mourned him as "Papa" Hemingway, not as a great writer. Why?

Ask: What will be the consequences? If a review gives reasons, you must understand what the outcome, or effect, might be. Hemingway became boastful and attention-grabbing. This behavior had certain results. What were they?

Examples

DIRECTIONS: Use the information on this page and the review from *Time* magazine on the preceding page to choose the one best answer for each item below.

1. According to the passage, Hemingway underwent marked changes in later life because

   (1) he had difficulty writing
   (2) he lived in Cuba
   (3) he won the Nobel Prize for Literature
   (4) he began acting out a role
   (5) he suffered serious injuries in a plane crash

Answer: (4) The changes noticeable in the older Hemingway were a consequence of a fame that was based increasingly on acting instead of writing. Lines 19–23 support this. Other choices are true but are not the *cause* of his behavior changes.

2. The public reacted to Hemingway in his later years as

   (1) the most distinguished writer of his time
   (2) an expert on big-game hunting
   (3) a war correspondent
   (4) an expert on bullfighting
   (5) an international star

Answer: (5) Because Hemingway presented himself more as a celebrity than a writer (cause), people began to think of him as a star (effect). His literary skill, choice (1), took second place. Choices (2) to (4) are factual but not mentioned in the passage.

Practice

HINT ▷ As you read a book review, be aware of the reason that certain things happen. You will be questioned on causes and their effects.

DIRECTIONS: Choose the one best answer for each item below.

Items 1–2 refer to the following review from The New York Times Book Review.

WHAT DOES AUDREY SEE IN A MAN LIKE CHARLIE?

Danielle Steel's new romance novel is a delicious, lightweight treat. Audrey Driscoll, age 26, with her coppery hair, creamy skin, passion for exotic places and sizable fortune, hardly seems a candidate for spinsterhood, but that seems to be her fate in San
(5) Francisco in the 1930's. She rebels and sets off for Europe with her stylish clothes and treasured Leica. Aboard the Mauretania, she meets Lady Vi and Lord James, a young, rich, beautiful couple who persuade her to spend a few champagne-drenched weeks at their villa in Cap d'Antibes. Here, Audrey is introduced to all
(10) sorts of amusing folk, including Picasso (who proclaims her a talented photographer) and Charles Parker-Scott. He's a tall, dark, handsome travel writer who, like Audrey, has adventuring in his blood. Obviously, the two are destined for each other, if their respective wanderlusts don't keep them apart. Not one to sit
(15) home knitting while Charles traipses off to interview Chiang Kai-shek, Audrey embarks on her own adventures, which include running an orphanage in China, adopting a child, traveling to Nazi Germany. . . . The plot is implausible, of course, and the dialogue what one expects: "Don't leave me here. My whole life is with you
(20) Charlie, it always has been." The characters' credibility leaves a lot to the reader's blind faith. But to question why the bright, nifty Audrey would fall for the self-centered Charles is, perhaps, to take "Wanderlust" more seriously than we should.

1. According to the passage, *Wanderlust* defies analysis because

(1) it is too sophisticated
(2) it is silly beyond words
(3) its realism is overpowering
(4) its characters are eccentric
(5) it deals with complex emotions

2. According to the review, reading *Wanderlust* would have the same effect on a reader as eating

(1) bacon and eggs
(2) meat and potatoes
(3) bon bons
(4) rice and beans
(5) bread and butter

GO ON TO THE NEXT PAGE.

Items 3–6 refer to the following review from Newsweek.

WHAT MAKES *MARYA* SO POWERFUL?

Not in years has Joyce Carol Oates written a novel as strong as this. In a mining town near the Erie Canal, eight-year-old Marya Knauer's father is bludgeoned to death. Her mother walks away from Marya and her infant brothers. Raised by her uncle's
(5) family, and sexually abused by her cousin, Marya develops a shell: she's quick-witted, sarcastic and (of course) friendless because she's so hard, so bright. She discovers that her reputation for brilliance serves as "a sort of glass barrier that would keep other people at a distance." Driven by work, Marya presses
(10) through graduate school, becomes a tenured professor at a college much like Dartmouth, then quits to become a lioness in the New York literary world.

Oates's professionalism eases her over the technical hurdles that she set for herself in this story. The first is to make us care
(15) for Marya, a humorless and arrogant girl. The second is to tell the story of this seemingly impermeable woman in a sequence of encounters with stronger characters, who all use Marya for their own purposes. The novel extends over 28 years and comprises chapters that are very nearly independent stories: Marya with her
(20) mother; her cousin; her high school teacher; her dying priest; her rich girlfriend at college; her lovers—a professor in one chapter, an editor in another. In summary, this may sound predictable, and it is. *Marya* isn't built on inspiration or on novelty, but on the contrast between Oates's adroitness with realistic detail and
(25) her insight into what these familiar situations involve.

3. In the reviewer's opinion, Oates's novel is powerful because

(1) she felt inspired by the subject
(2) it has an unusual theme
(3) she has a gift for description
(4) she has insight into ordinary events
(5) the characters are convincing

4. What is Marya's first occupation?

(1) lion-tamer
(2) book reviewer
(3) celebrated writer
(4) university teacher
(5) high school teacher

5. The story takes place over a period of

(1) eight months
(2) nearly three decades
(3) twelve years
(4) a weekend
(5) a half century

6. According to the excerpt, Marya reacts to the traumas of her early childhood by

(1) becoming a teenage runaway
(2) growing a protective covering
(3) developing a witty personality
(4) dominating her loved ones
(5) schizophrenia

Before you take the GED Mini-Test, check your answers on page 239.

DIRECTIONS: Choose the one best answer for each item below.

Items 1–6 refer to the following review from New York *magazine.*

WHAT IS THE MEAT AND POTATOES OF THRILLERS?

On balance, I would have to acknowledge that I prefer *The Aquitaine Progression* to Robert Ludlum's last few elephantine thrillers—though in the way that one might prefer a chronic lower-back pain to a lesion of the neck joints. . . .

(5) For Ludlum remains pretty much what he was ten books and fifteen years back: a no-frills, no-nonsense keyboard thumper who clearly couldn't care less about imagery, diction, cadence, or syntax. If there's a wrong word, an inert word, he will nearly always manage to find it. Ludlum and language are by now on such bad terms, in fact, that he

(10) seems to be out to punish every other sentence. . . .

No wonder Ludlum is happiest with data and documentation—with the number of seconds needed to open the forward door of an airplane; the speed of an elevator after it has been adjusted for room-service deliveries; the conversion rate from guilders to dollars . . .

(15) Granted, information is the bread and meat, the guts and glory of thrillers. We read them, after all, for the sneaky, low-life pleasure of learning as much as we can about lone-wolf types and exotic locales . . . But Ludlum's diligent detailing, his artless accretion of bleak, banal facts is simply more punishing than anything else. . . .

(20) All the same, nobody in the thriller trade can come up with a more promising idea than Ludlum. *The Aquitaine Progression* is an arresting example of his gift for tunneling into the American undermind and dredging out just the kind of paranoid perception that helps explain the harrowing complexities of modern history in terms a *National Enquirer*

(25) reader can understand. Its story, as near as I can follow without a manual, propels a well-placed, well-coordinated lawyer into hardball combat with a bunch of international totalitarian military-corporate types trying to "create widespread unrest, political crises, and enormous suffering everywhere." . . .

1. Why do people enjoy reading thrillers?

   (1) It beats watching TV.
   (2) They want to impress their friends.
   (3) They like to learn about fearless characters and flashy locales.
   (4) The books are engrossing.
   (5) They want to learn about literary types and techniques.

2. The reviewer says that Ludlum's writing suffers from

   (1) careless craftsmanship
   (2) routine plots
   (3) predictable endings
   (4) fangless villains
   (5) bad taste

GO ON TO THE NEXT PAGE.

3. This passage is primarily about

    (1) the plot of *The Aquitaine Progression*
    (2) the novelist's private life
    (3) the craftsmanship of good writing
    (4) political power
    (5) National Reading Week

5. When the reviewer describes Ludlum's thriller as "elephantine" (line 2), he means

    (1) suspenseful and absorbing
    (2) aristocratic and elegant
    (3) pretentious and boring
    (4) large and clumsy
    (5) poetic and soulful

4. The novel's main character is

    (1) president of a steel company
    (2) an attorney
    (3) a *National Enquirer* reporter
    (4) an airlines pilot
    (5) unemployed

6. Which of the following would be *most* likely to appear in a Ludlum thriller?

    (1) a description of a sunset
    (2) the number of diamonds in Queen Elizabeth's state crown
    (3) dream symbolism
    (4) a heartrending love story of deep significance
    (5) elegant satire

Check your answers to the GED Mini-Test on page 240.

Answers and Explanations

Practice   *pp. 236–237*

1. **Answer:** (2) The passage strongly implies that sophistication, realism and complexity are not to be found in the book. As a consequence, the mostly silly (but enjoyable) story has little connection with real life. That is why it must be accepted on faith instead of reason.

3. **Answer:** (4) The reason why Oates's novel is so strong owes much to her skill in writing about everyday situations. The reviewer also mentions inspiration and novelty but clearly states that these are *not* responsible for the power of the book. Choices (3) and (5) are true but irrelevant.

5. **Answer:** (2) The passage states that Joyce Carol Oates's story covers a period of some 28 years. This piece of information is mentioned in line 18. None of the other choices is found in the review.

2. **Answer:** (3) In the opening lines, the reviewer likens *Wanderlust* to a delicious, delicate treat. Only choice (3) is sugary enough to fit the description. All of the remaining choices refer to more substantial fare.

4. **Answer:** (4) Marya had two careers. First she was a college professor and then you can infer that she became a successful writer. You had to read carefully because choices (2) to (5) include two kinds of teachers and two types of writers.

6. **Answer:** (2) Throughout the passage you found words and phrases such as "shell," "glass barrier," and "impermeable," all of which should have suggested that Marya protected herself by developing a tough hide. Note that no details in the review would support any of the remaining choices.

GED Mini-Test *pp. 238–239*

1. **Answer:** (3)   This is the only correct choice that appears in the passage. It depends on understanding cause and effect. Reading thrillers produces enjoyment (effect). This is the result of reading about (and experiencing through your imagination) unusual characters, dangerous situations and exotic settings (cause).

3. **Answer:** (3)   The question asked you to grasp the main idea and then make an inference. The review is primarily a discussion of what the reviewer believes to be bad writing. By implication, good writing is careful writing. Less attention is paid to the thriller's plot.

5. **Answer:** (4)   The word "elephantine" is easy to figure out if you think of an elephant. It means big and awkward. The reviewer thinks that Ludlum's novels are not just big as elephants but that they also move clumsily.

2. **Answer:** (1)   The passage gives detailed criticism of Ludlum's writing. The reviewer's main objection is that a Ludlum thriller is sloppily made. The other choices are opposed by information in the excerpt, since you can infer that Ludlum's stories do not lack excitement.

4. **Answer:** (2)   This is a detail that occurs at the end of the passage, where it is stated that Ludlum's hero is a lawyer. There are no references to any of the remaining professions or to unemployment.

6. **Answer:** (2)   According to the passage, Ludlum's favorite technique is to stuff his books with great quantities of facts. It is the only choice that deals with odd facts. Other choices refer to common literary techniques, but none of them are mentioned in the review as being practiced by Ludlum.

30 Commentary Poetry & Drama

In these reviews on poetry and drama look for clues, words or phrases, to the reviewer's feelings on a subject.

Below is a review from the *New York Times Book Review* by David Kirby about the skill of the poet Mary Oliver. Use the Purpose Question to help you to understand the reviewer's feelings.

HOW HAPPY WAS MICHELANGELO'S BRUSH CLEANER?

Even before she was given the 1983 Pulitzer Prize for "American Primitive," much had been written about Mary Oliver's considerable powers as a nature poet and probably too little about the pain underlying her work. This is something she shares with
(5) others. . . . Thoreau went to Walden Pond to get away from a society that supported the Mexican War. The speakers in Ms. Oliver's "Dream Work" are troubled by more private concerns; for example, there is a father, brutal and unlovable, who shows up in two poems with telling titles, "Rage" and "A Visitor." Faced with such
(10) ugliness, one is given "the chance to love everything," to cite the title of a beautiful poem in which a camper is menaced by something huge and unseen (a bear, probably) and goes toward rather than away from it. . . .

One of Ms. Oliver's hallmarks is plain speech. The earnest
(15) questers in her poems know it is easy to state a goal—forgive the bad parent, seek out the bear—and hard to carry it out. They are ordinary people who are close to the elements:

> *Surely the sea*
>
> *is the most beautiful fact*
> (20) *in our universe, but*
>   *you won't find a fisherman*
>   *who will say so;*
> *what they say is,*
>   See you later.

(25) To work, to be a fisherman or a gardener or a writer, is exhausting, and in several of these poems there is an old and frightening idea—in the end art kills the artist. In her poem on Robert Schumann, Ms. Oliver notes that "everywhere in this world his music/explodes out of itself, as he/could not." In another
(30) poem, "death is the fascinating snake" . . . and artists who look too closely at it sometimes find themselves unable to look away. It makes one uneasy to hear a fine poet say perhaps we should be like the man who did nothing more than clean Michelangelo's brushes every day, and lived to be 100 years old.

Identify Techniques (Tone)

This skill identifies an author's attitudes, both stated and implied. From the tone of a writer's work, you receive clues to his or her feelings. The tone of a review or critical essay signals to a reader whether or not a creative work might be worthy of attention.

Identifying **tone** is something you do every day. When people speak to you, unless they try hard to conceal their feelings, you rarely have trouble interpreting their tone, meaning and underlying emotions. For example, your waiter at lunch says, "Watch out, the plate is hot!" You understand the situation from the sound of his voice, his choice of words and the details he uses.

Writers also talk to their readers. Although the sounds of their voices cannot be heard, they signal their meaning by use of language. They convey their feelings in the following ways:

By choice of words. The passage on page 241 has such adjectives as "brutal" and "frightening." You sense that the writer feels disturbed by some of the poems in the book he is reviewing.

By choice of details. In order to reveal emotion, the writer carefully selects certain details—and omits others. Notice also how the writer's tone influences *your* response to the play or poem.

Examples

DIRECTIONS: Use the information on this page and the review by David Kirby on the preceding page to choose the one best answer for each item below.

1. The general tone of this review is one of

   (1) modified admiration
   (2) utter disdain
   (3) straightforward description
   (4) exaggeration
   (5) tongue-in-cheek humor

Answer: (1) You know from the reference to Michelangelo's servant (line 33) that the poet's bitterness makes the reviewer slightly uncomfortable. Choice (3) is only partly true. Choices (2), (4) and (5) are incorrect.

2. The author compares Mary Oliver to Henry Thoreau in order to show that

   (1) the poet is gifted
   (2) she lives in a fishing village
   (3) the theme of pain is not unusual in nature writing
   (4) she objects to war
   (5) she understands the hardships facing artists

Answer: (3) Choice (1) is taken for granted throughout the review and choice (5) is also true, but neither has anything to do with Thoreau. Choices (2) and (4) are not supported by the passage.

Practice

As you read, ask yourself: What is the critic feeling? What does the critic want *me* to think or feel?

DIRECTIONS: Choose the <u>one</u> best answer for each item below.

Items 1–4 refer to the following New York *magazine drama review of* Arsenic and Old Lace.

IS *ARSENIC* STILL KILLING?

The play on which generations of America's high school students formed their taste in theater, *Arsenic and Old Lace,* wheezed onto Broadway as creaky as the day it was born. Written (one gathers) by Joseph Kesselring as a serious thriller, it was
(5) turned into a farce by the producers, Lindsay and Crouse. . . . the kick has gone out of this vintage 1941 elderberry wine. Especially so with the present cast, wherein only Mary Layne, a fine actress even under adverse circumstances, displays genuine class. . . .

Everyone, however, is surpassed by William Hickey, as the
(10) comic-villainous Dr. Einstein. Regardless of the part, a Hickey performance consists of the same dithering whines occasionally relieved by whiny dithers. I'd call him the worst actor in America, but fear doing him an injustice: He might not have his equal in the world. . . .

1. How would you describe the reviewer's tone?

   (1) noncommittal
   (2) pleased
   (3) disappointed
   (4) bored
   (5) irritated

2. The author implies that *Arsenic and Old Lace* would *most* likely be produced by

   (1) summer stock companies
   (2) schools
   (3) composers such as Leonard Bernstein
   (4) little theater groups
   (5) public television

3. When the play was first written in 1941, its author probably intended it to be

   (1) a TV sitcom
   (2) a film starring Rudolph Valentino
   (3) a controversial radio program
   (4) a frightening murder mystery
   (5) a sophisticated farce

4. In referring to a performance he particularly dislikes (lines 9–14), what technique does the reviewer use to express his feelings and make the reader laugh?

   (1) contrast
   (2) exaggeration
   (3) flashback
   (4) metaphor
   (5) irony

GO ON TO THE NEXT PAGE.

Items 5–6 refer to the following New Yorker *review.*

WHAT IF TOM SAWYER HAD A REUNION WITH HUCK FINN?

It will be merciful to devote but a paragraph or so to "The Boys in Autumn," a two-person play by Bernard Sabath. . . . In a program note, Mr. Sabath implies that he considers it proof of a lively imagination to wonder what becomes of the characters in a
(5) novel that one has read. The exact opposite is, of course, the case: a lively imagination takes delight in apprehending that nothing whatever can or should happen to the characters in a novel when the last sentence of the last chapter has been set down. Acting on his misguided notion of what a work of fiction is, Mr. Sabath has
(10) had the vulgar audacity to write a play about a meeting between Huckleberry Finn and Tom Sawyer in late middle age. . . .

5. In the critic's opinion, a dramatist who borrows his characters from a beloved work of fiction must be called which of the following?

(1) original
(2) foolish
(3) dishonest
(4) naïve
(5) adventuresome

6. *The Boys in Autumn* is a drama about Huck Finn and Tom Sawyer when they are

(1) adolescents
(2) senile old men in a nursing home
(3) over 50 years of age
(4) on the brink of 30
(5) five-year-old boys

Items 7–8 refer to the following commentary by Leo Sauvage.

DOES SAM SHEPARD DESERVE HIS REPUTATION?

Leaving aside the popularity Sam Shepard has gained from his other activities, strictly as a playwright he seems to have achieved a status near the top in American theater. I do not know why. If *Fool for Love* . . . had been his first play, I might have said
(5) its brute tension—despite unnecessary overtones of incest in the violent reactions of its loving, fighting couple—shows a promising young author whose next work is worth watching for.

Yet *Fool for Love* was not Shepard's first, or fifth, or tenth effort. . . .
(10)   . . . One day, perhaps with his 49th or 50th play, he will give us a fully thought-out masterwork, untrammeled by the self-indulgent digressions that merely scatter his talent.

7. The passage describes the playwright as a man who has been

(1) judged too advanced for his time
(2) forgotten over the years
(3) neglected by Hollywood
(4) highly acclaimed
(5) blacklisted for his views

8. How does the reviewer feel about Sam Shepard as a dramatist?

(1) He should write in a more mature fashion.
(2) He should give up writing.
(3) He should write less.
(4) He should write more.
(5) He should change his style.

Before you take the GED Mini-Test,
check your answers on pages 246–247.

GED Mini-Test

30

TIP

Before selecting an answer, you can narrow the choices by first eliminating any that seem silly or irrelevant. Then choose among those remaining.

DIRECTIONS: Choose the one best answer for each item below.

Items 1–6 refer to the following review from the Wall Street Journal.

WILL THE YOUNGERS GET $10,000?

There have been so many plays that start with someone staggering into the kitchen to make breakfast that you can watch the first few outwardly humdrum minutes of "A Raisin in the Sun" and not notice that you're in the presence of a masterpiece. An alarm clock rings, a mother
(5) awakens a schoolboy, she brushes her teeth at the kitchen sink, she scrambles some eggs—a poor black family in the midst of the morning's mundane ritual, no more scintillating on the stage than in real life.

But then, maybe 15 minutes into the Roundabout Theatre's solid revival, you find yourself thoroughly caught up in the hopes and dreams
(10) of the Younger clan as they await the $10,000 life-insurance check that promises to change their lives.

It wasn't innovative technique or groundbreaking style that made Lorraine Hansberry's play a Broadway sensation 27 years ago. It was the richness of her characters, the power of her perceptions. And these
(15) remain undiminished, however shopworn and familiar her kitchen-sink storytelling. Amazingly—or, perhaps, not so amazingly—the dilemma that concerned her and her characters, the profound contradiction at the heart of the modern black experience in modern white America, is no less urgent now than it was in 1959. Timely "Raisin" may have been
(20) then; now, clearly, it is timeless.

1. The Youngers' immediate escape from poverty is due to

(1) wise budgeting
(2) the grandmother's pension
(3) the mother's job
(4) room rental
(5) a death in the family

2. Judging by the tone of the review, we can assume that the critic feels

(1) discomfort
(2) mostly indifference
(3) indecision
(4) enthusiasm
(5) annoyance

3. The author refers to *A Raisin in the Sun* as "timeless." What does she mean?

(1) It describes historical events.
(2) It still has meaning for audiences.
(3) It makes us laugh and cry.
(4) It seems overly sentimental.
(5) It contains old-fashioned wisdom.

4. Which one of the following made the play a tremendous success in 1959?

(1) an offbeat story
(2) poetic language
(3) new methods of playwriting
(4) memorable characters
(5) an unforgettable ending

GO ON TO THE NEXT PAGE.

5. Which of the following does *not* explain why the Younger family wants $10,000?

(1) They plan to move to a white neighborhood.
(2) They work at dull jobs.
(3) They hate being poor.
(4) They want a good education.
(5) They plan to invest in rare antiques.

6. In line 15 the critic reveals a negative opinion about the play, implying that it is flawed and might be

(1) better with a first-class cast
(2) improved by a less emotional approach
(3) damaged by the passage of time
(4) making fun of television game shows
(5) helped by a more original story

Check your answers to the GED Mini-Test on page 247.

Answers and Explanations

Practice *pp. 243–244*

1. **Answer:** (5) Since the critic can find nothing favorable to say about the production, the most reasonable answer is choice (5). You might argue for choices (3) and (4), since the writer also may have felt disappointed and bored, or he *could* have been suffering from a bad toothache that evening. But these are weaker answers. Choices (1) and (2) are clearly not true.

2. **Answer:** (2) In fact, the play also has been popular with stock companies and amateur groups, choices (1) and (4), but this fact is not mentioned in the passage. By stating "generations of high school students . . ." the author implies that schools are the most likely to produce this play. No reference is made to Leonard Bernstein, who based his musical *West Side Story* on *Romeo and Juliet,* or to television, which were choices (3) and (5).

3. **Answer:** (4) This requires you to consider when certain events more or less occurred. In 1941, TV sitcoms were not yet commonplace, and Valentino died in 1926. There is nothing in the passage to back up choices (3) and (5).

4. **Answer:** (2) The actor named is not likely to be the world's worst. In reaching for an effect, the critic is using a common technique to indicate displeasure. Choice (3) is a method more often used in fiction; choices (1), (4) and (5) are not accurate.

5. **Answer:** (2) Possibly another critic might have applauded the dramatist's approach. But if you selected choices (1) or (5) you missed the author's disapproving tone, which he makes clear from the beginning of the review.

6. **Answer:** (3) Even though the play's title refers to "boys," the passage specifically talks about the ages when this imagined reunion was supposed to be taking place. None of the other choices is backed up by the information supplied in the excerpt.

7. **Answer:** (4)   The critic admits that Shepard is widely admired but goes on to express his skepticism in a restrained tone. In his opinion, he writes, Shepard's reputation is unjustified. All other choices are either completely untrue or do not apply.

8. **Answer:** (1)   According to the passage, Shepard has been slow to mature as a writer. The critic states a hope that in time he will learn self-discipline. Nowhere in the review does he suggest Shepard lacks talent, or should change his habits, as the remaining choices suggest.

GED Mini-Test   *pp. 245–246*

1. **Answer:** (5)   In this passage only choice (5) is totally correct. There has been a death in the family. This information is implied by the mention of the $10,000 life-insurance check the family is waiting for. Choices (2), (3) and (4) are not mentioned. Although choice (1) is a possible way out of poverty, it does not offer an *immediate* escape.

2. **Answer:** (4)   In this question there is no truth in choices (1), (2) or (5). Although the critic has a few reservations about the play, she is firm about her conclusion. Choice (4) is the best.

3. **Answer:** (2)   All the choices, except choice (1), contain an element of truth. But since the question asked for the meaning of the term "timeless," you should have selected choice (2). "Timeless" means that the play has not gone out of style. It does not sound as if it had been written three decades ago.

4. **Answer:** (4)   The key to this question is a careful reading of the critic's balance sheet as she lists the play's strengths and weaknesses. Rather than the language, theme or ending, it is the ordinary but unforgettable characters whom audiences remember.

5. **Answer:** (5)   This question requires you to recognize what the author means when she refers to "the hopes and dreams" of a black family in the 1950s. You must either know from experience or deduce what such a life was like. Parts of the answer can be found in each of the four choices.

6. **Answer:** (5)   You should have thrown out choice (4) as silly. Choices (1) and (2) ask for knowledge not contained in the passage, while choice (3) contradicts the reviewer's statement about the play's timelessness. Only choice (5) refers to a flaw—Lorraine Hansberry's commonplace story.

Commentary Television

As you read television reviews, look for conclusions that can be drawn. **A conclusion** is formed on the basis of information presented. Drawing conclusions follows logically once you have considered the evidence.

A conclusion can be for or against the review. Below is a *Variety* review about TV coverage of Liberty Weekend. Be aware of conclusions that are implied or stated by the reviewer. Use the Purpose Question above the passage to help you.

WILL ABC-TV BLITZ LOUISVILLE?

ABC-TV's "Liberty Weekend" coverage, stretching from July 3–6, was a stupendous logistic undertaking that ABC News pulled off rather well from a graphics standpoint, hosted graciously by Peter Jennings (with some occasional help from Barbara Walters).

(5)   As TV programming, the massive entertainments ... proved without a doubt that when it comes to overdoing it, the U.S. doesn't have to take a backseat to anybody.

Anyone who wasn't numb when the four-day TV event was over probably doesn't know the meaning of overkill.... The

(10) production maxim, for the entertainment sequences, seemed to be "if you can't do it better than it was done in the past, do it bigger."

The closing ceremonies from the Meadowlands was the worst culprit in this area, with hordes of people running around the stadium, including some 200 Elvis Presley imitators. It became

(15) hard to ascertain what the entertainment had to do with the Fourth and Miss Liberty but it was spectacular in an excessive sense.

There were some legitimate moments of honest emotion, such as when Pres. Reagan turned on the statue's lighting effects dur-

(20) ing the opening ceremony, along with the stately parade of the tall ships and the sensational fireworks display July 4....

A giant 20-tier backdrop stage, with two waterfalls, was the technical marvel of the show. The native American art form, jazz, was sloughed off as an all-white medium....

(25) The most effective moment came from a light show, when spectators turned on flashlights to ring the stadium with red, white and blue sections. One couldn't help wonder if they were going to bring the lions and the Christians on for a finale—or maybe bomb Louisville (with appropriate fireworks).

It came to an end, as all things do. It had been a Hollywood-like production, full of glitz, glamour and more celebrities than one could count—and surely no one was clamoring for more....

Draw Conclusions

This skill involves making a judgment about given facts, using the details in the article plus your own prior knowledge and reasoning skills.

Most reviewers form **conclusions.** You can accept them or not. (Have you ever read a negative review of a film that you thought was terrific?) Sometimes a judgment is implied. Again it is up to you to agree or disagree. Generally an author's conclusion is:

At the beginning.   In the first sentence or first paragraph the writer tells you that a judgment has been made and what it is. This is followed by examples to indicate how and why the conclusion was reached.

At the end.   The writer closes the review with a statement that summarizes the examples. In the review that you read on page 248, the writer supplies a conclusion at both the beginning and the end of the passage.

Occasionally a review presents evidence and allows you to make up your mind about a conclusion. In this case you must read critically, examine the relationship between the facts (read between the lines) and then arrive at your own conclusion.

Examples

DIRECTIONS: Use the information on this page and the review on the preceding page to choose the one best answer for each item below.

1. The conclusion formed about ABC-TV's coverage of Liberty Weekend is that

   (1) it turned out well in spite of many drawbacks
   (2) it added luster to our national heritage
   (3) bigger is always better
   (4) most viewers found it boring
   (5) American TV knows how to create tasteless spectacles

Answer: (1)   Although the reviewer complains that the event was too Hollywoodish to qualify as good taste, he gives credit where he believes it is due. Only choice (1) is supported by the information presented.

2. The author believes that the event was *most* memorable for

   (1) Operation Sail
   (2) the fireworks display
   (3) President Reagan's speech
   (4) dual waterfalls
   (5) red, white and blue lights flashing in the audience

Answer: (5)   There is no question that the author admired all of the above choices. But the one event singled out as particularly striking was the flashlight display. You should have selected choice (5).

Practice

HINT ▷ Is a conclusion at the beginning? at the end? not given at all? Look for stated or implied details or examples that suggest the conclusion.

DIRECTIONS: Choose the one best answer for each item below.

Items 1–4 refer to the following New York Times *television review.*

CAN JOAN RIVERS WIN THE BATTLE OF THE TALK SHOWS?

There she was, the star of "The Late Show Starring Joan Rivers," applauding her studio audience eagerly with outstretched hands and, in turn, getting a standing ovation for the premiere of her very own talk show. "So much has been said, so much has
(5) been written," she beamed, "I am so happy to be here." Another standing, screaming ovation. This may have been the first hour in the history of television that begged for a stiff tranquilizer.

For the past few months, Ms. Rivers has kept herself in scattered headlines because of a "feud" she triggered with Johnny Car-
(10) son, against whom she will now be competing directly in many television markets. It was Mr. Carson's "Tonight" show on NBC that brought Ms. Rivers into the megabucks league of show business. Was she being ungrateful, or was she simply struggling to prevail? Who cares? In today's world, it seems, go for the con-
(15) tract and get away with as much as you can.

Meanwhile, Thursday's premiere offered several clues as to what kind of "personality" the Rivers show wants to cultivate. Compared with the Carson product, the sound is younger. The music arrangements of Mark Hudson and the Party Boys are
(20) more partial to contemporary electronics than Doc Severinsen's band. The set is larger. . . . However, Ms. Rivers' desk and the seating arrangement for guests are strictly vintage Carson. The studio audience, at least as sampled in the first two shows, is considerably more frenetic. . . .
(25) . . . One practical note: despite the publicity and the big-name guests, "The Late Show" was considerably behind the "Tonight" show in the first head-to-head ratings. . . .

1. What word *best* describes the author's attitude toward the Rivers-Carson "feud"?

   (1) amusement
   (2) awe
   (3) mixed feelings
   (4) excitement
   (5) indifference

2. Joan Rivers' decision to host a rival talk show met with what sort of reaction from Carson?

   (1) displeasure
   (2) good-natured acceptance
   (3) mild enthusiasm
   (4) reluctant congratulations
   (5) strong encouragement

GO ON TO THE NEXT PAGE.

3. According to the passage, which personality was winning the talk-show war?

(1) David Letterman
(2) Mark Hudson and the Party Boys
(3) Johnny Carson
(4) Joan Rivers
(5) too soon to tell

4. If a restaurant were earning "megabucks" (line 12), it would mean

(1) an extremely large profit
(2) income not reported to the IRS
(3) popularity with teenagers
(4) bankruptcy was close
(5) it advertised heavily on TV

Items 5–8 refer to the following Vogue *magazine television review.*

WILL AGE IMPROVE THE *HOLLYWOOD SQUARES*?

Perhaps in an attempt to get with the post-modern swing of things, perhaps out of desperation (guess which), television producers have taken to cannibalizing this medium's distant past, regurgitating the hits of ten, twenty, thirty years ago in craven
(5) and embarrassing fashion. Which brings us to the new *Hollywood Squares*, gussied up for the 'eighties after a five-year hiatus.

When it debuted in 1966, the *Squares* was unquestionably TV's dopiest game show (not to be confused with its most humiliating, *The Newlywed Game*). Based on tick-tack-toe, the
(10) show featured nine minor celebrities, roosting in a precarious three-story grid, who responded to leading questions with either double entendres or blank stares, depending on whether or not they remembered the retorts the show's writers had "suggested" to them. "In *Alice in Wonderland*," went a typical question, "who
(15) complained of being late?" "Alice . . . and her mother's just *sick* about it," smirked the late Paul Lynde, a regular, to the giggles, cackles, and asthmatic snorts of, respectively, Karen Valentine, Rose Marie, and the late Charley Weaver. For sixteen years, this spectacle of buffoonery was unbeatable, a sublimely ridiculous
(20) expression of America's fascination with celebrity.

5. On the basis of the evidence, the author concludes that

(1) the new show will be much different
(2) people find celebrities boring
(3) he is going to watch regularly
(4) a better game show has never been invented
(5) the show will regain its popularity

6. According to the passage, *Hollywood Squares* is being revived because

(1) viewers demanded its return
(2) TV is anxious for a sure hit
(3) strong nostalgia for the sixties
(4) a Paul Lynde fan club insisted
(5) a toothpaste company suggested it

7. If *Squares* was the "dopiest" game show (line 8), *The Newlywed Game* was

(1) the most clever
(2) a favorite with kids under five
(3) the most degrading
(4) regularly watched by nurses
(5) a winner in the ratings

8. The author implies that this game show formula uses

(1) new and innovative ideas
(2) glamour and prestige
(3) challenging questions
(4) fascinating guests
(5) a children's game as its basis

Before you take the GED Mini-Test,
check your answers on pages 253–254.

31

DIRECTIONS: Choose the one best answer for each item below.

Items 1–6 refer to the following television review.

WHAT WOULD VOLTRON THINK OF SATURDAY MORNING TV?

Children's television is filled with furry bears and fruit-scented little girls, robots and Smurfs, muscle-bound blond princes and antiterrorist teams, talking unicorns and shrill chipmunks elbowing one another off the screen every half-hour or so to demonstrate their unique buyability
(5) while mouthing extracts from a random loop of recorded messages: be polite, be happy, be sure to hug, consult with others, respect your elders, cheating doesn't pay, don't fight, follow the rules.

Few adults, of course, look at children's television carefully. For any adult who looked, however, it would be hard to avoid the impression
(10) that the plots repeat each other continually, no matter who produces them. . . .

One would pardon visiting aliens from the planet Eternia (*He-Man*), Arcadia (*Voltron*), or Thundera (*Thundercats*) if they mistook such crude, repetitious, and heavy-handed fare for badly done propaganda put
(15) together by some unseen, and certainly uninspired, hand. But our aliens might then wonder, as critics of kids TV sometimes do: If it's meant to convince, why are these shows so lacking in conviction that even their most violent sequences are without resonance or emotional conse-quence? And finally, if these shows are so bad, why, as the industry
(20) constantly reminds us, do earthling young choose to watch them in such extraordinary numbers?

The fact is, there has probably never been a more creative moment in children's TV than the present one; more creative, that is, as long as what appears on the screen is seen as a listless by-product of an extraor-
(25) dinary explosion of entrepreneurial life force taking place elsewhere—in the business of creating and marketing toys. . . .

1. In this passage the author concludes that

(1) adults never watch children's TV
(2) children are crazy about the shows
(3) cartoonists are clever people
(4) the toy business is booming
(5) he feels nostalgic for Big Bird

2. On Saturday morning TV, children would be *least* likely to see shows with

(1) a variety of cartoons
(2) alien creatures
(3) positive messages
(4) emotional immaturity
(5) emotional maturity

GO ON TO THE NEXT PAGE.

3. In this passage the writer's tone is one of

    (1) scholarly objectivity
    (2) indifference
    (3) complaint
    (4) pride
    (5) admiration

4. Youngsters continue to be avid watchers of Saturday TV because

    (1) the shows seem to be highly creative
    (2) their parents encourage it
    (3) they are attracted to toy commercials
    (4) they are addicted to TV
    (5) they are too young to discriminate between good and bad

5. Based on the passage, the writer might possibly approve of a show that

    (1) carried no toy commercials
    (2) dramatized stories
    (3) showed more violence
    (4) taught fractions
    (5) used animated characters

6. The TV shows described in the passage are *primarily* interested in teaching children

    (1) good manners
    (2) cooperation
    (3) to obey their parents
    (4) to ask for toys based on the characters
    (5) to be physically affectionate

Check your answers to the GED Mini-Test on page 254.

Answers and Explanations

Practice *pp. 250–251*

1. **Answer:** (5)   The author may feel amused, choice (1), and also have mixed feelings, choice (3). But you should have concluded from his question "Who cares?" that he cannot take the "feud" seriously. There is no evidence for choices (2) or (4).

2. **Answer:** (1)   To arrive at the most likely answer, it is necessary to analyze the word "feud," which means people at odds. Only choice (1) infers that Carson was upset about competition from his one-time protégée. Choices (2) to (5) imply the opposite.

3. **Answer:** (3)   This is a straightforward question that is answered directly in the last sentence. Since the writer makes clear his conclusion, none of the other choices were possibilities.

4. **Answer:** (1)   This is a tricky application of getting meaning from context. You must know that "megabucks" means a great deal of money and then use the information in a different situation (food). No evidence for choices (2) to (5) appears in the review.

5. **Answer:** (5)   To find out the correct answer you had to read to the end of the passage. The writer concludes that America is fascinated by celebrity shows. It seems unlikely that he will watch regularly, choice (3). Choices (1), (2) and (4) do not reflect the author's point-of-view.

6. **Answer:** (2)   Eliminate choices (3) to (5) immediately as having no support from the review itself. In the passage the writer asks you to decide between the accuracy of choices (1) and (2) and he assumes you will be sharp enough to pick choice (2).

7. **Answer:** (3) Choice (5) sounds like a possible answer but you do not know this from the review. Choices (1), (2) and (4) are all unlikely. Only choice (3) reflects the reviewer's opinion.

8. **Answer:** (5) This choice is factually correct because the author mentions tick-tack-toe in line 9. Choices (1) to (4) are incorrect. Indeed, the author feels that many of these elements are missing from this show.

GED Mini-Test   *pp. 252–253*

1. **Answer:** (4) Choices (1) to (3) are not only true but also mentioned in the excerpt. But the question asked you to recognize a writer's conclusion. Therefore, the only correct answer is choice (4). Big Bird does not appear.

2. **Answer:** (5) This choice is implied in lines 18–19. Choices (1) to (4) are all mentioned or implied as being a part of Saturday morning TV programming.

3. **Answer:** (3) Obviously the author is examining facts but he is certainly not detached. He is working hard to sway readers to his viewpoint. The tones in choices (2), (4) and (5) are not possibilities. All this makes choice (3), complaint, the best.

4. **Answer:** (1) A case could be made for any of the five choices. But in line 22 the writer pays a backhanded compliment to the creativity of the shows, even though he is mainly referring to toymakers' energy. Choice (1) is closest to the target.

5. **Answer:** (1) Since the information for this question is not included in the passage, you had to understand the author's attitude and then make a judgment. It is possible that commercial-less programs *might* satisfy him, although he believes the general quality of children's TV is poor. Choices (2) to (4) are part of Saturday morning TV. Choice (5) is incorrect because the author does not object to animated characters.

6. **Answer:** (4) The author's conclusion appears at the end of the passage, when he infers that the real message—buy toys—is concealed. Choices (1), (2), (3) and (5) are mentioned as behaviors that the programs appear to teach.

32 Commentary Film

Writing film criticism involves making endless assumptions about films and actors. In reading criticism it is helpful to know the writer's prejudices.

The following review of a Beatles' film was written in 1970. Use the Purpose Question above the passage to help you understand the writer's feelings about his subjects.

BUT CAN THE BEATLES ACT?

The new Beatles film, *Let It Be*, is only for worshipful teenyboppers and middle-aging intellectuals hellbent on being with-it. Sloppily photographed and casually spliced together, it could pass for a home movie, except that an unfunny funhouse is

(5) not a home. One is aware, especially now that their break-up has been announced, . . . that their fingernail parings have become priceless. *Let It Be* is a collection of audiovisual nail parings, but not without a certain morbidly sociological interest. . . .

Paul McCartney, a chubbily handsome young man, appears

(10) quite pleasant . . . But the others! Particularly grubby are John Lennon and his worse half, Yoko Ono, who sits, smug and possessive, almost always within touching distance of him. Flouting, it would seem, even minimal sanitary measures, their hair looks like a Disneyland for the insect world . . .

(15) I am no inveterate Beatle-baiter, having enjoyed *A Hard Day's Night* and *Yellow Submarine*, as well as some Beatle records. But very little of this transcends the mass-culture, pop-music level . . . At one point, Lennon mumbles a bit of impromptu rhyme, something like "Isadora Duncan / Goes for Telefunken,"

(20) and that is about the height of wit in *Let It Be*.

We witness several recording sessions . . . ; we see the inscrutable smirking of Yoko (truly, in Wilde's phrase, a Sphinx without a secret); and there is much middling music-making and muddled smalltalk. Galt MacDermot, the composer of *Hair*, once

(25) told me during an interview that he expected rock to be a passing musical fashion, and I wonder whether it isn't about time for it to pass. But, I suppose, rock has become the international anthem of the youth revolution, and while that movement lasts, so will rock. Which brings us to the central point of the film: that the Beatles,

(30) visibly, are not that young any more. . . . I note a forced gaiety in Paul and John, a bemused quizzicality in Ringo, and downright gloom in George.

═ Identify an Implication ═

This skill identifies assumptions, facts or statements that are taken for granted (not proved), and that the author takes for granted.

Written material contains ideas that appear directly on the page. But it may also include additional information or meanings, **implications,** that *do not* appear in the text. Think of it as "reading between the lines." For example, in the film review on page 255 there is a mention of John Lennon reciting a rhyme about dancer Isadora Duncan. The reviewer is not amused. The assumption that Lennon is a poor poet is not proven and may be untrue.

Figuring out meanings from what is *not* said is a skill that you have used many times in your life. Keep these points in mind:

Rely on general knowledge.   In the Beatles' review, the writer assumes that readers are familiar with both the Beatles and the type of music they perform. He does not identify or explain.

Rely on common sense and judgment.   You can recognize the writer's assumptions (and prejudices) from the tone and choice of words. Common sense will clue you to ideas that do not appear in the text. (How does the reviewer feel about Yoko Ono?)

Examples

DIRECTIONS: Use the information on this page and the Beatles' review on the preceding page to choose the <u>one</u> best answer for each item below.

1. What can you assume about rock in 1970?

  (1) It appealed to all ages.
  (2) Only teens appreciated it.
  (3) Some thought rock a fad.
  (4) Rock had not gained popularity.
  (5) Films about rock singers did poorly.

Answer: (3)   The inference is that rock's popularity will last only as long as the "youth revolution" (line 28) and when this revolution ends, rock music will disappear with it. No other options can be inferred from the passage.

2. You can infer that the critic

  (1) enjoyed the rock musical *Hair*
  (2) lacks a good sense of humor
  (3) is compulsively neat and clean
  (4) is over the age of 21
  (5) has high critical standards

Answer: (4)   The writer is obviously over 21 and belongs to a different generation. He implies that the Beatles appeal mainly to youth or to adults who are behaving inappropriately for their age.

Practice

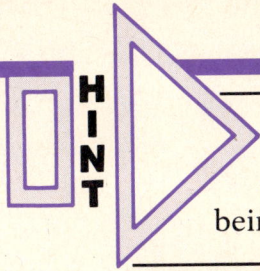

Keep your eyes open for any assumptions the writer may be making. What ideas are being taken for granted?

DIRECTIONS: Choose the <u>one</u> best answer for each item below.

Items 1–3 refer to the following review from Newsweek *magazine.*

WHY CRITIC WRITE REVIEW IN UGGA-MUGGA?

"The Clan of the Cave Bear" is dog. Jean M. Auel write big best seller about Neanderthals who live 35,000 years ago. Holly-woodheads buy movie rights, screw up movie. Holly-woodheads even more primitive than Neanderthals. Book make cave people
(5) talk in plain English. Holly-woodheads make cave people talk in fake ugga-mugga lingo like old Johnny Weissmuller movies, while audience read subtitles. Book like ice-age soap opera (no, soapless opera, cave people pretty grungy). Movie no zip, no zap, no zing. John Sayles good writer, why his screenplay so dull? Director
(10) Michael Chapman great camera man, why his movie so dull? Alan Silvestri write music sound like "Chariots of Fire," dumb Holly-woodhead move.

    Daryl Hannah play Ayla, girl from new Cro-Magnon people. Neanderthals found her when little child after big earthquake.
(15) Short dark Neanderthals uneasy with tall blond Cro-Magnon girl. But foster mother Iza (Pamela Reed), foster father Creb (James Remar) very kind to orphan girl. Ayla break Neanderthal taboos, use male weapons, become first woman hunter, defy male chauvinist pig Broud (Thomas G. Waites). Ayla become prehistoric
(20) Gloria Steinem. Daryl Hannah look great in animal skins, try hard show deep feeling in ugga-mugga talk. Pamela Reed look very hairy. James Remar more primitive as mob boss Dutch Schultz in "The Cotton Club." Jean Auel very mad at Holly-woodheads for screwing up her book. She bring suit. No, not animal-skin suit,
(25) legal suit. Good luck, Jean. Ugga-mugga.

1. How does the reviewer feel about the film?

(1) Jean Auel is a superb writer.
(2) The film made the subject seem silly.
(3) The book deserved big sales.
(4) Books should not be made into films.
(5) He had enjoyed reading the novel.

2. What was Ayla doing with the Neanderthals?

(1) She was orphaned by a disaster.
(2) The Neanderthals kidnapped her.
(3) She ran away from home.
(4) She was captured in battle.
(5) She was worshipped as a goddess.

GO ON TO THE NEXT PAGE.

3. Which of the following headlines *best* describes the reviewer's opinion of the film?

(1) AS EXCITING AS MOVIES CAN GET
(2) A STUNNING ACHIEVEMENT
(3) ONE OF THE YEAR'S WORST FILMS
(4) YOU WON'T WANT TO MISS IT
(5) DARYL HANNAH DESERVES AN OSCAR

Items 4–7 refer to the following review from Ms. *magazine.*

IS THE WORLD WAITING FOR MS. RAMBO?

Sly Stallone and Arnold Schwarzenegger had better get out of town. Sigourney Weaver is ready to take over as the number-one action hero. As Ripley in "Aliens," she is just as brave and competent with weaponry as the male Rambos. She is also smarter and
(5) capable of feeling. She is as close to believable as you can get in science fiction. That's because Weaver can act—more than can be said for the muscle-bound Katzenjammer Kids.

. . . Ripley . . . returns as a consultant with a fighting force of Marines to the planet taken over by the aliens. The human
(10) colonists have been wiped out, except for a little girl named Newt.

. . . The "top gun" pilot is a woman. The outfit's best fighting machine is a well-muscled woman named Vasquez, who in barracks-style banter puts the men in their place. A male Marine,
(15) eyeing her bulging biceps with envy: "Ever been mistaken for a man?" Vasquez: "No, have you?"

When the going gets rough, a number of the men come apart—panic-stricken, hysterical, cowardly. The women do not. Despite her own fear (something the thickheaded Rambo never
(20) feels), Ripley takes control from the mission's commander, paralyzed by the horror of it all, and, driving a space-age tank, rescues the Marines trapped inside the aliens' incubation room. It's a pleasure to root for her.

4. Throughout the passage, the reviewer assumes that his readers

(1) are studying karate
(2) would welcome a female Rambo
(3) plan to join the Air Force
(4) admire tough men
(5) dislike violence in films

5. What is implied in the opening paragraph?

(1) Male heroes dominate action films.
(2) War is heroic.
(3) Flying is for men.
(4) Female astronauts are cowardly.
(5) Women make poor combat soldiers.

6. According to the reviewer, the *main* difference between Stallone and Weaver is that Stallone

(1) earns more money
(2) never smiles
(3) is a male
(4) lacks acting ability
(5) is an accomplished pilot

7. According to the passage, the aliens killed all the planet's human colonists except

(1) two Mars explorers
(2) a Japanese space scientist
(3) the Italian ambassador
(4) a female child
(5) all women over six feet

Before you take the GED Mini-Test, check your answers on page 260.

32

TIP

Reading *slightly* faster than usual may improve your comprehension of a GED test passage and also help your concentration.

DIRECTIONS: Choose the <u>one</u> best answer for each item below.

Items 1–6 refer to the following review by Pauline Kael.

WHY CAN *SUPERMAN* NOT GET OFF THE GROUND?

The film rallies when [Christopher] Reeve takes over—especially when he gets out of the drably staged scenes at the offices of the *Daily Planet*, gets into his red cape and blue tights, flies over Metropolis, and performs a string of miracles. Yet after the first graceful feat, in which

(5) he saves Lois Lane, who has fallen from a helicopter that crashed on a skyscraper, and then steadies the fallen chopper (with the injured pilot inside) and gently lifts it to safety, the other miracles don't have enough tension to be memorable . . . When Superman takes his beloved up for a joyride in the sky, the cutting works against the romanticism that we're

(10) meant to feel, and, with Lois reciting Leslie Bricusse lyrics to convey her poetic emotions, even the magic of two lovers flying hand in hand over New York City is banalized. Lois Lane has always been one of the more boring figures in popular mythology: she exists to get into trouble. Margot Kidder tries to do something with this thankless part, but she's

(15) harsh-voiced, and comes across as nervous and jumpy; she seems all wrong in relation to Reeve, who outclasses her. He's so gentlemanly that her lewdness makes one cringe. (We aren't given a clue to what our hero sees in Lois Lane. It might have been more modern fun if he hadn't been particularly struck by her until she'd rejected his cowardly Clark Kent

(20) side for his Superman side—if, like any other poor cluck, he wanted to be loved for his weakness.)

. . . In order to sell the film as star-studded, a great many famous performers were signed up and then stuck in among the plastic bric-a-brac of Krypton; performers who get solo screen credits, with the full

(25) blast of trumpets and timpani, turn out to have walk-ons. Susannah York is up there as the infant Superman's mother, but, though Krypton is very advanced, this mother seems to have no part in the decision to send her baby to Earth. York has no part of any kind; she stares at the camera and moves her mouth as if she'd got a bit of food stuck in a

(30) back tooth. Of all the actors gathered here—all acting in different styles—she, maybe, by her placid distaste, communicates with us most directly.

1. From the passage, which of the following can you infer is the reviewer's main point?

   (1) The special effects are stunning.
   (2) The enchantment is missing.
   (3) Lois Lane was born for trouble.
   (4) Too many stars appeared.
   (5) More good actors would have helped.

2. It would be a reasonable assumption to believe this critic might award *Superman*

   (1) **** Extraordinary
   (2) *** Excellent
   (3) ** Very good
   (4) * Good
   (5) (none) Poor

GO ON TO THE NEXT PAGE.

3. Christopher Reeve's portrayal of Superman is described as

   (1) intelligent and insightful
   (2) courteous and well bred
   (3) crude and vulgar
   (4) boring and annoying
   (5) enthusiastic and playful

5. If you were asked to take a starring role in this film, other than the characters of Lois Lane and Superman, you would probably appear

   (1) throughout the entire film
   (2) only as a newspaper reporter
   (3) in the Krypton scenes
   (4) as a villain
   (5) very seldom

4. The reviewer feels that the Lois Lane character is

   (1) too silly for words
   (2) a poor sport
   (3) tense and unhappy
   (4) dull and uninteresting
   (5) peppy and sharp-tongued

6. The city of Metropolis is supposed to be which of the following real places?

   (1) Chicago
   (2) London
   (3) Milwaukee
   (4) New York
   (5) Houston

Check your answers to the GED Mini-Test on page 261.

Answers and Explanations

Practice   *pp. 257–258*

1. **Answer:** (2)   The answer is implied throughout. Choosing to compose a mocking review in "Ugga mugga" suggests a lack of seriousness toward the film. Therefore, choices (1) and (3) to (5) can be eliminated at once.

2. **Answer:** (1)   Line 14 states that the Neanderthals found Ayla after an earthquake, and line 17 explains that she is an orphan. Choices (2) to (5) should have been rejected as inaccurate.

3. **Answer:** (3)   There is not one statement in the passage that would suggest a favorable opinion. Daryl Hannah may look good in furs, but she receives no praise for her acting. The writer's implication is that this film is one of the worst films of the year.

4. **Answer:** (2)   The reviewer takes for granted that readers share his enthusiasm for a film in which women play roles usually reserved for men. Choices (1) and (3) to (5) are incorrect because the reviewer makes no assumptions about karate, the Air Force, tough men or violence.

5. **Answer:** (1)   You know from comparisons made in the opening sentences that the reviewer is enthusiastic about seeing women in action films. The main idea is that such roles have been limited to men in the past. This is assumed rather than stated directly in the passage.

6. **Answer:** (4)   The opinion that Weaver has more acting talent than Stallone (or Schwarzenegger) can be found in lines 6–7. According to the reviewer, it is Weaver's ability that makes the story believable. He does not think this is true in the case of male action films.

7. **Answer:** (4)   This detail is mentioned in lines 9–11. The only colonist who has not been killed by the aliens is "a little girl named Newt." No other survivors are mentioned in the passage.

GED Mini-Test   *pp. 259–260*

1. **Answer:** (2)   The main point is that the film lacks charm. Disappointment is implied when the reviewer writes that the miracles fall flat and even flights over the city lack the glamour they should have conveyed. Choices (3) and (4) are either details or minor objections.

2. **Answer:** (5)   Since the writer does not recommend the film, the only rating supported by the passage would have to be Poor. Susannah York's expression of distaste, cited in the last line, infers that this is an opinion shared by the reviewer.

3. **Answer:** (2)   The answer is courteous and well bred, which means "gentlemanly" (line 16). In contrast, Lois Lane is described as boring and crude. Close attention to details would rule out Reeve's portrayal as either smart or enthusiastic. Although these are implied, the passage never mentions them.

4. **Answer:** (4)   The answer is in lines 12–13 " . . . one of the more boring characters in popular mythology . . . " Dull and uninteresting is another way of saying boring. Choices (3) and (5) partially describe the way the actress played the role, but not the Lois Lane character that the reviewer objected to. Choices (1) and (2) are not discussed in the review.

5. **Answer:** (5)   This question required you to use ideas from the review in a different situation. In line 25, big stars are described as winding up with "walk-ons," a term meaning an insignificant part. If you had played a leading role in *Superman*, you would rarely be seen.

6. **Answer:** (4)   The fictional city of Metropolis is supposed to be based on New York City. This information is mentioned in line 12 when Superman takes Lois Lane for a "joyride in the sky." You may have had to go back and scan for this small detail.

33 Commentary Music

The viewpoint expressed in a review is always the author's.

Below is a *Rolling Stone* review about a rock concert. Use the Purpose Question to help you understand the author's viewpoint.

DOES HIGH-TECH LOWER LISTENER ENJOYMENT?

The first notes played on Lionel Richie's current world tour were wildly out of tune, but it wasn't his fault. The afternoon of the show . . . Richie's special-effects-laden $52,000 piano rolled off the stage and into the photographer's pit, and not all the damage
(5) had been repaired when the piano rose from under the stage, rotated and sounded the opening bars of "Hello."

. . . Richie grimaced at his piano's discordance. But when he heard one member of the audience yell, "Outrageous!"—his favorite expression—he knew everything would be all right. And
(10) sure enough, nobody . . . seemed bothered by the piano. They came to be dazzled and they were, by a show chock-full of glitz and hits.

Richie's stage was made up of interlocking wings that moved back and forth, rose into the air and slid aside . . . His piano came
(15) out of the floor and spun on its axis—and after it was repaired, it also tilted forward and spoke in Lauren Bacall's voice. . . . Two members of the crack backing band were pulled into the rafters, where they danced on the ceiling during "Dancing on the Ceiling." And for those who came to hear the music, the ninety-minute set
(20) was studded with tunes that have long been staples everywhere from radios to elevators.

But that kind of praise sounds condescending, which isn't fair to Richie. He may set his sights squarely on the pop charts, but Richie doesn't condescend to his audience: instead, he makes
(25) honest, good-hearted music, skillful explorations of the pop side of R&B . . .

And on those terms, the second of Richie's two . . . shows was a likable showcase of a body of hit songs . . . The key might be his boy-next-door personality: . . . Richie does have heart. But the
(30) emphasis should be more on that down-to-earth heart and less on the high-tech stage, which moved so often that it became hard to concentrate on the people it was supposed to be supporting. . . .

"We Are the World," the best-known song Richie ever co-wrote, was nowhere to be found. . . . Richie said he'd like to add
(35) the song at some point, "but I prefer it being something spontaneous, rather than planned."

Identify Techniques (Point of View)

This skill involves identifying and distinguishing whose thoughts and feelings are being revealed. The point of view expressed is the author's but this viewpoint may be seen through the eyes of a character and therefore hard to distinguish.

You should have no trouble identifying **point of view** in commentary if you remember one fact. The person who is speaking is the author. The situation is unlike a poem or a story, where the author must designate a narrator for the tale. Even when being ironic, the author is speaking directly to the reader.

When there is no need to disguise views by speaking through an invented character, the personality of the author is free to emerge. A common technique is boldly grabbing the reader's attention in the opening lines. Striving for effect may sometimes depend on shocking, or even repelling, the reader.

In the passage about the rock concert on the previous page, the critic captures attention with a provocative opening sentence: "The first notes played on Lionel Richie's current world tour were wildly out of tune, but it wasn't his fault." This should compel the reader to ask both "Why?" and "Why not?"

Examples

DIRECTIONS: Use the information on this page and the review from *Rolling Stone* on the preceding page to choose the <u>one</u> best answer for each item below.

1. The passage as a whole is presented from the viewpoint of a(n)

   (1) fan of elevator music
   (2) close friend
   (3) elder statesman
   (4) sympathetic admirer
   (5) Lauren Bacall fan

Answer: (4)   Based on the point of view revealed, it seems probable that the author has followed the singer's career for many years. His attitude toward Richie is respectful, admiring and sympathetic.

2. Based on this review, the author would *most* probably enjoy a

   (1) Las Vegas revue
   (2) classic ballet
   (3) tap dance extravaganza
   (4) Radio City Music Hall show
   (5) simply staged pop concert

Answer: (5)   Based on the reviewer's opinion about special effects overpowering the music, choices (1) and (4) can be eliminated. There is not enough information to support choices (2) or (3).

DIRECTIONS: Choose the one best answer for each item below.

Items 1–4 refer to the following review from Esquire *magazine.*

CAN TOM WAITS TURN A PRINCESS INTO A FROG?

Tom Waits sings as if he doesn't change his underwear daily. I've always liked him. But then my musical tastes have never been to everybody's liking. I've had friends look through my five-hundred-plus record collection and say they can't find one they

(5) want to hear. I purchased only four LPs last year (*Glenn Gould: Wagner, Billy Stewart: The Greatest Sides,* Nico's *Camera Obscura,* and *The Wonderful World of Sonny and Cher*), but Tom Waits's newest, *Rain Dogs,* would have been my fifth. It should carry an "attitude warning" on the cover. If you're debating whether to go

(10) to sleep early so you can be productive the next day or to go out to a bar and get drunk, don't play this record. Tom Waits brings out the derelict in us all, but his sense of humor elevates him above being merely a cult figure who specializes in wrist-slashing cocktail/sleaze music.

(15) . . . there's big talent playing behind him, but I'd be a fan even if he were singing with a high school combo. Imagine him terrorizing "New York, New York" or even "You Light Up My Life." Sometimes I wish he'd lighten up a bit and make us laugh out loud instead of through crocodile tears. But he's an original, all

(20) right; a white-trash prince in damaged armor who kisses the princess and turns her into a frog right before our bloodshot eyes.

1. The main idea of this review is

   (1) how Tom Waits could use a washer-dryer
   (2) the tragedy of the urban homeless
   (3) how a high school band made good
   (4) the author's enthusiasm for Waits
   (5) a cult figure's wicked sense of humor

2. Why does the author describe his record collection (lines 3–5) as uninteresting to his friends?

   (1) to brag about its size
   (2) to show that his friends are hard to please
   (3) to compare Tom Waits to Glenn Gould
   (4) to warn readers that he has offbeat musical tastes
   (5) to make fun of Sonny and Cher

GO ON TO THE NEXT PAGE.

3. Which of the following types of writing would *not* be likely to use an introductory sentence such as the one that appears in line 1?

(1) a short story
(2) a film star's biography
(3) a *New York Times* news story
(4) a *Rolling Stone* review
(5) a television sitcom

4. To demonstrate Waits's originality (line 19), the author describes him as a

(1) swashbuckling pirate king
(2) born-again Mozart
(3) former Rockette impersonator
(4) person with magical powers
(5) throwback to the Ice Age

Items 5–6 refer to the following review from the New York Post.

DOES MODERN MUSIC MEAN POPULAR MUSIC?

Luciano Berio does not seem to like captive audiences.

At least that was the impression the Italian composer-conductor gave at Wednesday night's Philharmonic subscription concerts at Avery Fisher Hall . . .

(5)   He sandwiched Haydn's 90th Symphony between two of his own compositions—the New York premiere of his "Voci" (Folk Songs II) and the Concerto for Two Pianos, with Katia and Marielle LaBeque as soloists.

At the least, Berio made life easy for those who wanted to come late and leave early.

(10)   Since he was conducting the concert and had his back to the audience, he missed the exodus of several hundred subscribers that began at the end of the Haydn and continued with somewhat diminished force during the concerto.

(15)   There were no boos or catcalls, but only about one-third of the patrons were on hand at the end.

Yet, ironically, if judged by duration and intensity of applause, the Haydn fared worst—a mere 60 seconds of polite clapping.

(20)   Response to the new Berio was a bit longer and stronger (70 seconds). And by far the biggest hand—a full two minutes and 30 seconds—saluted composer Berio and the LaBeques after the concerto. Clearly there are many different audiences with vastly different tastes.

5. The person most interested in the information found in this review would probably be

(1) a balletomane
(2) a piano teacher
(3) a Barry Manilow fan
(4) a lover of contemporary classical music
(5) a visitor from Rome

6. This review is an example of an author stating his opinion indirectly. Which of the following does he use to show point of view?

(1) vivid introduction
(2) description of audience reaction
(3) dialogue
(4) symbolism
(5) dialect

Before you take the GED Mini-Test, check your answers on page 267.

GED
Mini-Test

33

TIP

Before beginning, quickly skim the complete test, including the questions, to get a general idea of the material that will be covered.

DIRECTIONS: Choose the one best answer for each item below.

Items 1–6 refer to the following review from the Village Voice.

CYNDI LAUPER—KOOK OR COOKIE?

There's this Japanese snack, maybe it's even tasty. You boil a pot of water. Plop in a fistful of teensy eels. They'll fidget. Then, fast, throw in three or four very cold bean cakes. That's it for the eels, who'll burrow into the cool center, seeking refuge, though eventually that, too, gets hot.

(5) Cyndi Lauper's *True Colors* (Portrait) has one mischosen cover version, another tune puzzlingly revived from her time with Blue Angel. The sound lacks viscera . . . The vocals don't front the arrangements like they should. The songs are laden with bland language. Somewhere inside the bean cake, though, there's this wriggling—this voice even more reck-

(10) less than it was on *She's So Unusual*, a better album than *Houses of the Holy* or *The Best of Junior Parker*.

It's a willed blindness how so many—from zines that hate her to *Rolling Stone* scribes for whom she does no wrong—peg Lauper as simp kook or smart cookie. Either way the party line—*that Cyndi!*—makes her

(15) sound like the nurdish half of a double date where Madonna's on the other guy's arm. Lauper's more evasive than is realized and too few have seen how those crazy threads and beads keep things at a useful distance. Making a checkerboard on the side of her head . . . for the "Time After Time" video may label her as out to lunch, but this is a gambit: *you are*

(20) *not gonna figure her out*. No matter how many octaves she navigates, how she wails, the cartoonishness also makes fun of virtuosity. It doesn't sound like a *real* voice is supposed to. You can't trust the lyrics—Lauper wipes them out when she wants, but you have to trust the voice, which is anything but detached. The riotous operatics, the

(25) reverent nods to Ethel Merman and Big Maybelle, et al., are so furious and mutant in each song, the lines changing mood and character, she walks away from poses she hasn't defined yet.

1. The purpose of contrasting Cyndi Lauper with Japanese food is to

   (1) explain her popularity in Japan
   (2) indicate how many of her songs are about ethnic food
   (3) suggest the special qualities of her music
   (4) show the influence of Madonna
   (5) increase her album sales abroad

2. In the author's view, the album *True Colors* is sometimes flawed by

   (1) poor choice of tunes
   (2) trite lyrics
   (3) problems with arrangements
   (4) unconvincing sound
   (5) all of the above

GO ON TO THE NEXT PAGE.

3. Which factor about Lauper's appearance might be misleading to audiences?

   (1) green wig
   (2) sunglasses
   (3) clothing and jewelry
   (4) Cubist makeup
   (5) bare feet

5. Which phrase *best* expresses the reviewer's conclusion about Lauper?

   (1) the Marilyn Monroe type
   (2) the essence of Ethel Merman
   (3) an untrustworthy voice
   (4) an operatic pop singer
   (5) a hard singer to explain

4. The author of this passage would *most* likely agree that

   (1) Cyndi Lauper is a first-rate actress
   (2) some pop stars cannot handle success
   (3) behind every star is a smart manager
   (4) Lauper's songs are thoroughly dated
   (5) some singers succeed better on videos

6. When the writer calls Lauper "simp kook" and "smart cookie" (lines 13–14), he is stating

   (1) facts
   (2) his personal opinion
   (3) the public's perception
   (4) Lauper's view of herself
   (5) quotes from a publicity release

Check your answers to the GED Mini-Test on page 268.

Answers and Explanations

Practice   *pp. 264–265*

1. **Answer:** (4)   Since the author insists that his musical tastes tend to be unconventional, the only sensible answer is choice (4). Choice (1) is an example of an attention-getting technique, while choices (2), (3) and (5) are unrelated.

3. **Answer:** (3)   In their news sections, papers print information that can be proved or disproved. The author's provocative statement about the singer is neither fact nor opinion. Such an opening sentence properly belongs to fiction and might easily be found in any one of the remaining choices.

5. **Answer:** (4)   It it obvious that the composer's work falls into the category of advanced modern music, which would not appeal to all tastes. Balletomanes, choice (1), are devoted to the ballet. Choices (2), (3) and (5) might be true, but there is no way of knowing from the passage.

2. **Answer:** (4)   The reviewer does seem to be boasting, complaining about his friends and poking fun at Sonny and Cher. But the point he is making in the passage seems to be that Tom Waits is an acquired taste. Therefore, choice (4) is best.

4. **Answer:** (4)   In the final sentence of the review, you learn that Waits strikes the author as a prince whose kiss might turn a woman into a frog, a twist on the old fairy tale. This is your clue to the correct answer, choice (4).

6. **Answer:** (2)   You should have eliminated choices (3) to (5) because none of these literary techniques occurs in the passage. Choice (1) may be correct, but the author chiefly indicates point of view by focusing on audience response. The implication is that he is in agreement.

1. **Answer:** (3)   The question requires a close reading of the opening paragraph. Even then it is difficult to follow the author's logic and finally you have to accept it. But by process of elimination you can discard the other choices, none of which is justified by the passage.

2. **Answer:** (5)   Choices (1) to (4) can be found listed in the passage (lines 5–8), which should have led you to choice (5). No interpretation is needed. The writer thinks Lauper is good despite these faults.

3. **Answer:** (3)   All five choices could be possible because audiences might be affected (positively or negatively) by green hair or bare feet. But choice (3) is best because the only mention of Lauper's costume in the excerpt refers to "threads" and "beads."

4. **Answer:** (1)   Nowhere does the reviewer actually use the words "actress" or "role." But he refers to "poses" (line 27) and the idea is implied throughout. Choices (2) to (5) have nothing to do with the reading.

5. **Answer:** (5)   You should have picked choice (5) for two reasons: the writer states that people do not understand Lauper and he calls attention to the idea by italicizing *"you are not gonna figure her out."* Choice (3) is correct, but it is not the conclusion. Choices (1), (2) and (4) are wrong.

6. **Answer:** (3)   Here you were expected to distinguish between provable and unprovable information. "Kook" and "smart cookie" reflect neither facts, choice (1), nor the writer's own opinion, choice (2). The best answer is choice (3), public perception.

34 Commentary Dance

Critical essays contain a combination of fact and opinion. Factual statements can be proved or disproved. On the other hand, the author's ideas and feelings may or may not be true.

Readers must learn how to recognize the difference between fact and opinion. Be aware of statements that reflect the writer's opinion in this *Time* magazine review of choreographer Mark Morris. Use the Purpose Question to help you.

ARE THE MORRIS DANCERS ALL WASHED UP?

The title alone is provocative: *Soap-Powders and Detergents*. Will this be some arch exercise with dancers dressed up as bubbles or boxes? A soggy bit of social criticism? A spoof on Balanchine's *Snowflake Waltz* in *The Nutcracker*? No, Mark Morris'
(5) latest creation, . . . is a lighthearted, structurally elegant look at washday.

The dancers somewhat resemble fresh laundry themselves in their loose white costumes. Lying on the floor, they suggest the rotating wash cycle by briskly waving their arms and legs. Later,
(10) as the action speeds up, they swing rolled-up sheets that churn around Penny Hutchinson, who plays a sort of heroine-housewife. Set to words and music by Herschel Garfein, the fantasy moves from borderline silly to giddily lyrical. Morris laughs at soap-company ad pitches but not at the washday ritual. For the
(15) indomitable housewife he has open affection.

Soap-Powders is a brimming piece of choreography, filled with wit and invention and a certain brash confidence. At 29, Morris is the hottest young choreographer in the country. His Seattle-based troupe of 13 dancers is in heavy demand and other
(20) signs of success are visible . . .

Like many other modern and postmodern choreographers, Morris also dances with his company. He is a riveting performer, with a delicate, Chaplinesque face atop a strong, bulbous body. . . . In *One Charming Night,* a dance set to four Purcell
(25) songs, he presents his own outrageously funny version of the old warhorse *Le Spectre de la Rose,* leaping and swooping with abandoned ardor around his seated beloved (Teri Weksler). But unlike Fokine's blithe spirit, Morris does not finish by flying out the window. Instead, he and Weksler thrash out their all too mundane
(30) frustrations and resentments before he finally carries her off, high above his head, as if to reassert his ideal of love. *One Charming Night* shows both sides of Morris' creation: ingratiating invention and, occasionally, youthful overkill of a good idea.

Distinguish Fact from Opinion

This skill involves determining which statements can be proved.

People read reviews to find out what a critic thinks about an artistic work. This form of writing is heavily opinionated. At times, few actual facts are presented. Keep these points in mind:

Facts can be proved true or false Observation and testimony are used to establish the truth of a statement. For example, a reviewer might write: "Morris's dance troupe has 13 dancers." Clearly this is a fact.

Opinions cannot be established as true or false The reviewer might also write: "The twirling, whirling dancers seem like a hundred pieces of spin/dry laundry." This is an opinion.

Be aware of key words "In my opinion," "I thought," "it seems."

Examples

DIRECTIONS: Use the information on this page and the review from *Time* magazine on the preceding page to choose the one best answer for each item below.

1. On the basis of the passage, which of the following is the writer's opinion?

   (1) Mark Morris is 29 years old.
   (2) He performs with his troupe.
   (3) He resembles Charlie Chaplin.
   (4) Seattle is his home base.
   (5) *Soap-Powders* is about washday.

Answer: (3) This is an opinion. While Morris's face strikes the writer as Chaplinesque, it might not have the same effect on others. Information about Morris in the other choices cannot be argued against.

2. Which of the following states a fact about *Soap-Powders and Detergents*?

   (1) The work is cheerful.
   (2) The dancers look like clean white laundry.
   (3) At times the piece verges on silliness.
   (4) The dancers lying on the floor wave their arms and legs.
   (5) The choreography is full of wit.

Answer: (4) This is the only observable choice. All other choices reflect the critic's personal opinion.

Practice

HINT Remember to keep separating the facts from the reviewer's opinions. You may be surprised to see how few facts some reviews actually contain.

DIRECTIONS: Choose the one best answer for each item below.

Items 1–4 refer to the following review from the Village Voice.

WILL HIGH-TECH CHANGE TAP DANCING?

Hines dances on a specially miked platform-stage about seven by five feet, constructed to amplify the taps. Hines is trying to figure out how to bring tap up-to-date with technology, to tune the sounds of the percussions by experimenting with different

(5) surfaces and amplification. As an improviser, Hines's choices are *always* surprising and wild. He takes you in unpredictable directions, cutting into phrases in unexpected places, alternating rest periods with full-blown movement as he skitters over the surface of his soundstage. A tough, get-down tapper who hunches over his

(10) feet, Hines keeps his head low like a fighter, listening, focusing himself and us on the sound of his feet. Neither graceful nor light (although he makes his feet whisper sweet nothings when he wants to) Hines is something better and rarer in the tap dance world, a sexy and compelling performer. Of all the tappers I

(15) know, Hines is perhaps the most inventive because he is fearless. Almost single-handedly he is pushing tap's technology and is a true modernist in how he uses rhythms. Frequently, he'll wrench phrases out of rhythm to create tension. On the feet of a lesser performer it could be chaotic. On Hines, it is exhilarating.

1. Which of these is *not* a fact?

(1) Hines uses a special soundstage.
(2) His platform amplifies the taps.
(3) The stage measures five by seven feet.
(4) Hines is always surprising.
(5) He likes to experiment with sound.

2. Hines is an unusual tap dancer because of

(1) an ability to improvise
(2) his height
(3) his interest in high technology
(4) a fondness for Duke Ellington music
(5) his resemblance to Fred Astaire

GO ON TO THE NEXT PAGE.

3. Why does Hines dance with his head down?

(1) to show toughness
(2) to gain momentum
(3) because he is an ex-boxer
(4) because he is slightly deaf
(5) to focus attention on his feet

4. The reviewer concludes that this dancer is creative because

(1) he takes risks
(2) he studied with Martha Graham
(3) he starred in motion pictures
(4) he grew up in a musical family
(5) his hobby is building robots

Items 5–8 refer to the following review from New York *magazine.*

DO YOU TAKE THE D TRAIN?

The most picturesque way to get from Manhattan to a performance at the Brooklyn Academy of Music is to take the D train
over the Manhattan Bridge. The slow ride over the dark water,
the lights that outline the bridges and twinkle along the skyline—
(5) this is perhaps our last piece of 90-cent romance. The trip made a
perfect prelude to the opening program in the three-week season
of Twyla Tharp Dance, in which *Nine Sinatra Songs* was the high-
light of the evening.

Tharp suggests a make-believe ballroom, with midnight-blue
(10) curtains and a faceted globe that rotates over the heads of the
dancers, casting blurry diamonds into the space. To the caressing
"Softly As I Leave You," Shelley Washington and Keith Young, in
elegant evening clothes, float in each other's arms, a latter-day
Rogers and Astaire. He releases her, she spins dreamily into the
(15) distance, then rushes back toward him, and he plucks her out of
the air. The action is so easy, so tender, she seems to have no
more substance than a cloud. . . .

. . . [Tharp] has given the conventions of theatrical ballroom
dancing her laser-beam scrutiny and is delivering up, deadpan,
(20) both the nonsense and the beauty in them. The Sinatra songs are
perfect for her purpose—egregiously sentimental now that they're
heard out of their time context, and still irresistible.

5. Which of these states a fact?

(1) A Brooklyn subway ride is romantic.
(2) Shelley Washington looks weightless.
(3) Sinatra songs are irresistible.
(4) Deep-blue curtains adorned the stage.
(5) Tharp's staging is laser-beam sharp.

6. The writer of the review was probably

(1) a fan of Frank Sinatra's
(2) a reporter covering a pop concert
(3) a person who enjoys riding trains
(4) a first-time visitor to New York
(5) a resident of Brooklyn

7. The dancers who perform "Softly As I Leave You" remind the reviewer of

(1) dazzling jewels
(2) dream images
(3) two floating clouds
(4) a famous former dance team
(5) a couple of Sinatra fans

8. The main theme of the review is

(1) Sinatra is a wonderful singer
(2) Tharp is a brilliant choreographer
(3) *Swan Lake* looks tired
(4) the pas de deux was a fiasco
(5) Brooklyn is breathtaking

**Before you take the GED Mini-Test,
check your answers on pages 274–275.**

DIRECTIONS: Choose the <u>one</u> best answer for each item below.

Items 1–6 refer to the following review by Edwin Denby.

WHAT DOES CLARA RECEIVE FOR CHRISTMAS?

The New York City Ballet's *Nutcracker* is a smash hit . . . It is Balanchine's *Oklahoma*—a family spectacle, large and leisurely, that lasts two hours and sends people home refreshed and happy. . . .

(5) . . . Two children are sleeping in an armchair, left alone. Clara, the little girl, wakes up and goes to the door, peers through the keyhole. She wakes up her brother Fritz . . . In the next room Father and Mother and the maid are trimming the Christmas tree. Guests arrive, children and parents. For the children there are games and gifts, a box of sugarplums; for the grownups tea and conversation. Little girls behave, boys

(10) grow rowdy. An odd guest comes in late, bringing huge packages. He is an inventor, fascinating and a bit frightening, an artist who makes singular clocks and mechanical toys. He brings three that can actually dance; he also brings a wooden-headed nutcracker for Clara. And he brings his nephew, a boy of Clara's age . . . Clara and he get along very

(15) well, too well for Fritz. He grabs his sister's nutcracker and stamps on it. But it isn't badly hurt and Clara puts it to sleep in a new doll bed. There is a traditional party dance for everyone and Clara dances with the clock-maker's nephew. Then the party is over, the guests say goodbye. And the room is empty.

(20) Clara steals back in her nightgown to see her wounded nutcracker. But strange things happen. . . .

The Nutcracker is a fantasy ballet for children, like a toy that a grownup makes with thoughtful care. Grownups watching can slip back into a world they have left. The buried longings of it are there glittering

(25) still, but so charmingly, so lightly offered one doesn't have to notice. It is enough to notice the amusing family bits in the party scene, the fun of the transformations, the jokes in the dream, the sweet brilliance of the dancing, the pervasive grace of the music. And there is the pleasure of seeing children on stage who are not made to look saccharine or hys-

(30) terical, who do what they do naturally and straight.

1. The critic thinks that *The Nutcracker*

   (1) makes people feel depressed
   (2) is boring to twentieth-century viewers
   (3) treats animals with cruelty
   (4) seems excessively violent
   (5) makes people feel good

2. The tone of this passage can *best* be described as

   (1) sad
   (2) indifferent
   (3) pessimistic
   (4) sarcastic
   (5) pleased

GO ON TO THE NEXT PAGE.

3. Which of the following *best* describes the inventor of the nutcracker?

   (1) ridiculous
   (2) scary
   (3) humorous
   (4) crippled
   (5) arrogant

4. According to the passage, Clara's brother *most* likely takes the nutcracker because he is

   (1) imaginative
   (2) jealous
   (3) awed
   (4) clumsy
   (5) happy

5. Which one of the following impressed the reviewer?

   (1) admirable child dancers
   (2) the graceful chorus of swans
   (3) a parade of wooden soldiers
   (4) Cinderella's Ugly Sisters
   (5) can-can dancers

6. According to the passage, which of the following is a fact?

   (1) The dancing is spectacular.
   (2) The music is elegant.
   (3) The jokes are funny.
   (4) Ballet is family entertainment.
   (5) The inventor brings dancing gifts.

Check your answers to the GED Mini-Test on page 275.

Answers and Explanations

Practice   *pp. 271–272*

1. **Answer:** (4)   Declaring that Hines is *"always* surprising" presents the writer's belief. The information about Hines's special stage, given in choices (1) to (3), does not depend on agreement with the writer. They involve physical features of a platform. Likewise, choice (5) offers no opportunity for disagreement since Hines clearly *is* fascinated with experimenting.

2. **Answer:** (3)   Selecting the correct answer involved determining the main point of the passage. In the second sentence (line 3), the writer introduces technology and continues to pursue the idea that using elements of high-tech makes Hines an unusual tap dancer. Choice (1) is incorrect because all tap dancers improvise. The remaining choices do not appear in the excerpt.

3. **Answer:** (5)   Lines 10–11 mention that Hines keeps his head low to emphasize the tapping sounds, both to himself and his audience. Therefore, it could be the only correct answer. You will find no references to the remaining alternatives in the selection.

4. **Answer:** (1)   The passage contains no information about Hines's background or personal life, choices (2) to (5). But from the phrase "the most inventive because he is fearless," you should have inferred that part of his talent lies in a willingness to take risks.

5. **Answer:** (4)   The detail about the blue curtains is given in lines 9–10 when the writer is describing the stage set. This is a fact. Comments concerning subways, weightlessness, Sinatra's songs and Tharp's talent describe the critic's personal feelings and do not reflect facts.

6. **Answer:** (1)   Nowhere in the selection is there a direct answer to this question. But from the passage as a whole it is not hard to figure out her admiration for Frank Sinatra and from line 22 you know that the writer thinks Sinatra's songs are "irresistible." If you picked choices (2) to (5), you did not read the review with enough care.

7. Answer: (4)   This question called for remembering a specific detail about the dancers' style. The critic states that they remind her of Ginger Rogers and Fred Astaire. Choice (1) refers to lighting. Choices (2) and (3) are partially mentioned, but the passage deals only with the female dancer; "[she] . . . spins dreamily— . . . has no more substance than a cloud." Choice (5) is incorrect.

8. Answer: (2)   The review is about Twyla Tharp. While choice (1) looks like a possibility, the excellence of Sinatra's music is not the review's main idea. Admiring references to Sinatra lend support to the premise that she makes wise musical selections. Choices (3) to (5) are irrelevant.

GED Mini-Test   *pp. 273–274*

1. Answer: (5)   From the excerpt you can infer that the ballet delighted the audience as well as the reviewer. Words such as "refreshed" and "happy" should have led you to select choice (5).

2. Answer: (5)   The tone of this passage is pleased. The choice of words such as "pleasure" (line 28) suggest the writer's positive feelings. Nowhere does he indicate disapproval of the production.

3. Answer: (2)   Lines 10–12 describe the inventor of the nutcracker as an artist who is "fascinating and a bit frightening." All the other answers are totally incorrect.

4. Answer: (2)   Fritz is presented as a boy who resents his sister's new friend. She and the nephew get along "too well" to suit him. The excerpt implies that Fritz wants to break the nutcracker because he is jealous. It was not an accident, as the other choices imply.

5. Answer: (1)   The clues to choice (1) are found in the last line. The reviewer compliments the young dancers who behave without affectation or sugary cuteness. Swans, soldiers, Cinderella and can-can dancers are not mentioned in the passage.

6. Answer: (5)   See lines 10–13 where it is stated that the inventor brings three gifts that can dance. Choices (1) to (4) can be eliminated because they reflect the writer's personal opinion, and are not factual.

35 Commentary Art

Critics and commentators often use cause and effect when dealing with reviews in a historical context.

Be aware of the way art historian Norbert Lynton uses cause and effect in his commentary on ice age art, below. Use the Purpose Question to help you.

WHY DID ICE AGE ARTISTS MAKE ALL THOSE PAINTINGS?

The cave paintings of prehistoric man, done 15 to 20,000 years ago, began to be discovered in the last quarter of the nineteenth century. A world gradually coming to terms with the shocking new art of Impressionism . . . learned that there was art

(5) before the dawn of human history. Before humans learned to write or otherwise record their activities for posterity, when life meant living off whatever the environment provided, the plants that grew, the animals that could be killed (for tools made from their bones as well as for food), people had gone down into the

(10) bowels of the earth to paint large images of animals on to the walls and ceilings of natural caves, and paint them not like clumsy beginners but realistically, naturalistically.

. . . The cave paintings show animals—horses, bison and oxen and also, much less frequently, mammoth, deer and ibex. Occa-

(15) sionally they showed other things: crudely simplified human beings and signs for things that may be spears and traps.

It used to be said that these paintings were done to give the painter and the group power over the animals represented. . . . This is a satisfying explanation of why such lifelike images should

(20) have been painted deep down in dark places where they can hardly have been meant to be looked at, but doubt has been cast on it recently. For one thing, we know from other evidence that these hunters of long ago ate mostly reindeer meat and used reindeer bones as tools, yet they did not paint reindeer images.

(25) . . . It must have taken time to develop this art, and it is more or less certain that the painters were specialists who passed the knowledge and skill to each other. Perhaps they were also the tool makers of the group, thus giving power to their fellows. They may even have been spiritual as well as practical guides, the pre-

(30) historic equivalents of the medicine-men of the American Indians or the witch doctors of Africa.

What we call art and associate with pleasure and interest was then a basic necessity, part of the struggle to survive. Did it give pleasure as well? Did the painters ever say to each other, or the

(35) others say to them, 'That's a good one' and 'That one is not so good'? Again, we can only guess. . . .

Identify Cause and Effect Relationships

A cause and effect relationship indicates how one thing affects another. A cause is what makes something happen. An effect is what happens as a result.

The passage on the previous page made use of the **cause** and **effect** relationship. Ideas came up. These ideas made something else happen. A cause brought about a result, or an effect. For example:

> In 15,000 B.C. someone drew a picture of a horse. (**cause**)
> In 1900 A.D. someone found a horse drawn on a cave wall. (**result**)

The result above is that very old paintings exist in caves. What happened to cause these paintings?

When identifying cause and effect relationships, look for clue words or phrases. If these signal words themselves do not appear in the text, their meaning is still implied.

It is not unusual for the result to be presented before the cause or for a cause to appear in one paragraph and the effect to follow in another paragraph.

Clue Words

because	therefore
since	as a result
consequently	

Examples

DIRECTIONS: Use the information on this page and the review by Norbert Lynton on the preceding page to choose the <u>one</u> best answer for each item below.

1. According to the passage, prehistoric people produced much art. Why?

   (1) as an expression of creativity
   (2) to gain control over animals
   (3) nobody knows for certain
   (4) for religious purposes
   (5) as a means of education

Answer: (3) The reason that the Ice Age produced art is a mystery. The author states in the final sentence that all the theories are only guesses.

2. Which of the following can be concluded from the passage?

   (1) Gathering food was a problem.
   (2) Painters learned from other artists.
   (3) Probably it was too dark to view the paintings clearly.
   (4) Art was not important to survival.
   (5) Art was essential in people's lives.

Answer: (5) The last paragraph describes prehistoric art as a need rather than as a luxury, "a basic necessity."

Practice

HINT

As you read, ask: Why did this happen, and What were the effects or results?

DIRECTIONS: Choose the <u>one</u> best answer for each item below.

Items 1–4 refer to the following review by art historian Marshall B. Davidson.

WHY WERE THE MIDDLE AGES A GREAT NEW AGE OF ART?

It was in these late medieval years that wonderfully skilled metalworkers hammered out suits of armor for knights to wear in mortal combat or in jousting tournaments. These steel-plated trappings were things of beauty that were, as well, perfectly
(5) designed to protect the wearer from head to toe. Other crafts-workers wove the brilliantly colored tapestries that hung in castles and churches to help ward off the wintry chill of bare stone walls. And it was at this time, too, that talented artists painted the exquisite miniatures that illuminated the pages of religious books.
(10) The most complete and magnificent expression of the medieval spirit was incorporated in the Gothic cathedral. . . . The huge structures were decorated with sculptured images, stained glass windows, and spires that shot up toward the heavens, rising higher than any structures ever before imagined.
(15) The Middle Ages was not simply a middle period in history between classical and modern times. It was a time when the artistic talents of a wide variety of people were forged into shared creations.

1. According to the passage, what made the Middle Ages an important period in art history?

   (1) brave knights
   (2) protection by kings
   (3) the influence of the Crusades
   (4) gifted artists
   (5) Church support

2. The *most* significant artistic achievement of the medieval period was the construction of

   (1) walled cities
   (2) beautiful monasteries
   (3) giant churches
   (4) fortified castles
   (5) wooden bridges

3. The writer is *primarily* concerned with showing how the Middle Ages

   (1) practically destroyed Western art
   (2) cared about beautiful objects
   (3) waged barbaric wars
   (4) was more creative than people think
   (5) produced no good artists

4. Which of the following would *not* be incorporated into a Gothic cathedral?

   (1) tapestries
   (2) fireplaces
   (3) colorful windows
   (4) statues
   (5) steeples

GO ON TO THE NEXT PAGE.

278　PRACTICE

Items 5–6 refer to the following New York Times *art review.*

WHY HAS JOHN MARTIN MADE A COMEBACK?

Fifty years ago it was possible to buy a painting by John Martin for next to nothing. As for the books that he illustrated, they turned up on book barrows all over England and cost only pennies. Born in the year of the French Revolution, Martin lived until
(5) 1854, had moments of celebrity in his lifetime and then somehow fell through the floorboards of art history. The fact that he was a visionary artist who could match himself against the Old Testament and go the distance without apparent effort counted for nothing in the 1920's and 1930's.
(10) But in our own time, John Martin has come all the way back again. Curators, connoisseurs and book collectors stand in line for his work when it appears on the market. His visions were true visions—fiery and never-failing, with direct access to heaven, hell and all regions between. . . .

5. What cause renewed interest in John Martin's work during recent years?

(1) cheap prices
(2) his powerful imagination
(3) scarcity of his paintings
(4) luck
(5) nostalgia for the nineteenth century

6. Anyone could have bought a Martin painting in the 1920s

(1) for millions of dollars
(2) with great difficulty
(3) for practically nothing
(4) for a moderate price
(5) by lining up at auctions

Items 7–8 refer to the following review by Norbert Lynton.

WHERE DID POP ART GET ITS NAME?

Pop suggests popular. The movement got a lot of publicity from the media who saw that it was news, easy to enjoy and easy to write about. It was the time when pop stars like Elvis Presley and the Beatles were emerging, and this art in many instances
(5) was responding to that world rather than the world of deep human feelings and problems. Its idiom was in many cases borrowed from the media: whereas art normally proceeded by taking ideas from art and making something new of them, this came from commercial art and so was speaking a language created by
(10) experts to reach the whole consumer society. For the same reason many commentators, especially in the United States, hated it. It denied, or seemed to deny, all seriousness and attach itself to commonplace fantasies and the hard sell. . . .

7. According to the passage, the term "pop art" means that it

(1) appealed to fans of rock and roll
(2) was not expensive
(3) received TV and press coverage
(4) dealt with important issues
(5) was favored by religious groups

8. One reason that some people objected to pop art was because

(1) it was too romantic
(2) it lacked serious content
(3) pop artists copied Picasso
(4) it had no humor
(5) the subject matter was unpleasant

Before you take the GED Mini-Test,
check your answers on page 281.

GED Mini-Test

35

TIP
Use your reading skills to help you when answering test items. Remember that a key to passing the GED test is reading for understanding.

DIRECTIONS: Choose the one best answer for each item below.

Items 1–6 refer to the following review by Bernard Myers.

WHAT IS ONE OF THE MOST OVERESTIMATED PAINTINGS?

Unquestionably the most glittering personality of the High Renaissance in Italy and the pioneer in its new and magnificent form of expression was Leonardo da Vinci. Even as a youth he displayed an aptitude for all manner of achievement, a winning charm, and a personal
(5) strength and beauty which have become almost legendary. In time this brilliant boy would become not only one of the leading artists of the sixteenth century, but its greatest contributor to the advancement of modern ideas as well. Leonardo possessed a variety of artistic talents— he was architect, sculptor, musician. He also mastered and did original
(10) work in the fields of mathematics, geology, engineering, anatomy, and every other science known in his day. More than anyone else he had "taken all knowledge as his sphere." Leonardo spent the early part of his life in Florence and then stayed in Milan for a number of years working on many important projects, including the *Madonna of the Rocks* and
(15) the *Last Supper*. The latter (perhaps the best known painting in the world) offers one of the finest instances of a rigid geometric enclosure. Everything turns inward toward the head of Christ, even the expressive gestures of His own hands. In spite of the great excitement within the work, complete formal control is maintained. . . .
(20) In the *Mona Lisa*, one of the most overdiscussed and overrated pictures of all time (through no fault of its own), the same balance of monumental form and lyrical feeling is evident. This poetic sense, here as in many other works, is a definite Leonardo quality. It has little to do with portraiture, that is, with analysis of the sitter. If it is considered
(25) part of the painter's own personality and not that of the somewhat smug lady, the picture takes on a different meaning. Certainly it is mysterious, but so are Leonardo's other paintings. To this artist, all things, human and divine, were fit subjects for the searching analysis of his extraordinary mind.

1. According to the passage, Leonardo is considered a genius because

   (1) he painted the *Last Supper*
   (2) he designed a flying machine
   (3) people were dazzled by his beauty
   (4) he was gifted in art and science
   (5) his anatomical sketches were superb

2. The passage states that the organization of the *Last Supper* uses geometry to focus every element in the painting toward

   (1) Judas
   (2) the windows
   (3) Christ's head
   (4) the bread
   (5) the hands of Christ

GO ON TO THE NEXT PAGE.

3. By saying that Leonardo took "all knowledge as his sphere," the writer means that he

   (1) was a nervous person
   (2) felt confused
   (3) had varied interests
   (4) felt unhappy being a painter
   (5) had trouble concentrating on one subject

5. Leonardo would *most* likely paint

   (1) any subject that caught his imagination
   (2) any subject he was hired to do
   (3) portraits of medieval nobles
   (4) religiously significant scenes
   (5) mathematically based studies

4. In the writer's opinion, the importance of the *Mona Lisa* has been exaggerated because

   (1) Leonardo was a pioneer in art
   (2) Leonardo lived during the Renaissance
   (3) he is not to blame for the portrait's fame
   (4) Leonardo had an extraordinary mind
   (5) all his works have depth

6. When did Leonardo's remarkable abilities first arouse attention?

   (1) after his death
   (2) during his years in Milan
   (3) as a boy near Florence
   (4) in his last years
   (5) after painting the *Last Supper*

Check your answers to the GED Mini-Test on page 282.

Answers and Explanations

Practice *pp. 278–279*

1. **Answer:** (4) See the last paragraph. You know that the Middle Ages were important in art history and that this was expressed in a variety of ways. The writer mentions armor, tapestries, miniatures and cathedrals. Although the information is implied throughout the passage, it is summarized at the end.

3. **Answer:** (4) According to the passage, the Middle Ages is often regarded as an insignificant link between Roman and modern times. Since so much fine art was produced, this view is incorrect, according to the author.

5. **Answer:** (2) Martin's "fiery" visions were the cause of his revival in recent times. There is no suggestion of cheap prices, choice (1). You should have eliminated choices (3) to (5) as inaccurate.

7. **Answer:** (3) Choices (1) to (2) and (4) to (5) can be eliminated as incorrect by careful examination. All suggest that pop art had a serious approach to art. The message of the passage is the opposite, however, and states that pop art was promoted by the media.

2. **Answer:** (3) The correct answer is giant churches or cathedrals. This period also saw the building of monasteries, castles, walled cities and timber bridges, but these are not discussed in the excerpt.

4. **Answer:** (2) The first paragraph includes "castles and churches" as places where tapestries were hung. The second paragraph describes some of the artistic features found in Gothic cathedrals. The only answer that is not supported by the passage is choice (2), fireplaces.

6. **Answer:** (3) The artist's work sold for "next to nothing." This information occurs in the first sentence of the passage. All the remaining alternatives imply he was popular in the 1920s, which is the opposite of what the passage is saying.

8. **Answer:** (2) Actually the passage gives two reasons for criticism of pop art: It was frivolous, and its ideas were more commercial than artistic. From the name "pop art" it is possible to infer a lack of seriousness.

GED Mini-Test *pp. 280–281*

1. **Answer:** (4)   Each of the choices gives accurate information, but choice (4) is the only one to supply a reason for his brilliance that is also supported by the passage. The first paragraph explains that he was considered a genius because of his gifts in art and the sciences.

2. **Answer:** (3)   The information is in line 17. A careful reading of the text will reveal no mention of choices (1), (2) or (4). Choice (5) refers to the fact that even Christ's own hands are turned toward His head.

3. **Answer:** (3)   "All knowledge as his sphere" (line 12) means the desire for knowledge that knows no boundaries. Leonardo's genius was not limited to one area. Notice references in the passage to "an aptitude for all manner of achievement" (lines 3–4) and "all things, human and divine, were fit subjects . . ." (lines 27–28). The other choices suggest negative qualities not in keeping with the passage.

4. **Answer:** (5)   This question asks you to distinguish fact from opinion. The writer feels that all Leonardo's works convey depth and mystery. Therefore, it is not fair to single out the *Mona Lisa*. The other options are factual statements occurring in the passage. They do not reflect the writer's judgment.

5. **Answer:** (1)   Leonardo would most likely paint any subject that captured his imagination (lines 27–29). Choice (2) is incorrect. It can be inferred from the passage that his skill was so acknowledged that he did not have to take every assignment that came along. Choices (3) to (5) refer to *some* types of scenes and styles he used, but not all.

6. **Answer:** (3)   The passage speaks of Leonardo showing unusual aptitudes as a youth and he is called "this brilliant boy" (line 6). Only choice (3) accurately sums up this detail. The other choices are incorrect.

In the commentary section you have read criticism about fiction and poetry and the popular arts including television, film, dance, art, music and theater. You have seen how critics observe and describe these works. You also learned that the most important function of a critic is to assist the reader by offering a professional opinion of the work being reviewed. Another aspect of commentary is presenting the material in an effective and well-written personal style. Critics use various literary techniques. Some of the techniques you have studied in this section were cause and effect, implications, tone and the use of fact versus personal opinion. As you answer the review questions, be aware of the strategies you have studied.

DIRECTIONS: Choose the <u>one</u> best answer for each item below.

1. The film critic for the *Weekly Enquirer* comments on a movie about Marie Antoinette. Playing the queen is the popular actress Wendy Woebegone. The critic thinks Wendy's acting is nauseating and her long, sour face has an unfortunate resemblance to a horse. The *best* way to express all this would be to

   (1) compliment Wendy on her French accent
   (2) suggest a boycott of her films
   (3) imply Wendy should take acting lessons
   (4) use inference or tone to suggest disapproval
   (5) refuse to review the film

2. Linda Literary is asked to review a first novel about a British spy ring in Athens. Before willingly reading a first novel, Linda would rather inhale carbon monoxide. She also loathes spy stories, and she once had her luggage stolen in Athens. The book receives a poor review. These clues suggest that commentary can sometimes be influenced by

   (1) politics
   (2) sex
   (3) personal prejudices
   (4) education
   (5) marital status

3. In 1961 *The New Yorker* published the following remark about Walker Percy's novel *The Moviegoer*: "Mr. Percy's prose needs oil and a good checkup." The magazine's comment would be *best* described as

   (1) literary gossip
   (2) fact
   (3) metaphor
   (4) opinion
   (5) untruth

4. In 1986 *The New York Times Book Review* commented upon *Year Before Last*, a novel by Kay Boyle. The review included this sentence: "A young woman leaves her husband to run away to France with a consumptive young writer, but his rich aunt's jealousy complicates their lives and threatens their financial security." Which of the following *best* describes the comment?

   (1) literary gossip
   (2) fact
   (3) metaphor
   (4) opinion
   (5) untruth

GO ON TO THE NEXT PAGE.

Items 5–6 refer to the following commentary by a dance critic.

IS IT CRITICAL TO BE A GOOD CRITIC?

On the subject of dance criticism, I should like to make clear a distinction that I believe is very valuable. . . . And that is that there are two quite different aspects to it. One part of dance criticism is seeing what is happening on stage. The other is describing clearly what it is you saw. Seeing something happen is always fun for everybody, until they get exhausted. It is very exhausting to keep looking, of course, just as it is to keep doing anything else. . . .

Now the second part of criticism, that of expressing lucidly what happened, is of course what makes criticism criticism. If you are going in for criticism you must have the gift in the first place, and in the second place you must cultivate it, you must practice and try. Writing criticism is a subject of interest to those who do it, but it is a separate process from that of seeing what happens. . . .

5. According to the passage, a person who enjoys watching a dance performance would *best* be described as

(1) a dance coach
(2) a dance fan
(3) a dance critic
(4) a dance student
(5) a dance historian

6. A person who describes a dance performance would be

(1) a dance coach
(2) a dance fan
(3) a dance critic
(4) a dance student
(5) a dance historian

Items 7–8 refer to the following commentary from the New York Times.

HOW SERIOUS IS THIS SERIES COVERAGE?

Say this about the World Series: It has been intimate. Seldom before have so many seen so few so close; the television cameras stared at ballplayers' faces. What will be the best-remembered television image of the 1986 World Series? It will be . . . players with wads of tobacco, gum or

(5) sunflower seeds in their jaws. On television, this was the year of the big spit. . . .

. . . For the most part, it's not unseemly brown goo. Davey Johnson, the Mets' manager, tucks away a wad of Red Man chewing tobacco each time he changes pitchers, but we never see him discharge the juice.

(10) Nonetheless, it has been virtually impossible to get through an inning without watching one or more ballplayers let go. At bat, Dykstra, for one, is an intermittent fountain; Wilson isn't far behind. Keith Hernandez, meanwhile, pops bubble gum. Never have we seen so many moving jaws. . . .

7. The *best* example of cause and effect utilized in this review would be the relationship between the use of TV and

(1) Dykstra's batting average
(2) Johnson's managerial style
(3) extreme close-ups of players
(4) the enjoyment of the fans
(5) coverage of the Mets

8. The reviewer's tone on the subject of TV coverage of the World Series can *best* be described as

(1) amused and easy-going
(2) factual and hard-hitting
(3) bored and reserved
(4) passionate and intense
(5) sarcastic and displeased

GO ON TO THE NEXT PAGE.

DOES RAGGEDY ANN HAVE ROUGH EDGES?

Finally we have a show that adults and children can view with equal distaste. *Raggedy Ann* is a musical guaranteed to bore the pants, skirts, and diapers off anyone of any age with a halfway normal brain, and it may be that the family that walks out together, stays together. . . . This

(5)   is the musical that was originally produced by the Empire State Institute for the Performing Arts in Albany, and was sent to Moscow, though Siberia would have been more appropriate. Its co-producers include the Kennedy Center (it has been seen in Washington) and CBS (it has, I gather, been seen on television). Ready or not, the world is getting this

(10)   show, advertised as "the musical with a heart," crammed down its throat, and I can only hope that its body will reject this transplanted organ.

9. Which of the following adjectives *best* describes the critic's opinion of *Raggedy Ann*?

(1) entertaining
(2) heartbreaking
(3) thought-provoking
(4) dreadful
(5) inspiring

10. The critic reveals his judgment of *Raggedy Ann* by

(1) contrasting it with *Peter Pan*
(2) writing in a sarcastic tone
(3) using metaphors
(4) summarizing the plot
(5) relying on similes

11. Prior to the New York premiere, the musical was seen

(1) at a special White House gala
(2) in London
(3) in Boston and Philadelphia
(4) in Elmira
(5) in the Soviet Union

12. Based on the passage, *Raggedy Ann* had been advertised as a musical that had

(1) clever costumes
(2) appeal for children of all ages
(3) lots of good feelings
(4) two hours of nonstop laughs
(5) songs by Cole Porter

HAVE WE ENTERED THE AGE OF "INSTANT ART"?

Make way for the artists of the next fifteen minutes. The debut of Meyer Vaisman, Jeff Koons, Peter Halley, and Ashley Bickerton at the Sonnabend Gallery . . . is a masterpiece of performance art. I have never seen so much hype and hoopla directed at four artists whose resumes,

(5)   aside from student exhibitions, barely reach back to 1984.

There is literally nothing in this work that is not a rehash of twenty years of conceptualism and Pop Art—but no matter. Their insight lies in *emptying* their work of content, the better to meet the requirements of the media age, which demands buzzwords and quick zooms and creates

(10)   new stars out of gossamer electronic fuzz. A whole generation now arrives from its training grounds, the boob tube and the silver screen. . . .

GO ON TO THE NEXT PAGE.

13. According to the passage, the attitude of the four artists was influenced by

(1) 1960s music
(2) Picasso and his friends
(3) TV and movies
(4) space exploration
(5) the development of silicon chips

14. The person reviewing this art show appears to be

(1) disgusted
(2) sad
(3) full of admiration
(4) sympathetic
(5) indifferent

Items 15–18 refer to the following review from TV Guide.

WILL THE STORY OF ENGLISH TRANSLATE TO THE LITTLE SCREEN?

If you're missing these nine fascinating programs on PBS you ought to be forced to surrender forever your privilege to deride television as a boob tube filled with nothing but bubble gum for the mind.

(5) *The Story of English* is exactly what the title implies, the story of where English came from, how it developed, what has influenced it, where and why it is spoken in its many forms and finally, where it is going. The story is told with such brilliant use of the medium's ability to present sight, sound and motion that it becomes as riveting as a well-produced drama.

(10) The programs succeed not only in informing viewers in a delightfully entertaining way, but also in imbuing them with a new respect and even love for our language. More important, perhaps, we gain an understanding of the varieties of English—not "dialects," the series insists—spoken in our country. We learn, too, how black English and contribu-

(15) tions from our many ethnic groups have enriched American English; how poker games on Mississippi river boats, the joining of East and West by the railroads and the everyday work of cowboys added colorful and unique Americanisms to the language. . . .

The Story of English is a treat for the eyes, the ears and the mind—

(20) worthy of a place among high television achievements alongside *Civilization*, *The Ascent of Man* and, to our shame, too few other examples of the medium at its best.

15. The phrase "bubble gum for the mind" (line 3) means that

(1) TV viewers like to chew gum
(2) people will watch practically anything
(3) some programs require little thought
(4) TV viewers are objecting to dull programs
(5) fruit is a better TV snack than gum

16. The reviewer urges readers to

(1) stop criticizing television shows
(2) buy videocassette recorders
(3) watch *The Story of English*
(4) avoid TV soap operas
(5) see re-runs of *The Ascent of Man*

17. Based on the passage, black English and ethnic English are *most* accurately described as

(1) basically bad grammar
(2) dialects
(3) deliberate distortions of English
(4) genuine forms of English
(5) borrowings from foreign languages

18. *The Story of English* could be described as

(1) how gambling began on river boats
(2) the inside story on cowboys
(3) the history of American railroads
(4) how immigrants changed America
(5) everything to be known about our language

Check your answers to the Review on pages 292–293.

Answers and Explanations

Mini-Review   *pp. 81–83*

1. **Answer:** (4)   Choice (1) is the opposite of what the author says in the passage. There is no support in the passage for choice (2). The woman who invented white crane boxing did live at a Shao-lin temple, but this was not what made her an ideal. Choice (3) is false; the passage indicates that dangerous women had their feet bound, but not that having feet bound makes a woman ideal. There is no support for choice (5).

2. **Answer:** (5)   Choices (1), (2) and (3) are all related to how the woman who invented white crane boxing learned about it. The question asks how the author learned about it, so these choices are all wrong. Choice (4) is wrong, although it repeats a detail from the passage about an ideal woman. It is plain that this is not where the author learned about boxing. Only choice (5) fits the context of the passage.

3. **Answer:** (2)   The passage does not say that the woman who invented white crane boxing was a legend, but the context of the story shows that she was. Choice (1) is wrong; this passage uses very little figurative language. Choice (3) is wrong because the story of the woman is clearly not a true story from the history books. Choices (4) and (5) are false; there is nothing about a woman who failed or the author's own life in the passage.

4. **Answer:** (2)   Choices (3) and (4) have no support in the passage and the word "everyone" in these choices is a tip-off that they are wrong. Choice (1) is a possible inference from the passage, but choice (2) is a much stronger inference, since choice (2) is related to the swordswoman whom the author clearly admires. Choice (5) is false; the passage says that the Chinese woman fails if she is only a wife.

5. **Answer:** (1)   There is no support in the passage for choice (2), although it may be true. Choice (4) might also be true, but the man had the same views as the presidential candidate, so his being unknown does not make him necessarily unlike the presidential candidate. Choice (5) is false; it is not history that causes the choice of the unknown. Choice (3) is also false; they do not support him because he is a pig in a poke, but because he is their candidate.

6. **Answer:** (1)   There is simply no support in the passage for any of the other choices. Only choice (1) makes any sense at all within the context of the passage. You do not need to know that "a pig in a poke" means "something offered in a way that leaves it largely unknown" in order to be able to infer that choice (1) is correct.

7. **Answer:** (4)   Choice (1) is false; the language is not frightening. Choice (2) uses words from the passage, but not in the way they are used in the passage. Choice (3) has no support in the passage. Choice (5) is a possible inference, but choice (4) is a better answer since it has direct support from words like "enormous," "enlarged" and "awesome." In fact, choice (5) is false.

8. **Answer:** (2)   Choice (3) is wrong; it is plain from the context that the orchestra has not begun. Choice (5) is also wrong; even if they liked the music of Mahler they would not be clapping for that reason before a note had been played. Choice (4) might be true, but since the music had not begun, it is probably not true. Choice (1) could be true only if the figurative language about the bird was taken literally. Thus, only choice (2) fits the context of the passage.

9. **Answer:** (1)   Choice (2) would be true only if the figurative language about the bird were taken literally. For the same reason, choices (4) and (5) are false; you have to take figurative language literally for these answers to make sense. There is no support for choice (3).

10. **Answer:** (3)   It is plain from the passage that this is figurative language meant to add effect to the silence just before the conductor begins. There is no support in the passage for any of the other choices, and none of them makes any sense.

Popular Literature Review   *pp. 147–153*

1. **Answer:** (4)   Choice (1) is false; the man is already on the airplane and is trying to get off. Choice (2) fits the context, but it does not explain the man's fear, which is deeper than merely being on the wrong plane. Choice (3) is false; there is no indication that a plane has crashed. Choice (5) is also false; there is no indication that a plane is landing, rather a plane is about to take off. Only choice (4) fits the context of the first 20 lines and also fits the rest of the poem.

2. **Answer:** (3)   Although choice (1) is connected to these lines, since the Bay Bridge is in San Francisco, it is not what the poet is trying to say. There is no support for choice (2) or (4). Choice (5) is wrong since the poet is describing when his father's fear began, and this makes it plain that his father was not always a coward. Only choice (3) truly fits the context of the poem.

3. **Answer:** (2)   Choice (1) is false; there is no indication that the poet is ashamed of his father. Choice (3) is also false; the poem does not address whether the father deserves his fate. The poet simply describes his father's fear as it is and expresses the poet's sorrow that he cannot help. Choice (4) may be true, but it is not what the poet is saying in these lines. There is no support for choice (5).

4. **Answer:** (2)   Choice (1) was probably true of the man before he developed his fear. Choice (3) is not true; the poem indicates that the man used to be brave, but now is frightened of many things. Choice (4) is false. Even if the man is a coward now, he was not always a coward. There is no support for choice (5). The poem does not say anything about the man's anger or lack of anger for his son.

5. **Answer:** (4)   The poet uses all the other techniques and the only one that might not be obvious is choice (5). However, if you read the poem you will see that absolutely nothing is said about the children's clothes, while the feeling of tension becomes more obvious each time you read the poem.

6. **Answer:** (3)   There is no support in the poem for choice (1), although choice (1) may be a true statement. Choice (2) may also be a true statement, but it is not supported by the poem and it is not the main idea. Choice (4) is false; the poem has nothing to do with TV at all. Choice (5) is a possible inference from the poem, but choice (3) fits the context of the whole poem much better.

7. **Answer:** (4)   Choices (1) and (2) have some support since the poet uses figurative language about bankers and soldiers to describe the birthday party. But in fact it is plain from the poem that it is a birthday party. Choices (3) and (5) are thus false.

8. **Answer:** (4)   Choice (1) has no support; there is no indication that the poet thinks children are a burden. Choices (2) and (3) are also unreasonable inferences. The poet is not critical at all of the children, but simply compares them to adults. Choice (5) may be a possible inference, but the poet does not mean that bankers or children have colds when she says they clear their throats.

9. **Answer:** (1) While all the other choices are possible, only this choice fits the context of the passage as a whole. The author says the snake lived sixteen miles up the Brazos, and later that he was seen along the Brazos. Only a river really fits these descriptions. Also, the river ties in to the central event of the passage, which is the flood that brought the snake.

10. **Answer:** (4) You know this is the right choice because it describes the way he behaves in the passage. Thus, choices (1) and (3) are false. From the passage, it is doubtful that choice (2) is true. There is no support at all for choice (5). Even if there were support for this choice, it would not be as good an answer as choice (4), which describes Yancey perfectly.

11. **Answer:** (3) Choice (1) is false; there was no drought, but rather a flood. Choice (2) may be partly true in that the snake is old, but there is no indication he cannot get around. Choice (4) is a possible answer, but the passage does not directly support it. Choice (5) also has no support because there is no indication in the passage what season it is. Choice (3), on the other hand, has ample support.

12. **Answer:** (3) Choice (1) may be true, but it is not the reason the snake would strike Yancey. Choice (2) is false; the passage indicates that the snake avoided people unless threatened. For this reason, choice (4) is also false. Choice (5) is a possible guess, but the passage shows that the snake was not crazed since it tried to warn Yancey away.

13. **Answer:** (4) This is correct because of Oscar's complaints about lacking entertainment. Choices (1), (2), (3) and (5) may all be sources of disagreement but are not discussed here.

14. **Answer:** (3) This is correct because the directions refer to his constant cleaning up. None of the other choices refers to things about Felix that are mentioned in the stage directions.

15. **Answer:** (5) This is correct because of his long speech toward the end of the passage. Choices (1), (2) and (3) refer to things *Oscar* does. Choice (4) refers to things Felix does, but it is not the main idea.

16. **Answer:** (2) This is correct because of their arguments about cleaning and from stage directions, which also rules out choice (1). Choice (3) is unsupported, and they talk about what *is* fun, not who has *more* fun, ruling out choices (4) and (5).

17. **Answer:** (5) This is correct because he describes her behavior in the face of her problems. Choices (1), (2), (3) and (4) also describe Gene's mother, but they are not main ideas.

18. **Answer:** (2) This is correct because of his words in the last line, which rule out choices (1), (4) and (5). Since he does not mention their feelings for him, choice (3) is also incorrect.

19. **Answer:** (2) This is correct because he acts in a military way and tells everyone his life story. Choices (1) and (5) are not supported by the passage, though he likes to watch westerns and make investments. Choice (3) is true, but it is not a main idea. Choice (4) must be ruled out because he never was *in* the military.

20. **Answer:** (2) This is correct because of Gene's words about what happens to them if they do not go. Choice (1) is contradicted by the passage. Choices (3) and (4) are activities they do in Florida, not their reasons for going, and choice (5) is not supported by the passage.

21. Answer: (1)   This is correct because Esperanza is searching for dignity. Choice (2) is not supported by the passage, and choice (3) is too specific for a theme. Choice (4) is a theme statement but not appropriate here, and choice (5), referring to specific characters, is not a theme statement.

22. Answer: (3)   This is correct because of her words in lines 18–20, which would rule out choice (5). Choices (1) and (4) make valid comparisons, but they are not Esperanza's. Since, in this case, the Anglos are the bosses and the Mexicans the workers, choice (2) must also be ruled out.

23. Answer: (3)   This is correct because of his resistance to Esperanza's wish that he be her friend. Choice (1) can be ruled out since he obviously is on strike, and choice (2) is just as clearly incorrect. Choices (4) and (5) must be ruled out because of Ramón's current view of women.

24. Answer: (2)   This is correct because of her words in lines 23–26, which also rule out choice (1). Choice (3) is incorrect because of her obvious wish for equality. Choices (4) and (5) are contradicted by her statements in the passage.

25. Answer: (3)   This is correct because everything she says indicates a wish to think well of herself and others. Choice (1) is important to her, but only as a synonym for self-respect. Choice (2) is something Esperanza would do to *gain* self-respect and, from her words, she clearly does not wish to be independent, choice (4), or more powerful than others, choice (5).

26. Answer: (4)   This is correct because the stage directions indicate that he begins to strike her and then stops. Her lines reinforce that decision. Choice (1) is clearly not the case; she wants them to struggle together. Choices (2) and (3) must be ruled out because of the content of the passage. Choice (5) is incorrect because she already *is* Ramón's friend, although he does not believe it.

Classical Literature Review   *pp. 226–231*

1. Answer: (1)   This choice best sums up the author's style. Although he deals with such factual matter as the weather and terrain, in choice (4), he supplies the reader with these facts in an almost poetic, descriptive way. There is no basis for choices (2), (3) or (5).

2. Answer: (2)   The details—Yukon, unbroken views of ice and snow and fifty degrees below zero, among others—lead to the conclusion that the story takes place in the far north. Although Siberia, in the Soviet Union, choice (1), is also cold and desolate, line 1 mentions the Yukon territory, which is the Canadian far north. There is no evidence for the other choices.

3. Answer: (3)   The details—that the strangeness of the place made no impression on the man, that he did not think about anything much except factual matters, "That there should be anything more to it than that . . ." (line 30)—support the mournful mood the author creates. Choice (1) is hinted at by the graphic descriptions of desolate areas and extreme cold, but the *overall* mood is meditative or thoughtful. There is no basis for the other choices.

4. Answer: (1)   *Vulnerable* means capable of being attacked or wounded. *Frailty* means fragile or easily broken or destroyed. The context clues ". . . able to live within certain narrow limits of heat and cold" (lines 24–25) should have helped you define the term.

5. Answer: (5) The dealer appears to be soft-hearted and friendly in the first paragraph because he is fatherly and kindly and jokes or sympathizes with those he meets. Although choices (1) and (3) are closer to his true nature, the reader does not know this at the beginning of the passage. Choices (2) and (4) do not reflect his personality.

6. Answer: (4) The dealer's professional and obsessional use of the coin (a magician's or trickster's art) help clue the reader to the real personality behind the friendly image he originally projected.

7. Answer: (3) The poet's use of pleasant and positive images reflect a glad and joyful approach to the world. Although the poem has some quiet moments, it is never mournful, choice (1). No other choice is supported by the poem.

8. Answer: (5) This calls for careful reading and recall, since the sound of train whistles is not mentioned. Choices (1) to (4) are all mentioned in the poem.

9. Answer: (5) Mrs. Dudgeon's actions and statements towards both Judith and Essie reveal this. Though she may also be stingy, choice (4), there is no evidence of that characteristic trait in this excerpt. Choices (1) to (3) are incorrect.

10. Answer: (2) Lines 7, 11–13 and 16, all stage directions, reveal characteristics of Judith that show the reader she is smug and self-satisfied. If the reader only had the character's speeches to rely on, choice (1) would be correct. There is no basis for choices (3) to (5).

11. Answer: (4) Lines 19–33, both speeches and stage directions, reveal Essie to be a sad, defeated girl. There is no evidence for the other choices.

12. Answer: (4) Lines 28–30 reveal Essie to be a poor relation. Although she is treated like a servant, choice (1), she is technically not one. There is no basis for choices (2), (3) or (5).

13. Answer: (4) Lines 23–34 explain aspects of an "in crowd" as do many other references throughout the piece. Choice (1) may have looked correct at first glance because the passage begins by talking about army systems. There is no basis for choices (2), (3) or (5).

14. Answer: (3) The author's tone throughout implies that the idea and the unwritten rules of inner circles are humorous. He undoubtedly is a member of some inner circles, choice (5), as we all are, but this does not provide his basic attitude toward them. Choices (1), (2) and (4) are incorrect.

15. Answer: (4) Although the author touches on all other choices as he tells about his early school days, the idea of adapting to new situations is the main idea. Lines 36–38 support this.

16. Answer: (3) The author looks back on his early schooling with fondness and amusement. Although his initial reaction was anger and disbelief, choice (2), when he was faced with his first day of school, his remembrance of the experience as a whole is warm and positive. There is no basis for the other choices.

Commentary Review *pp. 283–286*

1. **Answer:** (4)   Suggesting an opinion through inference or tone would be the most effective way for a reviewer to air his or her views. Choice (1) does not reflect the reviewer's opinion. Choices (2) and (5) do not resolve how to deal with the film in question. Choice (3), though partially correct, does not include all the situations the reviewer is faced with.

2. **Answer:** (3)   A reviewer may let personal prejudices knowingly or unknowingly influence a review. Though the other choices may or may not influence some reviewers, they do not apply to the situation described.

3. **Answer:** (4)   This is an opinion, a personal feeling that cannot be proved true or false. All other choices are incorrect.

4. **Answer:** (2)   This is a fact, a statement that can be proved true or false by checking the novel in question to see if it is an accurate recital of the plot. All other choices are incorrect.

5. **Answer:** (2)   This is correct from implication. All other choices involve people who watch a performance probably for enjoyment, but also with a critical eye to their various professional roles as well.

6. **Answer:** (3)   This is correct by definition. A critic describes performances. Choice (5) may seem a likely choice, but a dance historian, if he or she were describing a performance, would place it in a broad historical context of the time and place it was performed in.

7. **Answer:** (3)   This is correct because, due to the capabilities of TV, the viewing public can now see the faces of players. Though the use of TV might affect fans' enjoyment and coverage of the teams, choices (4) and (5), this is not emphasized in the review. Choices (1) and (2) would not be affected by TV coverage.

8. **Answer:** (1)   This is the only choice that accurately describes the reviewer's opinion. He uses gentle humor to emphasize "the year of the big spit . . . ," lines 5–6. All other choices are incorrect.

9. **Answer:** (4)   Dreadful is the only adjective that would sum up the reviewer's opinion. He conveys this by direct statement in lines 1–2 and by implication throughout the review. No other choice reflects his opinion.

10. **Answer:** (2)   The reviewer's tone throughout is heavily sarcastic. All other choices are incorrect.

11. **Answer:** (5)   See line 6. Choice (1) might have been chosen due to careless or too rapid reading of the passage. The show was seen in Washington, but not at the White House. Choices (2) to (4) are not mentioned.

12. **Answer:** (3)   The advertising slogan "the musical with a heart" (line 10), means a musical full of good feelings. All other choices are incorrect.

13. **Answer:** (3)   See lines 8–12 "the better to meet the requirements of the media age, . . . " All other choices are incorrect.

15. **Answer:** (3)   The phrase "bubble gum for the mind" implies something without much substance or thought. Choices (1), (4) and (5) are incorrect. Although a common criticism of TV and its viewers is stated in choice (2), it does not pertain to this question.

17. **Answer:** (4)   See lines 14–18. Choices (1), (2), (3) and (5) may be opinions held by some people, but they are not the opinions mentioned in the passage.

14. **Answer:** (1)   The reviewer makes her opinion known by citing as facts that the artists have little experience, insight or originality. Although she might be sad about the situation, choice (2), her tone and attitude are established in her opening line. Choices (3) to (5) are not reflected in the review.

16. **Answer:** (3)   The whole tone of the review, both stated and implied, is very favorable. The reviewer urges people to see the show. Although elements of choices (1) and (5) are mentioned, they are done in the context of promoting the show being reviewed. Choices (2) and (4) are not mentioned.

18. **Answer:** (5)   This is the choice that most accurately sums up the show. Although gambling, cowboy and railroad terminology influenced the English language, as did immigrants, choices (1) to (4), the show is not about these topics as historical or documentary studies.

Tests of General Educational Development

7 TEST BOOKLET NO. _____

8 TEST TAKEN AT _____

> When completed this answer sheet must be treated as **Confidential Material.**

9 TEST FORM

☐

MN ○
MO ○
MP ○
MQ ○
MR ○
MS ○
MT ○
MU ○
MV ○
MW ○
MX ○
MY ○
MZ ○
SF ○
SG ○
SH ○
SJ ○
SK ○
SL ○
SM ○
AR ○
AS ○
MC ○
MH ○
LR ○
LS ○

10 TEST NUMBER

☐

① ② ③ ④ ⑤

TEST ANSWERS

Fill in the circle corresponding to your answer for each question. Erase cleanly.

DO NOT MARK IN YOUR TEST BOOKLET

1 ① ② ③ ④ ⑤   21 ① ② ③ ④ ⑤   41 ① ② ③ ④ ⑤   61 ① ② ③ ④ ⑤
2 ① ② ③ ④ ⑤   22 ① ② ③ ④ ⑤   42 ① ② ③ ④ ⑤   62 ① ② ③ ④ ⑤
3 ① ② ③ ④ ⑤   23 ① ② ③ ④ ⑤   43 ① ② ③ ④ ⑤   63 ① ② ③ ④ ⑤
4 ① ② ③ ④ ⑤   24 ① ② ③ ④ ⑤   44 ① ② ③ ④ ⑤   64 ① ② ③ ④ ⑤
5 ① ② ③ ④ ⑤   25 ① ② ③ ④ ⑤   45 ① ② ③ ④ ⑤   65 ① ② ③ ④ ⑤
6 ① ② ③ ④ ⑤   26 ① ② ③ ④ ⑤   46 ① ② ③ ④ ⑤   66 ① ② ③ ④ ⑤
7 ① ② ③ ④ ⑤   27 ① ② ③ ④ ⑤   47 ① ② ③ ④ ⑤   67 ① ② ③ ④ ⑤
8 ① ② ③ ④ ⑤   28 ① ② ③ ④ ⑤   48 ① ② ③ ④ ⑤   68 ① ② ③ ④ ⑤
9 ① ② ③ ④ ⑤   29 ① ② ③ ④ ⑤   49 ① ② ③ ④ ⑤   69 ① ② ③ ④ ⑤
10 ① ② ③ ④ ⑤   30 ① ② ③ ④ ⑤   50 ① ② ③ ④ ⑤   70 ① ② ③ ④ ⑤
11 ① ② ③ ④ ⑤   31 ① ② ③ ④ ⑤   51 ① ② ③ ④ ⑤   71 ① ② ③ ④ ⑤
12 ① ② ③ ④ ⑤   32 ① ② ③ ④ ⑤   52 ① ② ③ ④ ⑤   72 ① ② ③ ④ ⑤
13 ① ② ③ ④ ⑤   33 ① ② ③ ④ ⑤   53 ① ② ③ ④ ⑤   73 ① ② ③ ④ ⑤
14 ① ② ③ ④ ⑤   34 ① ② ③ ④ ⑤   54 ① ② ③ ④ ⑤   74 ① ② ③ ④ ⑤
15 ① ② ③ ④ ⑤   35 ① ② ③ ④ ⑤   55 ① ② ③ ④ ⑤   75 ① ② ③ ④ ⑤
16 ① ② ③ ④ ⑤   36 ① ② ③ ④ ⑤   56 ① ② ③ ④ ⑤   76 ① ② ③ ④ ⑤
17 ① ② ③ ④ ⑤   37 ① ② ③ ④ ⑤   57 ① ② ③ ④ ⑤   77 ① ② ③ ④ ⑤
18 ① ② ③ ④ ⑤   38 ① ② ③ ④ ⑤   58 ① ② ③ ④ ⑤   78 ① ② ③ ④ ⑤
19 ① ② ③ ④ ⑤   39 ① ② ③ ④ ⑤   59 ① ② ③ ④ ⑤   79 ① ② ③ ④ ⑤
20 ① ② ③ ④ ⑤   40 ① ② ③ ④ ⑤   60 ① ② ③ ④ ⑤   80 ① ② ③ ④ ⑤

Permission is granted to reproduce this form for student use.

Instructions for Using This Answer Sheet

To be sure that your test results are properly scored and recorded:

- Use a soft lead pencil (not a pen) to mark your answers.
- Erase completely any errors or answers you wish to change.
- Make no unnecessary marks or calculations on this answer sheet or in your test booklet.
- Be sure the marks you make to fill in the circles are dark and fill the circle completely.

Do this: ●   Not this: ⊙ ⊗ ✓

DO NOT FOLD OR CREASE THE ANSWER SHEET.

In the time provided before you start the test, fill in the information in sections 1–10 on the answer sheet. In sections 9 and 10, be sure to write the letters or number in the box provided and mark the appropriate circle. (This helps avoid later scoring errors!)

1

BEGINNING AT THE LEFT BOX, PRINT YOUR LAST NAME, LEAVE A SPACE, FIRST NAME, SPACE, MIDDLE INITIAL.

2a PURPOSE FOR TESTING (Mark 1 or more)

EDUCATION ○   MILITARY ○
EMPLOYMENT ○   OTHER ○

2b ARE YOU ON ACTIVE DUTY IN THE ARMED FORCES?

YES ○   NO ○

3

SOCIAL SECURITY NUMBER

4 AGE

5 HIGHEST GRADE COMPLETED

6TH OR LOWER ○
7 ○
8 ○
9 ○
10 ○
11 ○
12 ○

6 TODAY'S DATE

JAN ○	DAY	YEAR–
FEB ○	⓪	1980 ○
MAR ○	① ①	1981 ○
APR ○	② ②	1982 ○
MAY ○	③ ③	1983 ○
JUNE ○	④	1984 ○
JULY ○	⑤	1985 ○
AUG ○	⑥	1986 ○
SEPT ○	⑦	1987 ○
OCT ○	⑧	1988 ○
NOV ○	⑨	1989 ○
DEC ○		

TIP   Before you take this posttest, you may want to skim the test-taking tips presented in our program. Use it to remind you of the ways in which you can help yourself pass the GED test.

DIRECTIONS: Choose the one best answer for each item below.

Items 1–4 refer to the following passage by Anne Tyler.

WHAT IS SO DIFFICULT ABOUT RETURNING HOME?

While Sarah got dressed, Macon took the dog out. It was a warm, golden morning. Neighbors were trimming their grass and weeding their flower beds. They nodded as Macon walked past. He had not been back long enough for them to feel at ease yet; there was something a little too

(5)   formal about their greetings. Or maybe he was imagining that. He made an effort to remind them of how many years he had lived here: "I've always liked those tulips of yours!" and "Still got that nice hand mower, I see!" Edward marched beside him with a busybody waggle of his hind end.

(10)   In movies and such, people who made important changes in their lives accomplished them and were done with it. They walked out and never returned; or they married and lived happily ever after. In real life, things weren't so clean-cut. Macon, for instance, had had to go down to Muriel's and retrieve this dog, once he'd decided to move back home. He

(15)   had had to collect his clothing and pack up his typewriter while Muriel watched in silence with her accusing, reproaching eyes. Then there were all kinds of other belongings that he discovered too late he'd forgotten— clothes that had been in the wash at the time, and his favorite dictionary, and the extra-large pottery mug he liked to drink his coffee from.

(20)   But of course he couldn't go back for them. He had to abandon them— messy, trailing strings of himself cluttering his leavetaking.

1. Based on this excerpt, Macon's "leavetaking" (line 21) involved

   (1) leaving Muriel to return to Susan
   (2) returning to Muriel after leaving her
   (3) leaving Sarah to move in with Muriel
   (4) leaving Sarah to move in with Muriel and then returning to Sarah
   (5) leaving both Sarah and Muriel to be with Edward

2. Which of the following titles *best* describes how Macon sees his own life?

   (1) My Life: Just like in the Movies
   (2) The Steady, Clean-Cut Life of Macon
   (3) My Happy Return to the Neighborhood
   (4) A Happy Reunion with Muriel
   (5) What a Mess: This Is Not like Life in the Movies

3. The author's attitude toward Macon can be *best* described as

   (1) judgmental
   (2) sympathetic
   (3) envious
   (4) teasing
   (5) reproachful

4. Who is Edward?

   (1) Macon's teenage son
   (2) Sarah's son and Macon's stepson
   (3) a neighborhood boy
   (4) Macon's dog
   (5) Muriel's dog

GO ON TO THE NEXT PAGE.

HOW DOES FICTION RESEMBLE THE UNIVERSE?

Begin with the crucial observation here that, except as creatures of the imagination, characters in fiction do not exist. It is true that Mrs. Eustace may be based on, say, Trollope's Aunt Maude. But except in the writing of a biography (and, strictly speaking, not even there), a writer
(5) cannot take a character from life. Every slightest change the writer makes in a character's background and experience must have subtle repercussions. I am not the same person I would have been if my father had been rich, or had owned elephants. Trollope's Aunt Maude can no longer remain perfectly herself once she's married to Mr. Eustace. Sub-
(10) tle details change characters' lives in ways too complex for the conscious mind to grasp, though we nevertheless grasp them. Thus plot not only changes but creates character: By our actions we discover what we really believe and, simultaneously, reveal ourselves to others. And setting influences both character and plot: One cannot do in a thunder-
(15) storm what one does on a hot day in Jordan. (One's camel slips, or, from homesickness, refuses to budge; so the assassin goes uncaught, the President is shot, the world is again plunged into war.) As in the universe every atom has an effect, however minuscule, on every other atom, so that to pinch the fabric of Time and Space at any point is to
(20) shake the whole length and breadth of it, so in fiction every element has effect on every other, so that to change a character's name from Jane to Cynthia is to make the fictional ground shudder under her feet.

5. According to this excerpt, if a writer changes a character's name then

   (1) the rest of the story must stay the same
   (2) the fabric of Time and Space is cut and atoms shift in the universe
   (3) the writer is making a mistake
   (4) an earthquake occurs
   (5) the rest of the story will also change

6. If this author wrote about movies, with which of the following statements would he agree?

   (1) It makes no difference if a film is set in Morocco or Los Angeles.
   (2) The choice of actors does not matter.
   (3) Where you focus the camera affects the scene and character.
   (4) Characters' names are insignificant.
   (5) Whether a scene is shot in close-up or from far away is unimportant.

7. Why does Trollope's Aunt Maude change once she marries the fictional Mr. Eustace?

   (1) She loses her nephew, Trollope.
   (2) Trollope sends her to Jordan.
   (3) She becomes a writer.
   (4) She becomes a fictional character.
   (5) Her husband is a doctor.

8. A writer cannot take a character from life *except*

   (1) when he changes the person's name
   (2) if he knows the person well
   (3) in autobiography
   (4) in biography
   (5) when he asks permission

GO ON TO THE NEXT PAGE.

HOW DOES A STRANGER WIN THE HEARTS OF TWO YOUNG GIRLS?

So when Henry arrived on a Saturday night, we smelled him. He smelled wonderful. Like trees and lemon vanishing cream, and Nu Nile Hair Oil and flecks of Sen-Sen.

(5) He smiled a lot, showing small even teeth with a friendly gap in the middle. Frieda and I were not introduced to him—merely pointed out. Like, here is the bathroom; the clothes closet is here; and these are my kids, Frieda and Claudia; watch out for this window; it don't open all the way.

(10) We looked sideways at him, saying nothing and expecting him to say nothing. Just to nod, as he had done at the clothes closet, acknowledging our existence. To our surprise, he spoke to us.

"Hello there. You must be Greta Garbo, and you must be Ginger Rogers."

We giggled. Even my father was startled into a smile.

(15) "Want a penny?" He held out a shiny coin to us. Frieda lowered her head, too pleased to answer. I reached for it. He snapped his thumb and forefinger, and the penny disappeared. Our shock was laced with delight. We searched all over him, poking our fingers into his socks, looking up the inside back of his coat. If happiness is anticipation with

(20) certainty, we were happy. And while we waited for the coin to reappear, we knew we were amusing Mama and Daddy. Daddy was smiling, and Mama's eyes went soft as they followed our hands wandering over Mr. Henry's body.

We loved him. Even after what came later, there was no bitterness

(25) in our memory of him.

9. According to the author, happiness is

(1) a bright, shiny penny
(2) meeting a new friend for the first time
(3) nervous anticipation
(4) confident and pleasurable expectation
(5) a memory

10. Based on how the mother introduces her girls to Mr. Henry, how does she treat them?

(1) She lavishes attention on them.
(2) She likes to watch them talk to men.
(3) She wishes they were movie stars.
(4) She hates them.
(5) She takes them for granted.

11. Who is the person who tells this story?

(1) a little girl telling about her childhood
(2) a grown woman remembering her youth
(3) a child telling about being an adult
(4) a woman telling about her adulthood
(5) a man telling about his boyhood

12. Mr. Henry can be *best* characterized as

(1) charming
(2) shifty
(3) pathetic
(4) sickly
(5) sinister

GO ON TO THE NEXT PAGE.

13. Which of the following words *best* defines "laced" (line 17)?

(1) knotted
(2) intertwined
(3) poisoned
(4) delicately stitched
(5) unwound

14. When the girls search for the missing penny, they are

(1) frightened
(2) nosy
(3) excited
(4) pushy
(5) anxious

Items 15–20 refer to the following poem by Henry Wadsworth Longfellow.

WHAT IS THE POEM OF THE AIR?

Snowflakes

Out of the bosom of the Air,
  Out of the cloud-folds of her garments shaken,
Over the woodlands brown and bare,
  Over the harvest-fields forsaken,
(5)   Silent, and soft, and slow
    Descends the snow.

Even as our cloudy fancies take
  Suddenly shape in some divine expression,
Even as the troubled heart doth make
(10)   In the white countenance confession,
    The troubled sky reveals
    The grief it feels.

This is the poem of the air,
  Slowly in silent syllables recorded;
(15) This is the secret of despair,
  Long in its cloudy bosom hoarded,
    Now whispered and revealed
    To wood and field.

15. The air in this poem is described as

(1) a woman
(2) a snowy field
(3) the voice of divine expression
(4) a whisper
(5) a recording

16. The word "syllables" in line 14 means

(1) shapes
(2) letters
(3) units of spoken language
(4) the sound of snow falling
(5) tears

GO ON TO THE NEXT PAGE.

17. The poet compares the falling snow to

(1) a forsaken field
(2) a secret
(3) a cloudy bosom
(4) a troubled heart
(5) a whisper of grief

18. What might this poet call falling rain?

(1) a watery voice
(2) precipitation
(3) a troubled sky
(4) a heart's wet secret
(5) tears

19. In line 16, what does the word "hoarded" mean?

(1) a secret
(2) stored or hidden for future use
(3) worn as a garment
(4) presented
(5) a dream

20. What does the poet mean by the "cloudy fancies" in line 7?

(1) the cloud's imagination
(2) a snowy dream
(3) the shape of snow on the fields
(4) the images we see in the shapes of clouds
(5) the sadness we feel watching snow fall

Items 21–24 refer to the following passage by Nadine Gordimer.

WHAT WORRIES THIS WOMAN AS SHE WATERS HER GARDEN?

Pat Haberman likes to work in the garden for an hour when she comes home from work in the afternoons. When the evening newspaper flops through the slot in the gate onto the grass she looks at the headlines while guiding the jet of the hose with her other hand. She feels at
(5) this time of day and in this (she knows) frail set of circumstances—the soothing hiss of the water, the nearness of sunset bird-calls and the distance of the traffic breaking beyond the reef of the quiet suburb—a balance. She ventures out to earn her living every day, but no longer is one of those truly out there, driven by adrenalin and sex hormones,
(10) surging along, black skins, white skins, inhaling toxic ambitions, the stresses of solving, of becoming—what? The five-thirty to six-thirty hour is an illusion of peace in middle age just as the innocence of Cape thrush calls and the freshness of leaves spattered by water from the municipal supply is an illusion of undestroyed nature. Yet while she
(15) holds the nozzle of the hose against the snaking energy of piped water's pressure, and reads that a diplomat has been kidnapped, that oil has again been ransomed in the holy money war between arabs and the West, even that leaders of the black workers' walk-out at a steel foundry in this same city are being detained by the police, there is this interlude
(20) of feeling herself regarding from the base of the calm and eternal what is feverish and constantly whirling away. Later she will read the paper with the background knowledgeability, the watchfulness, the sense of continuity with statements and struggles of black and white, that reasserts involvement and rescues her from that strange pleasant lapse, dan-
(25) gerous white suburban amnesia.

GO ON TO THE NEXT PAGE.

21. Pat Haberman's "strange pleasant lapse" (line 24) can be *best* described as

(1) productive
(2) well deserved
(3) relaxing
(4) enviable
(5) dangerous

22. What saves Pat Haberman from her "strange pleasant lapse"?

(1) working in the garden
(2) the setting sun
(3) the kidnapped diplomat
(4) reading the newspaper
(5) her job

23. Based on this excerpt, what would the author recommend Pat Haberman do?

(1) increase her hours in the garden
(2) retire early
(3) become more active politically
(4) stay indoors
(5) not read the newspaper anymore

24. What time of day is most peaceful for Pat Haberman?

(1) five-thirty to six-thirty P.M.
(2) when she hears birdcalls
(3) at her nine-to-five job
(4) commuting home
(5) five-thirty to six-thirty A.M.

Items 25–28 refer to the following passage by Joseph Conrad.

WHAT WERE THE DYING MAN'S LAST WORDS?

"She said suddenly very low, 'He died as he lived.'

" 'His end,' said I, with dull anger stirring in me, 'was in every way worthy of his life.'

" 'And I was not with him,' she murmured. My anger subsided before
(5) a feeling of infinite pity.

" 'Everything that could be done—' I mumbled.

" 'Ah, but I believed in him more than any one on earth—more than his own mother, more than—himself. He needed me! Me! I would have treasured every sigh, every word, every sign, every glance.'
(10) "I felt like a chill grip on my chest. 'Don't,' I said, in a muffled voice.

" 'Forgive me. I—I have mourned so long in silence—in silence. . . . You were with him—to the last? I think of his loneliness. Nobody near to understand him as I would have understood. Perhaps no one to hear. . . .'
(15) " 'To the very end,' I said, shakily. 'I heard his very last words. . . .' I stopped in fright.

" 'Repeat them,' she murmured in a heart-broken tone. 'I want—I want—something—to—to—live with.'

"I was on the point of crying at her, 'Don't you hear them?' The dusk
(20) was repeating them in a persistent whisper all around us, in a whisper that seemed to swell menacingly like the first whisper of a rising wind. 'The horror! The horror!'

" 'His last word—to live with,' she insisted. 'Don't you understand I loved him—I loved him—I loved him!'
(25) "I pulled myself together and spoke slowly.

" 'The last word he pronounced was—your name.'

"I heard a light sigh and then my heart stood still, stopped dead short by an exulting and terrible cry, by the cry of inconceivable triumph and of unspeakable pain. 'I knew it—I was sure!' . . . She knew.

GO ON TO THE NEXT PAGE.

(30)   She was sure. I heard her weeping; she had hidden her face in her hands. It seemed to me that the house would collapse before I could escape, that the heavens would fall upon my head. But nothing happened. The heavens do not fall for such a trifle. Would they have fallen, I wonder, if I had rendered Kurtz that justice which was his due?

(35)   Hadn't he said he wanted only justice? But I couldn't. I could not tell her. It would have been too dark—too dark altogether."

25. The narrator imagines he hears the dead man's last words in the

  (1) woman's voice
  (2) heavens that fall upon his head
  (3) persistent whispers of dusk
  (4) the voice of the dead man's mother
  (5) the woman's tears

26. Based on the information in this passage, who is "Kurtz" (line 34)?

  (1) the woman's son
  (2) the narrator's brother
  (3) a judge
  (4) the dead man
  (5) a hero

27. When the narrator tells the woman the dead man's final words, she feels

  (1) angry and confused
  (2) carefree and elated
  (3) triumphant and pained
  (4) bitter and sad
  (5) jealous and vindictive

28. Which of these statements *best* describes the narrator's feelings toward the woman?

  (1) He pities her and so he lies to her.
  (2) He is angry at her and wants to punish her.
  (3) Because she boasts, he is jealous of her.
  (4) He wishes the woman loved him.
  (5) He wishes she loved the dead man.

Answers and Explanations

Literature Posttest *pp. 297–302*

1. **Answer:** (4)   Choice (1) is incorrect because there is no mention of Susan in this excerpt. Macon retrieves his things from Muriel's to return to his old neighborhood, which rules out choices (2), (3) and (5).

2. **Answer:** (5)   Choices (1) and (2) are incorrect because the author states Macon's life is unlike the movie ideal. His neighbors do not welcome him home, choice (3), nor is there evidence he is returning to Muriel, choice (4).

3. **Answer:** (2)   The writer wants us to feel sympathy, choice (2), toward Macon and not be judgmental, choice (1), or reproachful, choice (5). The author portrays Macon's life as more messy than ideal, so clearly we are not meant to envy him, choice (3). Macon may seem a bit foolish, but the author's tone is not critical enough to be teasing, choice (4).

4. **Answer:** (4)   By the description of the "waggle of his hind end" and the fact that Macon is taking him for a walk, we know Edward is a dog. That Macon retrieves him from Muriel suggests the dog belongs to Macon, choice (4), not to Muriel, choice (5).

5. **Answer:** (5)   Choices (1) and (3) contradict the main point of this excerpt. When the author writes of the "earth shuddering," choice (4), and the pinching of the "fabric of time," choice (2), he does not mean that these things actually occur.

6. **Answer:** (3)   Using the same standards with film as with writing, the author states that the choice of setting will affect the story, so choice (1) is incorrect. The same principle applies to choices (2), (4) and (5). Only choice (3) allows for the relationship between elements.

7. **Answer:** (4)   There is no mention of choices (1), (2), (3) or (5) in this excerpt. Aunt Maude does not lose her nephew Trollope, choice (1), because she remains a real person. Choice (4) explains the example the author uses of turning a real person into a fictional character.

8. **Answer:** (4)   In line 4, the author explains that a character cannot be taken from life, except in biography, thus making all other choices incorrect.

9. **Answer:** (4)   While a bright, shiny penny, choice (1), a new friend, choice (2), and the memory of a friendly meeting, choice (5), might make the author happy, she explicitly defines happiness as "anticipation with certainty"—as in choice (4). There is no mention of nervous anticipation, choice (3).

10. **Answer:** (5)   Based on how she introduces her daughters to Mr. Henry, the mother does not lavish attention on them, choice (1). She likes to watch them talk to a stranger, choice (2), but this does not explain how she treats them. There is no evidence to support choices (3) and (4).

11. **Answer:** (2)   While this is a story about a little girl, it is not told by one, choice (1). The subject of this passage is childhood, not adulthood, so choices (3) and (4) are incorrect. The excerpt describes a girl, not a boy, choice (5).

12. **Answer:** (1)   Nothing in this excerpt suggests Mr. Henry is shifty, choice (2), pathetic, choice (3), sickly, choice (4), or sinister, choice (5). Instead he is friendly and playful, so choice (1) best describes his manner.

13. **Answer:** (2)   When she writes that their "shock was laced with delight" (line 18), the author means shock and delight mixed in their responses. None of choices (1), (3), (4) and (5) suggests the intermingling of two feelings.

14. **Answer:** (3)   If the girls were frightened, choice (1), or anxious, choice (5), they would not boldly search for the coin. They do search for it, but not because they are nosy, choice (2), or pushy, choice (4). Excitement, choice (3), best describes their innocent curiosity.

15. **Answer:** (1)   The air has a "bosom" (line 1), and is described as wearing "the cloudfolds of her garment" (line 2), and later shows "a white countenance" (line 10), so the poet wants the air to embody human, and especially female, characteristics.

16. **Answer:** (3)   In line 13, the poet writes that "this is a poem of the air" that is "whispered and revealed" (line 17). The sound of the snow falling, then, is like a voice speaking. "Syllables" is defined as units of spoken language.

17. **Answer:** (5)   The snow falls on the "forsaken field," choice (1), from the "cloudy bosom," choice (3), of "the troubled heart," choice (4), but it is not compared to any of these. The sky "reveals the grief it feels" (line 12) in "a whispered" (line 17) show of despair.

18. **Answer:** (5)   Based on an understanding of this poem, in which snow represents a showing of sorrow from a troubled heart, if this poet were to write about rain he would most likely describe it as tears, another way in which the body "reveals" despair.

19. **Answer:** (2)   "Hoarded" means to hide or withhold for future use, to keep a hidden treasure. While a secret, choice (1), is withheld, it does not define the verb "to hoard." The other choices are incorrect.

20. **Answer:** (4)   The "cloudy fancies" are "ours," so choices (1) and (5) are incorrect. A snowy dream, choice (2), and the snow of the fields, choice (3), are both other snow formations, but not the ones we imagine, or "fancy," in the sky.

21. **Answer:** (5)   While she does have a job and tends her garden, this passage does not suggest her life is particularly productive, choice (1). Nor does the author say she has done anything to deserve it, choice (2). The lapse is not relaxing, choice (3), or enviable, choice (4), because she cannot ignore what worries her.

22. **Answer:** (4)   Working in the garden does not ease her mind, choice (1), nor does seeing the sun set, choice (2). The kidnapped diplomat, choice (3), does not have a direct effect upon her, although reading about him and other news does change her mood, choice (4).

23. **Answer:** (3)   All choices except choice (3) suggest Pat Haberman should become more reclusive, when it is clear from this excerpt that her isolation contributes to her uneasiness.

24. **Answer:** (1)   Although she relaxes when she hears the birds singing, choice (2), this does not define the time of day she enjoys most. Choices (3), (4) and (5) are not described in the passage.

25. **Answer:** (3)   While he does hear the woman's voice, choice (1), she does not convey the dead man's last words. He imagines the heavens fall, choice (2), as a result of telling the dead man's last words, not because the heavens contain those words. Choices (4) and (5) are mentioned in the passage, but are not relevant.

26. **Answer:** (4)   Although Kurtz was obviously close to the man and woman, no concrete clues suggest he was related to either of them, so choices (1) and (2) are incorrect. Kurtz said that he wanted only justice, but there is no evidence he was a judge, choice (3), or a hero, choice (5).

27. **Answer:** (3)   When she hears the narrator say her name she cries out, but not in anger, choice (1). Throughout this passage she seems excited, but she is not joyous or elated, choice (2). She would not be sad, choice (4), because he has told her what she wanted to hear. She is not jealous, choice (5), because she believes the dead man loved her the most.

28. **Answer:** (1)   Choice (2) is wrong because if he wished to punish her he would not have told her the dead man spoke her name. The narrator is not jealous of her, choice (3), because he thinks he knew the dead man better than she did. There is no evidence for choices (4) or (5).

Pretest/Posttest Diagnostic Chart

For the Pretest After you check your answers, look at the chart below. Circle the number of each problem you missed. Find the skills in which you need the most help. Then find those skills listed in the Table of Contents and begin your studying in those skill areas.

For the Posttest After you check your answers, look at the chart below. Circle the number of each problem you missed. Find the skills in which you still need help. Then find those skills listed in the Table of Contents and review those skill areas, paying special attention to the Strategies for Reading pages and the Answers and Explanations pages for the Practice items and the GED Mini-Test.

CONTENT AREAS

SKILLS	Popular Literature Pretest	Popular Literature Posttest	Classical Literature Pretest	Classical Literature Posttest	Commentary Pretest	Commentary Posttest
Identify Implications	5, 9, 10, 11, 28, 29	1, 4, 11, 12, 14, 21, 22	2, 3	26, 27		
Draw Conclusions	12, 21, 25	2, 3, 10, 23	1		16	
Restate Information	8, 20, 22, 27	9, 24		25	13, 14	7, 8
Identify Main Idea	6, 26				15	5
Get Meaning from Context	7, 17, 19, 24	13	4	19, 20		
Understand Consequences	18			28		
Transfer Ideas to New Context				18		6
Identify Effects	23			15, 16		
Identify Techniques	30			17		

Acknowledgments

Grateful acknowledgment is made to the following authors, agents and publishers for permission to use copyrighted materials:

American Council on Education for the GED Answer Form AS7010. Copyright © 1987, The GED Testing Service of the American Council on Education. Used with permission.

Atheneum Publishers, Inc. for Randall Jarrell, "The Woman at the Washington Zoo" from THE WOMAN AT THE WASHINGTON ZOO. Copyright © 1960 Randall Jarrell. Reprinted with the permission of Atheneum Publishers, Inc. Excerpt from THE MIRACLE WORKER by William Gibson. Copyright 1956 by William Gibson. Reprinted with the permission of Atheneum Publishers, Inc. and Flora Roberts, Inc.

James Baldwin for excerpt from his play THE AMEN CORNER. Copyright © 1968 by James Baldwin. Reprinted by permission of the author.

Bantam Books, Inc. for excerpt from "Leonardo Da Vinci" in FIFTY GREAT ARTISTS by Bernard Myers. Copyright 1953, by Bantam Books, Inc. Excerpt from HIGH HEARTS by Rita Mae Brown. Copyright © 1986 by Speakeasy Productions, Inc. Reprinted by permission of Bantam Books, Inc.

Gwendolyn Brooks for her poems, "First Fight, Then Fiddle" and "A Song in the Front Yard."

Chatto & Windus for excerpt from THE GOOD APPRENTICE by Iris Murdoch. Reprinted by permission of the author and Chatto & Windus. Extract from "Florence Nightingale" in EMINENT VICTORIANS by Lytton Strachey. Reprinted by permission of the author's estate and Chatto & Windus. Excerpt from CIDER WITH ROSIE by Laurie Lee. Reprinted by permission of Chatto & Windus and the Hogarth Press.

William Collins Sons & Co. Ltd. for excerpt from "The Inner Ring" in WEIGHT OF GLORY AND OTHER ADDRESSES by C. S. Lewis. Copyright 1946 by C. S. Lewis. Reprinted by permission of William Collins Sons & Co., Ltd.

Condé Nast Publications, Inc. for "Hollywood Squares Cubed." Courtesy VOGUE. Copyright © 1986 by The Condé Nast Publications, Inc.

Curtis Brown, Ltd. for A SEPARATE PEACE by John Knowles. Reprinted by permission of Curtis Brown, Ltd. and Macmillan Publishing Company, Inc. Copyright © 1959 by John Knowles.

Doubleday & Company, Inc. for "My Papa's Waltz" copyright 1942 by Hearst Magazines, Inc. from THE COLLECTED POEMS OF THEODORE ROETHKE by Theodore Roethke. Excerpt from THE STRANGER FROM THE SEA by Winston Graham. Copyright © 1981 by Winston Graham. Excerpt from MOVIES INTO FILM: FILM CRITICISM 1967–70 by John Simon. Copyright © 1971 by John Simon. Excerpt from BLUES FOR MISTER CHARLIE by James Baldwin. Copyright © 1964 by James Baldwin. Excerpt from COME NINEVEH, COME TYRE by Allen Drury. Copyright © 1973 by Allen Drury. "Morning Beads" and "Old Man, The Sweat Lodge" by Phil George from WHISPERING WIND edited by Terry Allen. Copyright © 1972 by The Institute of American Indian Arts. All reprinted by permission of Doubleday & Company, Inc.

Dow Jones & Company, Inc. for "Timeless Play about Black Experience in White America" from THE WALL STREET JOURNAL, 9/2/86. Reprinted by permission of THE WALL STREET JOURNAL © Dow Jones & Company, Inc. 1986. All rights reserved.

Dryad Press for "Migrants" from SOMETHING TUGGING THE LINE by Roderick Jellema. Reprinted by permission of Dryad Press.

Lawrence Elliott for excerpt from ON THE EDGE OF NOWHERE by James Huntington and Lawrence Elliott. Copyright © 1966 by James Huntington and Lawrence Elliott. Reprinted by permission of Lawrence Elliott.

Farrar, Straus and Giroux, Inc. for excerpt from "Dean of Men" in THE COLLECTED STORIES OF PETER TAYLOR by Peter Taylor. Copyright © 1940, 1941, 1948, 1949, 1950, 1951, 1955, 1957, 1958, 1959, 1960, 1961, 1962, 1963, 1964, 1967, 1968, 1969 by Peter Taylor. Copyright renewed © 1967, 1968 by Peter Taylor. Reprinted by permission of Farrar, Straus and Giroux, Inc. Excerpts from MY MOTHER'S HOUSE AND SIDO by Colette, translated by Una Vicenzo Troubridge and Enid McLeod. English translation copyright 1953, renewed copyright © 1981 by Farrar, Straus and Giroux, Inc. Reprinted by permission of Farrar, Straus and Giroux, Inc. and Martin Secker & Warburg Ltd., London. Excerpts from 5TH OF JULY by Lanford Wilson. Copyright © 1978 by Lanford Wilson.

Houghton Mifflin Company for "The Cruise" and "Charade" from NARCISSA AND OTHER FABLES by Louis Auchincloss. Copyright © 1983 by Louis Auchincloss. Excerpt from O PIONEERS! by Willa Cather. Copyright 1913 and copyright renewed 1941 by Willa Sibert Cather. "Ars Poetica" from NEW AND COLLECTED POEMS 1917–1976 by Archibald MacLeish. Copyright © 1976 by Archibald MacLeish. "God's Backside" from THE DEATH NOTEBOOKS by Anne Sexton. Copyright © 1974 by Anne Sexton. All reprinted by permission of Houghton Mifflin Company. Excerpt from COLD SASSY TREE by Olive Ann Burns. Copyright © 1984 by Olive Ann Burns. Reprinted by permission of Ticknor & Fields, a Houghton Mifflin Company.

International Creative Management for excerpt from I NEVER SANG FOR MY FATHER by Robert Anderson. Copyright 1966, 1968 by Robert Anderson as an unpublished dramatic composition Copyright © 1968 by Robert Anderson. Reprinted by permission of International Creative Management by Mitch Douglas.

Ari Korpivaara for excerpt from his article entitled "Roll Over, Rambo." Published in MS. magazine, 9/86. Reprinted by permission of the author.

Morton L. Leavy for excerpts from SPOON RIVER ANTHOLOGY by Edgar Lee Masters. Copyright © 1966 by Mrs. Edgar Lee Masters. Reprinted by permission of Morton L. Leavy as attorney for Ellen Masters.

Louisiana State University Press for "At Our Fingers' Tips There Are Small Faces." Reprinted by permission of Louisiana State University Press from ANGEL FIRE by Joyce Carol Oates. Copyright © 1973 by Joyce Carol Oates.

Macmillan Publishing Company, reprinted with permission of Macmillan Publishing Company from A SEPARATE PEACE by John Knowles. Copyright © 1960 by John Knowles, reprinted 1961.

William Morris Agency for excerpt from FIDDLER ON THE ROOF by Joseph Stein. Copyright © 1964 by Joseph Stein. Used by permission of William Morris Agency as agent for Joseph Stein. Excerpt from DON'T DRINK THE WATER by Woody Allen. Copyright © 1967 by Woody Allen. Used by permission of William Morris Agency. "CLOSE TIES" copyright © 1981 by Elizabeth Diggs. All Rights Reserved. Used by permission of William Morris Agency. The first professional production of CLOSE TIES was by The Long Wharf Theatre, New Haven, Connecticut on February 3, 1981. "GETTING OUT" © Copyright 1978, 1979, by Marsha Norman. ALL RIGHTS RESERVED. Used by permission of William Morris Agency. Originally Produced by Actors Theatre of Louisville, Inc., in Louisville, Kentucky. The West Coast Premiere of "Getting Out" was produced by the Center Theatre Group of Los Angeles Mark Taper Forum, Gordon Davidson, Artistic Director. Originally Produced in New York by The Phoenix Theatre, Produced Off-Broadway in New York City by Lester Osterman, Lucille Lortel and Mark Howard.

Samuel French, Inc. for excerpt from FIVE ON THE BLACK HAND SIDE by Charlie Russell. Copyright © 1969 by Charlie Russell. Copyright © 1977 (revised and rewritten) by Charlie Russell. Reprinted by permission of Samuel French, Inc.

New American Library for excerpt from "The Cherry Orchard" from CHEKHOV: THE MAJOR PLAYS translated by Ann Dunnigan. Copyright © 1964 by Ann Dunnigan. Reprinted by arrangement with New American Library, New York, New York.

New Directions Publishing Corporation for Carson McCullers, MEMBER OF THE WEDDING. Copyright 1949, 1951 by Carson McCullers. All rights reserved. Ezra Pound, "The River Merchant's Wife" from PERSONAE. Copyright 1926 by Ezra Pound. Dylan Thomas, "Do Not Go Gentle Into That Good Night," from THE POEMS OF DYLAN THOMAS. Copyright 1952 by Dylan Thomas. Tennessee Williams, THE ECCENTRICITIES OF A NIGHTINGALE. Copyright © 1948, 1964 by Tennessee Williams. All reprinted by permission of New Directions Publishing Corporation.

THE NEW LEADER for excerpt from "Acts of Insanity" by Leo Sauvage. Reprinted with permission of The New Leader. March 10, 1986. Copyright © the American Labor Conference on International Affairs, Inc.

NEW YORK magazine for excerpt from "Romance and Other Disturbances" by Tobi Tobias. Copyright © 1984 by News America Publishing, Inc. Excerpt from "Acts of Darkness" by John Simon. Copyright © 1986 by News America Publishing, Inc. Excerpt from Theater Commentary by John Simon and excerpt from Art Commentary by Kay Larson. Copyright © 1987 by News America Publishing, Inc. All reprinted with the permission of NEW YORK magazine.

NEW YORK POST for excerpt from "Berio's compositions cause a big exodus" by Robert Kimball, in the THE NEW YORK POST of October 10, 1986. Reprinted by permission of Robert Kimball.

THE NEW YORK TIMES for excerpts from "Joan Rivers's 'Late Show' Enters Talk-Show Fray" by John J. O'Connor, of Oct. 13, 1986, and from "Three Traditions, Two and a Half Heirs," by David Kirby of Oct. 12, 1986 BOOK REVIEW. Copyright © 1986 by The New York Times Company. Reprinted by permission. Excerpt from Art review by John Russell of Oct. 12, 1986 and from review of WANDERLUST by Jill Gerston of Aug. 3, 1986 BOOK REVIEW. Copyright © 1986 by The New York Times Company. Reprinted by permission. Excerpt from "NBC's Coverage of the World Series" by John Corry, October 28, 1986. Copyright © 1986 by The New York Times Company. Reprinted by permission.

The NEW YORKER MAGAZINE for excerpts from "Unhappy Tyrones" by Brendan Gill. Reprinted by permission; © 1986. Originally in the New Yorker.

NEWSWEEK magazine for excerpts from "When is a Bear a Dog," by Jack Kroll; "Madness or Genius," by Jack Kroll; and "Out of Her Shell," by Peter Prescott. Condensed from NEWSWEEK. Copyright 1986 by Newsweek, Inc. All rights reserved. Reprinted by permission.

North Point Press for "The Necessity of Faith" and "Traveling At Home" excerpted from: A PART, Copyright © 1980 by Wendell Berry. "The Wheel" excerpted from: THE WHEEL, Copyright © 1982 by Wendell Berry. Published by North Point Press and reprinted by permission. ALL RIGHTS RESERVED.

Harold Ober Associates, Inc. for excerpt from THE YOUNG JOHN ADAMS. Reprinted by permission of Harold Ober Associates, Incorporated. Copyright © 1949 by Catherine Drinker Bowen. Copyright renewed 1977 by Ezra Bowen.

Overlook Press for "Miami" from THE BOOK OF FORTUNE by Daniel Mark Epstein. Copyright © 1982 by Daniel Mark Epstein. Reprinted by permission of Overlook Press.

Oxford University Press, London for excerpt from "A Christmas Carol" by Charles Dickens. For excerpt from A DOLL'S HOUSE by Henrik Ibsen, translated by James McFarlane, from FOUR MAJOR PLAYS: Oxford University Press, 1981. Reprinted by permission of Oxford University Press.

Random House, Inc. for excerpt from "Saturday Morning Fever" by Tom Englehard in WATCHING TELEVISION, edited by Todd Gitlin. Copyright © 1986 by Pantheon Books, a Division of Random House, Inc. Specified excerpt from "Nimram" from THE ART OF LIVING AND OTHER STORIES by John Gardner. Copyright © 1981 by John Gardner. Reprinted by permission of Alfred A. Knopf, Inc. "Rite of Passage" copyright © 1983 by Sharon Olds. Reprinted from THE DEAD AND THE LIVING by Sharon Olds, by permission of Alfred A. Knopf, Inc. Specified excerpt from THE WOMAN WARRIOR: MEMOIRS OF A GIRLHOOD AMONG GHOSTS by Maxine Hong Kingston. Copyright © 1975 by Maxine Hong Kingston. Reprinted by permission of Alfred A. Knopf, Inc. Excerpt from THE KING MUST DIE, by Mary Renault. Copyright © 1958 by Mary Renault. Reprinted by permission of Pantheon Books, a Division of Random House, Inc. "Energy: A Villanelle" from FACING NATURE, by John Updike. Copyright © 1985 by John Updike. Reprinted by permission of Alfred A. Knopf, Inc. "Dragons We Are" and "Strange Season" from ALL THE NIGHT WINGS, by Loren Eiseley. Copyright © 1979 by the Estate of Loren Eiseley. Reprinted by permission of Times Books, a Division of Random House, Inc. "Man On Wheels" Copyright © 1968 by Karl Shapiro. Reprinted by permission of Random House, Inc. Excerpts from COLLECTED POEMS, 1940–1978 by Karl Shapiro, by permission of Random House, Inc. "To Be Of Use" copyright © 1972 by Marge Piercy. Reprinted from CIRCLES ON THE WATER, by Marge Piercy, by permission of Alfred A. Knopf, Inc. Excerpts from MUSEUMS AND WOMEN AND OTHER STORIES, by John Updike. Copyright © 1972 by John Updike. Reprinted by permission of Alfred A. Knopf, Inc. Excerpt from A RAISIN IN THE SUN by Lorraine Hansberry. Copyright © 1958 by Robert Nemiroff, as an unpublished work. Copyright © 1959, 1966, 1984 by Robert Nemiroff. Reprinted by permission of Random House, Inc. "Velvet Shoes" by Elinor Wylie. Copyright 1921 by Alfred A. Knopf, Inc. and renewed 1949 by William Rose Benet. Reprinted from COLLECTED POEMS OF ELINOR WYLIE by Elinor Wylie, by permission of the publisher. Excerpt from "Ile" copyright 1919 and renewed 1947 by Eugene O'Neill. Reprinted from THE PLAYS OF EUGENE O'NEILL by Eugene O'Neill, by permission of Random House, Inc. Excerpt from THE GLASS MENAGERIE, by Tennessee Williams. Copyright 1945 by Tennessee Williams and Edwina D. Williams and renewed 1973 by Tennessee Williams.

Reprinted by permission of Random House, Inc. Excerpt from THE CHILDREN'S HOUR, by Lillian Hellman. Copyright 1934 by Lillian Hellman Kober and renewed 1962 by Lillian Hellman. Reprinted by permission of Random House, Inc. Excerpts from RAGTIME, by E. L. Doctorow. Copyright © 1974, 1975 by E. L. Doctorow. Reprinted by permission of Random House, Inc.

From Act I of DON'T DRINK THE WATER by Woody Allen. Copyright © 1967 by Woody Allen. Reprinted by permission of Random House, Inc. Excerpt from THE YEARS OF LYNDON JOHNSON: THE PATH TO POWER by Robert A. Caro. Copyright © 1982 by Robert A. Caro. Reprinted by permission of Alfred A. Knopf, Inc. Excerpt from SPACE, by James A. Michener. Copyright © 1982 by James A. Michener. Reprinted by permission of Random House, Inc. "Harlem" copyright 1951 by Langston Hughes. Reprinted from THE PANTHER AND THE LASH: POEMS OF OUR TIME by Langston Hughes, by permission of Alfred A. Knopf, Inc. Excerpt from THE ODD COUPLE by Neil Simon. Copyright © 1966 by Nancy Enterprises, Inc. Reprinted by permission of Random House, Inc, and DaSilva & DaSilva, attorneys.

Flora Roberts, Inc. for excerpt from PAINTING CHURCHES by Tina Howe. Copyright © 1982 by Tina Howe. Reprinted by permission of Flora Roberts, Inc.

ROLLING STONE magazine for excerpt from "Lionel Richie Goes High-Tech" by Steve Pond. From ROLLING STONE, November 6, 1986. By Straight Arrow Publishers, Inc. © 1986. All Rights Reserved. Reprinted by Permission.

St. Martin's Press, Inc. for excerpt from HUYSMAN'S PETS by Kate Wilhelm. Published by Bluejay Books, New York. Copyright © 1986 by Kate Wilhelm. Reprinted by permission of St. Martin's Press, Inc. Excerpt from THE FAR PAVILIONS by M. M. Kaye. Copyright © 1978 by M. M. Kaye. Reprinted by permission of St. Martin's Press, Inc.

Scapegoat Productions, Inc. for excerpt from CATCH-22 by Joseph Heller. Copyright © 1971 by Scapegoat Productions, Inc. Reprinted by permission of the publisher.

Schocken Books Inc. for excerpt from "Silent Snow, Secret Snow" by Conrad Aiken. Reprinted by permission of Schocken Books Inc. from THE COLLECTED SHORT STORIES OF CONRAD AIKEN by Conrad Aiken. Copyright © 1950, 1952, 1953, 1955, 1956, 1957, 1958, 1959, 1960, 1961, 1962, 1964.

Charles Scribner's Sons for excerpt from THE GREAT GATSBY by F. Scott Fitzgerald. Copyright 1925 Charles Scribner's Sons. Copyright renewed 1953 by Frances Scott Fitzgerald Lanahan. Reprinted with the permission of the publisher. Excerpt from "A Day's Wait" from WINNER TAKE NOTHING by Ernest Hemingway. Copyright 1933 Charles Scribner's Sons; copyright renewed © 1961 Mary Hemingway. Reprinted with the permission of the publisher.

Simon & Schuster, Inc. for excerpt from CONTACT by Carl Sagan. Copyright © 1985 by Carl Sagan. Excerpt from LONESOME DOVE by Larry McMurtry. Copyright © 1985 by Larry McMurtry. Excerpt from "Marty" in TELEVISION PLAYS by Paddy Chayefsky. Copyright © 1955 by Paddy Chayefsky, renewed © 1983 by Susan Chayefsky. Reprinted by permission of Simon & Schuster, Inc.

Alexander Speer for excerpt from TALKING WITH . . . by Jane Martin. Copyright 1980 by Alexander Speer, as Trustee. All rights reserved.

The Society of Authors for extract from THE DEVIL'S DISCIPLE by Bernard Shaw. Copyright © 1941 by George Bernard Shaw. Reprinted by permission of The Society of Authors.

Time, Inc. for excerpts from "Seattle's Young Spellbinder" and from "A Quarter-Century Later, the Myth Endures." Copyright © 1986 Time, Inc. All rights reserved. Reprinted by permission from TIME.

TV Guide for excerpt from review of "The Story of English" in issue of 10/4/86. Reprinted with permission from TV Guide Magazine. Copyright © 1986 by Triangle Publications, Inc., Radnor, Pennsylvania.

Vanguard Press for excerpt from "Daisy" in NIGHTSIDE by Joyce Carol Oates. Copyright © 1977 by Joyce Carol Oates. Reprinted by permission of the publisher.

Variety, Inc. for excerpt from "Television: Review of Liberty Weekend" by Bok in issue of July 9, 1986. Reprinted by permission of Variety, Inc.

The Village Voice for excerpts by R. J. Smith and Sally Sommer. Reprinted with permission of the authors and the Village Voice © 1986.

Viking Penguin, Inc. for excerpt from WINESBURG, OHIO by Sherwood Anderson. Copyright 1919 by B. W. Huebsch. Copyright renewed 1947 by Eleanor Copenhaver Anderson. Excerpt from

"Murder is Corny" from TRIO FOR BLUNT INSTRUMENTS by Rex Stout. Copyright © 1963, 1964 by Rex Stout. Excerpt from "The Hazards of Science" in THE MEDUSA AND THE SNAIL by Lewis Thomas. Copyright 1977 by Lewis Thomas. Originally published in the New England Journal of Medicine. Excerpt from THE PEARL by John Steinbeck. Copyright 1945 by John Steinbeck. Copyright renewed © 1973 by Elaine Steinbeck, Thom Steinbeck and John Steinbeck IV. Excerpt from "The Dead" in DUBLINERS by James Joyce. Copyright 1916 by B. W. Huebsch. Definitive text Copyright © 1967 by the Estate of James Joyce. Excerpt from "The Rockinghorse Winner" in THE COMPLETE STORIES OF D. H. LAWRENCE. Copyright 1933 by the Estate of D. H. Lawrence. Copyright renewed © 1961 by Angelo Ravagli and C. Montague Weekley, Executors of the Estate of Frieda Lawrence Ravagli. Excerpt from THE GOOD APPRENTICE by Iris Murdoch. Copyright © 1985 by Iris Murdoch. Excerpt from "Good Climate, Friendly Inhabitants" in NOT FOR PUBLICATION AND OTHER STORIES by Nadine Gordimer. Copyright © 1964 by Nadine Gordimer. Excerpt from LAKE WOBEGON DAYS by Garrison Keillor. Copyright © 1985 by Garrison Keillor. Excerpt from "A Correspondence Course" from SOMETHING OUT THERE by Nadine Gordimer. Originally published in The New Yorker. Excerpt from IRONWEED by William Kennedy. Copyright © 1979, 1981, 1983 by William Kennedy. Excerpt from Act I of CRIMES OF THE HEART by Beth Henley. Copyright © 1981, 1982 by Beth Henley. All reprinted by permission of Viking Penguin, Inc.

John Waters for an excerpt from "Tom Waits' Gutter Guitar" by John Waters, first published in ESQUIRE, April 1986. Reprinted by permission of the author.

A. P. Watt Ltd. for excerpt from ON THE BEACH by Nevil Shute. Copyright © 1957 by Nevil Shute. Reprinted by permission of the publisher on behalf of the Trustees of the Estate of Nevil Shute, Norway.

Every effort has been made to trace the ownership of all copyrighted materials in this book and to obtain permission for their use.

Index